BEHIND THE RED LINE

Political Repression in Sudan

Human Rights Watch/Africa

Human Rights Watch
New York · Washington · London · Brussels

Library of Congress Catalog Card Number: 96-75962
ISBN 1-56432-164-9

Cover photograph © June 1995 by Jemera Rone. The remains of a squatters' shanty town in Omdurman, Sudan, after government forces demolished it as part of an "urban renewal" effort.

Human Rights Watch/Africa
Human Rights Watch/Africa was established in 1988 to monitor and promote the observance of internationally recognized human rights in sub-Saharan Africa. Peter Takirambudde is the executive director; Janet Fleischman is the Washington director; Suliman Ali Baldo is the senior researcher; Bronwen Manby and Alex Vines are research associates; Kimberly Mazyck and Lenee Simon are associates; Alison DesForges, Binaifer Nowrojee and Michele Wagner are consultants. William Carmichael is the chair of the advisory committee and Alice Brown is the vice chair.

Addresses for Human Rights Watch
485 Fifth Avenue, New York, NY 10017-6104
Tel: (212) 972-8400, Fax: (212) 972-0905, E-mail: hrwnyc@hrw.org

1522 K Street, N.W., #910, Washington, DC 20005-1202
Tel: (202) 371-6592, Fax: (202) 371-0124, E-mail: hrwdc@hrw.org

33 Islington High Street, N1 9LH London, UK
Tel: (171) 713-1995, Fax: (171) 713-1800, E-mail: hrwatchuk@gn.apc.org

15 Rue Van Campenhout, 1000 Brussels, Belgium
Tel: (2) 732-2009, Fax: (2) 732-0471, E-mail: hrwatcheu@gn.apc.org

Gopher Address://gopher.humanrights.org:5000
Listserv address: To subscribe to the list, send an e-mail message to majordomo@igc.apc.org with "subscribe hrw-news" in the body of the message (leave the subject line blank).

HUMAN RIGHTS WATCH

Human Rights Watch conducts regular, systematic investigations of human rights abuses in some seventy countries around the world. Our reputation for timely, reliable disclosures has made us an essential source of information for those concerned with human rights. We address the human rights practices of governments of all political stripes, of all geopolitical alignments, and of all ethnic and religious persuasions. Human Rights Watch defends freedom of thought and expression, due process and equal protection of the law, and a vigorous civil society; we document and denounce murders, disappearances, torture, arbitrary imprisonment, discrimination, and other abuses of internationally recognized human rights. Our goal is to hold governments accountable if they transgress the rights of their people.

Human Rights Watch began in 1978 with the founding of its Helsinki division. Today, it includes five divisions covering Africa, the Americas, Asia, the Middle East, as well as the signatories of the Helsinki accords. It also includes five collaborative projects on arms transfers, children's rights, free expression, prison conditions, and women's rights. It maintains offices in New York, Washington, Los Angeles, London, Brussels, Moscow, Dushanbe, Rio de Janeiro, and Hong Kong. Human Rights Watch is an independent, nongovernmental organization, supported by contributions from private individuals and foundations worldwide. It accepts no government funds, directly or indirectly.

The staff includes Kenneth Roth, executive director; Cynthia Brown, program director; Holly J. Burkhalter, advocacy director; Barbara Guglielmo, finance and administration director; Robert Kimzey, publications director; Jeri Laber, special advisor; Gara LaMarche, associate director; Lotte Leicht, Brussels office director; Juan Méndez, general counsel; Susan Osnos, communications director; Jemera Rone, counsel; and Joanna Weschler, United Nations representative.

The regional directors of Human Rights Watch are Peter Takirambudde, Africa; José Miguel Vivanco, Americas; Sidney Jones, Asia; Holly Cartner, Helsinki; and Christopher E. George, Middle East. The project directors are Joost R. Hiltermann, Arms Project; Lois Whitman, Children's Rights Project; Gara LaMarche, Free Expression Project; and Dorothy Q. Thomas, Women's Rights Project.

The members of the board of directors are Robert L. Bernstein, chair; Adrian W. DeWind, vice chair; Roland Algrant, Lisa Anderson, Alice L. Brown, William Carmichael, Dorothy Cullman, Gina Despres, Irene Diamond, Edith Everett, Jonathan Fanton, James C. Goodale, Jack Greenberg, Vartan Gregorian, Alice H. Henkin, Stephen L. Kass, Marina Pinto Kaufman, Bruce Klatsky, Harold Hongju Koh, Alexander MacGregor, Josh Mailman, Andrew Nathan, Jane Olson, Peter Osnos, Kathleen Peratis, Bruce Rabb, Sigrid Rausing, Orville Schell, Sid Sheinberg, Gary G. Sick, Malcolm Smith, Nahid Toubia, Maureen White, and Rosalind C. Whitehead.

ACKNOWLEDGMENTS

This report was researched and written by Human Rights Watch Counsel Jemera Rone. Human Rights Watch Leonard H. Sandler Fellow Brian Owsley also conducted research with Ms. Rone during a mission to Khartoum, Sudan, from May 1-June 13, 1995, at the invitation of the Sudanese government. Interviews in Khartoum with nongovernment people and agencies were conducted in private, as agreed with the government before the mission began. Private individuals and groups requested anonymity because of fear of government reprisals. Interviews in Juba, the largest town in the south, were not private and were controlled by Sudan Security, which terminated the visit prematurely. Other interviews were conducted in the United States, Cairo, London and elsewhere after the end of the mission. Ms. Rone conducted further research in Kenya and southern Sudan from March 5-20, 1995. The report was edited by Deputy Program Director Michael McClintock and Human Rights Watch/Africa Executive Director Peter Takirambudde. Acting Counsel Dinah PoKempner reviewed sections of the manuscript and Associate Kerry McArthur provided production assistance.

This report could not have been written without the assistance of many Sudanese whose names cannot be disclosed.

CONTENTS

GLOSSARY

Ansar	Sudanese Muslim religious sect headed by Sadiq al Mahdi; base of the banned Umma Party
Ansar al Sunna	a traditional Islamic sect calling for the revival of the traditions of the prophet Mohamed
Anya-Nya	the southern Sudanese rebel army of the first civil war, 1955-72
Anya-Nya II	rebel south Sudanese forces who, together with former members of the Sudanese army, formed the SPLA in 1983; also, some of those forces that defected from the SPLA later in 1983 and became a militia force of Nuer in Upper Nile province supported by the Sudanese government; several Anya-Nya II groups over the years were wooed back to the SPLA
Baggara	Arabized tribes of western Sudan; their name means cattle herders
Citibank Ghost House	a secret detention facility run by Sudan Security, called "Citibank" because it was in a house behind the high-rise office building where Citibank used to have its Khartoum office
DUP	Democratic Unionist Party, junior partner in several 1986-89 coalition governments, associated with the Khatmiyya traditional Islamic sect and its spiritual leaders, the Mirghani family
Dawa Islamiyya	large Islamic nongovernmental organization that engages in relief work in over fifteen African countries
Dinka	a southern Nilotic people originating in Bahr El Ghazal and Upper Nile
E.U.	European Union

xi

"ghost house"   secret place of detention

hudud - offenses of   six major offenses in Islamic law with penalties prescribed in fixed terms in the Qur'an or the Sunna (traditions of the prophet Mohamed)

Hunger Triangle   a name adopted by relief organizations in 1993 for the area defined by Kongor, Ayod, and Waat, in Upper Nile province, where hunger was especially acute

ICRC   International Committee of the Red Cross

ILO   International Labor Organization

jihad   holy war

Khatmiyya   Sudanese Muslim religious sect headed by Mohamed Osman al Mirghani; base of the banned Democratic Unionist Party

mujahedeen   holy warriors or participants in jihad

murahiliin   Arab tribal militias

NGO   Nongovernmental organization

NIF   National Islamic Front, the militant Islamist political party which came to power in 1989 after a military coup overthrew the elected government

National Assembly   legislative body as of March 1996

National Service   agency within the ministry of defense responsible for conscripting men who under law are obliged to serve one or two years in the armed forces

Nuba   the African people living in south Kordofan's Nuba Mountains; some are Muslims, some Christians, and some practice traditional African religions

OFDA	Office of Foreign Disaster Assistance, within the U.S. Agency for International Development
OLS	Operation Lifeline Sudan, a joint United Nations/NGO relief operation for internally displaced and famine and war victims in Sudan which began operations in 1989. It serves territory controlled by the government and by the SPLA. Much of its work in southern Sudan is through cross-border operations conducted by OLS' Southern sector based in Nairobi.
PDF	Popular Defense Forces, a government-sponsored militia
RASS	Relief Association of Southern Sudan, the relief wing of Southern Sudan Independence Movement
SPLA-United	the name that SPLA dissidents adopted after they united on March 27, 1993, until their organization was renamed in October 1994 as Southern Sudan Independence Movement/Army
SPLA-United (Western Upper Nile)	rebel movement formd by Dr. Lam Akol after his February 1994 expulsion from SPLA-United, based in Tonga, Upper Nile
SPLM/A	Sudan People's Liberation Movement/Army, the political organization and army of the Sudanese rebels formed in 1983, of which John Garang is chairman
SRRA	Sudan Relief and Rehabilitation Association, relief wing of the SPLM/A
SSIM/A	Southern Sudan Independence Movement/Army; this is the faction of the SPLA, led by Cmdr. Riek Machar Terry Dhurgon, that broke away from the SPLM/A and Dr. John Garang's leadership in August 1991. It was based in Nasir, Upper Nile, and for a time was referred

to as "SPLA-Nasir;" on March 27, 1993, others joined it and it was renamed "SPLA-United." In November 1994, it was renamed Southern Sudan Independence Movement/Army

Three Towns	Khartoum, Omdurman and Khartoum North; their combined population is estimated at four million
Toposa	southern Equatorian people originating in the Kapoeta area of eastern Equatoria
Transitional National Assembly	legislative body until March 1996
Triple A camps	displaced persons camps in Ame, Aswa and Atepi created in 1992 in Eastern Equatoria and evacuated in 1994 due to government military advances
UNDP	United Nations Development Program
UNHCR	United Nations High Commissioner for Refugees
UNICEF	United Nations Children's Fund
Umma Party	a banned political party which was the senior mainstream political party in the coalition governments between 1987-89, associated with the traditional Islamic sect of the Ansar and its spiritual leaders, the Mahdi family
WFP	World Food Program

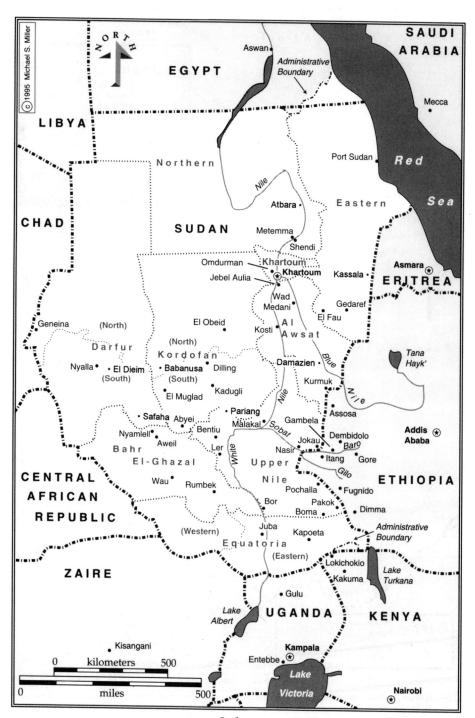

Sudan

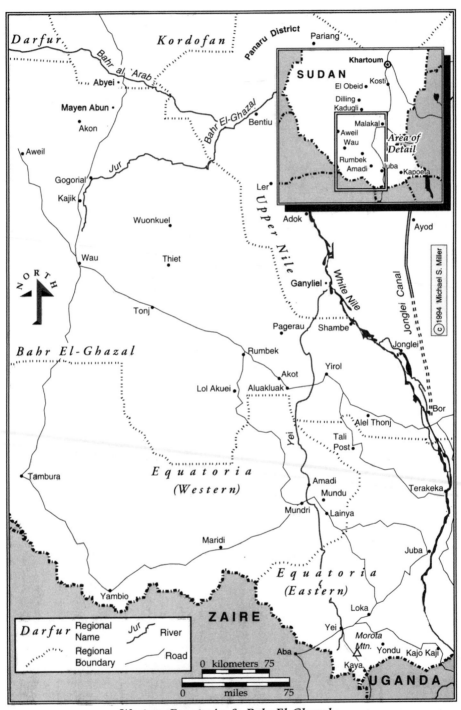

Western Equatoria & Bahr El-Ghazal

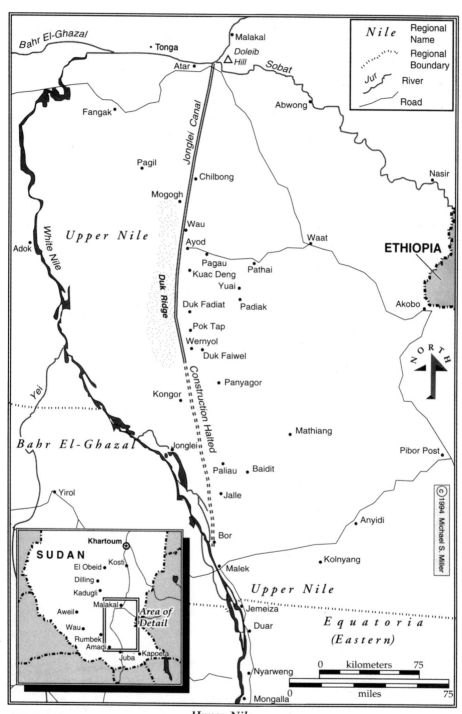

Upper Nile

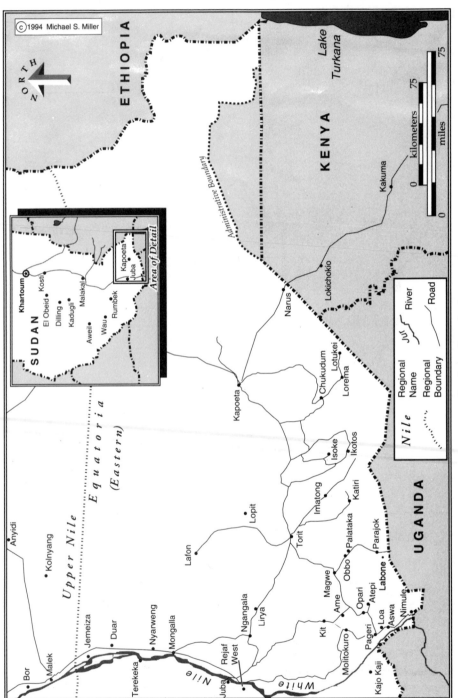

Eastern Equatoria

1
SUMMARY AND RECOMMENDATIONS

Violation of political and civil rights in Sudan remains the norm almost seven years after the elected government was toppled by a military coup backed by the National Islamic Front (NIF) party. A state of emergency was imposed on the date of the coup, June 30, 1989, which has never been lifted. The transitional constitution of 1985 was abolished and although elections for president and some members of the assembly were held in 1996, these elections were held without political parties, which remained banned since the 1989 coup, and in a climate of denial of basic freedoms of speech, assembly, and association, with the threat of arbitrary arrest by an ever-present security apparatus and detention with possible torture or ill-treatment. The limits to political participation were bluntly described by President (Lt. Gen.) Omar Hassan al Bashir in a January 1996 speech, where he said, "When we talk of handing power to the people, we mean the people will be within certain limits but no one will cross the red lines which are aimed at the interest of the nation."[1] This anomalous situation provides no effective protection for human rights.

When President al Bashir warned that "no one will cross the red lines," he was commenting on a lecture that Abel Alier, a prominent southern politician and former vice-president of Sudan, gave to a university audience on the sensitive issue of self-determination for southern Sudan, the non-Muslim and non-Arab third of the national territory where oil resources lie. Self-determination is off-limits for discussion even though the country has been involved in a civil war for much of the period since independence in 1956 (with the exception of eleven years from 1972-83 when the south had autonomy). The rebels, mostly southerners and including Christians and practitioners of traditional African religions, and Muslims from the Nuba Mountains in central Sudan, belong in large part to the Sudan People's Liberation Movement/Army (SPLM/A) led by Cmdr.-in-Chief John Garang. The rebel SPLM/A controls substantial territory in the south, which is about three times the size of neighboring Uganda. Sudan is the largest country — 2.5 million square kilometers — in Africa. Although the SPLM has demanded a "united, secular Sudan" since 1983, that goal has been eroded within the south in favor of demands of independence.

Long-standing complaints of southerners about discrimination against them in the north and under northern rule in the garrison towns of the south — on

---

[1]Nhial Bol, "Sudan, No News is Good News for the Government," InterPress Service, Khartoum, January 22, 1996.

1

the grounds of religion, ethnic origin, language, and race — have not been heeded nor seemingly understood by the northern political class, traditionally composed of those riverain Sudanese who define themselves as Arab. Sudan, with a 1992 population estimated at 26.7 million, is one of the most diverse countries in the world. According to the 1956 census (the only one which included ethnic origin), there were nineteen major ethnic groups and 597 subgroups in Sudan. In 1956 those who identified themselves as Arabs formed the largest ethnic group, at 40 percent of the population, followed by Dinka (12 percent), Beja (7 percent), and West Africans (6 percent). Islam is the state religion but only about 60 percent of the population are Muslims. Christians account for 4 percent of the national total (15 percent of the southern population), and traditional religions the rest.[2] The official language, Arabic, is spoken by about 60 percent of the population. There are over 115 tribal languages, of which over twenty-six are spoken by more than 100,000 people.[3]

Since 1989, when the present government took power through a military coup, the diversity of Sudan's peoples has not been respected or encouraged, although prior governments did not have a good track record on respect for diversity either. Unlike previous governments, however, the NIF's stated aspiration is to create an Islamic state with one language, Arabic, and one religion, Islam — although it hedges on the rights of religious minorities. For instance, Minister of Education Kabashour Kuku announced in 1995 that the government would introduce changes in the school curriculum aimed at bringing up children according to the tenets of Islam and requiring Arabic as the language of instruction in all parts of Sudan, including the south where the majority of the population is non-Muslim and where the medium of instruction has been the vernacular or English.[4] International human rights norms which require protection and respect for religious, racial, ethnic, linguistic and other minorities, and forbid discrimination on such grounds, are routinely violated in the course of government efforts to impose conformity on the population.

---

[2] "Sudan: Country Profile 1994-95," *The Economist Intelligence Unit* (London 1995), p. 9.

[3] English is used commercially and as the lingua franca in the south. Ibid.

[4] Nhial Bol, "Sudan-Education: Islamic Education for the Non-Muslim South,"InterPress Service, Khartoum, August 1, 1995. The Ministry of Education said that two million copies of textbooks (used before independence in 1956) would be burned in furtherance of the Arabization policy. Ibid.

Arbitrary arrests

The National Security Act of 1995 provides for prolonged arbitrary detention in "security" cases of up to six months without judicial review, with detainees in the custody of Sudan Security, in violation of international standards prohibiting arbitrary arrest and detention. The government has also misrepresented the status of this law to the U.N. It said in its November 1995 response to the U.N. human rights report that the 1992 National Security Act was in effect, and failed to disclose that it was replaced by a more restrictive act signed into law in May 1995.

The new 1995 law was quickly applied that month to detain arbitrarily the former prime minister and leader of the banned Umma Party and the Ansar sect on which it is based, Sadiq al Mahdi, on account of a speech he gave during the religious holiday Al Eid in which he criticized the NIF and the government. The violation of Sadiq al Mahdi's right to free expression was followed a week later by mass detentions of other Umma Party leaders. These detainees were released, never having been charged, in August; the time the prisoners spent in incommunicado detention appeared designed to remind the party, its leader, and Sudanese civil society that there was a certain "red line" beyond which criticism would not be tolerated.

Many other mass and individual arrests followed in the same fashion, of students during the September 1995 demonstrations and of suspected political opponents and those believed to be in league with the northern armed rebel movement based in Eritrea in late 1995 and early 1996.

Torture and death in detention

Detention conditions, especially for Sudan Security detainees, violate international law and standards requiring safeguards against torture, "disappearance," and unlawful detention. Detainees are regularly held for interrogation and prolonged detention incommunicado, often in unacknowledged detention places known as "ghost houses." These places of detention are administered by Sudan Security, which also is responsible for the interrogation of the detainees, with no supervision by the courts or other independent authorities with power to order a release of the detainees, in violation of international standards.

Mohamed al Fatih Abdel Moneim Taifor died in suspicious circumstances in July 1995 while in the custody of Sudan Security in Khartoum: fellow detainees reported hearing his cries as he was beaten the night he died.

These "ghost house" torture centers became so notorious that in March 1995 the government greatly remodeled the notorious "Citibank" ghost house, located near the former Citibank branch office in Khartoum, transferring the sixty detainees held there to a specially-renovated section of Kober Prison in Khartoum North. The special section at Kober was under the jurisdiction of Sudan Security. Despite the notoriety of the "ghost houses," political detainees continued to be taken back and forth from Kober, and some were subjected to torture and other ill-treatment during interrogation in these ghost houses.

Although it appears that torture is not used as routinely as it was in the early years of this government, it has not been abandoned. The worst reports of torture and ill-treatment continue to come from the war zones and border areas. A former rebel boy soldier who wanted to leave Khartoum and return to southern Sudan in 1995 was stopped at Kosti, the northern Nile river terminal for the trip south, when he tried to board a barge. Military intelligence agents arrested him because he did not have a travel permit. After interrogation they handed him over to Sudan Security in Kosti, where he was subjected to further questioning and severe torture. Sudan Security agents burned his naked back and body, among other things.

Impunity

The lack of prosecution of Sudan Security agents and army personnel for torture and murder continues to be the norm, with some few exceptions. As of June 1995, the conviction of only one army soldier — not an officer and not a Sudan Security member — was upheld by the Supreme Court during the year for unlawfully killing a civilian at a checkpoint. Other similar convictions were still pending Supreme Court review. An announced pardon of thirty-seven military personnel on August 31, 1995, may, however, have resulted in the release of the Sudan Security and army personnel in jail for abuses against civilians in June 1995.

Torture has been tolerated by the courts in a virtual guarantee of impunity. Testimony and medical examinations established at trial that the defendants in a high-profile 1994 case (known as the "Explosives Case") had been tortured, but the court violated international standards when it admitted the confessions in evidence and used them to convict the defendants. Moreover, it took no steps to initiate criminal prosecutions of the torturers. This case was doubly offensive since one of the torturers identified in court — Abd al Hafiz Ahmed al Bashir — had been accused of an arbitrary checkpoint killing a year earlier; had he been suspended from his job then, he would not have been able to engage in torture in 1993.

Nor has the government lived up to its obligations under international law to undertake a prompt and impartial investigation of serious torture allegations in the case of Brig. (Ret.) Mohamed Ahmed al Rayah al Faki. Brig. al Rayah was detained in 1991 and with several others convicted of a coup attempt. He filed a complaint of torture while he was still in jail, and as a result was not released in the release of political prisoners in August 1995. The government, through various agents, tried to persuade him to withdraw his complaint several times, but he refused. He was finally released in February 1996, having been punished by spending six months in jail beyond the time his peers, who did not file any torture complaints, served. His complaint remains uninvestigated.

The future impunity of Sudan Security agents has been further reinforced. The National Security Act as now amended bars all civil and criminal actions against Sudan Security members for anything they did during their employment, unless the agency's director gives prior approval in cases where the conduct was not related to employment. Under this law, torture conducted in the course of employment is not actionable.

Fundamental fairness in the judicial system

The Sudanese judicial system, which in the past has capably defended fundamental rights using Sudanese law, has been weakened by the perennial inability of the body politic to agree upon a constitution, three military coups that suspended basic rights and ruled by decree, and the difficulty of transition, starting in 1983, of the legal system from one based on the British system to one based on Islamic law, *shari'a*.

Immediately after the June 1989 military coup, the de facto government dismissed some fifty-seven judges. Others in the judiciary were winnowed out after that. New judges purportedly sympathetic or loyal to the NIF were recruited. When the number of states was increased to twenty-six, more new judges were appointed to fill the increased need in the states.

In September 1995, the government announced that it was creating a committee to review the cases of all those who were "sent into retirement for the public interest" after the 1989 coup. Whether any dismissed judges will be reinstated bears watching.

The death penalty is still in use, and executions continue. It is difficult to know what the rate is since military tribunals, which appear to use the death penalty much more frequently than the civilian courts, do not make their proceedings public. It appears that justice is much more summary and rendered with considerably fewer procedural safeguards in military tribunals than in civilian courts, often with no advocate or counsel permitted, and no effective appeal from a death sentence. This summary "justice" violates due process and excludes the additional safeguards required by international standards in death penalty cases, which standards are designed to minimize the possibility of error. Human Rights Watch opposes executions under law whenever and wherever carried out, irrespective of the crime and the legal process leading to the imposition of the death penalty, because of its inherent cruelty.

Even though some military tribunal sentences have been softened by executive action, substituting life sentences for the death penalty, and ultimately in some cases by pardons, the summary military trial and execution of twenty-eight army officers and others in 1990 (for an attempted coup) still stands out as an abuse without remedy. The government has never released any information about the trials, nor has it even disclosed the burial place of those officers.

Military tribunals also were responsible for the summary executions of many persons, civilian and military, in Juba in 1992 after the SPLA military incursion into that southern city. There has never been an accounting of any of these trials nor a disclosure of where the bodies are buried. It appears that in many cases there were no trials at all before executions. Several hundred persons remain unaccounted for, and the investigation frequently promised by the government has never materialized. These reported unacknowledged detentions should be considered disappearances.

The right to due process and privacy has been arbitrarily denied by Sudan Security when it confiscates homes and other property belonging to political detainees, in some cases without any written order; in other cases it has not returned the property, even after acquittal. Some property is reportedly kept and used by Sudan Security.

Freedom of expression and the press

The government of Sudan told the United Nations in November 1995 that freedom of expression has been guaranteed by the Press and Printed Materials Law and there are many daily newspapers where opinions different from those of the Government are freely expressed. Although under the 1993 press law a few more independent newspapers have been allowed to open, several of those have since been closed, their presses confiscated, and their owners and journalists arrested. In many other cases, following hard on the publication of critical articles the government disliked, publications have been closed for periods of time. The government has enforced stringent financial and ownership requirements under the press law to close newspapers that criticize the government. Some newspapers published before June 1989 have not been permitted to reopen since they were banned.

In June 1995, the independent *Akhir Khabar* (Latest News) published an editorial highly critical of the 1993 Press and Printed Materials Law which the publisher said threatened small independent papers like his with extinction. This editorial followed the publication, in May 1995, of an interview with newspaper owner Mahjoub Erwa about his 1994 arrest and the government confiscation of his newspaper, *Al Soudani al Doulia*. The Press and Publications Council established under the press law ordered *Akhir Khabar* off the streets for two weeks in July 1995 and on January 18, 1996, the council ordered *Akhir Khabar's* permanent closure, accusing it of publishing articles it said "incited animosity, social disintegration and a spirit of intolerance." Its publisher said the real reason the paper was closed was because it had announced that it intended to publish a serialized interview with former elected Prime Minister Sadiq al Mahdi. The council also decided to bar the same publisher's forthcoming *Sabah Al Kheir* (Good Morning) newspaper. The publisher accused the government of banning these newspapers to keep them out of the debate preceding the March 1996 elections. These permanent closures are restrictions on the press that go far beyond what is permissible under the free expression guarantees in international human rights law.

Several newspapers published during the 1986-89 period of multiparty government have never been permitted to reopen after they were banned in 1989 at the time of the coup. Journalists believed to be associated with the Umma Party's underground *Sawt El Umma* (Voice of the Nation) newspaper were detained and grilled about the paper in November 1994. A man suspected of coordinating *Al Maidan*, the underground journal of the banned Sudan Communist Party (SCP), was detained in April 1995 and held in a "ghost house" then in the Sudan Security section of Kober Prison for a total of four months of warrantless incommunicado detention. Following the large street demonstrations in September 1995, at least thirteen journalists were arrested on suspicion of publishing *Al Shabiba*, the underground journal of the Sudan Youth Union, affiliated with the SCP.

There are limits, vaguely admitted by the government, on what the press can publish in Sudan. These limits shift. Notwithstanding the press closures described above, during the March 1996 elections these limits appeared to be slightly relaxed, and the Sudanese press — with the exception of those newspapers already suspended or permanently closed — jumped into the electoral fray with articles harshly criticizing the ruling party. This freedom is not considered a right, however, and it remains to be seen if the banned newspapers will be reopened and if this latitude continues after the elections.

Freedom of association

Immediately after the June 1989 coup, the junta banned free association. Constitutional Decree No. 2 stated that "all political parties and groups are to be disbanded, and it is illegal for them to be established or to remain active." The decree also banned all trade unions and federations and confiscated their funds and properties, and canceled all licenses issued to non-religious institutions and societies.

In 1996 the ban on political parties remains intact, although seven years have passed and the elimination of political parties appears intended to be a permanent political arrangement, not a temporary measure. The NIF justifies this by what it describes as a need to do away with sectarian political parties; in past multiparty elections, the largest vote-getters were parties based on Sufi Muslim religious sects whose followers voted for their religious leaders — usually men who inherited their positions. These parties were the Umma (Ansar sect) and the Democratic Unionist Party (Khatmiyya sect). The ban on political parties, however, extends also to nonsectarian political parties, such as the Sudan Communist Party and the Republican Brothers.

All parties are banned, with the de facto exception of the NIF. It is an open secret that the government has been run from behind the scenes by this technically "banned" political party. Elections for president and some legislative seats were held in March 1996 but no political parties were allowed to participate, and many NIF leaders were elected. NIF leader Dr. Hassan al Turabi became speaker of the National Assembly.

Other associations, such as professional groups, have been permitted to reconstitute themselves under post-1989 laws, but their independence is severely limited and their freedom restricted by the "red line." The government maintains that they are subject to their own administrative regulations but subjects professional associations and trade unions to close control: it was precisely these organizations that played a leading role in the peaceful overthrow of two Sudanese dictatorships in 1964 and 1985. Other civic associations, such as trade unions and student unions, have been taken over by NIF supporters through tactics including the detentions of rival leaders, dirty tricks and violence.

A neighborhood network of popular committees, created by the current government, provides a means to control residential areas where demonstrations also played a political role in toppling past governments. These committees, too, cannot go beyond the "red line" to defend the interests of residents against the government — such as opposing government demolitions of its members' homes.

Freedom of assembly

The government of Sudan has stated that freedom of assembly is fully guaranteed by law. In fact, the law is administered to permit only government-sponsored or pro-government assemblies and demonstrations. Anti-government assemblies, both indoors and outdoors, remain illegal because the government will not grant permits to its opponents and violently represses their demonstrations, so opponents rarely seek such permits. Their assemblies, or indoor meetings, take place clandestinely, if they are held at all, to prevent Sudan Security from observing and arresting the participants. This repression of the right of peaceable assembly has been going on for almost seven years; citizens know where the "red line" is, and continue to cross it at their peril.

The outer limits of the right of assembly have been explored by the relatives of twenty-eight army officers who were summarily executed for an alleged coup attempt in 1990. They demonstrate publicly once a year on or near the anniversary of the executions. Sudan Security has used excessive force illegally to break up their demonstrations, which have been peaceful. In 1995 a demonstration in a Khartoum street quickly disbanded when Sudan Security arrived, but the authorities proceeded to beat and detain six women. In 1996 Sudan Security refrained from physically attacking the demonstrators. However, it continued its harassment and intimidation campaign to prevent the relatives from exercising their rights by approaching them before the day of the demonstration and asking them to sign statements agreeing not to demonstrate. The government still does not accept their right to peaceably demonstrate, and in 1996 only grudgingly tolerated their short annual demonstration.

In late 1994 police used lethal force to break up a demonstration of squatters protesting the bulldozing of their homes in Khoder, Omdurman. The police killed about eleven shanty town residents and injured many more; some protesters reportedly threw stones at the bulldozers, but all available evidence indicates that the use of firearms was a grossly disproportionate response. After a storm of international protests, the government managed to conduct the next large demolition of squatters' homes in Angola, Omdurman, in March 1995 without the use of lethal force.

Right to movement

The right to freedom of movement inside Sudan has been severely restricted, with the southern region placed off-limits to many, including southerners living in the north whose families are in the south. Restrictions are particularly hard on southerners who were politically active during the period of multiparty government. Those citizens and foreigners working in relief or development agencies, including the U.N., are subjected to very strict limitations on movement in Juba and other southern garrison towns, and thus on the work they can do there. Movement to the Nuba Mountains is tightly controlled on the limited occasions it is permitted, making relief or development programs there out of the question, except by agencies aligned with the government's Islamization program.

Even in Khartoum there are restrictions on movement for certain categories of people, although in the past year those restrictions seem to have eased. Former political detainees — never charged with or convicted of any crime — frequently must sign a written undertaking agreeing to limitations on their residence and not to travel abroad or sometimes, even outside a designated city, without prior approval.

Since an exit visa is required for citizens and residents leaving Sudan, departure is never problem free for certain categories of people. They include former political detainees and those who intend to attend conferences abroad. Even after the issuance of an exit visa, the authorities have stopped travelers from leaving with no reason given.

Women's rights of movement and travel outside the country are subjected to discrimination in that adult women, unlike adult men, must have the permission of a male family member or guardian to travel.

Freedom of religion

Being a Muslim does not guarantee freedom of religion in Sudan's Islamic state. The two large Muslim sects, the Ansar and the Khatmiyya, from which, in the past, the two largest political parties drew their members — the Umma Party and the Democratic Unionist Party, both banned since 1989 — have been subjected to government attempts at control and confiscation of their mosques. Some Muslim religious groups critical of the government and the National Islamic Front — as being insufficiently religious — have been subjected to harassment.

The government took a step forward in its relations with the churches when it repealed the Missionary Society Act of 1962 in late 1994, under which foreign missionaries were expelled from Sudan in 1964. Subsequently, however, the president issued a decree the churches feared would require each Christian congregation to register separately and secure approval from a government minister to continue worshiping, while imposing other controls on their daily affairs that threatened to violate the freedom of religion. When the churches rose in protest against the decree's unfairness, the decree was not enforced.

The government's move to grant more exit visas to Christian clergy is counter-balanced by heavy-handed government tactics to restrict the movement and freedom of expression of clergy. The arrest and televised release in January 1996 of a priest who the government said was involved in "sabotage" plans in Juba marked a recent heightening of tension between the government and the Christian community. The priest and a student detained about the same time — both members of a southern tribe, the Toposa — were reportedly tortured into making false confessions in court and before the video cameras of Sudan Security.

The most serious religious rights violations, however, occurred in conjunction with the government's efforts to proselytize in prisons, the armed forces, the civil service, the universities, and other sectors of society. The PDF is the principle vehicle for carrying out this agenda. Participation in forty-five days of its religious-military training program, intended to create holy warriors to fight in a holy war in the south, is mandatory for civil servants, university students, and others. The mandatory training, infused as it is with Islamic religious fervor, creates an atmosphere of coercion on all participants to convert to Islam in violation of freedom of religion, or if they are already Muslim, to join in the government's particular interpretation of Islam.

Students' free association and expression rights and police conduct

The largest anti-government demonstrations in the six years since the army and NIF seized power started on university campuses in September 1995. Up to thirty anti-government protesters were killed and at least seventeen wounded as the demonstrations spread to the center of Khartoum and other towns. Many hundreds were beaten and detained without charges.

Crowd control does not appear to have been conducted in compliance with United Nations guidelines on the use of force and firearms by law enforcement officers. Security forces used live ammunition and tear gas on the first and second days of the demonstration to disperse the demonstrators, some of whom reportedly smashed windows and caused other damage to property. The principle that the intentional lethal use of firearms be permitted only when strictly unavoidable in order to protect life does not seem to have been followed.

The government also used NIF security forces and NIF youth militias, neither of which are lawfully established and regulated public forces, alongside police and Sudan Security forces to control and attack the student demonstrators. Where those allowed to use firearms are not part of public law enforcement bodies, but are members of ruling party militias, supervision and control of their conduct and use of force is particularly difficult to regulate and accountability for official misconduct is sidestepped.

Human Rights Watch received reports that up to 2,000 students and others were detained incommunicado without any criminal charges brought against them. Some detainees reportedly were beaten and tortured; more than three had their arms deliberately broken, according to later evidence. After local and international protests, most detainees were released after a few days, but the government reiterated its determination to try several on unspecified charges. Several prominent advocates (lawyers) were arrested at the same time and released without explanation a few days later.

Ahliya University in Omdurman became the target of a security force raid on September 23, 1995, in which agents deliberately brutalized a student who was admitted to Omdurman Hospital the same day with several broken limbs. The agents destroyed college computers and ransacked offices. Ahliya University, a private university, had refused to enforce the policy of making Arabic the language of instruction (which the Ministry of Higher Education mandated throughout Sudan), employed lecturers purged from public universities, and had a liberal attitude toward women's dress. The greatest issue of contention between Ahliya University and the government's however, was reportedly the tolerance of a student movement that the authorities considered too rebellious. In late November 1995, armed members of NIF student and other militias attacked anti-government students at Ahliya; the Student Union Activity Center was burned down and many students were injured. The government refused to intervene to halt the assault.

Abuses by the government in the war

The government's approach to the war is divisive: its aim appears to be a military victory in which the dominant Islamic and Arabic culture is imposed on militarily defeated non-Islamic and non-Arabic speaking southern and other peoples. The south is to be "brought to the light" — an expression frequently used in conversation by government officials and NIF supporters — through conversion, assimilation and abandonment of southern cultures, languages and religions. The war against the south is characterized as a Holy War (*jihad*). At frequent government mass rallies the head of state and other government officials address the participants as Muslims and encourage them to continue with the Holy War against the south. On the fortieth anniversary of the independence of Sudan, for example, President Lt.-Gen. al Bashir

> reaffirmed that Sudan was entering a renaissance, which is an embodiment of real independence, so that Sudan could perform its Arab, Islamic and international roles. . . . [He] referred to the spirit of jihad which has engulfed the entire people of Sudan. He said that sectors of the society were currently competing with each other in the fields of jihad in defense of the faith and the homeland.[5]

---

[5]"Sudan: President Bashir Says All Citizens 'Engulfed' by Spirit of Jihad," Republic of Sudan Radio, Omdurman, in Arabic, 1300 gmt, January 1, 1996, excerpts quoted by BBC Monitoring Service: Middle East, January 3, 1996.

The government refers to Muslims who die in battle against the south as holy warriors (*mujahedeen*) and martyrs (*shu'hada*), celebrating their deaths by "weddings" as promised in the Qur'an.

The army provides Islamic religious training to national service conscripts and Popular Defense Forces (PDF) militia. There is little respect for the right to maintain one's own non-Muslim religion in this environment, and the pressure to conform by adapting to Muslim religious practices is great. Civil servants, aspiring university students and others are required to join these ostensibly voluntary PDF forces for forty-five days and receive military/religious training. All students, male and female, wishing to enter any university must first have completed PDF training, and have a certificate to prove it; this requirement is in addition to national service obligations imposed on male students.

The government has manipulated differences between different southern peoples and financed several ethnic breakaway rebel factions to serve as its proxies in attacks on the main rebel group, the SPLM/A. In March 1996, Cmdr. Riek Machar, leader of the mostly Nuer Southern Sudan Independence Movement/Army (SSIM/A) forces who lead a breakaway from the SPLM/A in 1991, signed a peace agreement with the government. Joining him was Cmdr. Kerubino Kuanyin Bol, formerly of SSIM/A, a Dinka from northern Bahr El Ghazal who has terrorized his region for more than a year, looting and killing Dinka civilians and sometimes members of the SPLA, with the support of the Khartoum government. From the beginning of the war in 1983, the government has always supported militias composed of southerners disaffected with the SPLA and its commander-in-chief, John Garang. The government is responsible for the atrocities committed by the militias working with it.

As the government army has — with one exception — denied taking any combatants prisoner during the thirteen years of civil war, it appears likely that summary executions are committed in the field. The army has indiscriminately bombed civilian areas in the south, including landing strips where displaced civilians gathered to receive relief food from U.N. and other agencies. Army and government militia have committed abuses of humanitarian law such as beating and torturing prisoners, and conducting scorched earth campaigns of indiscriminate firing at villages and civilians, looting, and kidnaping women and children for use as slave or forced domestic labor. Government forces occupy garrison towns in the south surrounded by a sea of rebels.

Slavery

Slavery is even more forbidden as a topic for discussion inside government-controlled Sudan than is self-determination for the south and religious discrimination. Historically, southern peoples, including the Dinka, Nuer and Shilluk, were captured in slave raids by the Turko-Egyptian empire and by northern and western Sudanese, including by the nomadic Baggara tribes of Darfur.

Slavery experienced a resurgence when the Baggara were armed with automatic weapons by the central government to attack their Dinka civilian neighbors in the mid-1980s. The Dinka are the largest of the southern peoples, and the top leadership of the SPLM/A is Dinka. Following a common but illegal counterinsurgency theory of draining the "sea" or people so the "fish" or rebels cannot swim, the tribal militias were given a free hand to raid the Dinka, killing those who resisted, looting cattle, and violently capturing women and children — war booty — to be used as slaves in unpaid domestic labor, enforced by beatings. This practice continues today. Testimony from children who escaped from slavery, and the relatives who sought the freedom of captive family members held as house servants, was collected by Human Rights Watch during its 1995 visit to Sudan. See *Children of Sudan: Slaves, Street Children and Child Soldiers* (New York: Human Rights Watch, 1995).

The government has been under investigation by several U.N. bodies and mechanisms with regard to the allegation of condoning slavery and forced labor for several years, notably the International Labor Organization, the U.N. Committee on the Rights of the Child, the U.N. Working Group on Contemporary Forms of Slavery, and other mechanisms of the U.N. Commission on Human Rights.

The government in response to a U.N. report has claimed that, with regard to slavery, "the element of intention is decisive." In the Sudan, it maintains, tribal fights normally result in captives and prisoners of war on both sides of the conflict, but there is no intention to take slaves. Testimonies of scores of escaped slaves taken over several years by different organizations and journalists rebut the premise that there is no intention to take slaves. Captured women and children are transported hundreds of kilometers from the victims' homes to the homes of the attackers, forced through physical punishment to work for no pay, and tracked down when they try to escape.

The government has taken the inexcusable attitude that slavery must be "proven" to it, instead of living up to its obligations under international human rights law to seriously investigate the grave and frequently well-documented reports on this practice, and protect its citizens from this abuse.

Abuses by the rebels in the civil war

The rebel forces also have a history of human rights and humanitarian law abuses including holding fellow rebels prisoner in prolonged arbitrary detention, confiscating food from civilians, looting, and summary executions. Indiscriminate fighting between and among rebel factions has led to numerous civilian casualties and enormous displacement of the population.

The highest number of civilian casualties caused by fighting between rebel factions in 1994 was an attack on Akot in the Lakes region of Bahr El Ghazal, in Dinka territory, in October 1994, where 106 bodies were counted, mostly civilians: forty-eight women and children and fifty-eight men (twenty of the dead were identified as SPLA soldiers). Thousands of cattle were stolen by the raiders. The attacks were by a Nuer militia believed to be backed by the government of Sudan, and the SSIM/A.

Despite the "permanent" cease-fire agreed in April 1995 between the SPLM/A and the SSIM/A, and probably in retaliation for the attack on Akot and to regain stolen cattle, forces believed to be under SPLA command from the Akot area raided Ganyliel in July 1995, killing 210 people, mostly civilians (thirty men, fifty-three women, and 127 children), and destroyed thirty-five villages. This was the highest number of civilian casualties from the fighting between rebel factions in 1995. Over 3,500 head of cattle were looted. Operation Lifeline Sudan (OLS) (Southern Sector), the United Nations-coordinated disaster relief program, undertook an investigation and the SPLA promised to investigate and report on the incident. No SPLA report was ever produced but some of the stolen property was returned.

Looting of civilians and of U.N. and non-government (NGO) relief supplies by the parties has continued, often on a large scale. When the OLS evacuated relief staff from Nasir on February 10, 1996, their equipment and property were extensively looted, including boats and generators, almost certainly by SSIA forces. In 1995 almost forty relief personnel were taken hostage in three separate incidents, according to the OLS.

The SPLA admits it has taken government soldiers and officers and Popular Defense Forces militia members prisoner in combat. It permitted a visit from the International Committee of the Red Cross (ICRC) to 229 such prisoners in January 1996, and 102 prisoners in April 1996; the SPLA acknowledged holding about 600 persons in detention. To date, however, it has not permitted the ICRC to visit rebels accused by the SPLA of "treason" or other crimes.

Equal treatment for the displaced and squatters

The rights of the poor to due process before their homes are demolished is nonexistent. Since 1990, access to the courts or to any tribunal to adjudicate property claims regarding land registered in the name of the state has been flatly denied by government decree. This gave the government a free hand to deal with the squatters and displaced persons who occupied state and unregistered land —

since under the same decree, all unregistered land was to be considered to be registered or held in the name of the state. Hundreds of thousands of squatters and displaced persons have been denied due process as part of a systematic government campaign of "relocation" in high gear since 1992 in Khartoum. Their homes are bulldozed, and they are forcibly relocated to unprepared sites far from Khartoum and any employment possibilities. In 1994, eleven persons were shot dead when squatters and displaced persons resisted home destruction and forcible relocation in Omdurman.

The displaced or squatters who arrived in Khartoum after 1990, almost all southerners and Nubas, are denied all relocation and property rights when they are forcibly evicted and their homes in "unauthorized settlements" destroyed. They are forced to live in sites in which they have no right of tenure and no guarantee they will not be displaced again.

Recommendations to the government of Sudan:
The right to life and to physical integrity

- Institute a high level program to halt torture, including official directives condemning its use, routine criminal investigations to be instituted into reports of torture, the prosecution of torturers, the protection of those making complaints of torture, and legislation to prohibit the use of confessions or other evidence obtained through torture in criminal proceedings.
- Introduce safeguards against torture in law and in administrative procedures including requirements that all detainees be brought promptly before a judicial authority, that prompt and regular access to families, defense counsel and a doctor of one's choice be assured, and that incommunicado detention outside the supervision of the courts never be tolerated.
- Safeguards should include legislation to prohibit the holding of detainees anywhere that has not been publicly acknowledged as a place of detention and to provide accurate and up to date central records of all detentions, the latter to be available for consultation by the families and lawyers of detainees.
- The same authorities should not be responsible both for the interrogations of detainees and for the custodial care of these detainees, in order to increase the protection of detainees by introducing a further element of supervision; the responsibility of Sudan Security both for the maintenance of detention centers and for interrogations should be ended.

- Detention facilities under the sole supervision of Sudan Security or other security agencies, notably the unacknowledged centers known as "ghost houses," should be closed, and no further detention facilities should be established that are not publicly acknowledged and regulated in accord with the law. Unrestricted access to the former "ghost houses" should be allowed for members of the human rights community, the press and the diplomatic corps to verify their closure.

- The section of Kober Prison built especially for security detainees should be removed from the jurisdiction of Sudan Security and restored to the jurisdiction of the General Administration of Prisons.

- Halt the execution of punishments that are inherently cruel, inhuman or degrading, in particular the death penalty in any form, whether prescribed through some form of legal process law or through extrajudicial executions, with a view towards the effective abolition of these punishments in law and practice.

- In the context of measures to eliminate cruel, inhuman or degrading treatment, halt the use of shackling within the prison system except in situations permitted under international standards, such as to prevent escape during transfer from one facility to another.

- Fully disclose the record of military trial proceedings against the twenty-eight officers tried and executed in April 1990 for alleged involvement in a coup attempt; disclose to their families the locations of their graves and permit the families to rebury these officers. If there were others tried and executed in connection with the same attempted coup, publicly disclose their names, ranks and the trial records, and permit their families to rebury them.

- Establish an independent commission of inquiry, composed of representative experts drawn from civil society, to investigate evidence of torture, summary executions, and forcible "disappearances" with full powers to receive official information, its report to be made public. The scope of this enquiry should include the summary executions of twenty-eight army officers and possibly others with them in April 1990, the scores of executions and "disappearances" reported in Juba in 1992, as well as well-documented cases of torture such as that of Brig. al Rayah and the accused in the so-called "Explosives Case." The procedures of such an enquiry should include provisions to protect the safety of witnesses.

- Discontinue pardons or amnesties for military or security persons convicted of grave abuses of civilians or captured combatants.

The right to a fair trial and not to be arbitrarily detained

- Abolish detention solely for the exercise of freedom of expression, association and assembly as protected in international human rights law.
- Halt prolonged detention without charge in preventive detention and other forms of administrative detention; repeal or amend the National Security Act of 1995 so that warrantless arbitrary detention without charge or trial and prolonged incommunicado detention without judicial review is no longer tolerated.
- All detainees, including those now held under detention provisions in the National Security Act, should either be promptly charged or released; prisoners sentenced in unfair trials should be given the opportunity to appeal their sentences in proceedings meeting international standards for a fair trial or released.
- Discontinue trials of civilians in military courts.
- Guarantee all defendants a fair and public trial within a reasonable time, in accord with international fair trial standards, including the right to defense counsel, access to the evidence to be used against them, the right to an appeal, and sufficient time to fully exercise these rights.

Freedom of expression, opinion and association

- Lift the prohibition on political parties and permit their members to engage in free speech, free association and free assembly without harassment.
- Lift restrictions on the independence of trade unions, professional associations, ethnic. religious and other associations.
- Permit independent human rights monitors and organizations to function without interference.
- Lift arbitrary restrictions on the press and revoke the 1993 Press and Printed Materials Law; permit newspapers publishing before June 30, 1989, to reopen, including but not limited to those newspapers formerly affiliated with political parties.
- Allow free expression of independent opinion in the media, including such media as leaflets and handbills.
- Put an end to the current practice of summary closure of publications and the detention and harassment of journalists and writers for the nonviolent expression of opinions.
- Guarantee academic freedom; cease the dismissal on political grounds of academic and administrative staff in state institutions and reinstate all those who have been arbitrarily dismissed.

- Guarantee freedom of association for students in national and private universities.

Freedom of religion

- Permit adherents of all religions to worship freely and to build, purchase or rent houses of worship without obstruction. Non-Muslim congregations and churches should be permitted to carry out religious activities freely, on the same terms applying to Muslims, without discriminatory governmental interference.
- Respect the right of religious organizations to maintain charitable or humanitarian institutions, to acquire materials related to religious rights, to teach, to train leaders, and other activities; cease imposing on some religions and their activities regulations and requirements not imposed equally on all religions.
- If religious instruction continues to be offered in schools, facilitate instruction in non-Muslim religions and beliefs, so that they are available to students readily and without discrimination or coercion in their choice of religion. Respect the rights of students to receive no religious instruction if they or their families so choose.
- Convicted prisoners of all faiths should have equal access to provisions for early release offered those who take religious instruction, based on their own religions; this program now applies only to those who memorize the Qur'an (take instruction in Islam).
- Abolish criminal punishment for the offense of renouncing Islam.
- Establish the equality in law of women and of non-Muslims and punish discrimination against them.
- Protect the rights of practitioners of all religions and beliefs to equal treatment and nondiscrimination in the army, civil service, schools and other aspects of public life.

Freedom of movement

- Lift foreign travel bans established on political grounds, including those imposed through the requirement of exit visas to leave the country, and permit the movement of Sudanese to any part of their country.
- Reduce controls on travel between the north and the south; facilitate north-south travel by those current or former southern residents who wish to relocate or visit their families.

- Facilitate access to all parts of the country, particularly the Nuba Mountains and the south, for human rights monitors, human rights educators, and relief workers.

The use of force in the control of demonstrations and other public assemblies

- Train police, including the People's Police Force, in the U.N. guidelines on the use of force, and incorporate these guidelines into police regulations and training materials concerned with crowd control.
- Prevent National Islamic Front forces and other forces not established and regulated by law from taking any part in the suppression of demonstrations or other police work
- Protect those exercising their freedom of expression, association and assembly from attacks, including attacks by government supporters.
- Investigate reports of the excessive use of force in the context of government programs to clear communities of squatters and the displaced, in the government response to student demonstrations in September 1995, and in the raids on the Omdurman Ahliya University campus in September and November 1995, and make the findings public.
- Disband and disarm National Islamic Front militias and security forces and other such quasi-governmental forces that are not formally established and regulated by law and open to public scrutiny and accountability before the law.

Human rights and the internally displaced

- Halt the destruction of homes of the internally displaced and squatters in Khartoum and other urban areas until the right to judicial review and appeal, suspended by the 1990 Amendment to the Civil Transactions Act, is restored; award compensation without discrimination on account of social origin, race, religion, or other status.
- Halt the forced relocation of internally displaced and squatters from the Khartoum area to areas far distant from urban centers and work opportunities.
- Halt the arbitrary relocation of persons living in rural areas from their villages under the pretext of military operations , and permit those who have been relocated in the past to return to their homes.
- Allow freedom of movement and residence, so that displaced people and squatters can return to their former homes if they wish.
- Compensate those who have lost homes and possessions in past relocations.

National service and the Popular Defense Forces (PDF)

- End conscription of those under the age of eighteen into the armed forces and the nominally voluntary PDF militia; prevent the participation in hostilities of those aged under eighteen. Conscription should be enforced only through procedures established in law, and without resort to the use of force in violation of international standards.
- Introduce legislation and procedures to provide alternative civilian service for those who object to national service in the military on conscientious grounds.
- Eliminate measures to compel non-Muslims performing national service or undergoing PDF training and service to take part in Islamic education programs and worship.
- Eliminate the requirement that any person serve in the Popular Defense Forces as a condition of government employment, university matriculation or similar activities unless and until its training programs are modified to respect the right of all participants freely to exercise their own religion.
- PDF training programs offering prisoners who choose to participate early release should be modified to allow participation by non-Muslims without prejudice to their rights not to be compelled to change their religion.
- Establish full accountability for abuses committed by the Popular Defense Forces and associated tribal militias, through transparent disciplinary and criminal procedures.

Stopping slavery and related practices

- Establish urgently a program to put an end to the capture and exploitation of children and other civilians during army and militia raids and their confinement in slavery-like conditions, to include public reporting of the measures taken.
- As an urgent priority, identify and release those held in captivity by members of tribal militias (including militias of the Baggara), Popular Defense Forces, military, and others; investigate all reports of the kidnaping and/or enslavement of civilians, especially children, with a view to releasing all those held against their will and/or forced to work without compensation, and prosecuting those in any way responsible for their capture or captivity or who benefited from their forced labor.
- Investigate all reports of children and adults held against their will as servants or laborers, paid or unpaid, and all reports of their physical or sexual abuse, and prosecute those found responsible;

- Establish, in consultation with international agencies with experience in locating missing persons, a central agency responsible for assisting family members to locate their missing relatives, and assure funding necessary for its operations, including publicity and full cooperation with community representatives seeking to trace community members taken in army and militia raids.

- As part of a comprehensive program to eliminate slavery and slavery-like practices, enforce fully Sudanese law punishing child abuse, kidnaping, hostage-taking, and forced or child labor, with regular, public reports on relevant criminal investigations, prosecutions and convictions. Investigate and prosecute officials and police officers who fail to enforce criminal laws in this regard.

- Ensure that the armed forces, security agencies and militia issue and enforce orders to halt the capture of children and other civilians who are not detained for recognizable criminal offenses, their exploitation and their transfer within and from the war zones.

- Institute procedures to prevent military personnel, militia and others under military jurisdiction from taking unrelated persons with them from war zones or garrison towns, and especially prevent such persons from using government transport to move unrelated persons.

- Prevent transportation by adults of unrelated children from state to state without appropriate authorization. Where the adult is of a different ethnic background from the child, the circumstances of such transport should be closely scrutinized.

- Introduce legislation to provide increased safeguards against slavery, including measures outlawing the unpaid the employment of non-family members of whatever age, and ratifying the International Labor Organization (ILO) Minimum Age Convention of 1973 (No. 138).

- Cooperate fully with the U.N. Committee on the Rights of the Child, the ILO, the United Nations Children's Fund (UNICEF), the U.N. Working Group on Contemporary Forms of Slavery, and the U.N. Commission on Human Rights' Special Rapporteur on Sudan in their investigations of reported slavery-like abuses.

- Request international cooperation, particularly technical assistance and advice, to pay urgent and due regard to reports of slavery and forced labor.

The rights of children

- Continue with the family reunification program for street children held in government camps.
- Halt the random capture of children from the streets and their transfer to closed camps without notification of their families. Children presently in the camps should be reunified with their families where possible, while care for homeless children and those whose families cannot be traced should be provided through programs which respect freedom of religion.
- Investigate the allegations of ill-treatment in the government's closed camps for street children and punish those responsible.
- In any detention of street children believed to be at risk, a first priority should be to establish contact with the child's family or guardian; prolonged custodial care of street children should be subject to judicial supervision, while due process guarantees should be present in any case in which children are brought into the criminal justice system. Alternatives to incarceration or confinement in closed custodial establishments should be provided where feasible.
- Ratify the African Convention on the Rights of the Child and introduce legislation to implement its provisions for the protection of children.

Human rights protection and the war in the south

- Respect international humanitarian law and human rights law, prohibiting the targeting of civilian and civilian objects in military operations, indiscriminate attacks, looting and unnecessary destruction of civilian property.
- Accord members of the SPLA or other rebel groups who are captured or otherwise *hors de combat* humane treatment; cease government secrecy concerning the capture and fate of suspected combatants.
- Investigate abuses committed by members of the Sudan Armed Forces, security services, militias and associated former rebel groups working with them. Bring to trial those held responsible for such abuses.
- Compensate those whose property has been looted or deliberately destroyed in violation of international standards during military or other government operations.
- Affirm the right of non-combatants in war-affected areas to receive food, medicine, and other relief, and cease actions that might prejudice their receipt of such relief. The U.N. Operation Lifeline Sudan, the ICRC and other relief programs should be allowed to proceed in accordance with

humanitarian need, without hindrance. Provide safe land, river and air access for the provision of humanitarian aid.
- Permit the ICRC to visit persons detained in connection with the conflict according to its specific criteria.

Recommendations to the Sudan People's Liberation Movement/Army and other armed rebel groups:

- Respect international humanitarian and human rights law, particularly the prohibitions on targeting civilians, indiscriminate attacks on civilians, and destruction or looting of civilian property.
- Refrain from involuntarily recruiting anyone.
- Refrain from using children under the age of eighteen as combatants and prevent them from participating in hostilities.
- Facilitate voluntary family reunification.
- Permit the ICRC to visit persons detained in connection with the conflict according to its specific criteria.
- Cease taking hostages.
- Provide safe land, river and air access for the provision of humanitarian aid.
- Cooperate with human rights monitors and educators, and facilitate their access to all parts of the country.
- Affirm the right of noncombatants in war-affected areas to receive food, medicine, and other relief, and not undertake any action that might prejudice their receipt of such relief. In particular, cease looting relief barges and the equipment of relief agencies.
- Refrain from taking food or non-food items, directly or indirectly, from civilians, particularly those at or below the subsistence level; any supplies taken by military personnel should be paid for.
- Abolish political detention, torture, ill-treatment and the death penalty in any form.
- Launch public investigations and permit investigations by others into allegations of human rights abuses committed by each rebel force's own members, and take disciplinary action against those responsible for such abuses, including but not limited to the July 1995 attack on Ganyliel, the October 1994 attack on Akot, the disappearance of Dr. Karlo Madut in 1994, the killing of Martin Majieur in 1993, and the killings of three relief workers and one journalist in 1992.
- Cooperate with international agencies willing to provide instruction in humanitarian law to combatants.

Recommendations to the United Nations Security Council:

- Institute an arms embargo on the parties to the conflict in Sudan, with special attention to bombs and aircraft used to deliver them.

Recommendations to U.N. Commission on Human Rights and High Commissioner for Human Rights:

- Assure that the proposals of the special rapporteur on human rights in Sudan for establishing three U.N. human rights monitors to be based in Eritrea, Kenya and Uganda are accepted by all necessary parties and appropriately funded, and that their duties include observation, investigation, bringing to the attention of the responsible authorities, and making public violations of humanitarian and human rights laws by all parties. The monitors should have access to all parts of Sudan.
- Establish a civilian-directed and staffed program of human rights education for all regions of Sudan. This program should be a supplement to, not a substitute for, the human rights monitors.
- Persuade the government to continue and expand upon its "open-door" policy in the field of human rights.
- Recommend to the government that it permit the extension of OLS emergency relief operations to all areas where war-affected civilians live in the Nuba Mountains and other disputed areas of the country.

Recommendations to UNICEF, ILO, U.N. Committee on the Rights of the Child, the Working Group on Contemporary Forms of Slavery, the U.N. Commission on Human Rights, and other concerned U.N. bodies, mechanisms and agencies:

- conduct voluntary family reunification; where small groups of minors are separated from their larger tribe, efforts should be made to reunite them in the safest location, even if that means reuniting them outside of Sudan or from one country of refuge to another. This task should receive the cooperation of all U.N. and NGO agencies.
- UNICEF and the ILO should establish and fund programs to effectively promote the adoption of national legislation and implementing programs to ban child labor, slavery, and slavery-like practices.
- UNICEF, the U.N. Committee on the Rights of the Child, the Working Group on Contemporary Forms of Slavery, the U.N. Commission on Human Rights' special rapporteur on Sudan, and the ILO monitor the application of the slavery and forced labor conventions to Sudan, and that

all send fact-finding missions to investigate the reported abuses and the mechanisms the government is employing to confront the problem.

- UNICEF, the ILO, and the Working Group on Contemporary Forms of Slavery should work with the government of Sudan to establish government mechanisms to effectively assist families in the search for kidnaped or missing family members.

Recommendations to the African Commission on Human and People's Rights

- Conduct, as soon as possible, a fact-finding mission to Sudan with regard to its emergency situation and serious violations of human and people's rights, and make a public written report to the session of the African Commission to be held in October 1996, on the following topics: summary executions; torture and ill-treatment; arbitrary arrests and fundamental fairness at trial; slavery and slave-like practices; freedom of religion, expression, assembly, association, and movement; treatment of displaced persons and squatters in Khartoum; and observance of human rights in the war in southern Sudan, the Nuba Mountains, and eastern Sudan.

Recommendations to the "Friends of IGAAD" (the United States, United Kingdom, Canada, the Netherlands, Italy, Norway), the European Union, and other concerned governments and bodies

- Support an arms embargo on all parties to the conflict, including by urging major exporters China, Russia, Iran, North Korea, South Africa, and others, to stop arms sales or transfers to Sudan. Similarly urge countries or others supplying arms to the SPLA and other armed rebel groups to cease their arms sales or transfers. Establish a multilateral monitoring mechanism for the implementation of an arms embargo. Members of the European Union should enforce the E.U. arms embargo of Sudan established as the common position of the European Union by council decision of March 16, 1994.
- Support the creation of a full-time U.N. human rights monitoring team, and provide financing for it.
- Support the creation of a civilian directed and staffed program of human rights education for all regions of Sudan. This program should be a supplement to, not a substitute for, the human rights monitors. The recommended U.N. human rights monitors and educational program should not be funneled through the government, the SPLA or other rebel factions or their agencies.

- Maintain pressure on the Sudan government and the SPLA and other rebel factions to permit access to relief operations.
- Use their votes in international financial institutions to freeze Sudanese requests for loans or disbursements, including from the African Development Bank, until patterns of gross human rights abuses are eliminated.
- Kenya, Uganda, Ethiopia, Eritrea, Zaire and other countries receiving Sudanese refugees should permit those unaccompanied boys in Sudan or in other countries to be reunited with their parents or closest surviving relatives who are refugees in their territories pursuant to their obligations under the United Nations Convention on the Rights of the Child, Article 10.

Recommendations to nongovernmental organizations working in Sudan

- Bring to the attention of the appropriate bodies, including the parties to the conflict, U.N. agencies, and donors, abuses committed by the parties to the conflict in possible violation of international standards of humanitarian law and human rights.
- Routinely include the human rights situation and the human rights consequences of a relief operation in field reports, country reports, and reports to the public of all the relief agencies concerned.

2

ARBITRARY ARREST AND ADMINISTRATIVE
OR PREVENTIVE DETENTION

The National Security Act of 1995 provides for prolonged arbitrary detention in security cases of up to six months without judicial review. This is a violation of the International Covenant on Civil and Political Rights (ICCPR), Article 9.[1] The judicial review that takes place after six months of warrantless incommunicado detention is inadequate; an appointee of the chief justice, who takes a very passive view of these supervisory duties, is supposed to conduct this review.[2] The government has misrepresented the status of this law to the U.N. It said in November 1995 that the 1992 National Security Act was in effect, and failed to disclose that it was replaced by a more restrictive 1995 act signed into law in May 1995.

The new law was quickly applied to facilitate the detention of the former prime minister and leader of the banned Umma Party and the mass detentions of suspected Umma Party leaders, all released, without charges, in August 1995. It was used again to cut off student protests against the government in September 1995 in the streets of Khartoum. Hundreds were detained, sometimes by NIF party security and militias; in 1996, the act was used to detain persons suspected of connections with the nascent armed opposition movement based in Eritrea, and representatives of civil society.

Sudan is in the throes of an internal armed conflict in the south and other areas, but the absence of combatants captured by the army in the thirteen years of war raises the troubling possibility that they might have been killed as a matter of government policy. The burden of explaining this anomalous situation lies heavily on the government.

THE APPLICABLE LAW

The Universal Declaration of Human Rights, in Article 9, states simply that "No one shall be subject to arbitrary arrest, detention or exile." Article 9 of the

---

[1]Sudan acceded to the ICCPR on March 18, 1986.

[2]Chief Justice Obeid Haj Ali appointed Deputy Chief Justice Mohamud Abu Geseesa to perform this function. Human Rights Watch/Africa interview, Chief Justice Obeid Haj Ali and Deputy Chief Justice Mohamud Abu Geseesa, Supreme Court of Sudan, Khartoum, June 10, 1995.

ICCPR is designed to further protect against arbitrary arrest and detention. It provides:

> 1.   Everyone has the right to liberty and security of person. No one shall be subjected to arbitrary arrest or detention. No one shall be deprived of his liberty except on such grounds and in accordance with such procedures as are established by law.
>
> 2.   Anyone who is arrested shall be informed, at the time of arrest, of the reasons for his arrest and shall be promptly informed of any charges against him.
>
> 3.   Anyone arrested or detained on a criminal charge shall be brought promptly before a judge or other officer authorized by law to exercise judicial power and shall be entitled to trial within a reasonable time or to release. It shall not be the general rule that persons awaiting trial shall be detained in custody, but release may be subject to guarantees to appear for trial, at any other stage of the judicial proceedings, and, should occasion arise, for execution of the judgement.
>
> 4.   Anyone who is deprived of his liberty by arrest or detention shall be entitled to take proceedings before a court, in order that court may decide without delay on the lawfulness of his detention and order his release if the detention is not lawful.
>
> 5.   Anyone who has been victim of unlawful arrest or detention shall have an enforceable right to compensation.

The African Charter provides similar protection against arbitrary arrest.[3]

The purpose of ICCPR Article 9 (1) is to require states to spell out in legislation the grounds on which an individual may be deprived of his liberty and the procedures to be used. This is to make clear that "[n]ot every policeman (or

---

[3]African Charter on Human and People's Rights, Article 6: "Every individual shall have the right to liberty and to the security of his person. No one may be deprived of his freedom except for reasons and conditions previously laid down by law. In particular, no one may be arbitrarily arrested or detained." Sudan acceded to the African Charter on February 18, 1986.

other state functionary) is entitled to decide at his discretion, and on his own responsibility, who can be arrested, why and how."[4]

Even where the government has complied with its own laws, an arrest may still be regarded as arbitrary. An "arbitrary" arrest is not limited to an "illegal" arrest. "Arbitrary" also means "unjust."

> Arbitrary arrest or detention implied an arrest or detention which was incompatible with the principles of justice or with the dignity of the human person irrespective of whether it had been carried out in conformity with the law.[5]

Other commentators have emphasized that the purpose of the ICCPR's prohibition on arbitrary arrest is to protect individuals from despotic legislation and to establish that deprivations of liberty as occurred under the Nazi regime are not consistent with human rights merely because they were enacted into national law.[6]

"Political" detainees are generally those held in preventive (or administrative) detention in Sudan. They are rarely charged with any crime or brought before a court by the authorities. Article 9 (4) of the ICCPR provides that such detainees have the right to judicial supervision of the lawfulness of their arrest. It states that anyone "deprived of his liberty by arrest or detention shall be entitled to take proceedings before a court, in order that that court may decide without delay on the lawfulness of his detention and order his release if the detention is not lawful."

The U.N. Human Rights Committee, created under Article 28 of the ICCPR, has found that the purpose of Article 9 (4) of the ICCPR is to ensure that it is a court that reviews detention, not merely any authority regulated by law, and that the reviewing authority must possess a degree of objectivity and independence to exercise adequate control over detention. It held that a person detained by order

---

[4]Yoram Dinstein, "The Right to Life, Physical Integrity, and Liberty," in Louis Henkin, ed., *The International Bill of Rights: The Covenant on Civil and Political Rights* (New York: Columbia University Press, 1981), p. 130.

[5]Ibid., citing the position of the American Delegation in the Third Committee of the General Assembly (footnote omitted).

[6]Ibid., p. 131 (footnote omitted).

of an administrative body or authority has the right to have that decision reviewed in a court of law.[7]

Significantly, Article 9 (4) gives the detainee the right to go to court for a decision "without delay." Even during states of emergency, a remedy like habeas corpus must be available.[8] Thus the government may not erect barriers to a prompt judicial decision on the lawfulness of the reasons for detention. "Judicial" means providing the fundamental guarantees of judicial procedures, including an "opportunity to be heard either in person, or where necessary, through some form of representation."[9]

To exercise this right to a hearing under Article 9 (4), the detainee must have notice of the reasons for the detention and access to legal counsel. The right to counsel, recognized in Article 14 (3) of the ICCPR and in the U.N. Basic Principles on the Role of Lawyers,[10] is necessary to make the other rights in Article 9 of the ICCPR effective. The rights to a hearing and to acknowledgment of the detention are also essential to prevent forcible "disappearance."[11]

---

[7]See *Antti Vuolanne v. Finland* (265/1987) (7 April 1989), *Official Records of the General Assembly, Forty-fourth Session, Supplement No. 40* (A/44/40), annex X, sect. J; and *Mario I. Torres v. Finland* (291-1988) (2 April 1990), ibid., *Forty-fifth Session, Supplement No. 40* (A/45/40), vol. II, annex IX, sect. K, cited in Centre for Human Rights and Crime Prevention and Criminal Justice Branch, Professional Training Series No. 3, *Human Rights and Pre-trial Detention* (New York: United Nations, 1994), p. 40.

[8]Centre for Human Rights, *Human Rights and Pre-trial Detention*, p. 40.

[9]Dinstein, "The Right to Life, Physical Integrity, and Liberty," p. 135, citing the European Court for Human Rights in Winterwerp case, judgment of October 24, 1979, *Publication, European Center for Human Rights*, Ser. A, para. 30.

[10]United Nations Basic Principles on the Role of Lawyers:

> Principle 7. Governments shall further ensure that all persons arrested or detained, with or without criminal charge, shall have prompt access to a lawyer, and in any case not later than forty-eight hours from the time of arrest or detention.
>
> Principle 8. All arrested, detained or imprisoned persons shall be provided with adequate opportunities, time and facilities to be visited by and to communicate and consult with a lawyer, without delay, interception or censorship and in full confidentiality. . . .

Basic Principles on the Role of Lawyers, Eighth United Nations Congress on the Prevention of Crime and the Treatment of Offenders, Havana, 27 August to 7 September 1990, U.N. Doc. A/CONF.144/28/Rev.1, p.118 (1990).

[11]U.N. Declaration on the Protection of All Persons from Enforced Disappearances, Article 9:

(continued...)

In order to prevent torture, the Convention Against Torture and Other Cruel, Inhuman, Or Degrading Treatment or Punishment provides in Article 10:

> 1. Each State Party shall ensure that education and information regarding the prohibition against torture are fully included in the training of law enforcement personnel, civil or military, medical personnel, public officials, and other persons who may be involved in the custody, interrogation or treatment of any individual subjected to any form of arrest, detention or imprisonment.[12]

Where there are complaints of torture, the Convention against Torture requires that the competent authorities promptly investigate.[13] In order to have safeguards against his or her rights not to be tortured, the detainee must have access to these authorities.[14] This obligation may not be suspended in times of emergency.

---

[11](...continued)
> 1. The right to a prompt and effective judicial remedy as a means of determining the whereabouts or state of health of persons deprived of their liberty and/or identifying the authority ordering or carrying out the deprivation of liberty is required to prevent enforced disappearances under all circumstances, including those referred to in article 7 above.
> 2. In such proceedings, competent national authorities shall have access to all places where persons deprived of their liberty are being held and to each part of those places, as well as to any place in which there are grounds to believe that such persons may be found.

U.N. General Assembly Declaration on the Protection of All Persons from Enforced Disappearances, G.A. res. 47/133, 47 U.N. GAOR Supp. (No. 49) p.207, U.N. Doc. A/47/49 (1992), adopted by General Assembly resolution 47/133 of 18 December 1992.

[12]Article 10, Convention against Torture and Other Cruel, Inhuman or Degrading Treatment or Punishment, G.A. res. 39/46, annex, 39 U.N. GAOR Supp. (No. 51) at 197, U.N. Doc. A/39/51 (1984), entered into force June 26, 1987. Sudan signed this convention on June 4, 1986, but has not yet ratified it.

[13]Convention Against Torture, Article 12: "Each State Party shall ensure that its competent authorities proceed to a prompt and impartial investigation, wherever there is reasonable ground to believe that an act of torture has been committed in any territory under its jurisdiction."

[14]Convention Against Torture, Article 13.

THE NATIONAL SECURITY ACT OF 1995

The National Security Act of 1995, as amended by the Transitional National Assembly (TNA),[15] on its face violates the prohibition on arbitrary arrest and detention of Article 9 of the ICCPR. The act does not permit prompt review by a judicial authority of the reasons for detention. Instead, it makes judicial review of preventive detention impossible before six months of incommunicado detention have elapsed, and erects a bar to proceedings against any official responsible for this and other human rights violations. It also violates international law in that it does not provide for any effective supervision of security detention, particularly in unacknowledged places of detention, known as "ghost houses." It permits a situation in which torture and disappearance may occur unchecked.

This National Security Act of 1995 is labeled "Top Secret" and government officials, when asked for a copy, claimed they did not have one. Nevertheless, Human Rights Watch obtained a copy of the act and its amendment through unofficial channels in Sudan. For unknown reasons, the government of Sudan, in its statement submitted to the U.N. in response to the interim November 1995 human rights report by the U.N. special rapporteur on human rights, refers not to the 1995 National Security Act but to the act of 1990, as amended in 1991 and 1992.[16] To the best knowledge of Human Rights Watch, the National Security Act of 1990 and its amendments were abrogated by the provisional National Security Act order of November 1994.

---

[15]The TNA was appointed by the Revolutionary Command Council in June 1989 (Constitutional Decree No. 4) to assume federal legislative powers until such a time as a permanent parliament (National Assembly) would be elected. Members of the TNA are appointed by the president, some after recommendation from state legislatures known as popular salvation committees. Under this government, which functions without a written constitution but on the basis of "constitutional decrees" issued by the president which remove rather than grant rights, legislation is decreed by the president and is effective from the date of his signature for two months while the TNA acts upon it. The TNA may approve, revise or take no action. If the TNA takes no action, the presidential decree is null and void.

Constitutional Decree No. 13 established a National Assembly with 275 seats (direct election) and 125 seats (indirect election) that was installed after the March 1996 elections. Legislation since that time is enacted according to a different scheme. Articles 51 and 52, Constitutional Decree No. 13 (1995).

[16]"The Response of the Government of the Sudan to the Interim Report on the Situation of Human Rights in the Sudan Contained in Document (A/50/569) of 16 October 1995, Prepared by Mr. Gaspar Biro the Special Rapporteur of the Commission on Human Rights," November 21, 1995, New York, pp. 18-19.

The National Security Act in effect at the time of our May-June 1995 visit to Sudan, and still in effect as of the date of this report, was the act of 1995, as promulgated by the president in November 1994, amended by the TNA in its thirty-fifth session on April 11, 1995, and signed by President al Bashir and TNA Speaker Khalifa on May 2, 1995. Indeed, General Administrator of Prisons Maj.-Gen. al Shaikh al Rayah referred to the National Security Act of 1995 in a statement published by the official news agency during a release of security detainees on August 26, 1995.[17] We analyze the provisions of the 1995 act because we conclude that the prior acts are not in effect, despite the government's representation to the U.N.

The 1995 act divides up the security apparatus into internal and external security sections.[18] According to a list of detainees given by the government to the International Commission of Jurists (ICJ) on May 3, 1995, persons then detained pursuant to the National Security Act were suspected or accused of offenses in the following security categories: economic security (*iqtisadi*), state security (*wilayat*), security of the apparatus (*amn al jihaz*),[19] African countries (*al Ifrikiyeh*), Arab countries (*al Arabiyeh*), the south (*al janoub*),[20] operations (*al amaliyat*),[21] and central administration (*al idarah al markazia*).[22] This suggests that security's internal and external divisions include these departments.

There are two provisions pursuant to which persons may be detained without a court order under the National Security Act of 1995. One is Article 37 (1), permitting the National Security Council to authorize "preventive detention" to "preserve public peace" for a period of three months, renewable for another

---

[17]"Sudan: Former Prime Minister Sadiq al Mahdi Among Released Detainees," SUNA News Agency, Khartoum, in English, 1725 gmt, August 26, 1995, quoted in BBC Monitoring Service: Middle East, August 28, 1995.

[18]The text of the law does not give any specific name to the combined entity of Internal Security and External Security. The 1995 amendment passed by the TNA calls the umbrella body "Security Apparatus." We refer in this report to "Sudan Security" for convenience, and because it is popularly known by this term.

[19]This refers to protection of the institution.

[20]The central office of this department reportedly is located in Khartoum 2 near the Farouk Cemetery.

[21]The central office of this department reportedly is located in Khartoum, in Hay al Maatar neighborhood near the Kuwaiti Embassy and army headquarters.

[22]International Commission of Jurists, "ICJ Mission Obtains Names of Administrative Detainees in Sudan," press release, Geneva, Switzerland, May 5, 1995, attachment.

three months. This six-month period is renewable only with the consent of a "competent judge."[23]

Art. 37. Preventive detention and judicial supervision.

1. The Council may order the preventive detention of any person to preserve public peace for a period of three months, renewable for another three months.

2. Renewal of detention is not permitted after the expiration of the period stated in section (1) without the approval of the competent judge.[24]

Sudan Security thus may avoid judicial review for six months by simple order of the National Security Council, a body composed of the president and other members of the executive branch appointed by him, and the speaker of the assembly, a position held since March 1996 by Dr. Hassan al Turabi.[25] It is not a court of law, which is the sole authority that may review the detention decision. This violates Article 9 of the ICCPR's requirement of judicial supervision "without delay" of the reasons for administrative detention. Nor is the requirement of notice and a hearing met.

Article 36 of the National Security Act of 1995, the second provision for detention without court order, permits the director of security to extend the period of detention from seventy-two hours[26] to one month, and requires the director to explain the reasons for an extension beyond the first seventy-two hours.

Article 36 (1) states that each member shall have the following powers:

---

[23]Article 3 of the act defines "competent judge" as "the justice of the Supreme Court appointed by the chief justice to supervise preventive custody and inspection of detention facilities."

[24]Before its amendment by the TNA in May 1995, this Article 37 read: "(1) The Council may order any person to be held in preventive detention for a period which may not exceed three months so as to preserve public security; (2) Renewal of the detention is not permitted after the expiration of the period stated in section (1) without the approval of the competent judge." In its amendment, the TNA deferred judicial review another three months by adding to Article 37 (1) the words, " renewable for another three months."

[25]The National Security Council's members, under Article 39 of the National Security Act, are the president of the republic, advisor to the president on security affairs, speaker of the TNA (now the National Assembly), ministers of defense, foreign affairs, interior, attorney general and minister of justice, and directors of internal and external security.

[26]Any security member may detain a person for the initial seventy-two hours. See Article 36 (1) (B).

B. With the exception of cases where the accused is caught in the act or in emergency situations, to arrest or detain any person for a period of seventy-two hours for purposes of interrogation and investigation, provided that the director [of the combined entity of security] may issue an order to extend the period of interrogation and investigation for a period not exceeding one month, explaining the reasons for such an extension.[27]

Although the act says the director must explain his reasons, it does not say to whom the explanation is to be given. Even if it were to be given to the detainee, the period of one month in the act between detention and notice of reasons for detention is also too long a delay under the ICCPR. Nor does the director of security qualify as a "court" under Article 9 (4) of the ICCPR. In any event it is impossible to establish who acts when because none of these proceedings are public nor does the detainee have any notice of them, if indeed they are held.

The only possibilities for legal review are by a designated justice of the Supreme Court after the statutory period of six months has elapsed under Article 37, or under the mandate apparently given to this appointee of the chief justice of the Supreme Court in Article 3 of the National Security Act of 1995, to "supervise preventive custody and inspect detention facilities."

While Article 37 provides for judicial review of the preventive detention, it does not say who has standing to bring a complaint. Most attorneys interviewed agree that the detainee does not have standing to bring a petition for his release. This conclusion is reinforced by the fact that the articles of the 1991 National Security Act giving the detainee the right to petition the court (or the attorney general[28]) were deleted from the 1995 act. When asked specifically by Human Rights Watch whether a detainee or his advocate could bring suit if he were in security custody, the chief justice and deputy chief justice of the Supreme Court —

---

[27]As set forth above, the exception to the limitation on security member detention powers, which may swallow the rule, is that in cases where the accused is caught in the act or in an undefined "emergency situation," a member may detain a person for more than seventy-two hours without the director's order.

[28]National Security Act of 1991, Article 40 (A) (3): "The detainee shall be enabled whenever he so wishes to send a petition to the Council about his detention or his treatment." Article 40 (A) (5) states: "The detainee may complain to the representative of the attorney general's chamber or to the judge about the failure to observe checks on detention specified in this article, and the judge may, after expedited review, issue any order he deems suitable to correct the injustice." Both sections are omitted from the 1995 National Security Act.

the supervising justice appointed under the act — avoided the question with a rhetorical shrug, "Why can't someone bring a suit to court?" and claimed lack of knowledge of the recently enacted National Security Act.[29]

The public officials responsible for the detention are immune from suit. Article 38 of the National Security Act of 1995 bars all civil and criminal proceedings against security members, except for those not related to their work. Criminal acts related to the work of the security agent are not punishable in any civil or criminal proceeding.

Article 38: Members and collaborators shall enjoy the following privileges:

> (b) Without prejudice to the provisions of this law and without prejudice to any right of compensation from the state, it shall not be permissible to take any civil or criminal proceedings against the member except after the approval of the director who shall give such approval whenever it becomes evident that the issue is not related to the official work of the member.[30]

Nor will any court take jurisdiction of such a case. The National Security Act has achieved its deterrent intent. No attorney will petition a court for relief if he knows beforehand that his client has no standing, that the only court with jurisdiction is indifferent to security detainees, and that the relevant public officials are immune from suit.[31]

---

[29]Human Rights Watch/Africa interview, Chief Justice Obeid Haj Ali and Deputy Chief Justice Abu Geseesa, June 10, 1995.

[30]The Article 38 the president sent to the TNA reads, "b. *With the exception of cases of being caught in the act*, it shall not be permissible to take any civil or criminal proceedings against the member except after the approval of the director who shall give such approval whenever it becomes evident that the issue is not related to the official work of the member. (Emphasis added.) Again, the TNA provided a bill more favorable to security personnel than that forwarded by the president.

[31]In one case, nevertheless, we learned that attorneys for detainees in Damazien attempted to petition the district court for release of their clients one month after the arrests in late 1994; that court refused to act, claiming it did not have jurisdiction. Human Rights Watch/Africa interview, Khartoum, May 27, 1995.

THE REALITY

Security detainees released in 1995 uniformly relate that they were not informed of the reasons for detention and had no right to counsel. Those detained longer than six months had no judicial review or remedy. One security detainee, whose case is described below, was told that he would not be released in the general amnesty of August 1995 because there was (ostensibly) no paperwork done on his case — despite the fact that he was detained on January 29, 1995, and his detention already exceeded the six-month limit.

Detainees released in late 1995 said that security officers led them to believe that the law applicable to preventive detention included a one hundred-day limit — less than the statutory maximum of six months, but still too long to meet due process requirements.

Security detainees were told that any agent of "officer" rank was empowered to extend the initial seventy-two hour detention period to a total of ten days. A "department" director may add one month to the ten days, for a total of forty days. The director of security may extend that period by two additional months, one month at a time. These limits do not appear in the 1995 National Security Act and seem to have been self-imposed by security.

Accordingly, based on what their captors told them, detainees expected to be released one hundred days from the date of arrest, and this timetable seems to have been followed in many cases, although not all. Some detainees spent up to two additional weeks in detention, awaiting the completion of formalities and paper work. Furthermore, since some detainees were told they were not officially entered in the records at the beginning of their detention, their day count could start whenever the officer in charge chose. As long as the detainee is not "registered," or registration is not acknowledged, security may maintain total deniability should it decide to disappear or kill the detainee.

The detainees might be held all or part of the time in "ghost houses," which are unofficial Sudan Security detention places, in security offices, or in military custody on a base or in a military intelligence facility. Detainees usually are moved several times before they are released. It appears in early 1996 that Khartoum security detainees are kept for fewer days in the ghost houses. Most are sent to the security section in Kober Prison after that.

THE ROLE OF THE SUPREME COURT

While in theory there is judicial review of preventive detention under Article 3 which outlines the supervisory duty of the Supreme Court over preventive custody, in reality this review does not function. The chief justice of the Supreme Court, whose duty it is under this statute to appoint a justice of the Supreme Court to supervise preventive custody, said he was unaware of the terms of this act in June 1995, six months after it was issued by the president and one month after it was amended by the TNA and passed into law. He protested that it was not the duty of the Supreme Court to monitor those in security detention and free those who had been in detention longer than the maximum statutory periods, absent a petition to the Supreme Court.[32]

He is wrong. Under Article 3 of the act, it is the duty of the designated justice of the Supreme Court to "supervise" preventive custody. This means the Supreme Court must take an active role, not merely wait passively for someone to bring a case to its attention. The judiciary also has an obligation to supervise preventive detention pursuant to the ICCPR, Article 9 (4), the Convention against Torture and Other Cruel, Inhuman, or Degrading Treatment or Punishment, Article 11,[33] and the U.N. Declaration on Forced Disappearances, Article 9 (1).[34]

It appears that the Supreme Court has never taken any serious action with regard to an illegally prolonged preventive detention under the prior version of the National Security Act. The deputy chief justice said in June 1995 that, in the ten months since he had been appointed under the prior act to receive complaints of detentions, he had received a petition from only one attorney. He said he had then inquired of the situation at Sudan Security, and the detainee was freed before security replied.[35] We understand several weeks elapsed between the judicial inquiry and security's release of the detainee. The deputy chief justice took no affirmative steps to prevent prolonged security detentions, nor did he think he had any obligation to do so. In a later case, Hasan Ahmad Osman was detained by

---

[32]Human Rights Watch/Africa interview, Chief Justice Obeid Haj Ali and Deputy Chief Justice Abu Geseesa, June 10, 1995.

[33]Convention Against Torture, Article 11: "Each State Party shall keep under systematic review interrogation rules, instructions, methods and practices as well as arrangements for the custody and treatment of persons subjected to any form of arrest, detention or imprisonment in any territory under its jurisdiction, with a view to preventing any cases of torture."

[34]U.N. Declaration on Forced Disappearances, Article 9 (1): "The right to a prompt and effective judicial remedy as a means of determining the whereabouts or state of health of persons deprived of their liberty and/or identifying the authority ordering or carrying out the deprivation of liberty is required to prevent forced disappearances under all circumstances . . . ."

[35]Human Rights Watch/Africa interview, Deputy Chief Justice Abu Geseesa, June 10, 1995.

security on June 12, 1995. His family appealed to Deputy Chief Justice Abu Geseesa and the detainee was released in January 1996, more than six months after detention.

Past public statements by spokespersons for the judiciary indicate that the judicial blind eye currently turned to security detainees' legal rights is not a new phenomenon. In August 1992 Supreme Court Judge Abdel Rahman Sherfi, the official spokesman of the judiciary, when asked about political detainees held by security, said that the judiciary carried out inspection visits to ensure that the rights of political prisoners were respected. He denied the existence of unacknowledged detention centers where detainees were tortured and carefully confined his remarks to the situation of convicted political prisoners held in official prisons under the jurisdiction of the General Administration of the Police of Prisons and Reformation of the Ministry of Interior.[36]

A follow-up question on whether the judiciary had received any complaints about torture in the first year of this government (1989-90) elicited this answer: "We don't deny the probability of some individual cases [of torture in detention], circulated by some people, but no real complaints about torture in prisons reached us. Even if such cases existed, they wouldn't go beyond being isolated or unfamiliar cases with no relevance."[37] This assertion is not borne out by the facts chronicled in many human rights reports on the practice of torture during those years.

In the belief that attempting to use a feckless judicial system to seek a detainee's release would be beating a dead horse, detainees and their families fall back on traditional ways of approaching officials to ask for their help — through family, personal and regional ties. They make the rounds from the attorney general's office to the ministry of the presidency to the TNA and its human rights

---

[36]He said the judiciary constantly monitored the situation of political prisoners, distinguishing them from common law prisoners. He said they lived in quarters comparable to hotels, not in underground dungeons. He avoided answering the question about pre-trial (and pre-indictment) security detainees, whose conditions have always been worse than those of convicted prisoners, according to released detainees and prisoners. Interview of Judge Sherfi in the government-owned daily *Al Ingaz al Watani* (National Salvation), August 6, 1992.

[37]Ibid. The judge also commented in the same interview on the seventy-four persons condemned for crimes against state security who were being amnestied on that day. He said that their liberty was not conditional, but they were aware that "they will face a dangerous destiny if they return to fighting the regime since [such conduct] will be considered as an aggravating factor of punishment. The punishment for the recidivist could be the death penalty without hesitation."

committee to those reputed to hold power in the NIF, seeking to locate someone with the power to act on their behalf. All these informal avenues of redress depend on the mercy — or whim — of the powerful, not upon legal rights. Those with no strong family influence or contacts in powerful circles risk being neglected and spending comparatively longer periods in detention. Southerners and the poor are the primary victims of this arbitrary system of petition, since they do not have powerful contacts.

The deputy chair of the TNA and chair of its human rights committee, Angelo Beda, regularly receives petitions from relatives of those held in preventive detention. This committee writes letters of inquiry to Sudan Security, and in some cases, Beda says, is successful in winning the release of the detainee. He provided copies of his correspondence to Human Rights Watch, which showed that inquiries were in fact made on behalf of several security detainees.[38] These formal and informal efforts made on behalf of detainees are worthwhile, but they provide only the slimmest thread of restraint on security, and are no substitute for a real judicial remedy such as a habeas corpus procedure.

TREND TOWARD RESTRICTION OF RIGHTS

In our meeting with the chair of the TNA Human Rights Committee, we were told that the TNA's 1995 amendments to the National Security Act improved the proposed 1994 act by diminishing the amount of time a person could be held in preventive detention before being brought before a judge. That was not born out by a reading of the act and its amendment, however. In Article 37 the TNA lengthened the time in preventive detention before judicial review from the proposed three months to six months.

Indeed, the National Security Act of 1995 has omitted several safeguards provided to detainees under the National Security Act of 1990, as amended,[39]

---

[38]We saw letters concerning three cases. In one case, security denied that Louis Gore and others were arrested by General Security in December 1994. We received information that in this incident, where six public officials and others were detained in Juba in December 1994 in connection with land disputes, three were held and tortured by Sudan Security in Juba. (See Chapter III). In a second case, security said that a named detainee was released several weeks before the TNA inquiry. In the third case, security denied that a female Umma Party member detained by security had been mistreated.

[39]The National Security Act of 1990 was amended in 1991 and 1992. We refer to the act as amended in 1991 and 1992 as the 1991 National Security Act and the 1992 National Security Act, respectively.

although these were in practice rarely honored. For instance, under the 1991 National Security Act a security detainee could be held for three months without an order. At the end of that time any order of extension of the preventive detention had to be submitted, with reasons justifying the extension, to representatives of the attorney general's chamber or the judge within three days of the issuance of the extension order.[40] The attorney general's representative or the judge were required to assess the reasons after "hearing from" the detainee or reading a memorandum by the detainee, and could "summarily" order the extension of the detention period, or could order the detainee's release.[41]

The flaw under the National Security Act of 1991 was that this procedure might be held by the representative of the attorney general, an executive, not a judicial official, although the ICCPR, Article 9, requires the hearing be held before a judicial official. The choice of the official — whether an attorney general representative or judge — conducting the hearing was up to security or other detaining authority. The 1992 amendment deleted reference to the attorney general, so that only the judge could order an extension of the detention period. The deletion of the reference to the representative of the attorney general was the only significant amendment to the act in 1992.

Even under the 1992 National Security Act, however, there was no obligation to hold a hearing at which the detainee had the right to be present, nor was there any right to counsel, nor to examine witnesses, or any other due process rights. The judge could "summarily" renew detention in three month periods, indefinitely, without any due process protections whatsoever, if he decided that "national security" called for it.[42]

The only approximations to due process in that act were the provisions that the detainee "shall be informed after a reasonable period of his detention of the reasons justifying his detention" (Article (A) (2), and that he had the explicit right "whenever he so wishes to raise a memorandum to the council about his detention

---

[40]The judge refers to "the judge appointed by the Chief Justice to supervise orders of preventive detention." National Security Act of 1991, Article 40 (A) (11).

[41]The National Security Act of 1991, Article 40 (A) (1), gave the council or its delegate the power to order preventative detention for a period not longer than three months. Extensions after that period were to be presented to the judge or a representative of the attorney general.

[42]National Security Act of 1990, Article 40 (A) (8): "The judge may, after assessment of the reasons and hearing of the detainee or examination of a memorandum from him, summarily agree to the extension of the preventive detention period if he considers that national security requirements call for such an extension, or he may order the release of the detainee if he sees otherwise."

or his treatment." (Article 40 (A) (3)). This falls far short of the right to a hearing, however.

With regard to the detainee's physical integrity, the 1991 National Security Act specified that "it shall not be permitted to expose the detainee to any physical harm or to treat him in a beastly manner." (Article 40 (A) (4)). To enforce that prohibition, the next article added that "The detainee may complain to the representative of the attorney general's office or to the judge against the nonobservance of limitations on detention specified in this article and the representative of the attorney general or the judge may, after expedited examination, issue the order that he deems suitable to correct the injustice." (Article 40 (A) (5)).

These are some of the provisions favorable to the detainee that the government of Sudan quoted in its submission to the U.N. in November 1995 in reply to the special rapporteur's human rights report.[43] The others are that any released security detainee or acquitted person shall not be re-detained for one month from the date of release or acquittal or with the prior permission of the judge.[44] All these provisions, however flawed and unobserved in practice, were deleted from the National Security Act of 1995: it makes no reference to any right to know the accusations, opportunity to petition any authority, or judicial review after three months. The 1995 act is also conspicuously silent about physical harm to the detainee and places no limit on the power of security to redetain someone who has just been acquitted or released from security. The National Security Act of 1995 is a step backward.

PROLONGED ARBITRARY DETENTION

Even though the person detained under the National Security Act of 1990 as amended had theoretical rights, in practice these were not respected. It is unlikely, judging from past performance and interviews with officials and others, that the 1995 act's requirement for judicial review after six months of detention will be honored, either.

Security detainees who have been released without charges claim never to have had hearings of any kind, no matter how long they have spent in detention. Several ex-detainees interviewed by Human Rights Watch, or whose cases were reviewed by Human Rights Watch, were held in preventive detention for two years

---

[43]"The Response of the Government of the Sudan," November 21, 1995, New York, pp. 18-19, paras. 75-76.
[44]See National Security Act of 1991, Article 40 (A) (9) and (10).

while the 1991 act was in effect. They were held in security detention, usually in unofficial places of detention or "ghost houses" and often moved around between states, without any authorization ever being sought from any court, unless it was in a secret proceeding of which the detainee had no notice. Their detention was illegal not only under the ICCPR but also under the national security laws of Sudan.

Among those released in 1994 and 1995 who as far as is known were held for more than three months without any judicial order — as provided by the National Security Act of 1992 then in effect — were alleged Communist Party leaders Yusif Hussein Mohamed (detained December 1992, released May 1995), Mohamed Babikr Mukhtar (secretary general of the banned Sudan Employees Union, detained May 1994, released May 1995)[45] and Farouk Ali Zakaria (detained December 1992, released October 1994); and Salah Samared, Mustafa Abd al Rahman, Abdul Raouf Ebn Oaf, Fadlalla Burma Nasir (minister of defense under the Transitional Military Council in April 1985); two businessmen detained in 1991, Abdulmoniem Awad Allah Salih (engineer) and Muhsin Abdel Hamid (ex-army officer), and others. Some had been arrested several times before;[46] several have been rearrested, including Yusif Hussein Mohamed and Mohamed Babikr (see below). There are reports of others held for extended periods without any charges or judicial recourse, including Mostafa Abdel Rahman Mostafa (in detention since December 1992, first in a ghost house then in early 1994 sent to Suakin Prison, denied family visits and necessary medication).[47]

On May 3, 1995 the government released to the Geneva-based International Commission of Jurists a list of persons detained pursuant to the National Security Act; there were eighty persons on the list, which was compiled at the request of the ICJ. This list quickly became outdated by the security detentions of hundreds of Umma Party members following the May 16, 1995 detention of Umma Party leader and former prime minister Sadiq al Mahdi.

The list given to the ICJ omitted several well-known long term detainees such as Yusif Hussein Mohamed and Mohamed Babikr Muktar and others who were released two weeks later on the occasion of the Al Eid holiday in mid-May

[45]See Human Rights Watch/Africa, "Sudan, 'In the Name of God': Repression Continues in Northern Sudan," *A Human Rights Watch Short Report*, vol. 6, no. 9 (November 1994), pp. 32-33. Mohamed Babikr Mukhtar was re-arrested in September 1995 following student demonstrations and only released in March 1996.

[46]Human Rights Watch/Africa interviews, Khartoum, May 20 and 27, 1995.

[47]SOS-Torture, "Case SDN 201094," International Secretariat of OMCT (World Organization Against Torture)/SOS-Torture, Geneva, October 20, 1994.

1995, and other less well-known detainees, some of whom Human Rights Watch sought to visit in May and who were not released for several months.[48] Other people omitted from the ICJ list include a group of members of the Arab Ba'thist (Revival) Party: Mohamed Salman, Adil Fouad, Mohamed Babiker Musa, Fathi Nouri, and Abu Ras (who spent more than a year in detention when he was released May 7, 1995). The reason for omitting these security detainees from the ICJ list was not stated. If political detainees were held by security pursuant to legislation other than the National Security Act, it is not clear just what legislation that could be.

Furthermore, the director of Kober Prison said that before the release of thirty security detainees from Kober on the Al Eid holiday in mid-May 1995, there were ninety security detainees in Kober, ten more than appeared on the list given to the ICJ.[49] Security detainees also were held in other cities and other Khartoum locations.

ARRESTS OF SADIQ AL MAHDI AND UMMA PARTY MEMBERS

The arbitrary nature of security detention under the 1995 National Security Act was illustrated by the crackdown on Sadiq al Mahdi, the former prime minister of Sudan (1986-89), who was deposed by the government now in power, and some 200 members of the banned Umma Party of which he is head. Al Mahdi was detained at his home in Omdurman on May 16, 1995. This was a high profile detention due to Sadiq al Mahdi's status as former prime minister and the Umma Party's history as one of the two largest political parties in Sudan before all parties were banned in 1989. Family members pursued various formal and informal avenues in seeking his release, but received no response to their many petitions to many government authorities. Al Mahdi also is the leader of the Ansar (Helpers) religious sect on which the Umma Party is based.[50]

---

[48]In a letter to the Ministry of Foreign Affairs of May 20, 1995, Human Rights Watch requested permission to visit Mustafa Zaki, Isak Makur Boc, and Faisal al Shabbu, all of whom were detained by security prior to May 2, 1995. In a letter of May 21, 1995 to the Ministry of the Presidency, we included the additional name of security detainee Abdula Rahim Min Allah. All were detained in the weeks prior to May 3, 1995, but none of them appeared on the list of detainees given to the ICJ on that date.

[49]Human Rights Watch/Africa interview, Maj. Gen. Abu Bakr Mohamed Ashrriya, Kober Prison, Khartoum North, May 29, 1995.

[50]Human Rights Watch/Africa interview, Sarah al Mahdi, wife of Sadiq al Mahdi, Omdurman, May 30, 1995.

The detention came less than a week after al Mahdi, speaking during the important religious holiday of Al Eid as a religious leader, delivered a sermon highly critical of the government. When taken into custody he sent a note that he was not going to talk to security and that he wanted a fair, open trial of any charges against him.[51]

He was held in incommunicado detention for more than three months, until his release in late August 1995 during a visit of European trade negotiators to Khartoum. Initially he was held in the security section of Kober Prison. His family was permitted to give food and clothes to security, but they never received, as they had during his prior detentions, any note from him acknowledging receipt of these items.

Human Rights Watch inquired about the reasons for his detention, as al Mahdi was never charged with any crime. Some government officials claimed they were not privy to the reasons. TNA Deputy Chair Angelo Beda said al Mahdi had been detained because he had been in "negotiations" with the government in early 1995 and had betrayed the confidential nature of these negotiations in his speech during Al Eid. He claimed that al Mahdi could have made the same speech without being arrested but for his negotiations.[52] The TNA chair was, in contrast, cited in a press interview two months later stating that Sadiq al Mahdi would be tried shortly for attempting to overthrow the government, having links with the SPLA leader John Garang, and helping to organize a military force to take the war to the north.[53] Another government official suggested that the detention was in relation to the preparation of an opposition meeting in Asmara, Eritrea, aimed at launching an invasion of Sudan, although no charges were ever brought.[54] It appears to Human Rights Watch that he was detained on account of his exercise of his free speech rights.

After Umma Party and Ansar leaders addressed a memorandum to the government calling for their leader's release, the authorities unleashed a campaign of arrests of Umma Party and Ansar leaders throughout Sudan. An estimated 200

---

[51]Ibid.

[52]Human Rights Watch/Africa interview, TNA Deputy Chair, Angelo Beda, Omdurman, June 10, 1995.

[53]Kathy Evans, "Sudan: Sudan's Ex-Prime Minister to be charged with Attempt to Topple Regime," *The Guardian* (London), August 16, 1995.

[54]"Sudan: Official Comments on Release of Sadiq al Mahdi, Return of Opposition Figure," SUNA news agency, Khartoum, in English, 1710 gmt, August 26, 1995, quoted in BBC Monitoring Service: Middle East, August 28, 1995.

were detained, some for as long as four months.[55] In Atbara, at least fifty other Umma leaders were in prison in mid August 1995.

These prisoners, held arbitrarily and without legal process since May, were discreetly released in the months after their detention, starting with the oldest first. The government held on to Sadiq al Mahdi as external pressure mounted, and finally released him and thirty-one other security detainees in late August 1995, on the eve of a visit to Sudan by the African, Caribbean and Pacific States-European Union (ACP-EU) to evaluate whether the European Union should resume financial cooperation with Sudan under the Lome Convention. The ACP-EU delegation made human rights one of its top priorities.[56]

MASS RELEASES OF MAY 1995 AND AUGUST 1995

One of the ways in which those detained without legal process are freed is by virtue of the "largesse" of the powerful, often in the context of international pressure. Releases are represented as "humanitarian" measures or other generous acts. Thus thirty detainees were released from prolonged preventive detention in Kober Prison on the holiday of Al Eid in May 1995, but also immediately after the U.N. Commission on Human Rights met and expressed its deep concern over human rights in Sudan,[57] and as Sudan was attempting to better its human rights image through these releases and through a series of visits paid by international human rights organizations. Amnesty International, in addition, was then waging a major campaign against human rights violations in Sudan.

Similarly, President al Bashir announced the release of all women prisoners who had children, on August 17, 1995 at the preparatory proceedings on

---

[55]At least the following Umma Party members were detained in Kober Prison: Abu Bakr Abdel al Magid al Amir Yagoub, Abdalla Ishag, Abdalla Abdel al Rahman Barakat, Abdalla Abdel al Rahman Salih, Abdel Nabi, Abdel Mahmoud Abo, Mubarak Osman al Sheikh, Ali Abd al Magid al Umda, Tibeira Abd al Gadir Habani, Fadlalla Burma Nasir, Hussein Salama, Teirab Tindil, Al Hadi Hamid, Said Ganat, Ali Hassan Taj al Din, and Seid Ahmad Abdalla. In addition, there were three Umma detainees transferred to Kober Prison from El Obeid, one from each of Sennar and al Simeih, four from Gedaref and six from Atbara, one of whom was seventy-three years old.

[56]Lord Plumb, Mr. Boulle, Mrs. Kinnock and Mrs. Robinson, "Report on the mission to Sudan, Eritrea and Ethiopia, 26 August - 2 September 1995," African Caribbean Pacific States-European Union Joint Assembly, September 25, 1995.

[57]U.N. Economic and Social Council, Commission on Human Rights, "Situation of Human Rights in the Sudan," 1995/77, 61st meeting, March 9, 1995.

the Beijing world conference on women's rights.[58] Reportedly, there were more than 1,000 women in jail[59] and 300 children who were held with their mothers. The director general of prisons in July had warned of a marked deterioration in the country's jails with prisoners going hungry and some dying for lack of medicine and urged that women with children and others be released.[60]

The release in August 1995 of former prime minister Sadiq al Mahdi and thirty-one other persons, all held in security detention without charges since May 1995, followed repeated written requests by a delegation from the African Caribbean Pacific States-European Union to meet with al Mahdi while in Sudan in late August to evaluate what assistance, if any, the E.U. would give Sudan.

The government claimed that these thirty-two were all the security detainees held.[61] That is not correct, since at least Hasan Ahmad Osman, detained on June 12, 1995, remained in security detention in August: his family appealed to Deputy Chief Justice Abu Geseesa for his release. He was released in January 1996. Another security detainee not released in August was Marial Musher Klweil, detained on January 29, 1995. The thirty-two released were said to include nineteen members of the dissolved Umma Party, eight members of the dissolved Communist Party and five of the dissolved Arab Socialist Ba'thist Party.[62]

On the eve of the ACP-EU delegation's arrival, the president also issued a decree pardoning eighteen persons classified as political prisoners by the government, convicted in connection with the coup attempt of 1991 and the Explosives Case of 1994.[63]

---

[58]"Sudan: Sudanese President Orders Mothers Released from Prison," Sudan TV, Omdurman, in English, 1545 gmt, August 17, 1995, quoted in BBC Monitoring Service: Middle East, August 19, 1995.

[59]"Sudan: Authorities Begin Implementing Bashir Directive to Release Women Prisoners," Radio National Unity, Omdurman, in Arabic, 1730 gmt, August 20, 1995, quoted in BBC Monitoring Service: Middle East, August 22, 1994.

[60]"Jailed Sudanese Mothers and Children Set Free," Reuter, Khartoum, August 4, 1995.

[61]Minister of State of Foreign Affairs Dr. Ghazi Salah al Din said that the total number of security detainees was thirty-two. "Sudan: Minister on Contacts with Opposition, Political Prisoners," SUNA news agency, Khartoum, in Arabic, 1530 gmt, August 28, 1995, quoted in BBC Monitoring Service: Middle East, August 30, 1995.

[62]"Sudan: Information Minister Gives Details of Party Affiliation of Released Prisoners," SUNA news agency, Khartoum, in English, 1715 gmt, August 26, 1995, quoted in BBC Monitoring Service: Middle East, August 28, 1995.

[63]"Sudan: President Issues Decree Pardoning 18 'Political Prisoners,'" SUNA news agency, Khartoum, in English 1011 gmt, August 30, 1995, quoted in BBC Monitoring
(continued...)

These releases, although to be welcomed, in fact tend to show that imprisonment is not governed by the rule of law in Sudan, that caprice and political expediency rule in its stead, and that personal ties and influence trump everything else.

OTHER ARRESTS: 1995 AND 1996

Within weeks of the prisoner and security detainee releases, in September 1995, student demonstrations broke out in Khartoum and several lawyers and others among the capital's "usual suspects" were detained by security, including advocates Mustafa Abdel Gadir, Ali Ahmed al Sayyid, Bushra Abdel Karim,[64] and Siddiq Yousif, Abdallah Meshawi, al Bagir Hassab al Rasoul, and Kamal al Juzuuli;[65] all were the subjects of international protest, and most were released after several days in detention. Yusif Hussein Mohamed and Mohamed Babikr Mukhtar (both just released in May 1995 after prolonged arbitrary security detention), were detained again; Yusif Hussein was not released until December 6, 1995, and Mohamed Babikr and Siddiq Yousif remained in detention until mid-March 1996.[66] Mohamed Hassan Wahba was arrested during the burial of Sudan Communist Party leader Izz al Diin Ali Amir. An unknown number of street children were also subjected to short-term detention by security on account of the demonstrations.

Others arrested after the demonstrations in September 1995, however, remained in security detention (in the security section of Kober Prison), including Awad Bashir, Adlaan Abdel Aziz,[67] and Al Sir Ossman Babu, all university graduates apparently considered by security to have been leaders of the student

---

[63](...continued)
Service: Middle East, August 30, 1995. Finance Minister Abdalla Hassan Ahmed also noted that the releases improved the negotiating position of Sudan at the level of the International Monetary Fund and the Lome Agreement. *Akhbar al Youm* (Khartoum), October 29,1995 (in Arabic).

[64]Amnesty International, "Sudan: Prisoners of Conscience," UA 218/95, AI Index: AFR 54/31/95 (London: September 15, 1995).

[65]Ibid., UA 224/95, AI Index: AFR 54/35/95, September 20, 1995.

[66]SOS-Torture, "Follow-up of Cases SDN 301095.1 and SDN 301095," International Secretariat of OMCT (World Organization Against Torture)/SOS-Torture, Geneva, May 3, 1996.

[67]They were among the twenty-two arrested in a security raid on a house in al Thawra, an Omdurman suburb, on September 2, 1995, which arrests sparked student demonstrations that month. Amnesty International, "Sudan: Possible Prisoners of Conscience," UA 222/95, AI Index: AFR 54/33/95 (London: September 18, 1995); see Chapter VII, Students, below.

demonstrations.[68] Adlaan Abdel Aziz was released on April 25, 1996, and Al Sir Ossman Babu was still being detained.[69]

In early 1996 security seemed to shift its focus to persons suspected of connections with the armed opposition based in Asmara, Eritrea, the National Alliance Forces led by Gen. Abdul Aziz Khalid. No Umma Party or Democratic Unionist Party member was known to be held in security detention in early 1996, but security detained some suspected of being associated with Gen. Abdul Aziz through the National Congress Party (al Muutamar al Watani) and/or the Union of Nationalist and Democratic Forces (Ittihaad al Quwa al Wataniyya al Democratiya), both small parties that emerged during the 1986-89 period of multi-party government.

Others reportedly detained included Mustafa Awad al Karim, a pharmacist and director of a pharmaceutical company, detained at his office on January 20, 1996. He was held and interrogated in Sudan Security department of operations (al amaliyat), in Hay al Mataar section of Khartoum. He was reportedly severely beaten and tortured during the period he spent in ghost houses, Sudan Security reportedly accusing him of leading a "ring" of former union activists.[70] He was transferred to the security section of Kober Prison and thereafter his family was permitted to visit him on April 23, 1996, for the first time since his January detention.[71]

Others, detained on January 15, 1996, included Al Sir Makki Abu Zeid, a former teacher and businessman, Ahmad Al Toam, Farah Hasan Suleiman Hajjaana, and Walid Yusuf Abu Sefeif,[72] were in the security section of Kober Prison. No charges were brought against any of them and they remained in detention as of late February 1996.

According to Amnesty International, reports were received that Moslih Salim Said, a truck driver, was arrested in Kassala at the end of January and was tortured. Six other men were subsequently detained, apparently on the basis of this interrogation and torture: Lt. Gen. Ahmad al Badawi (air force, retired) and Farah Hassan Suleiman (lawyer) were detained on January 29, 1996, and Atif Mohamed Idris (medical doctor), Mohiadin Ali Daoud (former civil servant), Babiker

---

[68]Confidential communication to Human Rights Watch/Africa, February 1996.

[69]SOS-Torture, "Follow-up of Cases SDN 301095.1," May 3, 1996.

[70]He served as the elected chair of the Trade Union of Pharmacists during 1985-89.

[71]Confidential communication to Human Rights Watch/Africa, April 1996.

[72]See also Amnesty International, "Sudan: Urgent Action," UA 43/96, AI Index: AFR 54/05/96 (London: February 22, 1995). This report refers to Hassabu Ibrahim, farmer and trade unionist.

Mohamed Gharib and Osman Mohamed Gharib (mechanics) were detained on January 31, reportedly suspected of being linked to the National Alliance Forces and alleged to be responsible for organizing recruitment of northern Sudanese youth for military training in Eritrea.[73]

Awad al Karim Muhammad Ahmed, an engineer and the secretary general of the Trade Unions Alliance that led the 1985 uprising that overthrew President Nimeiri, was detained on February 4, 1996, and released the same month, without charges.[74] In early February 1996, army officers Khalid Naasir, Abdel Waahid al Taahir, and Ibrahim Bilaal, who had been dismissed by the current government, were detained, reportedly suspected of links with the Alliance Forces.[75]

Among the foreigners held in the Sudan Security section of Kober Prison in early 1996 were reportedly several Egyptian Islamic militants (said to have criticized NIF leader Hassan al Turabi); a Ugandan formerly employed by the Ugandan Embassy, Muhi al Din Nasim (in detention since May 1995, suspected of being a spy); and several suspected members of the Chadian National Front, a Chadian opposition group, Abdul Malik, Abdul Maaruuf, and Adam, detained on September 15, 1995.[76]

Al Haadi Tanjjuur, sixty-eight, a Minister of Health employee, reportedly was taken from his sickbed in his home in Khartoum by security agents in January 1996. He is the head of the Association of North and South Funj — Southern Blue Nile (Ittihaad Shamaal wa Januub al Funj); the Funj, a marginalized ethnic group, were politically active during the period of multi- party government (1986-89).[77]

NO ICRC ACCESS TO PERSONS DETAINED IN CONNECTION WITH THE CONFLICT (PRISONERS OF WAR)

The Sudanese government has now admitted — for the first time, to our knowledge, and perhaps inadvertently — that it has taken prisoners in the armed

---

[73]Amnesty International, "Urgent Action: Sudan," UA 36/96, AI Index: AFR 54/01/96 (London: February 14, 1996).

[74]Confidential communication to Human Rights Watch/Africa, February 1996.

[75]Also detained in Kassala a few months before, and suspected of being en route to join Gen. Abdel Aziz Khalid in nearby Eritrea, was dismissed army officer Awad Ahmad Mirghani Gharbaawi. He was transferred to the security section of Kober Prison on January 24, 1996, according to a witness. Ibid.

[76]Ibid.

[77]Ibid. This list of security detainees is not intended to be a complete list of all security detainees; many others have been registered by other human rights organizations.

conflict. In November 1995 the Sudanese government reported what it said were the statements of captured Sudanese rebels and Ugandans, claiming these prisoners said that Ugandan troops, Eritrean tank crews and "African mercenaries" took part on the side of the SPLA in the November 1995 battles with the government in Eastern Equatoria.[78] Nevertheless, the government of Sudan has always rejected all requests by the ICRC to visit captured combatants and others held in connection with the conflict, steadfastly maintaining that it has no such prisoners.

Captured combatants are at great risk of being summarily executed since the government denies that it has any in captivity. They are far from their families or other institutions that might be sources of protection.

Many others, not combatants, have been detained by the government for suspected "subversive" activities. They are considered by the ICRC to be within its mandate, as persons deprived of their liberty for reasons connected with the conflict. Since these detainees are usually not detained in areas of combat, there often are witnesses to their capture and the government cannot easily deny that it has them in custody. They include those detained in Wau in April 1995, mentioned below.

Although the term "prisoners of war" is reserved for combatants captured in international armed conflicts, it is used by the parties to this conflict. Any party to the conflict is free to treat its captives as prisoners of war and accord them the rights in the Third Geneva Convention of 1949, regarding prisoners of war in international armed conflicts. Neither the government nor the rebels, however, have chosen to do so.

In many noninternational armed conflicts around the world, with the permission of the detaining government and/or the insurgents, the ICRC has come to the aid of persons deprived of their freedom in connection with the conflict — including captured combatants and those suspected of being aligned or involved with them. ICRC delegates conduct strictly humanitarian visits: they observe the material and psychological conditions of detention and the treatment accorded to detainees, provide them with relief supplies if required (medicines, clothing, toilet articles) and ask the authorities to take any steps deemed necessary to improve the detainees' treatment. The results of the visits are provided by the ICRC to the government in confidential reports not intended for publication.

ICRC visits to places of detention are carried out according to specific criteria ICRC: its delegates must be allowed to see all the detainees and talk freely

---

[78]"Uganda: Sudanese Report on 'Shattering' Defeat of Force of SPLA, Ugandans, Eritreans," SUNA news agency, Khartoum, in Arabic, 1510 gmt, November 11, 1995, quoted in BBC Monitoring Service: Africa, November 13, 1995.

to them without witnesses, to have access to all premises used for detention and to repeat their visits, and must be provided with a list of the persons to be visited (or be permitted to draw up such a list during the visit). The delegates hold discussions at various levels of the government before and after these visits.[79] In 1994 the ICRC visited 99,020 detainees in fifty-five countries,[80] most of them in the context of noninternational armed conflicts.

Despite the confidential nature of any ICRC visit, the Sudan government has refused the ICRC humanitarian access to any and all persons detained in connection with the conflict.

The absence, in a war that has lasted over a decade, of any acknowledged captured combatants on the government's side raises the possibility that captured or incapacitated combatants might routinely have been killed as a matter of government policy. The burden is on the government to explain this troubling lack of captured combatants.

DAILY REPORTING AS A FORM OF HARASSMENT

Persons perceived as opponents of the government are frequently ordered to report to one branch or another of the various security agencies on a daily basis in what constitutes a pattern of harassment and intimidation. This is particularly prevalent with the political section branch of the Department of Centralized Security, which is part of Sudan Security. Suspects are served with an official written and stamped order to present themselves the next day to the security offices of political security, in the army headquarters in Khartoum. A daily average of thirty to forty persons are called to that branch alone. They are required to arrive at the start of the working day at eight in the morning, and are sometimes made to wait well into the evening. They frequently are told they have been called for interrogation: weeks or even months of consecutive days of waiting in daily visits may be required before any questioning ensues. The suspects are not allowed to talk to each other or to read.

One advocate told us that he had been called to security on several different occasions. He was summoned to the Sudan Security building in Khartoum North, which is three or four stories high but has no sign on it. When he was called there in January 1995, he was directed by reception to an office (number seven or eight), where he found a table and two or three chairs and a bed. No one was there. After a half hour someone entered, with a mask (ski cap) over his face, who asked

---

[79]International Committee of the Red Cross, *Annual Report 1994* (Geneva), p. 8.
[80]Ibid., p. 21.

him questions: such as why he went to visit his client on Monday, the nature of his discussions with him, and so forth. The advocate said he could not tell the interrogator what the discussion was about without receiving the client's permission. The interrogator verbally abused the advocate, his family, his political party, and his client, before leaving. After one hour, the advocate was escorted back to the reception area. He was required to return each day for seven days at 8:00 a.m. and stay until the end of the business day, although no one returned to question him. He insisted on receiving a summons for each day because he had to have an excuse for not appearing in court.

In the reception area the same source said he observed hundreds of people waiting and coming and going. They included women, merchants, doctors, school boys; the security building was full of people. Outside security agents came and went in vehicles and on motorcycles.[81]

These procedures represent a form of undeclared detention outside the supervision of the judiciary. They disrupt the victims' professional and family lives, exert undue pressure on them and constitute a violation of their rights not to be arbitrarily detained.

---

[81]Human Rights Watch/Africa interview, Khartoum, May 6, 1995.

3
TORTURE AND DEATH IN DETENTION

Security detainees are kept in secret detention places known as "ghost houses" administered by Sudan Security, which also is responsible for investigation of crimes — including by interrogation — and the apprehension of suspects under the National Security Act, and these detentions are not supervised by a judicial authority, in violation of international standards.

Although it appears that torture is not used as routinely as it was in the early years of this government, it has not been abandoned. Torture in "ghost houses" became so notorious that the government dismantled most of the famed "Citibank ghost house" in Khartoum and transferred the sixty Sudan Security detainees held there to a specially-renovated section of Kober Prison in Khartoum. Since then, many Sudan Security detainees have been taken back and forth from Kober to ghost houses or other security facilities, where some were subjected to torture and other ill-treatment during interrogation. The worst reports of torture and ill-treatment, however, continue to come from the war zones and border areas.

THE APPLICABLE LAW

There is no dispute that torture and cruel, inhuman or degrading treatment or punishment are forbidden in international law. Article 7 of the International Covenant on Civil and Political Rights, to which Sudan is a party, provides:

> No one shall be subjected to torture or to cruel, inhuman or degrading treatment or punishment. In particular, no one shall be subjected without his free consent to medical or scientific experimentation.

Article 10 (1) states "All persons deprived of their liberty shall be treated with humanity and with respect for the inherent dignity of the human person."

Deaths resulting from torture or mistreatment in detention also violate the individual's right to life set forth in Article 6 (1) of the ICCPR:

> 1. Every human being has the inherent right to life. This right shall be protected by law. No one shall be arbitrarily deprived of his life.

The Convention Against Torture or Other Cruel Inhuman or Degrading Treatment, which Sudan has signed but not ratified, states in Article 2:

> 2. No exceptional circumstances whatsoever, whether a state of war or a threat of war, internal political instability or any other public emergency, may be invoked as a justification of torture.
> 3. An order from a superior officer or a public authority may not be invoked as a justification of torture.

In Article 4, the Convention Against Torture also provides that each state party "shall ensure that all acts of torture are offences under its criminal law." Its Article 12 also provides that each state shall ensure

> that its competent authorities proceed to a prompt and impartial investigation, wherever there is reasonable ground to believe that an act of torture has been committed in any territory under its jurisdiction. Article 13 requires that each state shall ensure that any person alleging torture has the right to complain to, and to have his case promptly and impartially examined by, its competent authorities. Steps shall be taken to ensure that the complainant and witnesses are protected against all ill-treatment or intimidation as a consequence of his complaint or any evidence given.

Furthermore, that convention is quite explicit about requiring states to provide a legal remedy for torture, in Article 14.[1] It requires each State Party to prohibit any statement made as a result of torture being used in evidence in any proceeding, except in a proceeding against the torturer.[2]

---

[1]Convention Against Torture, Article 14:

> 1. Each State Party shall ensure in its legal system that the victim of an act of torture obtains redress and has an enforceable right to fair and adequate compensation, including the means for as full rehabilitation as possible. In the event of the death of the victim as a result of an act of torture, his dependants shall be entitled to compensation.
> 2. Nothing in this article shall affect any right of the victim or other persons to compensation which may exist under national law.

[2]Convention Against Torture, Article 15: "Each State Party shall ensure that any statement which is established to have been made as a result of torture shall not be invoked as evidence in any proceedings, except against a person accused of torture as evidence that the statement was made."

The U.N. Human Rights Committee issued General Comment 7 (1) under the ICCPR, stating

> Complaints about ill-treatment must be investigated effectively by competent authorities. Those found guilty must be held responsible, and the alleged victims must themselves have effective remedies at their disposal, including the right to obtain compensation.

When a death in custody occurs, and complaints by relatives or other reliable reports suggest unnatural death, the authorities have the responsibility under international standards to conduct a thorough, prompt and impartial investigation, to determine the cause, manner and time of death, the person responsible, and conduct an autopsy. The scene of the death should be preserved for full forensic investigation and for police and coroners' inquiries.[3]

The Human Rights Commission has held that a state violated Article 6 (1) of the ICCPR where a detainee died in custody and was given an autopsy by military authorities, but where the state did not submit any information on the circumstances of death or the inquiries it had made into those circumstances. While the commission could not determine if it was a case of suicide or murder, the state authorities violated Article 6 (1) by not protecting the detainee's life and not investigating impartially how his death occurred.[4]

The U.N. has recommended that places of detention should not be administered by the same division of government that supervises officers with responsibility for the investigation of crime and the apprehension of criminals, whether in the police, security forces or military units. States should ensure that there is effective oversight of the status of detained persons and places of detention,

---

[3]U.N. Centre for Human Rights, *Human Rights and Pre-trial Detention*, p.36; see United Nations Principles on the Effective Prevention and Investigation of Extra-Legal, Arbitrary and Summary Executions, Economic and Social Council resolution 1989/65, annex, 1989 U.N. ESCOR Supp. (No. 1) p.52, U.N. Doc. E/1989/89 (1989), Principles 9, 12-14; United Nations Body of Principles for the Protection of All Persons under Any Form of Detention or Imprisonment, G.A. res. 43/173, annex, 43 U.N. GAOR Supp. (No. 49), p. 298, U.N. Doc. A/43/49 (1988), Principle 34.

[4]*Guillermo Ignacio Dermit Barbato and Hugo Haroldo Dermit Barbato v. Uruguay*, (84/1981) (21 October 1982), *Human Rights Committee, Selected Decisions under the Optional Protocol, Volume 2, International Covenant on Civil and Political Rights (Seventeenth to Thirty-Second Sessions)* E.89.XIV.1, vol. 2, p. 112, and p. 115, para. 9.2, cited in Centre for Human Rights, *Human Rights and Pre-trial Detention*, p. 36.

in order to protect the rights of all detainees. The officials responsible for such oversight should have the authority to compel judicial review of a person's detention. Oversight of the application should be done by a judicial or similar authority independent of the police, security forces and other officials responsible for the apprehension of offenders or the investigation of offenses. These authorities should also be responsible for keeping track of the status of all persons in detention to ensure that their cases are being processed appropriately.[5]

The practice of maintaining unacknowledged, concealed or unofficial places of detention such as "ghost houses" is a violation of international standards; this practice makes it difficult to supervise the treatment detainees receive, and makes it impossible for the detainee to assert his rights. As U.N. criminal justice authorities have found,

> Effective supervision of places of detention by impartial authorities interested in maintaining humane treatment is vital for the protection of human rights of detainees. . . . Looking after the well-being of detained persons is an obligation under the Covenant on Civil and Political Rights. . . . The location of detainees should also be known at all times so that their treatment may be supervised. This supervision is in addition to the rights of detainees to take judicial proceedings to challenge the basis and conditions of their detention.[6]

Rule 36 of the U.N. Standard Minimum Rules for the Treatment of Prisoners requires that certain measures be taken to facilitate complaints by a detainee to the proper authorities.[7] Principle 29 of the U.N. Body of Principles for the Protection of All Persons Under Any Form of Detention also requires that

> places of detention shall be visited regularly by qualified and experienced persons appointed by, and responsible to, a

---

[5]Ibid., p. 36, para. 156 (D. Practical Guidelines).

[6]Ibid., p. 35, para. 151.

[7]United Nations Standard Minimum Rules for the Treatment of Prisoners, adopted Aug. 30, 1955 by the First United Nations Congress on the Prevention of Crime and the Treatment of Offenders, U.N. Doc. A/CONF/611, annex I, E.S.C. res. 663C, 24 U.N. ESCOR Supp. (No. 1) p. 11, U.N. Doc. E/3048 (1957), amended E.S.C. res. 2076, 62 U.N. ESCOR Supp. (No. 1) p. 35, U.N. Doc. E/5988 (1977), Rule 36.

competent authority distinct from the authority directly in charge of the administration of the place of detention or imprisonment.[8]

It is but a short step from unacknowledged detention to torture and disappearance. The U.N. General Assembly has condemned forced disappearance as a constellation of violations of recognized human rights: the right to life, the right to liberty and security of the person, the right not to be subjected to torture and the right to recognition as a person before the law. In order to prevent disappearances, the General Assembly Declaration on the Protection of All Persons from Enforced Disappearances, Article 9,[9] requires:

1.The right to a prompt and effective judicial remedy as a means of determining the whereabouts or state of health of persons deprived of their liberty and/or identifying the authority ordering or carrying out the deprivation of liberty is required to prevent enforced disappearances under all circumstances . . . .
2. In such proceedings, competent national authorities shall have access to all places where persons deprived of their liberty are being held and to each part of those places, as well as to any place in which there are grounds to believe that such persons may be found.
3. Any other competent authority entitled under the law of the State or by any international legal instrument to which the State is a party may also have access to such places.

Article 10 of the same declaration on protection from disappearance states:

1. Any person deprived of liberty shall be held in an officially recognized place of detention and, in conformity with national law, be brought before a judicial authority promptly after detention.
2. Accurate information on the detention of such persons and their place or places of detention, including transfers, shall be

---

[8]U.N. Body of Principles for the Protection of All Persons under Any Form of Detention or Imprisonment, Principle 29.

[9]U.N. General Assembly Declaration on the Protection of All Persons from Enforced Disappearances, G.A. res. 47/133, 47 U.N. GAOR Supp. (No. 49) p.207, U.N. Doc. A/47/49 (1992), adopted by General Assembly resolution 47/133 of 18 December 1992.

made promptly available to their family members, their counsel or to any other persons having a legitimate interest in the information unless a wish to the contrary has been manifested by the persons concerned.

3. An official up-to-date register of all persons deprived of their liberty shall be maintained in every place of detention. Additionally, each State shall take steps to maintain similar centralized registers. The information contained in these registers shall be made available to the persons mentioned in the preceding paragraph, to any judicial or other competent and independent national authority and to any other competent authority entitled under the law of the State concerned or any international legal instrument to which a State concerned is a party, seeking to trace the whereabouts of a detained person.

In other cases, the danger from unacknowledged detentions and secret places of detention is not disappearance but summary execution. Thus, under the U.N. Principles on the Effective Prevention and Investigation of Extra-Legal, Arbitrary and Summary Executions, Principle 2 states:

In order to prevent extra-legal, arbitrary and summary executions, Governments shall ensure strict control, including a clear chain of command over all officials responsible for apprehension, arrest, detention, custody and imprisonment, as well as those officials authorized by law to use force and firearms.

Those same principles also require that governments ensure that "persons deprived of their liberty are held in officially recognized places of custody." Governments also must make accurate information on the detainee's custody and whereabouts, including transfers, promptly available to their relatives and lawyer or other persons of confidence.[10]

---

[10]Principle 6, U.N. Principles on the Effective Prevention and Investigation of Extra-Legal, Arbitrary and Summary Executions.

SECURITY DETENTION FACILITIES AND CONDITIONS OF DETENTION

Torture, ill-treatment and death usually occur while the detained are held incommunicado in Sudan Security or military custody, rather than in the prison system. Security members are able to operate with relative impunity for many reasons: there is no judicial or other supervision of their practices or detention centers; authorities such as the Supreme Court and the attorney general's and minister of justice's offices, which should play a role protective of detainees, have shown no inclination to do so, and apparently acquiesce in whatever security wants to do. Nor is a right such as habeas corpus available whereby an advocate for the detainee might press the courts to establish his or her physical condition. They do not allow visits by family or advocates and the detainee is generally kept in incommunicado detention.

The detainees remain under the jurisdiction of security, rather than other executive agencies that have a better record of treatment of prisoners, such as the Ministry of Interior's General Administration of Police of Prisons and Reformation. This administrative arrangement violates international standards recommending that places of detention not be administered by the same division of government that is responsible for investigation of the crime and detention of suspects.

Under these conditions, there is no institutional brake on security. The human rights movement, however, has been credited with improving the treatment of detainees by former detainees themselves. They believe the government, while belittling foreign concern about this issue, is nevertheless sensitive to external criticism of torture and ill-treatment.

Ghost Houses

"Ghost houses" are secret detention centers run by Sudan Security or anyone else with official or semi-official power who wants to hold detainees without warrant or court order. The detention "facilities" may be former homes or offices; at one time the former office of the Sudan Bar Association was even used as a "ghost house." They are used to provide deniability, the first step on the unacknowledged detainee's path to torture, murder and/or disappearance.

Their existence became so well known, however, that by 1994 deniability was weakened. The practice and many locations became known, although security still frequently refused to acknowledge having the detainees in custody. The most notorious of the "ghost houses" was the "Citibank ghost house," so called because it was in a government-owned house behind the high-rise office building where Citibank used to have its Khartoum office; it was also known as the Oasis (*Al*

Waha). Before June 1989, when it was taken over by security, it served as the head office of the Sudan Council of Voluntary Agencies, an NGO umbrella group established by the government.

The "Citibank ghost house" was just one of many "unofficial" detention facilities in Sudan. It acquired a central and legendary place in the secret detention system controlled by security. However, other evident unacknowledged detention locations in 1994-95 were within the head office of security, inside the army headquarters complex in Khartoum, and in the government houses previously used for technical services of Sudan Airways and the National Elections Commission, also near the army complex. A security facility near the Kuwaiti Embassy in Khartoum, the department of special operations of internal security (al amaliyat), also was used. Detainees at this location in May 1995 were subjected to ill-treatment: they were forced to do kneebends for hours while lifting chairs above their heads, and were whipped.[11]

CITIBANK GHOST HOUSE BEFORE MARCH 1995

Many former detainees have given accounts of their torture inside the Citibank ghost house. Others, not tortured themselves, witnessed the torture of their fellow inmates.[12]

Security initially renovated the Citibank ghost house, building cells to hold dozens of detainees. Up to 150 detainees are believed to have been held there at one time.

In the courtyard of the house, security built eighteen cells of bricks and cement for the walls, iron sheets for the doors, and corrugated iron for the roofs. The cells were in a U shape, facing north. The cells were numbered from one to eighteen. According to former detainees, cells number one to five (the western arm of the U) each had a maximum capacity of three people. Cells six to sixteen, the center of the U, were individual detention cells. Cells seventeen and eighteen had a holding capacity of fifteen persons each, although detainees were routinely packed in greater numbers. At any given time, some fifty detainees could be found in the cells. Inside the main house, many others were detained in rooms less like cells; they were generally the ones whose interrogation was finished.

---

[11]Human Rights Watch/Africa interviews, Khartoum, May 1995.

[12]The account of conditions at the Citibank ghost house is based on several Human Rights Watch/Africa interviews, including in Khartoum, May 20, 22, 27, and 29, 1995, and New York, March 1996.

All cells in the courtyard had narrow doors of sheet metal with a narrow barred ventilation strip on top. Opposite each door was a square window twenty by twenty centimeters. The corner cells, numbers six and sixteen, had the least ventilation.

Former detainees said that the heat inside the ghost house cells was unbearable; during many months of the year Khartoum temperatures reach above 40 degrees Celsius (104 degrees Fahrenheit) in the day and are not cool at night. This heat is intensified by metal doors, corrugated iron roofing, lack of ventilation and overcrowding. For each cell there was only a jug of drinking water. They did not allow detainees to change clothes nor to wash (except the ritual washing preceding prayers).

Detainees, usually denied mattresses by the guards, slept on the cement floor of the cells, using their shoes as pillows. They were allowed out of the cells six times a day, for breakfast and for prayers, although the times did not coincide with the five daily prayers. They were not allowed to talk to each other and had to return to their locked cells immediately after prayers. They were only allowed to go to the bathroom during prayer breaks.

Detainees were not allowed to receive any visits or even food packages from their families; usually the families knew only that security was holding them, but not where they were held.

Medical care was minimal, even for those who were injured in torture sessions or who suffered from preexisting ailments. One older detainee, Abdel Rassoul El Nour, an Umma party leader and ex-minister, did not leave his individual cell for two days. Only when other detainees pressured the guards did they open the cell and find him unconscious; the detainees believed he had passed out some time before. He was taken to the health unit of Sudan Security and after several days recovered enough to be released from security in late June 1994. He then required treatment for another three weeks in Mulazmein Hospital.

Interrogation sessions in other security locations provided the only occasions for which detainees were taken outside the ghost house. The detainees were blindfolded and made to stay out of sight in the cars taking them outside the ghost house.

The account of one detainee, held from the end of 1992 until late 1994, illustrates the plight of long-term detainees in ghost houses during that period. This man, whom we shall call Mustafa, was held without charges, trial, family visits, access to a judge or an attorney for almost two years and was moved around among facilities and states as it suited security.[13]

For more than two weeks, they held him in Citibank, on a closed veranda with others, including several soldiers from the Nuba Mountains. After sixteen days, they put him into an individual cell. Although he was not beaten — he had been tortured during prior detentions — the young guards shouted at and insulted him, trying to provoke him, and made him stand for hours. He said they taunted him with not being a Muslim, with being a leftist. His warning to the young guards, that they should be careful "since when his government was overthrown, the torturers would all be tried," caused a guard who frequently taunted him to remove his mattress, making him sleep on the bare floor, to punish him.

After the first sixteen days of detention they removed him to an individual cell, number sixteen, where he was kept alone. Cell sixteen was very small, only one by two meters, and was in a closed and very hot corner area with ventilation provided only by the small opening above his head.

He was in this cell for the first time for forty days, and for the second time for two months. They did not release him for his prayers or meals at the same time as the other detainees, to increase his isolation. They locked the other detainees up when they let Mustafa out of his individual cell. They let him out sometimes to wash his clothes, the guards telling him he could wash five pieces. He told us he never had time to wash more than one piece, however, and that the guards often took that one clean piece and threw it in the mud.

They did not give him daily medicine he had to take for high blood pressure until, toward the end of his time in detention, he threatened to go on a hunger strike. They finally brought it, but insisted he pay for the medicine.

He said he was questioned for just two days, and asked about his alleged activities in a banned political party and other members' names and activities. During interrogation, they referred to his condition as "preventive detention." When he asked for his rights and to be taken before a judge, they said, "We'll keep you for whatever time we want. Don't even dream of being taken to a judge or asking for your rights. We are the ones who will decide, not a judge. We will decide to try you and we can even execute you. We can keep you whatever time we want to keep you, one year, two years. You won't work again in the [banned] party."

He rarely saw a security officer in the ghost house. Although the guards did not wear names on their uniforms, they rarely covered their faces. He saw only one officer who came to the ghost house to supervise the guards, most of whom

---

[13]Human Rights Watch/Africa interview, May 29, 1995.

were between nineteen and twenty-four years old. Some guards were educated and most were Islamists, although he characterized some as "more fanatical" than others. They rotated the group of guards.

After the initial period of detention in Citibank ghost house, he and twenty other detainees were taken to Kassala Prison in eastern Sudan, where he stayed for nine months, still under the jurisdiction of security. When they prepared the detainees for transfer from the Citibank ghost house, they were also photographing detainees, and he could see that there were about 150 detainees at the Citibank ghost house at that time. Not all ghost house detainees were "political"; there was always a group of "economic" detainees (who had allegedly violated import/export or foreign currency restrictions) in the Citibank ghost house, and foreigners (accused of many crimes, from spying to financial offenses) also.

In Kassala Prison the prison guards did not mistreat them. In fact, perhaps because their group included five Umma Party members who had held high positions in the past government, the prison director met them and told them that the prison authorities were not aligned with any party, that they treat all the prisoners the same and that they have "the best prison regulations in the world." The political detainees in Kassala did, in fact, have the right to a bed, bedding, a refrigerator for food, and better rations than in security. They were able to receive visits from their families, although families needed a permit from security in Khartoum to do so. In Mustafa's case, the long distances his family had to travel and the difficulty of securing visiting permits meant he had only three visits from his family in the nine months he was held in Kassala. During that period, security released some of the twenty-one detainees who were transferred with him from the ghost house in Khartoum, so that by February 1994 their numbers were down to six.

It was during Mustafa's time in Kassala Prison, in September 1993, that Gaspar Biro, the special rapporteur on Sudan for the U.N. Human Rights Commission on Human Rights, was supposed to visit that prison. The authorities temporarily closed down the security section at that time and obliterated the evidence that these security detainees had been there; all security detainees in Kassala Prison were moved to a security house in Kassala until the authorities were sure Biro had left town.

While Mustafa was in Kassala Prison, he and others wrote twice to President al Bashir, informing him of their detention and asking him to order their immediate release and punishment for those responsible for their detentions. They received no reply. They believed, however, that since human rights groups published their names abroad and people wrote to the Sudan government about them, their treatment was better than it would have been.

In early 1994 security sent Mustafa and the other five remaining security detainees from Kassala Prison back to Kober Prison. Then they were taken back to Citibank ghost house for eighteen days. Security did not interrogate them there but treated them very badly. Upon arrival at the Citibank ghost house, the guards lined the detainees up against a wall and beat them all in turn. At that time, he counted more than sixty detainees in the cells and about sixty in the house itself.

According to his testimony, he observed others being tortured and mistreated while was in the Citibank ghost house. He saw some being kept in the sun, and others kept standing outside all night. Others were deprived of water and kept from going to the toilet for more than twenty-four hours at a time. They would not let people bathe for a week or ten days, although some were forced to roll in the mud in the courtyard. Many were beaten with hoses and plastic pipes. Others were forced to squat and then forced to hop like a hare. Many were "boxed" or punched. The guards also used a high powered water hose to spray water directly on the body, eyes and ears. The ones who were beaten the worst were young men, about fifteen or sixteen years of age, usually suspected members of banned mass movement organizations.

Mustafa and one other security detainee were taken about a month later to Al Damar Prison, about 200 kilometers north of Khartoum, and were treated according to prison regulations, as in Kassala Prison. They were there for four months and then sent back to Kober Prison. From there, Mustafa was brought back to the Citibank ghost house for the third time, where he stayed for two months until his release.[14]

Another man detained in June 1993 and not released until May 1995 had a similar story of harsh and arbitrary treatment. He spent three and a half months in the Citibank ghost house, was transferred to Kober Prison for three months, returned to Citibank for two months, and was transferred to Atbara prison. No charges were ever pressed against him.

He was strictly confined inside the Citibank ghost house, kept locked in his individual cell day and night, except when it was opened four or five times a day for ten minutes each time. He had no newspaper, radio, medicine, or medical care, although he had medical problems due to his age and severe torture during his first arrest under this government when "my life was at stake." Because of the cumulative effects of his detentions, he had serious health problems upon release in May 1995.[15]

---

[14]Human Rights Watch/Africa interview, Khartoum, May 29, 1995
[15]Interview, Khartoum, May 30, 1995.

"CLOSING" OF CITIBANK GHOST HOUSE IN MARCH 1995

Apparently responding to international criticism, the government quietly dismantled most of the Citibank ghost house in March 1995, without, however, acknowledging its past use. It dismantled the cells specially built in the courtyard — except two cells that continued to be used to lock up detainees — and transferred the estimated sixty detainees there at the time to the newly-created security section of Kober Prison.

After its nominal closure in March 1995, detainees continued to be taken to the Citibank ghost house immediately after detention, kept there for interrogation for as long as the officer in charge wanted, but often no more than two days. Then they were transferred to the security section of Kober Prison. The Citibank ghost house continued to be used for interrogation, however, and some detainees would be taken from the security section of Kober Prison back to the ghost house for interrogation for weeks at a time. Confinement in the Citibank ghost house in its reduced form was also used as a punishment and a means to isolate selected detainees. After the March 1995 remodeling of the facility, some security detainees granted family visits were taken there and then to the head office of security to meet their families.

Kober Prison Security Facilities

To say that the security detainees are "in Kober Prison" is misleading. They are held under conditions of detention different from those of other Kober inmates, be they convicts or detainees awaiting trial. The security detainees are held in a specially-built section in the northwest corner of Kober, totally cut off from other prisoners and from the protection of the prison system for the most part.

Security detainees do not have the protection from torture that prisoners in Kober traditionally have enjoyed while they are on the premises,[16] although most

---

[16]Indeed, we were told by some political detainees captured immediately after the June 1989 coup that they were not tortured because they were taken directly to Kober Prison, where the prison guards were "all right" with them. Later groups of security detainees, starting with the trade union leaders and members captured in September 1989 in a crackdown on unions, were not taken directly to Kober Prison for reasons of overcrowding, but were taken to secret unofficial security detention places. They were tortured badly there. When word of this reached the political detainees already in Kober, they went on strike, demanding that the newer detainees be brought to Kober Prison regardless of the overcrowding, in order to protect them from further torture. Thus the prison administration received a back-handed vote of confidence from political detainees. Human Rights
(continued...)

of the ill-treatment they suffer is still administered in "ghost houses" or other security facilities, not in Kober. Visits by families and lawyers are exceptional, and require special permission. Usually those favored with family visits meet their family outside Kober Prison, for example in the head office of security. Nor do the security detainees have the right to see their advocates, unless the advocate secures an order from Sudan Security.[17]

The security detainees do not have the same rights to visits as other Kober prisoners. For example, the "political prisoners" — a group arbitrarily defined by the government whose composition is unclear but seems to include those convicted by military tribunals for involvement in various coup attempts — are entitled to receive visits on Fridays from any visitor, without pre-clearance. The common criminals sentenced to death receive visits on Thursdays. Homicide detainees awaiting trial see their visitors on Wednesdays.[18]

When Human Rights Watch visited Kober Prison on May 29, 1995, the prison director said we could not visit the security section of Kober Prison without permission from security. We were allowed to tour the grounds of the main prison, which remains under the jurisdiction of the minister of interior, and to speak privately to convicts, including "political prisoners. "

The security section of Kober Prison, at the time of our visit, reportedly held sixty-four detainees, among them former Prime Minister Sadiq al Mahdi; our specific request to talk to him was denied by the prison authorities. Although the director of Kober Prison told us that he was responsible for the safety, food and health of the security detainees, he said he did not have the authority to permit anyone to visit them or send them packages of food, clothes or medicine. These prisoners are still under investigation; Sudan Security, he said, takes them out of Kober for questioning, and then brings them back.

The security detainees are sent to Kober Prison with an order from the director of security stating that the named detainee is in custody, and requesting the Kober Prison director to keep him in Kober until further orders. The director of

---

[16](...continued)
Watch/Africa interview, Khartoum, May 6, 1995.

[17]According to the prison director, only those detained in connection with the Explosives Case — a case brought in 1994 against over twenty defendants accused of conspiracy and possession of explosive devices, among other things — had permission to receive visits from their advocates, before and during trial. This permission appeared to have been given once the accused had been charged and were under the jurisdiction of the court. No other security detainee in Kober had seen his advocate as of June 1995.

[18]Human Rights Watch/Africa interview, Maj. Gen. Ashrriya, May 29, 1995.

Kober told Human Rights Watch that in early May 1995 Sudan Security had ninety prisoners in the security section, the highest number at any one time since 1993 when he became prison director. He compared this with President Gaffar Nimeiri's era (1969-85), when at various times, he said, there were more than 1,000 security prisoners.

These detainees are supposedly better off in Kober than they were in the Citibank ghost house with regard to medical care. There is a resident doctor at Kober who is available to them and their health is the responsibility of the prison director.

Those released from the Kober security section said it has three wards or barracks, each with a place for twenty or more detainees. These detainees are said to be under the "special treatment" regime mandated for (convicted) "political prisoners" and therefore have the right to beds, books, and food and cigarettes from their families — although these items have to be transmitted from the families through security, not through the Kober Prison director, and security has not always respected the detainees' rights. They may wear their own clothes (unlike the common crime convicts in Kober, who wear uniforms) and have their own yard for exercise, but are not permitted to mix with the other prisoners. We observed walls more than two stories high between the security section and the rest of Kober Prison.

The security section, closed off from the rest of the prison, abutted three sections not in use: the "Nimeiri Pavilion" (a wooden scaffold erected for hangings, and a concrete amputation block, built under Nimeiri's regime and preserved unused) and the educational wing, under repair at the time of our May 1995 visit. There was a small locked metal door between this wing and the security section. The security section also abuts a third area where those accused of homicide are held awaiting trial.

In September 1993, there were only five in Kober's security section, which at the time was much smaller; two of the five were long-term detainees, leaders of the Sudan Community Party, Mohamed Babikr and Yusif Hussein. These five were taken back and forth frequently from security offices for interrogation and possibly torture; they were never charged with a crime.

In March 1995 they were joined by the large influx of security detainees from Citibank ghost house. By late May there were sixty-four security detainees in Kober as some were released and new arrests were made.[19]

---

[19]Human Rights Watch/Africa interview, Maj. Gen. Ashrriya, May 29, 1995.

Other Places Of Detention

Detention centers in Sudan apart from police stations and Sudan Security facilities appear to have proliferated. The army and military intelligence also have detention facilities throughout the country. The People's Police have detention facilities and police courts. Their judgments are often rendered on the spot and usually involve noncustodial punishments such as flogging.

Human Rights Watch has received reports that the NIF has its own security apparatus; indeed, before they were banned, most political parties were believed to have such divisions.[20]

Members of the NIF security division (*amn al jabha*) were believed by some observers to have attacked student demonstrators in Khartoum in September 1995, and were alleged to have carried out the arrests of seventy-four people involved in demonstrations in Atbara that same month. In Atbara, the NIF reportedly already held twenty-four detainees in its own security detention center in Atbara, and shaved the heads of all detainees while taunting them, according to a reliable source.[21]

Other detention facilities are part of specially-created units that include a court with a judge, police, and attorney general representatives. Places of detention are maintained by the agencies that regulate taxes, electricity, customs, exports, banking, and others. They have the power to arrest, hold in detention, try and sentence the accused.

One example is the unit set up to expeditiously process complaints relating to banking law violations, particularly writing bad checks. The prosecutor general, Dr. Abdel Rahman Ibrahim El Khalifa, referring to the taxes electricity, customs, exports, and banking detention places, claimed that these are the "ghost houses" denounced abroad, but they are not ghost houses at all and anyone could visit them. He granted Human Rights Watch permission to visit the banking law violations center, at the far eastern end of Zubair Pasha Street in Khartoum.[22]

---

[20]A North American Muslim observer wrote, "Intelligence gathering is, however, an entrenched part of the political game in Khartoum. Most of the political parties had their own secret divisions that were funded to gather and fabricate information, as well as guard against infiltration from the outside." T. Abdou Maliqualim Simone, *In Whose Image? Political Islam and Urban Practices in Sudan* (Chicago: University of Chicago Press, 1994), p. 147.

[21]Confidential communication to Human Rights Watch/Africa, February 1996.

[22]Human Rights Watch/Africa interview, Dr. Abdel Rahman Ibrahim El Khalifa, Director of Public Prosecution (Prosecutor General), and Dr. Ahmed M. O. Elmufti, Director General of the Department of Public Law and Rapporteur from the Ministry of Justice to the

(continued...)

Human Rights Watch was permitted to look into the detention cells there. They appeared to be clean but one large cell was crowded with six men who had just enough room to put a mat each down on the floor. There were no more than ten detainees.

We spoke to one detainee in English, in front of the guards; he had no complaint about the conditions but complained that "there are too many authorities to talk to." He said he had been detained for six days and had seen the judge once; he had spoken to his advocate and was represented by him in court. He was ill and was taken to a hospital the day before our visit but was not admitted.[23] The First District Attorney knew that the medical officer at the hospital had recommended that the detainee be admitted to the hospital, but he said it was not possible because a medical commission composed of three doctors had to authorize the admission of a detainee. When the detainee asked the judge to permit him to go to the hospital (an alternative to convening the three-person committee), the detainee told us, "the judge insulted me."

Human Rights Watch raised this case with the prosecutor general, who insisted that a three-doctor panel had to be convened, but that they had not convened the panel. Sudan was not like the U.S., he said, and calling together the appropriate persons was not so easy.[24]

If, as the prosecutor general admits, convening three doctors is so difficult, then they should drop that requirement. The requirement appeared to be a convenient pretext for not providing medical treatment even if the detainee is seriously ill.

DEATHS IN DETENTION

Among the 1995 cases of possible deaths under torture was that of Mohamed Al Fatih Abdel Moneim Taifor, who died in suspicious circumstances in July 1995 while in the custody of Sudan Security in Khartoum.[25] The department of the security apparatus dealing with the south (*amn al janoub*) arrested Taifor on

---

[22](...continued)
[government] Advisory Council on Human Rights, Khartoum, May 27, 1995.
    [23]Human Rights Watch/Africa interview, Banking Law Violations Detention Center, Khartoum, May 28, 1995.
    [24]Human Rights Watch/Africa interview, Prosecutor General Dr. Ibrahim, May 28, 1995.
    [25]Taifor, from a politically influential family, was number forty-four on the government's list of detainees under the National Security Act presented on May 3, 1995, to the ICJ.

April 20, 1995, in the south, and he was accused of "Impersonation."[26] Another detained during the same time later hold Human Rights Watch of Taifor's experience and death in custody, and this account follows.

Taifor said he was arrested because he had differences with an influential NIF member over money from trafficking of official contracts. In a series of incidents, some dealing with money, Taifor was repeatedly insulted by guards in front of other detainees, and was taken frequently to the ghost house for interrogations. He seemed to be particularly shaken by accusations and insults touching on his family honor.

On Friday, July 28, Taifor quarreled with the Sudan Security guard at Kober. Although it was against prison regulations to transfer prisoners after 5:00 p.m., he was removed at about 7:00 p.m. that night to the ghost house.

About twenty detainees at the ghost house on the night of July 28 reportedly heard Taifor's groans and screams throughout a long session of severe beatings. Following the beating ordeal in the ghost house, Taifor was taken to a solitary confinement cell in the same ghost house where other detainees heard him recite the Qur'an for some time. After that there was only silence. A commotion occurred in the morning when security guards opened his cell and found him dead. They quickly moved all other detainees from the ghost house to another place used as a storeroom. They removed the body, already in an advanced stage of decomposition due to the extreme heat, in the early hours of Sunday, July 30, 1995.

Doctors who treated him after a possible suicide attempt (overdose of pills) ten days before his death reportedly warned security guards not to leave him alone. Other Kober security detainees tried to warn the guards who picked him up at Kober on the fatal day of July 28 that his condition was very fragile and that they should not take him to the ghost house. Security did not heed these warnings. The immediate reaction of the authorities was to maintain a total blackout about the death. The guards who originally quarreled with and insulted him on Friday, July 28, and the two other guards who took him to the ghost house that day, continued their duties at the Sudan Security wing of Kober Prison.

According to a reliable source, on the night of September 14, 1994, Abdel Muniem Rahma, a trade unionist, was arrested in Wad Medani. At the time, he was sick and in bed on a quinine drip, an intravenous treatment for malaria. The security agents reportedly pulled the needle out of his arm and took him way.

---

[26]This term refers to falsely claiming to be a security agent for the purpose of extortion of money and trafficking of influence. Security agents often attribute to "impersonators" crimes of which they are accused.

It appears he was suspected of involvement in the anti-government demonstrations that occurred at the University of Wad Medani two weeks before the detention, and was known as a local leader of the banned Communist Party. The victim's refusal to become a member of a popular committee in Wad Medani dominated by NIF supporters may have been a further element in his detention. The local authorities had jailed him several times before for suspected political activities.

He was taken to Hasa Hiisa Prison not far from Wad Medani. The day after his detention, people who had been to visit relatives who were prisoners in Hasa Hiisa prison came to his family and reported that Abdel Muneim was dead. The family went as a group to the prison and demanded the body. The prison guards turned it over to them.

According to the family, the body had clear signs of beating and torture on the testicles and head. Before burial, the family displayed the body in their home to other family members and friends of the victim, so many residents of Wad Medani saw the condition of the body. There was a demonstration in protest of his death, and reportedly the army was called in to protect government offices and security forces buildings from attacks.[27]

Sources told Human Rights Watch that the Ministry of justice said Abdel Muneim Rahma was brought to Hasa Hiisa Prison only after he recovered from malaria, arriving there in good health. The government reportedly maintained that the medical report showed he died of a heart attack because of a state of "severe shock."[28] Although the government reportedly claimed it had initiated an investigation of the matter, Human Rights Watch received no information when it asked government officials about the case.

In a similar case, Mahamad Saleh Fadul Mahamed Saleen reportedly died in security custody in Port Sudan in August 1994. A post mortem was reportedly held, establishing that he sustained wounds and deep cuts on various parts of his body.[29] We asked the government about this case, and for a copy of the post mortem report, but received no reply. A forensic report is apparently required on all deaths in custody, although compliance with the regulation cannot be

---

[27]Human Rights Watch/Africa interview, Khartoum, May 27, 1995.

[28]In another version of events, security supposedly claimed that Muniem Rahma died of malaria and tried to make the local hospital take the body, which it refused to do. Human Rights Watch/Africa interviews, Khartoum, May 1995.

[29]Sudan Human Rights Organisation, *Sudan Human Rights Voice*, vol. 4, issue 1 (London, January 1995), p. 8.

confirmed. According to sources, there are only two forensic pathologists in Khartoum for all of Sudan.

We received a report that Khalid Ghariib Alla, a fourth year medical student at Kassala University, was detained by security in Hasa Hiisa near Wad Medani in November 1995, and died under torture, but are as yet unable to verify this. Similarly, it was reported that in late 1995 Ibrahim Mohamad, a resident of Damazien who was a merchant involved in the border trade between Ethiopia and Sudan, was accused by security of being an intelligence agent in the employ of Ethiopia, was tortured, and died. Allegedly his body was put in a sack that was thrown into a reservoir of the Roseires Dam, and was accidentally picked up by a cleaning crane the following morning and seen by many laborers. The police reportedly opened an investigation and an initial medical report said the victim died of head injuries caused by falling on the reservoir. We have not yet been able to confirm this reported death.[30]

TORTURE AND CRUEL, INHUMAN OR DEGRADING TREATMENT

Southerners continue to receive very harsh treatment in detention. A pensioner from Wau, Bahr El Ghazal, whom we shall call Lual, was detained in Khartoum in January 1995 as a "returnee from the rebellion," and reportedly severely beaten by security.

Lual was held in the department of Sudan Security responsible for all detainees from southern Sudan and southern affairs (al janoub), housed in an ordinary residential building in Khartoum 2 district near Farouq Cemetery. In front of the building there are empty freight containers in which security agents reportedly locked Lual and other detainees. When he was brought to Kober from an unofficial detention center, he still bore physical signs of torture.

Lual told fellow detainees that his was a case of mistaken identity. He repeatedly asked security agents to verify his claim with the department from which he had retired, but this simple check reportedly was not run. At the end of his initial detention period, guards told him that he did not have "papers" and that his official detention was only beginning. They did not release him in the general amnesty of August 1995.[31]

In another case reported in 1996, David was reportedly tortured by Sudan Security in Kosti in mid-1995. David is a former SPLA boy soldier who was sent for education to Cuba, as described in our 1995 report, *Children of Sudan: Slaves,*

---

[30]Confidential communication to Human Rights Watch/Africa, February 1996.
[31]Human Rights Watch/Africa interview, October, 1995.

Street Children and Child Soldiers, pp. 69-70. Because of the factional fighting still going on in 1993 when he returned from Cuba to Uganda, he and seven other boys in his group decided to return to Khartoum instead of southern Sudan. The government promised them continuing education in Khartoum, then used their defection in its propaganda war against the rebel movement. These seven Nuer and one Dinka boy soldiers experienced attempts of coerced Islamization, and suffered neglect once they served the propaganda purpose.[32]

By mid-1995, David wanted to return to southern Sudan. He was told in Khartoum that the travel permit to board a barge at Kosti, the northern Nile river terminal for the trip south, was a formality; he therefore did not obtain any permit. As he boarded the barge in Kosti, military intelligence agents arrested him because he did not have a permit. They interrogated him about his reasons for going south and later handed him over to Sudan Security in Kosti, where he was subjected to further questioning and tortured to admit he was a rebel.

Security agents dropped plastic from burning plastic bags on his naked back and body, among other things. The skin on his back had peeled off and his wounds were still raw where the plastic burned him when he arrived in the Sudan Security section of Kober prison in mid-July, according to someone who saw him there and talked to him. He was not released during the general amnesty of August 1995; the authorities apparently promised he would be released when his wounds healed.[33]

Several reports of torture by Sudan Security in Juba have been received. On December 4 and 5, 1994, at least six and possibly as many as fourteen civil servants and relief workers were detained in Juba, the largest town in war-torn southern Sudan. At least three of them were tortured, according to relatives and others. Five were civil servants working in the Equatoria state ministries of engineering (town planning), agriculture and housing. They were Louis Gore, town planner; Christopher Gore, former Commissioner of Juba; Tobias Atede, relief coordinator for a Christian-oriented Sudanese NGO; Richard Roman, civil servant; Luke Subek, agriculturalist; and Dr. Venusto, civil servant. Eight other civil

---

[32]He was sent to work in Port Sudan, but since he did not know Arabic, he returned to Khartoum to take lessons. The government, however, reportedly did not want to pay for his instruction, we are told by a source who knows him well. Human Rights Watch/Africa interview, Khartoum, May 19, 1995.

[33]Confidential communication to Human Rights Watch/Africa, October 1995.

servants were believed to have been detained at the same time.[34] They spent two months in detention. Those who were taken to military headquarters in Juba were reportedly made to lie on their stomachs while their captors stepped on their backs, and held guns to their heads at the military detention center close to military headquarters known as the White House,[35] the place to which hundreds were brought who "disappeared" in 1992.

Those of the same group of detainees who were taken to Sudan Security in Juba were tortured systematically. They were locked in an extremely hot container without ventilation on the grounds of Sudan Security. At times they were hung by the hands from the top of the container, so that their feet did not touch the ground. Two of them were badly beaten, and not allowed to sleep. They were subjected to mock executions to force them to talk. Beatings often took place at night.[36]

Relatives believe that swift denunciation of the detentions by human rights organizations saved the lives of these men. Since their releases, however, they have been under tight travel restrictions and as of mid-1995 were not allowed even to travel to Khartoum.

An informant said that the arrests were the result of a local dispute between southern civil servants and a group of Muslims over land use. Juba and the land around it have traditionally been inhabited by Bari, Acholi, Mandari, and other southern peoples. Under the British (until 1956), Muslim missionaries were banned from the south; after independence, Sudanese Arab Muslims came to Juba and the south as civil servants and traders. The large Juba garrison includes many northern soldiers and members of the Popular Defense Forces (PDF). Thus the Muslim population of Juba, while still in the minority, has grown.

A group of Muslims had apparently asked the Juba town planner, Louis Gore, to allocate to them a certain site belonging to the Catholic church, in order to build a mosque. Gore said the land was already allocated but that the town could give the Muslim group another plot. The Muslim group replied that they already had permission for the first site from the Juba representative of the ministry of engineering affairs. Gore advised the official in question that the first site had already been allocated, and the official revoked his permission to the Muslim group.

---

[34]Amnesty International, "Urgent Action," UA 12/95, AI Index AFR 54/07/95 (London: January 17, 1995).

[35]Human Rights Watch/Africa interview, Khartoum, June 9, 1995.

[36]Human Rights Watch/Africa interviews, Khartoum, May 15 and June 9, 1995.

There was another dispute about the land around Juba. Several Islamic nongovernmental organizations wanted land to the north and west of Juba for their own agricultural use. This land was occupied and used by those native to the area, and under Sudanese law, such land could only be taken from them by the government for governmental purposes. The same town planner was said to have blocked transfer of this tribal land to the Islamic nongovernmental organizations.[37]

Also in Juba the arrests of the civil servants followed in late 1995 and early 1996. Sudan Security in Juba reportedly tortured young Toposa men to implicate a priest in anti-government activities. (See Chapter VII, Freedom of religion).

Accounts of torture have also come from some of the Umma Party leaders detained without charges following the May 16, 1995 detention of the party's leader Sadiq al Mahdi. Sayed Abdel Gadir Ganat, a physician and retired army brigadier, was reportedly tortured with lit cigarettes in a ghost house in Khartoum. Sayed Ganat, who had already served a two-year prison sentence on charges of participating in a coup attempt, was taken to the ghost house after detention although scores of Umma Party security detainees in Khartoum were taken directly to the Sudan Security section of Kober Prison. When Sayed Ganat was finally transferred to Kober, fellow detainees saw recent marks from cigarette burns on his abdomen, according to a former detainee.

Sadiq al Mahdi himself, a former prime minister, was ill-treated during his 1995 detention; he had been detained before under previous governments and under this government. He said that his imprisonment was "the worst that I have been subjected to. I was kept in solitude in a room exposed to the sun all day. I was prevented from receiving visits or contacting my family."[38] He was detained from May 16 to August 26, 1995.

Accounts of torture and ill-treatment in Sudan Security secret detention places are not limited to the south or Khartoum. In Damazien, for instance, Sudan Security detained some thirty-seven people in December 1994 in connection with an election for the municipal council where the detainees had tried to raise issues of economic policy toward local agriculture as well as official corruption. They were giving out leaflets urging a boycott of the 1995 elections, which seemed to be the event that triggered the detentions. There was no court order for their arrests or the searches and seizures conducted in some of their offices. None of them were

---

[37]Human Rights Watch/Africa interview, Khartoum, May 15, 1995.
[38]Amnesty International, "Sudan: Urgent Action," UA 119/5, AI Index: AFR 54/37/95 (London, September 26, 1995).

ever tried although they were held for one month in a private house used as a secret security detention center.

According to one detainee, other detainees were tortured with electric shock during that month. One said he had been blindfolded and his arms tied before he was given electric shocks, which he described as "terrible." He said he had received electric shocks and complained of difficulty concentrating; a fellow detainee observed that this young man either stared continually into space or looked down, and did not speak much, which was not his usual state.

Other forms of torture and mistreatment reportedly inflicted during that month included sleep deprivation, prolonged standing (for up to nine hours at night), and beatings with a stick or fists by two security members. Fellow detainees heard others crying in pain at night, mostly after they had been interrogated.

In this Damazien security detention facility there were several other detainees, including two accused of gun-running from Ethiopia to Khartoum; they had fresh, deep wounds on their heads. One, who was about nineteen, said he was tortured with electric shocks.

Attorneys for the leafleting group tried to file a petition in the Damazien court under the National Security Act. The judge refused to accept the case, saying he had no jurisdiction. The attorneys then asked the chief justice to appoint a judge for the case, but there was no answer and eventually these detainees were released.[39]

---

[39]Human Rights Watch/Africa interview, Khartoum, May 27, 1995.

4
IMPUNITY

The past pattern of prosecution of security and army personnel for torture and murder is discouraging. There is only one recent case in which the conviction of a soldier, Yousif Ali Yousif — not an officer — for unlawfully killing a civilian has been upheld by the Supreme Court. This was not an abuse in detention, but a shooting at a checkpoint. Two other similar convictions were still pending Supreme Court review. The director of Kober Prison, who had more complete information on security, army and police agents convicted of abusing civilians than did any other government official interviewed, said that two police privates, Adil Abbas and Ismaeil Abdullah, were convicted in May 1995 in the same case for torturing and killing a man, and given the death sentence.[1] Also according to the prison director, a soldier, Lance Corp. John Adam Rabeh, was convicted in a civilian court in 1994 of killing a civilian in Khartoum. Three army members were involved in the crime but two escaped from police custody before trial.[2] Security agent al Juzuuli Idris Abdulmajid was convicted of killing a student in a school in 1994.

Despite our requests for such information, the government was unable to provide any other examples of prosecution of its agents for killing civilians, despite many documented cases of deaths in detention. Furthermore, we have been unable to establish whether the small number of security and military defendants actively prosecuted for abuses were released in a pardon of thirty-seven military personnel in August 1995; neither the names nor the ranks of those pardoned were published, and the government has not replied to our written requests for more information.

Torture also has been tolerated and torturers guaranteed impunity. Testimony and medical examinations established at trial in the 1994 Explosives Cases, for example, that the defendants had been tortured by security agents. Despite this fact, criminal prosecution was not initiated by the government in this case, although Attorney General Shiddu said that he asked for an investigation. One of the torturers identified in court had been accused of an arbitrary checkpoint killing. He was not suspended from his job then, and he therefore was able to torture the Explosives Case detainees a year after the checkpoint killing.[3]

Nor has the government lived up to its obligations in the case of Brig. (Ret.) Mohamed Ahmed al Rayah to undertake a prompt and impartial investigation of serious torture allegations under international human rights law.

---

[1]Human Rights Watch/Africa interview, Maj. Gen. Ashrriya, May 29, 1995.
[2]Ibid.
[3]This is the case of Abd al Hafiz Ahmed al Bashir.

The future of security accountability in Sudan looks even bleaker because the National Security Act as amended now bars all civil and criminal actions against security members — except for when that the abuse "is not related to the official work of the member." International norms prohibit such impunity.

The cases described below are far from the only cases of abuse at the hands of security or military personnel; other cases are detailed in other chapters of this report. They include the cases of southerners such as "Lual," a group of civil servants detained in Juba in December 1994, a priest and several students from the Toposa tribe detained in Juba in December 1995, Umma Party leaders such as Sayed Abdel Gadir Ganat, groups of persons detained in Damazien and Atbara in 1994, and hundreds of students and others detained in Khartoum in September 1995, among many other cases.

CASES OF IMPUNITY

Torture of Brig. (Ret.) Mohamed Ahmed al Rayah al Faki
One of the best known and documented cases of torture in Sudan in recent years was that of Brig. (Ret.) Mohamed Ahmed al Rayah al Faki. Human Rights Watch/Africa in 1994 reprinted sections of his graphic letter of complaint to the minister of justice and attorney general.[4] He alleged he was tortured with electric shock, severe beatings, and rape in 1991 and 1992. A medical certificate from August 1993 detailed physical injuries consistent with the allegations.[5] In November 1995, the government admitted to Human Rights Watch that Brig. al Rayah was not released in an August 1995 general pardon extended to others convicted with him because he had complained about being tortured.[6] Brig. al Rayah told many people that government representatives visited him in jail and tried to pressure him into withdrawing his case in exchange for his release. Six months later, however, in February 1996, al Rayah finally was released, still not having withdrawn his complaint of torture. While his unconditional release is a step forward, the next step must be a full investigation of his torture.

The government of Sudan is extremely defensive about this case, in part because it involves a high-ranking military man. It refused to permit the United

---

[4]Human Rights Watch/Africa, "In the Name of God," pp. 26-28.

[5]Ibid.

[6]Human Rights Watch/Africa interview, Dr. Ahmed M.O. Elmufti, Director General of the Department of Public Law and Rapporteur from the Ministry of Justice to the [government] Advisory Council on Human Rights, New York, New York, November 29, 1995.

Nations special rapporteur on human rights to interview Brig. al Rayah during the rapporteur's September 1993 visit to Sudan, although the special rapporteur met with the victim in December 1993.

The government first told the special rapporteur that there would be a judicial inquiry into the complaint.[7] Judge Aliahia, a provincial judge in Khartoum, was assigned by then Chief Justice Jalal Ali Lufti to conduct the investigation.[8] To date this investigation has not been completed and no results have been announced.

In the course of its attack on the 1995 Amnesty International report on Sudan, the government made two assertions regarding the al Rayah case that do not hold up to scrutiny. First, the government asserted that, since the special rapporteur met with Brig. al Rayah in December 1993 and did not mention the meeting in his subsequent report, "the only logical explanation for such omission . . . is that he was convinced that the allegation was not true, otherwise he would have enjoyed reporting the facts to the last minute detail."[9]

This is not the only logical explanation. Human Rights Watch asked the special rapporteur about this comment. He said that the complaint of Brig. al Rayah appeared in an earlier report and it is not the practice to repeat, report after report, the details of cases that have already been described. He said he was satisfied that the interview bore out the written allegations of Brig. al Rayah.[10]

The second assertion the government made about the al Rayah case that is not proved was that "there was no report because Mr. al Rayah has requested in writing that the judicial investigation be discontinued."[11] Dr. Ahmed Elmufti, the

---

[7]U.N. Economic and Social Council, Commission on Human Rights, Fiftieth session, "Final Report of Special Rapporteur on Human Rights in Sudan," E/CN.4/1994/48, February 1, 1995, p. 12.

[8]Human Rights Watch/Africa interview, Khartoum, May 22, 1995.

[9]U.N., Economic and Social Council, Commission on Human Rights, Fifty-first session, Agenda item 12, Letter dated 17 February 1994 from the Permanent Representative of the Sudan to the United Nations Office at Geneva, E/CN.4/1995/174 (29 March 1995)(entitled "The Crocodile Tears, A response by the Government of the Sudan to the highly dramatic book published recently by Amnesty International under the title 'The Tears of Orphans'"), p. 12.

[10]Human Rights Watch/Africa interview, London, July 2, 1995.

[11]The government accused Amnesty International of trying to "sow confusion" with its statement that no report of the judicial investigation has been published. "We have every reason to believe that Amnesty International is fully aware of the interview between Mr. al Rayah and the Special Rapporteur which proved that the allegation is not true, but it would like to confuse the issue to the detriment of the Sudan by claiming that no report of the

(continued...)

special rapporteur for the government's Advisory Council on Human Rights, told Human Rights Watch that he had looked into the torture allegations. He said that the government was in possession of a handwritten letter from al Rayah requesting that the attorney general intervene to stop the investigation of the torture allegations. Human Rights Watch asked for a copy of the letter. It was never produced. We asked if al Rayah was represented by an attorney; government officials said they were not sure.[12]

Human Rights Watch told Dr. Elmufti that we had met recently with a family member who informed us that al Rayah had not withdrawn the complaint. Dr. Elmufti and Dr. Ibrahim were skeptical, claiming that the family wanted nothing to do with him and had no way of knowing these things.[13]

The director of Kober Prison, where al Rayah was imprisoned flatly contradicted the assertions of these other government officials that al Rayah had withdrawn the complaint. Al Rayah was still receiving medical treatment in connection with his complaint, he said. He was most certain that the complaint had not been withdrawn, even when presented with the contrary statements made by the prosecutor general.[14] A fellow inmate also confirmed that al Rayah was still pursuing his complaint, adding, "He was tortured too much. He suffered too much. He is really sick. He has continual headaches."[15]

Although we had requested several times in writing to speak to Brig. al Rayah, when we visited Kober Prison we were told that he was not in that day because he had gone to the hospital for his regular medical treatment — in connection with his torture complaint.

Several reliable sources said that the authorities had been trying for some time to persuade Brig. al Rayah to withdraw his complaint, even offering him in

---

[11](...continued)
investigation has been published. Actually, there was no report because Mr. al Rayah has requested in writing that the judicial investigation be discontinued." "The Crocodile Tears," p. 12.

[12]Human Rights Watch/Africa interview, Prosecutor General Dr. Ibrahim and Rapporteur Dr. Elmufti, May 27, 1995. We were told by others that Brig. al Rayah is represented by Mustafa Abdel Gadir, a prominent defense attorney who has defended a series of political clients with some success and a great deal of flourish. Abdel Gadir has been detained by Sudan Security any number of times, most recently in September 1995, during the student demonstrations in Khartoum.

[13]Ibid. The prison director, however, said that al Rayah went home on leave once a month. Human Rights Watch/Africa interview, Maj. Gen. Ashrriya, May 29, 1995.

[14]Ibid.

[15]Human Rights Watch/Africa interview, Kober Prison, Khartoum, May 29, 1995.

exchange certain benefits, such as permission to travel abroad for medical treatment and money. He reportedly refused.

When the government pardoned political prisoners in August 1995, the name of Brig. al Rayah was not among those being released. Other prisoners convicted with him in connection with the same coup attempt were released then. As noted, the government admitted to Human Rights Watch that Brig. al Rayah was not released because he had a complaint pending. Human Rights Watch noted that the complaint could be processed even if he were not in prison and that this was a punishment for exercising his right to be free from torture, as well as a deterrent to others who might have valid torture complaints.

Brig. al Rayah was released in February 1996; his persistence in pursuing his case cost him an extra six months in prison. He announced that he was intent on pursuing his complaint. We await the government's thorough investigation into this serious matter.

Abd al Hafiz Ahmed al Bashir

Abd al Hafiz Ahmed al Bashir, a member of Sudan Security, was first accused of unlawfully killing Abu Bakr Mohy al Din Rasikh, an engineer, at a checkpoint in October 1992; he was not dismissed nor suspended from the force. His case is a stark illustration of what may happen when a brutal officer is not suspended. After this murder, he remained on active duty and took part in the ghost house interrogation and torture of several of the accused in the Explosives Case in 1993; the torture victims identified him during their trial in 1994. He was then convicted at his own trial for the checkpoint killing. His death sentence was being reviewed in June 1995 by the Supreme Court under highly irregular circumstances.

Apparently the killing of Engineer Rasikh took place in front of many people in the Haj Yussef neighborhood of Khartoum North. We were told by the prosecutor general that in this case the security member turned himself in to a police station shortly after the killing and told his story, claiming self defense. This security member's immunity from prosecution was lifted,[16] a result impossible today under the 1995 National Security Act unless it was evident that the killing was not related to the official work of the agent.

We mentioned this case in a 1994 Human Rights Watch report as an example of one of the very few cases where there had been an investigation and prosecution of a security member.[17] On appeal however, the case lost its force as an example in the fight against impunity. Under Sudanese law, intentional

---

[16]Human Rights Watch/Africa interview, May 27, 1995.
[17]Human Rights Watch/Africa, "In the Name of God," p. 29.

homicide is punishable by retaliation or retribution (*qisas*, which means the taking of a life in cases of deliberate homicide) or by payment of blood money (*dia*) to the victim's relatives.[18] We were told by lawyers familiar with the case that compensation was set in the amount of Ls. 250,000 (U.S. $473).

The appellate court found that negligent homicide had been committed, rather than intentional homicide.[19] It reduced the sentence to two years; in negligent homicide the maximum penalty is three years. The accused was never in custody.[20]

The case of the killing of Engineer Rasikh was on appeal to the Supreme Court in June 1995. One of the grounds for appeal was that there was a conflict of interest in the case. The defendant was represented on appeal by a legal advisor for Sudan Security (a staff attorney with the attorney general's office) at the same time that the prosecutor from the attorney general's office represented the state, according to those familiar with the case. He was also represented by the private advocate who represented him at trial.[21]

In the Explosives Case this same security officer was identified by the defendants as one of the security agents who tortured them. This identification was possible because the defendants saw the torturers when they were in the ghost house, and the same security agents appeared at the trial to provide evidence against the defendants.[22]

The three-judge court in the Explosives Case found that the defendants or some of them had been tortured but nevertheless admitted their confessions in evidence on the grounds that the torture did not influence their confessions. The

---

[18]Intentional homicide is defined in the Criminal Act of 1991, section 130. Penalties are established in the Criminal Act of 1991, Article 28 (3) (in case of intentional murder, retribution shall be death by hanging) and Article 43 (a) (the court shall pass judgment of dia in intentional murder if retribution is remitted). The relatives of the victim may pardon the killer with or without compensation (dia) and he will not be executed. Article 31.

[19]Negligent or culpable homicide is defined in Article 1323, Criminal Act of 1991. The maximum penalty is three years in jail, without prejudice to the right of dia. There is no retribution or retaliation available in cases of negligent homicide.

[20]Human Rights Watch/Africa interview, Khartoum, May 22, 1995.

[21]Ibid.

[22]Human Rights Watch/Africa interview, Khartoum, May 27, 1995. Other security agents said to have been identified at the trial as having participated in the torture were Salah Abdullah Mohamed, Ali Hassan, Abdelhafiz, Yassir Hasan Osman, Hamid Farah al Haj, Mohamed Ahmed Mohamed al Haj, and Imad Akod. The Explosives Case defendants also alleged on the record that Sudan Security officers Hassan Dahawi, now chief of Internal Security, and Nafi Ali Nafia, then Chief of Internal Security, supervised and observed the torture.

court took no further action with regard to this serious finding of torture. The minister of justice and attorney general, however, told Human Rights Watch that he asked Sudan Security to investigate this case even though the victims did not come to him with information;[23] the trial court record had the sworn statements of the victims, however. The status of the attorney general's request to Sudan Security is not known.

Human Rights Watch will continue to monitor the progress of the investigation into the torture of the Explosives Case defendants. Since the April 1994 trial in the Explosives Case, however, the National Security Act has been amended to prohibit criminal and civil proceedings against security members. Not only is it doubtful that Maj. Abd al Hafiz Ahmed al Bashir will ever be punished for murder in the Rasikh case, it is also likely that he and the others named in the Explosives Case will evade punishment for the documented use of torture in that case. He reportedly is still on active duty as a security officer.

Abdul Wahab al Beshir

Abdul Wahab, a lance corporal in the army, was convicted on April 17, 1994 by a one judge civilian court for the killing of a man he shot fleeing a checkpoint.[24] This killing, as related by the defendant himself, was a violation of international standards regarding the use of firearms.[25] Although he received a sentence at trial of death by hanging for culpable homicide, by virtue of an unprecedented maneuver in the Supreme Court he may not be punished at all for the crime.

Human Rights Watch was allowed to interview Abdul Wahab in Kober Prison where he was confined. He consented to the interview (translated by an

---

[23]Human Rights Watch/Africa interview, Minister of Justice and Attorney General Abdel Aziz Shiddu, May 2, 1995.

[24]Criminal courts trying homicide cases ordinarily are composed of three judges. There is no jury in Sudan. That this court had one judge suggests that it was specially appointed by the chief justice of the Supreme Court.

[25]The U.N. Code of Conduct for Law Enforcement Officials, Article 3, provides, "Law enforcement officials may use force only when strictly necessary and to the extent required for the performance of their duty." Code of Conduct for Law Enforcement Officials, G.A. res. 34/169, annex, 34 U.N. GAOR Supp. (No. 46), p. 186, U.N. Doc. A/34/46 (1979). The commentary on Article 3 stated: "In general, firearms should not be used except when a suspected offender offers armed resistance or otherwise jeopardizes the lives of others and less extreme measures are not sufficient to restrain or apprehend the suspected offender. In every instance in which a firearm is discharged, a report should be made promptly to the competent authorities."

official of the Ministry of Foreign Affairs). He admitted that he killed a man. He was acting as a soldier, he said. "The bullet shot the man." He did not intend to kill him. The shooting took place at 12:30 a.m. on December 29, 1992, after curfew. Although he initially said he did not know the victim's name, when pressed he recalled that it was Abdullah Khidir. He said the car, with two passengers, did not stop at the checkpoint. It stopped after the checkpoint and the two inside ran out and into a building.[26] Abdel Wahab shot one man in the back to prevent escape. He took the man to the hospital, but he died.

Abdel Wahab said that after the incident he spent two years on duty. He was not jailed until the time of the trial in April 1994. He was then detained in the military section of a military unit for about one year, and during that time did not work as a soldier.

At trial he was represented by "an attorney from the ministry of justice, an advocate with the title of brigadier." In our conversation Abdel Wahab said that he had killed a man and deserved to die, to receive the punishment of death as required by shari'a law. His case was on appeal to the Supreme Court.[27] At the time, however, it was likely that his death sentence would be quashed by the Supreme Court.

A panel of Supreme Court judges received this case on appeal in early 1995. The three judges disagreed on the verdict; two were in favor of confirming the death penalty and the third, said to be a National Islamist Front sympathizer, was opposed.[28] Under Sudanese law, only a majority is required to affirm a death sentence. The Supreme Court panel does not have the option of setting a lesser penalty. Its role in this limited appeal is solely to affirm or strike the death sentence. If the death sentence is not affirmed, the case is remanded for further proceedings.

In an extraordinary move, the chief justice of the Supreme Court removed the case from this panel before the final decree was signed, and assigned it to another panel. When asked why he did this, he admitted that this was not a common practice. He said that he dissolved the first panel because "they did not want to sit down and listen to each other and deliberate." The deputy chief justice added that this was the first time a panel had refused to deliberate. Denying that the fact the defendant was an army soldier was relevant, the chief justice said a death

---

[26]Often persons who have been drinking will try to escape the police, since consumption of alcohol by Muslims is a crime.

[27]Human Rights Watch/Africa interview, Abdul Wahab al Beshir, Kober Prison, Khartoum, May 29, 1995.

[28]Human Rights Watch/Africa interview, Khartoum, June 7, 1995.

penalty case was a serious matter that the judges should discuss. It was a matter of "court discipline."[29]

We agree that the death penalty is a serious matter, and indeed we oppose its application in any case. There is some question as to whether or not the judges deliberated according to formula, as it was presented to us. We were told by a well-placed source that the chief justice tried to persuade the two judges in the majority in the first panel to change their votes, and they refused, suggesting that it was the result and not the methodology that was at issue in this particular case. The real issue is with the precedent set when the Supreme Court's procedures and deliberations are subject to arbitrary interference on political grounds.

Faisal Hassan Omar

Faisal Hassan Omar was a National Islamic Front member who killed a student at the University of Khartoum in 1989. He was convicted of murder but on appeal the conviction was quashed — on the grounds that the killing of the student was found by the court to be an act of jihad or Holy War.[30]

The Supreme Court set aside that extraordinary appellate decision unanimously and reinstated the trial court verdict of guilty, in an opinion by Justice Ahmed Jaafar Hamid (later dismissed with no reason given).

The case was remanded by the Supreme Court to the trial court for the question of dia (compensation) for the relatives. The relatives refused dia and insisted on the death penalty, as is their right under Sudanese law. The verdict went back to the Supreme Court for confirmation. It was sent not to the panel that originally heard the case, as was the practice, but to another panel, which quashed the conviction and set the accused free in 1992. This second panel apparently was composed of Supreme Court Justices Hashim Abdul Gasim (now retired), Sadiq Abdullah (now retired) and Hussein Awad Abul Gasim.

Faisal Hassan Omar later was said to have volunteered for battle in the south and to have been killed there, as a "martyr." It was not possible to verify this information, however.

The jihad defense to intentional murder of a civilian gives great cause for concern. Killing a combatant during armed conflict is not considered homicide when it occurs in international conflicts where combatants are protected from prosecution for acts that do not violate international humanitarian law by the

---

[29]Human Rights Watch/Africa interview, Chief Justice Obeid Haj Ali and Deputy Chief Justice Abu Geseesa, June 10, 1995.

[30]This account was provided primarily by a source whose identity must be withheld. Human Rights Watch/Africa interview, Khartoum, June 7, 1995.

"combatants' privilege."[31] In internal armed conflicts, such as the one in Sudan, there is no combatants privilege but a government soldier may lawfully, under domestic and international law, kill an armed rebel combatant under a range of circumstances. In neither international nor internal armed conflicts, however, may any combatant deliberately kill a civilian.

In this case, the killing of a civilian is unlawful for many reasons: the victim was not a combatant or otherwise presenting a real and immediate threat to life or security of the attacker or others; the attacker was not a member of the armed forces; and there was no armed conflict occurring in Khartoum, nor has the civil war ever reached the capital.

Permitting killing of unarmed civilians pursuant to notions of a "holy war" is a serious deviation from international law. The opening it provides for self-appointed vigilantes to commit crimes with impunity is a threat to the stability of any society.

Relief Agency Employees and Others: Juba, 1992

The SPLA made two surprise military incursions into the garrison town of Juba in Eastern Equatoria in June and July, 1992. Juba is the largest town in the south. In reaction to these incursions, Sudan Security and military intelligence took very heavy-handed measures that included extrajudicial executions and disappearances.[32] Hundreds of persons disappeared and are presumed dead; Amnesty International documented 230 men who were arrested by the government in Juba between June and August 1992 but were never accounted for.[33] The government, responding to international pressure, appointed a judge to investigate the allegations, but that investigation was never finished.

---

[31]The combatants' privilege "provides immunity from the application of municipal law prohibitions against homicides, wounding and maiming, or capturing persons and destruction of property, so long as these acts are done as acts of war and do not transgress the restraints of the rules of international law applicable in armed conflict." Michael Bothe, Karl Josef Partsch, Waldemar A. Solf, *New Rules for Victims of Armed Conflicts* (London: Martinus Nijhoff Publishers, 1982), p. 243.

[32]See Human Rights Watch/Africa, *Civilian Devastation: Abuses by All Parties in the War in Southern Sudan* (New York: Human Rights Watch, June 1994), pp. 56-65.

[33]Amnesty International, "Sudan: Deaths and detentions: The destruction of Juba," AI Index: AFR 54/26/92 (London, September 23, 1992).

Four of the victims were employees of the U.S. Agency for International Development (AID),[34] two were employees of the United Nations Development Program (UNDP),[35] and another was an employee of the European Economic Community (now European Union).[36] The U.S. government requested the Sudan government to provide information on the U.S. employees after they went missing. The Sudan government eventually claimed that one was executed as a spy after a trial before a military tribunal; it later orally admitted that a second was also executed. The others were never accounted for, but the Sudan government promised a judicial inquiry into the "incidents" in Juba of mid-1992.

President al Bashir appointed a committee of five headed by Judge Abu Sin to investigate the case, but no report was ever issued. We inquired about the status of the investigation. The minister of justice and attorney general, Dr. Abd el Aziz Shiddu, while admitting in 1995 that the investigation commenced in 1992 had been "delayed," was defensive. He wanted to know why, with so many executions in the war, the U.S. was making such an issue of four employees, one of whom had been convicted of being a spy[37] — although no record of any trial or hearing in his case was ever produced.

The Minister of Justice told Human Rights Watch that there had been a delay in the preparation of the Juba report because the judge in charge was transferred from the Supreme Court to a court in Gedaref (420 kilometers from Khartoum) in 1994, and did not finish the report. "The judge said that every time he was about to conclude the report, he received many telexes with new names [of disappeared] on it."[38] Human Rights Watch asked to interview the judge, but no response was received.

The U.N., the E.U., and the U.S. government continued to be dissatisfied with the unfulfilled promise of investigation. In 1995, the Sudan government

---

[34]Andrew Tombe and Baudoin Tally were arrested in July 1992 when they protested the government's entry into the U.S. AID compound (which had been left under their care) and the commandeering of U.S. government vehicles. Both were summarily executed. Dominic Mobris and Chaplain Lako were arrested in August 1992 and disappeared. Human Rights Watch/Africa, *Civilian Devastation*, pp. 56-65.

[35]One was Michael Muto Alia, the highest ranking United Nations Development Program representative in Juba. Both UNDP employees were arrested and disappeared. Ibid.

[36]Mark Laboke Jenner admittedly was summarily tried and executed. Ibid.

[37]Human Rights Watch/Africa interview, Attorney General Shiddu, May 2, 1995. He alleged that Tombe had directed the rebel forces' attack on Juba using a U.S. AID radio.

[38]Ibid.

publicly proposed the name of Fateh Erwa as ambassador to the U.S.[39] It is not disputed that Fateh Erwa, in his capacity as security advisor to the president with status of state minister, was present in Juba during the events in question in 1992, as was Ibrahim Shamsa al Din, a lieutenant colonel in the army and member of the governing Revolutionary Command Council. The two were the top-ranking government officials on the scene.

Human Rights Watch received a hearsay account of killings during the first days of the June 1992 SPLA incursion into Juba in which both officers were implicated. A well-placed source alleged that one person summarily executed was an army major of Bor Dinka origin, John Amour. According to this account, Maj. Amour was recalled by radio from the front because he was suspected of being an SPLA collaborator. After an exchange of words during which a fellow officer spoke up for him, Amour was told to go to the detention unit. He was shot dead one hundred meters from the First Division Army headquarters in Juba as he was walking to the detention unit (a building originally used for armored units). Supposedly Fateh Erwa and Ibrahim Shamsa al Din were standing right in back of him and gave the signal to another officer who shot Amour. This reportedly was witnessed by several soldiers. We were not able to verify this account.

The U.S. government delayed several weeks and ultimately did not accept Erwa as ambassador. No reasons were given but apparently one factor was the admitted presence of Fateh Erwa as the highest-ranking security officer in Juba during the incidents in 1992. In this case, there was an unexpected price to pay for impunity and failure to complete a promised investigation.

CASES IN WHICH CONVICTIONS HAVE BEEN UPHELD OR ARE BEING REVIEWED

Yousif Ali Yousif

Security agent Yousif Ali Yousif was convicted by a court in Sennar and given the death penalty for the murder of Hassan Haj Billel, a merchant shot dead in 1993 at a checkpoint, apparently because he resisted confiscation of goods Yousif believed were suspicious. The Supreme Court confirmed the death penalty

---

[39]Making public the name of a new ambassador before his acceptance is not customary diplomatic procedure. In this case, the government of Sudan may have believed there would be no problem with the appointment of Fateh Erwa, because he was well known to the U.S. He reportedly coordinated the exit of the Falasha Jews from Ethiopia through Sudan to Israel, and had received military and intelligence training in the U.S. Human Rights Watch/Africa interviews, Khartoum, May and June, 1995.

and remanded the case to the Sennar court to permit the heirs of the victim to decide if they wanted to forgive him.[40] The heirs declined to forgive him, and the soldier was executed on or about June 18, 1995.[41] The government has mentioned this case to the U.N. as an example of government punishment of a soldier accused of a killing in detention.[42]

Al Juzuuli Idris Abdulmajid

Al Juzuuli Idris Abdulmajid is a security agent who shot dead a seventeen-year-old secondary school student, Ahmed Hassan Saad, on March 19, 1994. The shooting took place inside Ali al Said School in Sahafa, Khartoum. Many students witnessed it because it occurred during the day, when school was in session.

According to a relative of the victim, security members came regularly to the school, where the student union was controlled by the National Islamic Front. The victim was an elected member of the Student Union although he was not a member of any party or movement.

The killing occurred during a cultural week held at the school. The victim was in charge of some of the activities. He and the head of the student union (a NIF member or sympathizer) disagreed over whether there should be one day for male students and a separate day for female students, Ahmed taking the position that the activities should be open to all students at all times.

Apparently the student union called in security agents from outside the school to speak to Ahmed about this. The security members asked him to step into a room to discuss the problem; in the past students had been beaten by security in this room. Ahmed refused to go and one security man went inside the room and came out with a pistol with which he threatened Ahmed, who continued to refuse. He was shot there and then in the stomach, was taken to the hospital, and died after one day. The bullet produced injuries to the spine as well as to the stomach.

After his death, his father, who had been minister of agriculture under Nimeiri, made great efforts to see that the killer was brought to justice. He managed, after three months, to convince security to send the case to the attorney general for prosecution. The case was then forwarded to the police and an investigation was commenced. The father hired three attorneys to follow the

---

[40]Human Rights Watch/Africa interview, Chief Justice Obeid Haj Ali and Deputy Chief Justice Abu Geseesa, June 10, 1995.

[41]"Sudan: Security Man Executed in Sudan," Reuter, Khartoum, June 20, 1995.

[42]"The Response of the Government of the Sudan," November 21, 1995, p. 19. The killing did not, however, take place in a detention facility, according to reports.

investigation. The accused was held in a building belonging to security for one year.

The police investigation took only one week since there were many witnesses. There was a trial and the defendant was convicted in March 1995, receiving the death sentence. Since his conviction, al Juzuuli Idris Abdulmajid has been in Kober Prison.

Those close to the case said that the family was pressured by several different persons, including some government ministers, to drop the case; they were told that the defendant worked in the headquarters of security and had the backing of important people. Since the death penalty was given, the case is being mandatorily reviewed by the Supreme Court.[43] If this is a case that escapes impunity, it may be due in no small part to the social position and persistence of the victim's family.

---

[43]Human Rights Watch/Africa interview, Khartoum, May 18, 1995.

5

FUNDAMENTAL FAIRNESS IN THE JUDICIAL SYSTEM AND THE NORTH-SOUTH DIVIDE

Sudan, unlike many newly independent African countries, had a functioning judicial system with trained advocates and judges at the time of its independence in 1956, and they proved capable of defending fundamental rights using Sudanese law. The rule of law has been weakened, however, by the lack of a written constitution, three military governments suspended basic rights and ruled by decree, and the transition, accelerated since the 1989 coup, of the legal system from one based on colonial law inherited from the British to one based on Islamic law, shari'a. Most of the abuses of due process and fair trial that Human Rights Watch noted, however, were unrelated to shari'a. They are instead abuses common to de facto governments wishing to stay in power and ruling by decree in prolonged states of emergency.

Immediately after the June 1989 military coup, the government purged ("sent into retirement for the public interest") fifty-seven judges.[1] Others were dismissed after that. Some who have served in the judicial system for many years observed that the criteria for selecting judges under the current government seemed more heavily weighted to the candidates' legal and political commitment to shari'a than was the past practice, where academic standing and, for the Supreme Court, extensive judicial experience were, they said, more valued.[2] When the number of states was increased from nine to twenty-six, additional judges were appointed to fill the new positions in the states (although more than a few judges are seconded to serve in the Gulf).

The government announced in September 1995 the creation of a committee to review the cases of all those who were purged.[3] Whether any judges dismissed in 1989 will be reinstated is unknown.

Abuses of due process surveyed in this chapter include denial of counsel and the right of appeal in trials before military tribunals. Military tribunals have been responsible for the execution after summary trial of many persons, civilian

---

[1]The dismissal was said to have been done pursuant to a list prepared by one of the National Islamic Front loyalists on the bench. Many so dismissed were known secularists. Human Rights Watch/Africa interview, Khartoum, May 27, 1995.

[2]Human Rights Watch/Africa interviews, Khartoum, May 27 and June 7, 1995.

[3]"Sudan: Human Rights Group Meets, Says it Will Not Cooperate with Amnesty," SUNA news agency, Khartoum, in English, 1750 gmt, September 2, 1995, quoted in BBC Monitoring Service: Middle East, September 5, 1995.

and military, although it is impossible to know how many because the military proceedings are not made public. The summary trial and execution of twenty-eight army officers in 1990 (for an attempted coup) still stands out as an abuse without remedy as do the executions in Juba in mid-1992.

The death penalty is still in use, and executions continue even in civilian courts.

Finally, southern advocates, judges, and others in the judicial system remain concerned that the south is being marginalized and its people reduced to second-class citizenship, by the way in which the law is administered as well as by shari'a as the law of the land — five Islamic penalties not yet enforced in the south. Customary laws, recognized in family matters (marriage, divorce, custody, inheritance),are not taught in law school curricula, and no customary law except Dinka has been codified.

THE APPLICABLE LAW

The right to due process and a fair trial is set forth in the International Covenant on Civil and Political Rights, Article 14.

> 1. . . . In the determination of any criminal charge against him, or of his rights and obligations in a suit at law, everyone shall be entitled to a fair and public hearing by a competent, independent and impartial tribunal established by law.
> 2. Everyone charged with a criminal offense shall have the right to be presumed innocent until proved guilty according to law.
> 3. In the determination of any criminal charge against him, everyone shall be entitled to the following minimum guarantees, in full equality:
> (a) To be informed promptly and in detail in a language which he understands of the nature and cause of the charge against him;
> (b) To have adequate time and facilities for the preparation of his defense and to communicate with counsel of his own choosing;
> (c) To be tried without undue delay;
> (d) To be tried in his presence, and to defend himself in person or through legal assistance of his own choosing. . . .
> (e) To examine, or have examined, the witnesses against him and to obtain the attendance and examination of witnesses on his behalf under the same conditions as witnesses against him; . . .

(g) Not to be compelled to testify against himself or to confess guilt. . . .

5. Everyone convicted of a crime shall have the right to his conviction and sentence being reviewed by a higher tribunal according to law.

The African Charter also protects due process.[4]

Sudan also is bound by Article 6 of the International Covenant on Civil and Political Rights, protecting the right to life and regulating the use of the death penalty:

1. Every human being has the inherent right to life. This right shall be protected by law. No one shall be arbitrarily deprived of his life.

2. In countries which have not abolished the death penalty, sentence of death may be imposed only for the most serious crimes in accordance with the law in force at the time of the commission of the crime and not contrary to the provisions of the present Covenant and to the Convention on the Prevention and Punishment of the Crime of Genocide. This penalty can only be carried out pursuant to a final judgement rendered by a competent court.

---

[4]The African Charter, Article 7:

1. Every individual shall have the right to have his cause heard. This comprises:

(a) the right to an appeal to competent national organs against acts violating his fundamental rights as recognized and guaranteed by conventions, laws, regulations and customs in force;

(b) the right to be presumed innocent until proved guilty by a competent court or tribunal;

(c) the right to defense, including the right to be defended by counsel of his choice;

(d) the right to be tried within a reasonable time by an impartial court or tribunal.

2. No one may be condemned for an act or omission which did not constitute a legally punishable offence at the time it was committed. No penalty may be inflicted for an offence for which no provision was made at the time it was committed. Punishment is personal and can be imposed only on the offender.

The United Nations Economic and Social Council has also promulgated certain safeguards guaranteeing protection of the rights of those facing the death penalty. Among other things, it requires that anyone sentenced to death "shall have the right to appeal to a court of higher jurisdiction, and steps should be taken to ensure that such appeals shall become mandatory."[5]

Where summary executions have been alleged, it is the duty of the government to investigate[6] and to prosecute.[7]

The right to due process before being deprived of a home pursuant to a criminal punishment is protected in Article 14 of the ICCPR. Furthermore, confiscation of property as a punishment for exercising other protected rights, such as free speech or freedom of association, is a violation of those protected rights.

FAIR TRIAL

Military Tribunals
Summary Execution of Twenty-Eight Officers Tried by Military Tribunal in 1990
The tribunal where offenses against due process and fair trial are most egregious is the military tribunal. Unknown numbers of members of the armed forces and civilians — perhaps in the hundreds — have been summarily convicted of treason or other charges for involvement in coup plots in secret trials by ad hoc military courts without counsel, appeal, or other fundamental elements of due process. Many have been summarily executed, often on the same day as the conviction.

---

[5]U.N. Safeguards Guaranteeing Protection of the Rights of Those Facing the Death Penalty, Economic and Social Council res. 1984/50, annex, 1984 U.N. ESCOR Supp. (No. 1), p. 33, U.N. Doc. E/1984/84 (1984), Article 6.

[6]Ibid., Article 9:
> There shall be thorough, prompt and impartial investigation of all suspected cases of extra-legal, arbitrary and summary executions . . . Governments shall maintain investigative offices and procedures to undertake such inquiries. The purpose of the investigation shall be to determine the cause, manner and time of death, the person responsible, and any pattern or practice which may have brought about that death. It shall include an adequate autopsy, collection and analysis of all physical and documentary evidence and statements from witnesses. The investigation shall distinguish between natural death, accidental death, suicide and homicide.

See also Articles 10-16.

[7]Ibid., Articles 17-19.

An abortive coup d'etat on the night of Sunday-Monday April 22-23, 1990 was followed by the arrests of dozens of officers and soldiers suspected of participating in the coup. Three officers were arrested two or three days before the alleged coup. Twenty-eight officers were summarily tried and promptly executed.[8] The government refuses to disclose information about the trials or to turn over the bodies to the relatives.

A military tribunal was believed to have been hastily constituted from four or five officers in government circles of high military rank on Tuesday, April 24, 1990. According to the information that reached the families later, the names of the accused officers were called out in groups of five and each group of five was brought before the tribunal and briefly questioned. All plead not guilty. The verdicts were handed down immediately and the twenty-eight were sentenced to execution.[9] Each group of five was chained together and then the condemned men were taken out by group and executed, allegedly by members of the NIF security, in front of a freshly-dug pit. The trials lasted only minutes. No defense counsel was permitted.[10]

---

[8]The widow of one told Human Rights Watch that her husband left home on Sunday night and when he did not return home on Monday night she went to his base the next day where they told her there had been an attempted coup and her husband had been executed. These officers necessarily had a very short trial and no real appeal. Human Rights Watch/Africa interview, Khartoum, May 27, 1995.

[9]The executed officers are Maj. Gen. (ret.) Khalid al-Zein Ali, Maj. Gen. (ret.) Osman Idriss al Balol, Maj. Gen. (ret.) Hussein Abdel Gadir al Kadru, Brig. (ret.) Mohamed Osman Ahmad Karrar, Staff Col. Ismat Mirghani Taha, Staff Col. Bashir Mustafa Bashir, Staff Col. (rtd.) Mohamed Ahmad Gassim, Col. Salah al Sayyid Hussein, Lt. Col. Bashir Amir Abu Dik, Lt. Col. Mohamed Abdel Aziz Ibrahim, Lt. Col. (ret.) al Sayyid Hussein Abdel Rahim, Lt. Col. (ret.) Abdel Moneim Hassan Ali Karrar, Lt. Col. (ret.) Bashir al Tayib Mohamed Saleh, Maj. Salah al Dardiri Babiker, Maj. el Fatih Khalid Khalil, Maj. Osman al Zein Abdullah, Maj. Babiker Abdel Rahman Nugudallah, Air Force Maj. Akram al Fatih Yusuf, Maj. al Sheikh al Bagir al Sheikh, Maj. Mu'awiyah Yasin Ali, Maj. Nihad Ismail Hamidah, Maj. Isam al Din Abu al Gassim Mohamed, Maj. (ret.) al Fatih Ahmad Ilyas, Maj. (ret.) Sid Ahmad Salih, Maj. (ret.) Taj el Din Fatih al Rahman, Capt. Muddathir Mohamed Mahjub, Air Force Capt. Mustafa Awad Khawajali, and Capt. (ret.) Abdel Moniem Khasr Kumeir. Africa Watch, "Sudan: Officers Executed and Doctor Tortured to Death," *A Human Rights Watch Short Report*, April 26, 1990.

[10]Ibid. In its notice of derogation to the U.N. Treaty Office, the government stated that the army officers "executed on July 26, 1990," were charged not with violation of the state of emergency regulations but with sections of The People's Armed Forces Act and The Penal Code of 1983. This may refer to the executions of April 1990. Sudan Ministry of

(continued...)

Regardless of the charges against them, these officers had a right to a fair hearing. The haste of the courts martial and firing squad is ample evidence that there was no fair hearing and no right to appeal. Due process was utterly lacking.

This case is rather exceptional for several reasons and still remains open since the government, aside from an announcement read on television by President Bashir naming those twenty-eight officers who had been executed for a coup attempt, never notified the families formally or in writing of their deaths. Some family members formed a committee called the Ramadan Martyrs' Family Organization which is demanding that the details of the trials be made public along with the names of those who presided over the trials and the names of the executioners.

The government has not, to this day, turned the bodies of the officers over to their families for a proper burial. The place where they were buried is kept secret. The families continue to demand the remains so they can be decently buried.[11]

Other Military Tribunal Cases

In another summary proceeding in connection with a 1991 coup attempt, one officer convicted by a military tribunal told us that his trial lasted about sixty seconds. The court's questions were "Name, rank, please go, we will see you again." He was never called back. He was "tried" with three other officers whom he said he did not know: a colonel, a major, and a lieutenant colonel. Forty-six persons were tried at the same time, with three courts martial proceeding simultaneously in the same place. None of the accused had a representative, friend or advocate to speak for them. The ten civilians among the forty-six were tried by courts martial also.[12]

According to the officer interviewed by Human Rights Watch, a colonel told him — two months after he was asked to state his name to the court — that he would be executed by a firing squad. His sentence later was decreased from death

---

[10](...continued)
Foreign Affairs, "Notification in Accordance with Article (4) of International Covenant on Civil and Political Rights," Khartoum, August 21, 1991, on file with U.N. Treaty Office, New York.

[11]Human Rights Watch/Africa telephone interview, March 6, 1996. Family members of the officers say that they were told that between seventy and ninety-six soldiers captured with the officers were also tried and executed at the same time. Ibid. We have no verification of this information.

[12]Human Rights Watch/Africa interview, Khartoum, May 29, 1995.

to twenty years imprisonment, and then to ten years.[13] He and most other convicted 1991 coup plotters were released from prison in August 1995.

Summary proceedings in military courts have been used under other Sudanese governments as well. Four Nuba rank and file army soldiers, El Nour Armin Degash, Osman Mahmud, Abdel Hadi Makki and Abdul Rachman Khalifa, among others, were detained in 1985 and convicted in 1986 in Khartoum by a military court of a "racist conspiracy" to overthrow the government by force.[14]

In 1992, while already serving sentences for (racist) conspiracy and after the NIF came to power, these Nuba prisoners were further accused of conspiracy and tried before another military court, convened inside Sudan Security headquarters in Khartoum. They were convicted and given life sentences. They had no attorney and no right to appeal aside from the right to go to the minister of defense for a confirmation or rejection of the verdict.[15] These four men were released from prison in August 1995.

In reaction to the SPLA's two armed incursions into the garrison town of Juba in Eastern Equatoria in June and July, 1992, security and military intelligence conducted sweeps of neighborhoods and made mass arrests of southerners in the military and the population of Juba, culminating in several hundred extrajudicial executions and disappearances. Some were alleged to have been tried by military tribunal and executed as spies, but although requested by various governments, records of those trials were never provided, if indeed there were any records or there was any trial.[16]

Only a handful of those convicted by a military tribunal on accusations of involvement in the mid-1992 SPLA attacks on Juba were transferred to Kober Prison. Among those were two southern game wardens, Gadi Jerry Angelo and Nixon Lemi Jobson. Their trial before a military tribunal in Juba reportedly was held the same night as their arrest, and they had no advocate and no right to appeal. They were sentenced to ten years although the charges against them were not clear

---

[13]Ibid.

[14]An attempted coup by southern and Nuba soldiers in 1985 prompted the accusation by some in the (Arab) elite in Khartoum that the "blacks wanted to take power." The prime minister at that time called it a "racist conspiracy." This in turn is held to have fueled the army's suspicion of the largely southern and Nuba displaced and squatters as part of a subversive "fifth column" in the northern towns. Peter Verney et al., "Sudan: Conflict and minorities," Minority Rights Group Report (London: 1995), p. 85.

[15]Human Rights Watch/Africa interview, Khartoum, May 27, 1995.

[16]Human Rights Watch/Africa, *Civilian Devastation,* pp. 58-63.

to them. They wrote an appeal to the military court but have received no response.[17] Because of the limited and expensive nature of travel to and from Juba — even Juba residents need security permission to come and go, and space on the flights in and out of the garrison town is limited — they have received no family visits since they have been in Kober.[18]

Civilian Court: The Explosives Case

The Explosives Case was a landmark case under the current government.[19] The defendants were arrested in 1993, tortured, and confessions secured. There were about twenty-five defendants, some tried in absentia. Apparently the government believed it had a watertight case with physical evidence that explosives were possessed pursuant to a conspiracy, concocted with agents of Egypt, Israel, and the U.S., to overthrow the government. A special court formed by Chief Justice Jalal Ali Lufti consisted of three young judges said to be sympathetic to the National Islamic Front.[20]

The trial, held in March and April 1994, unexpectedly attracted prominent and experienced members of the bar — some twenty-five in number — who stepped forward to defend the accused. Among the leaders of this defense team were Ali Mahmud Hassanein and Mustafa Abdel Gadir, outspoken advocates who had been arrested several times by several governments during their long careers.

The defense advocates fought hard for their clients from the very beginning of their involvement in the case. They walked out of court when they were not allowed access to their clients with enough time to prepare the defense in this complicated case, for which the government had months to prepare. They argued that the confessions obtained were inadmissible since they had been produced as a result of torture.

These advocates succeeded in having the court hear the testimony of the defendants about their torture, order a medical examination of the defendants, and call witnesses they requested, who could corroborate the testimony of torture — including one witness, Farouk Zakaria, who was in a ghost house when he was summoned to court. Indeed, he gave the ghost house as his place of residence. When Sudan Security denied in writing that a second torture witness, Salah Hassan

---

[17]Human Rights Watch/Africa interviews, Khartoum, May 27, 1995.

[18]Gadi Jerry Angelo suffers from an ulcer for which the prison authorities are said to provide inadequate treatment.

[19]Human Rights Watch/Africa, "In the Name of God," pp. 28-29.

[20]This account is based on Human Rights Watch/Africa interviews with several lawyers and others familiar with the case.

Samaret, was in its custody, an advocate elicited from Zakaria that he had seen Samaret in the ghost house that morning. The advocates asked the court, in writing, to take note of Sudan Security's lie about having the witness in custody.

The defendants, under oath, named the names of the Sudan Security agents who tortured them. This proceeding was the first time that torture by security was exposed in court under the current government.

The court, composed of younger judges, apparently ceased to resist the force of the defense arguments midway through the trial, and permitted the advocates to do and say what they wanted on behalf of the accused. This permitted much greater observance of the defendant's due process rights, and was a positive step forward.

Ultimately, however, the court admitted the confessions taken from the tortured defendants as evidence, on the grounds that the torture did not affect the will of the accused. This was the first time in which confessions obtained from tortured defendants were ruled admissible in Sudan, we are told; in any case, this is a major step backward. In August 1995 the president issued a decree pardoning eighteen "political prisoners," including those convicted in the explosives case of 1994.[21]

Security summoned Ali Mahmud Hassanein, the lead defense counsel, to their offices on several consecutive days while the defense was preparing the oral argument and final submission to the court. They asked no questions but claimed that he was a criminal himself, and asserted that they would never let "those criminals," the Explosives Case defendants, out of jail, according to someone who heard the exchange. Some thirty security agents attended each session of the trial.

Hassanein was summoned to security again on the day of his final oral summation. He decided to ignore the summons and, in court, showed the summons to those present. The judge ruled that he did not have to go to the security offices that day and permitted him to stay in court.

Security still was not through with the defense advocates, and sought to intimidate Hassanein, who was arrested and held for four days at the Sudan Security headquarters in the army base in Khartoum in May 1994, after the end of the trial. Security personnel hit him, angrily referring to his in-court criticism of them. "You said this in summation, you attacked us." A young security member beat him severely on the head.

The news of the detention and beatings spread. Pressure built and Hassanein was released. This was not the end of it, however. He was rearrested in the fall of 1994 and then, too, security kept mentioning the Explosives Case during

---

[21]"Sudan: President Issues Decree Pardoning 18 'Political Prisoners,'" August 30, 1995.

his interrogation. This time fellow Explosives Case advocate Mustafa Abdul Gadir and he were held in the Special Operations Section (al amaliyat) near the Kuwaiti Embassy, to the south of Sudan Security headquarters. They were made to face the wall for six hours. Hassanein was interrogated from 9:00 a.m. until about 4:00 a.m.; Abdel Gadir was beaten on the head and interrogated. They were made to stay on a veranda at night and ordered not to sleep. It was very cold and no blankets or beds were provided. The next day they were ordered to go home and return the same day. When they returned there were more references to the Explosives Case, or rather the statements the advocates made about security during the case: "You said this about us, you are against the NIF." The two advocates were released after four days of coming and going.

In December 1994, the two advocates were again harassed by security. Fifteen security members thoroughly searched the home and office of Hassanein. Abdel Gadir's house was searched at 4:45 a.m., without a search warrant. The next day his office was searched and documents removed without any receipt or identification of what was taken. Both Abdel Gadir and Hassanein were taken to a ghost house for interrogation, which began after midnight. They were permitted to go home after more than twenty-four hours in custody during which they were not allowed to sleep, were forced to do exercises and threatened; Abdel Gadir was beaten with fists and struck with a wooden rod. In September 1995, Abdel Gadir and other lawyers were again arrested by security during the Khartoum student demonstrations and released after a few days, after various human rights organizations issued special alerts on their behalf.

The animus toward the defense advocates carried over to the next notorious trial, of those accused of the February 1994 killing of sixteen persons in a Omdurman mosque of the Ansar al Sunna sect, a conservative sect religiously aligned with the Wahabi sect in Saudi Arabia and critical of the National Islamic Front. This case was tried in a civilian court. Under Sudanese law, the relatives of the victim in a criminal case may retain an advocate to represent their interest in a criminal matter, to work with the prosecution. Under shari'a, the heirs of the victim may pardon the accused, in which case the court must set him or her free; the heirs, not the state, have the paramount interest in a murder case. But the heir's advocate, unlike an advocate for the defendant, must have the permission of the attorney general to become involved in the case.

Some relatives of the Ansar al Sunna victims asked Hassanein to represent them. The attorney general's office adamantly refused to permit this. The prosecutor general told another advocate that they refused because Hassanein would make this into a political case and try to "take over" the prosecution. The case already had political overtones: the chief defendant, Mohamed Abdel Rahmal al Khuleifi, was a Yemeni raised in Libya who fought with the mujahedeen in Afghanistan. He had no visible means of support in Sudan but was said to be supported by Ussama Ben Lauden, a former Saudi citizen who is an opponent of the Saudi government and a NIF supporter. In the hands of a skilled advocate, the witnesses could have been cross-examined about the relationship between the anti-Saudi Ben Lauden group, the NIF government, and the animosity toward Ansar al Sunna leaders, who had received funding for proselytization from Saudi Arabia.

DEATH PENALTY

Death Sentences in Civilian Courts
Sudan has not abolished the death penalty and executions continue pursuant to Sudanese law after trial in civilian courts.[22] Under the 1991 Criminal Act, the death penalty may be given in cases of undermining the constitutional system (Article 50), waging war against the state (Article 51), espionage (Article 53), the offenses of homicide (Article 130), homosexuality (third-time offenders, Article 148), rape (in the case of adultery or homosexuality, Article 149), incest (in the case of rape, adultery or homosexuality combined with incest, Article 150), and running a house of prostitution (third-time offender, Article 155).

Islamic law recognizes six major offenses, each of which has a penalty prescribed in fixed terms in the Qur'an or the Sunna (the traditions of the Prophet

---

[22]The death penalty is set forth in the Criminal Act of 1991, Section 27:

> (1) Death penalty shall be by hanging, stoning, or in the same manner in which the offender caused death, and it may be by way of hudud (fixed penalty), qisas (retribution) or ta'zir; and it may be accompanied by crucifixion.
>
> (2) With the exception of hudud and retribution offenses, the death sentence shall not be passed against any person who has not attained the age of eighteen or who exceeds seventy years of age.
>
> (3) Death sentence with crucifixion shall not be passed except for hiraba (armed robbery).

Ta'zir is "discretionary punishment to be delivered for transgression against God, or against an individual for which there is neither fixed punishment nor penance." Mohamed S. El-Awa, *Punishment in Islamic Law* (Indianapolis: American Trust Publications, 1993), pp. 96-97.

Mohamed).[23] These major offenses are known as the offenses of hudud.[24] In the penal context, hudud (plural of *hadd*) offenses receive a punishment with three main aspects. The first is that the punishment is prescribed in the public interest. It cannot be lightened nor made heavier. It may not be pardoned after being reported to the judge, either by him, the political authority, or the victim.[25] The hudud crimes of apostasy (*riddah*, Article 126), adultery (*zina*, Article 146),[26] and armed robbery (*hiraba*, Article 168)[27] may carry the death penalty.

Although the government vigorously defends its right to use the death penalty, apparently the death penalty in civilian courts is neither frequent nor well-publicized since Nimeiri was deposed in 1985.

The director of Kober Prison told us that there were nine executions in Kober in the twenty-one months he had been the director.[28] At least one other execution occurred in 1995 in Sennar. These were executions pursuant to sentences by civilian courts. Human Rights Watch did not receive a reply to its inquiry to the government for the total numbers of executions.

International standards require a right to appeal in the case of a death sentence. Sudanese civilian law provides for an automatic review of death sentences by the Supreme Court, we were told. The case will go directly from the trial court to the Supreme Court for review of this penalty. If there is an appeal on other grounds, the case will go first to the appellate court and then to the Supreme Court for review of the death penalty, unless the decision has been reversed by the appellate court.

According to Attorney General Shiddu, there are a number of safeguards to the death penalty, making it less likely that a person receiving a death sentence

---

[23]See Abdullahi Ahmed An-Na'im, *Toward an Islamic Reformation* (Syracuse: Syracuse University Press, 1990), pp. 21-22.

[24]El-Awa, *Punishment in Islamic Law*, p. 1. The six offenses are the drinking of alcohol, theft, armed robbery, illicit sexual relations, slanderous accusation of unchastity, and apostasy. Many scholars believe that apostasy and alcohol-drinking are not properly classified as hudud offenses since the punishment for them is not strictly defined in words in the Qur'an or the Sunna. Ibid., pp.1-2.

[25]Ibid.

[26]In the southern states, adultery may be punished with imprisonment for a term not exceeding one year or fine or both, and when the offender is married, with imprisonment for a term not exceeding three years, fine or both, but not with death. Article 146 (4), Criminal Act of 1991.

[27]In the southern states, armed robbery may be punished with death if the act results in causing death, and imprisonment in other cases. Article 168 (2), Criminal Act of 1991.

[28]Human Rights Watch/Africa interview, Maj. Gen. Ashrriya, May 29, 1995.

will actually be executed. He said that there were grounds in shari'a law for holding that a long wait between the death sentence and its execution is cruel treatment and therefore the death sentence should not be carried out after a certain period of time has passed. He said he made a recommendation not to carry out a death sentence on these grounds in one case, but unfortunately it was too late and the man was executed.[29]

The attorney general told us during our May 1995 visit that only one person had been executed recently: Mohamed Abdel Rahman Al Khuleifi, the Yemeni convicted for the February 1994 killing of sixteen people at the Ansar al Sunna mosque referred to above. He and others were alleged to have entered the mosque and opened fire. He was tried with an accomplice; two Sudanese who directly participated in the attack were killed the following day in a confrontation with security forces. (See Chapter 7, Religion.) He was convicted and was the only one executed.[30] The date of his execution in Kober Prison was September 19, 1994.[31]

The prosecutor general explained that in cases considered of particular urgency, as the case of the killings in the Ansar al Sunna mosque, the chief justice has discretion to assign a trial judge. This case was judged by one judge of first instance, Abdul Rahman Sherif, instead of the ordinary three-judge court for homicide. An appeal was taken to the appellate court and the Supreme Court, and the latter court confirmed the death sentence.[32]

Regarding the execution of the death sentence, Attorney General Shiddu said that, among other things, the death penalty will not be carried out if the relatives of the victim (or the victim, if surviving) forgive the convicted man and agree to accept monetary compensation instead. A sentence of execution will not be carried out until all the heirs of the victim have been surveyed by the court to determine whether or not they wish to forgive the convicted man. If one heir pardons the man, then there can be no execution. If one heir is under eighteen, then the court must delay execution of the sentence until that heir reaches the age of eighteen, according to the attorney general. Since there were sixteen victims in the Ansar al Sunna case, it was most likely that more than one had an heir under age

---

[29]Attorney General Shiddu did not refer to the case by name.

[30]Human Rights Watch/Africa interview, Attorney General Shiddu, May 2, 1995.

[31]"Detailed List of Prisoners On Which Al Hidia Trials Have Been Applied," undated, Ministry of Justice, Khartoum. Mohamed Abdel Rahman Al Khalifa was listed here as having been executed on September 19, 1995; Human Rights Watch believes that this name refers to the defendant in the Ansar al Sunna case, Al Khuleifi, who was executed after trial.

[32]Human Rights Watch/Africa interview, Prosecutor General Dr. Ibrahim, May 27, 1995.

eighteen. We were unable to find out if the court had taken steps to ascertain the ages of the heirs and whether those over eighteen had pardoned the assailants.

The prosecutor general and the director general of the department of public law, both in the ministry of justice, had a different interpretation of the law. They told Human Rights Watch that if the family of the deceased comes forward and forgives the defendant, then there will be no execution. The court may contact the families to assure that there is no forgiveness, but this is not required. They referred us to Article 31 (b) of the Criminal Act of 1991, which says that retribution (qisas)[33] shall be remitted in a case where the victim or some of his relatives have pardoned the convicted person, with or without consideration. Therefore they doubted if the families of the victims in the Ansar al Sunna case were all canvassed.[34] This case suggests that the usual safeguards to the death penalty may not be applied in politicized cases — or that the provisions for clemency under shari'a are less rigorous than the attorney general claimed.

Death Sentences in Military Tribunals

The procedural opportunities for clemency under shari'a and civil law do not appear to have been applied to cases tried before military tribunals. In addition to the case of the executions after the alleged coup on April 24, 1990 and the executions in Juba in 1992, there is the case of businessman Magdi Mahjoub Mohamed Ahmed, whose one-day trial inside a military compound in December 1989, for the possession of foreign currency, resulted in the death penalty. Witnesses reported that Maj. Ibrahim Shams al Din, a member of the governing Revolutionary Command Council, attended the trial and influenced the judges to order the defendant's lawyer to leave the military compound where the trial was taking place, a serious violation of due process. Mahjoub received the death sentence. On the day the sentence was carried out, December 14, Maj. Shams al Din was seen outside Kober Prison reportedly awaiting confirmation of the execution. Contrary to regulations of the General Administration of Prisons — whereby executions are carried out immediately after the dawn prayer, about 3:00 a.m. — on this day the sentence was executed at thirty minutes past midnight. This

---

[33]Retribution (qisas) is defined as "the punishment of an intending offender with the same offensive act he has committed." Criminal Act of 1991, Article 28 (1). It states, "In case of murder, retribution shall be death by hanging and, if the court sees fit, it shall be in the same manner in which the offender has caused death." Ibid., Article 28 (3).

[34]Human Rights Watch/Africa interview, Prosecutor General Dr. Ibrahim and Director General of the Department of Public Law Dr. Elmufti, May 27, 1995.

speed in execution was possibly an effort to avoid any last-minute review of the case or clemency.[35]

In early 1990, apparently to deter nonviolent resistance to the junta as well as army coup plotters, President Omar Hassan al Bashir said he would not commute any sentence of capital punishment. During a state visit to Bahrain, President al Bashir told the press that he would have Dr. Mamoun Mohamed al Hussein, the jailed head of the Sudan Medical Association, hanged. Dr. Mamoun was tried without counsel by a military tribunal with evidence reportedly obtained by torture. Dr. Mamoun was reportedly beaten so badly he was in a coma for four days.[36] President al Bashir said that whoever else went out on strike, as most members of the Medical Association had done a few months before, deserved "execution and would not [be] allowed to appeal."[37] This statement received wide international coverage which may have caused the president's plan to backfire. A national and international campaign was mounted to save Dr. Mamoun's life, and he was eventually pardoned.[38]

The death sentences of a number of political prisoners, many of whom were tried by a military tribunal, have been reduced to life imprisonment by executive act since 1991. Some of these prisoners' sentences were further reduced and, finally, they were released in amnesties. This was the sequence of sentence reductions in the case of some of those convicted in the 1991 coup attempt.

Conditions of Executions

Executions of prisoners tried in civilian courts (which sometimes include military personnel) are carried out in Kober Prison in Khartoum North and in the prisons in the nine old regional capitals. (See below.) Executions in Kober Prison are conducted by hanging in a small room isolated from the rest of the prison, constructed for this purpose when the British built this prison. The condemned man spends the night before his death in a room adjacent to the execution room. The execution is witnessed by the prison warden, a doctor, a judge, and a religious representative. The family is notified prior to the execution of the day fixed, and is allowed to take possession of the body and bury it. The prisoner director said two persons were executed for currency law violations in this way in 1993.

---

[35]Human Rights Watch/Africa interview, March 1996.

[36]Africa Watch, "Political Detainees in Sudan - Medical Doctors," *A Human Rights Watch Short Report*, January 12, 1990, p.2.

[37] Ibid.

[38]Human Rights Watch/Africa interview, New York, March 1996.

There is no death row where those condemned to death await execution for weeks or months. There is, however, a section of Kober Prison where those condemned to death are housed together with those condemned to life imprisonment. Dozens of people resided there on May 29, 1995, the day of our visit to Kober Prison.

During the Kober visit, we were shown a part of the prison referred to by prison authorities as "Nimeiri's Pavilion." It had a gallows on a high platform, constructed higher than the prison walls so that a hanging could be seen from outside the prison. This was the place of execution of seventy-five-year-old modernist Islamic scholar Mahmoud Mohamed Taha.[39] The "Pavilion" also had an elevated cement "chopping block," and a chair where prisoners whose hands were to be amputated sat and were tied down. Neither has been used, the prison authorities told us, since President Nimeiri was overthrown in 1985.[40]

International law does not bar all death sentences but requires safeguards that appear to be lacking in practice in Sudan. Human Rights Watch opposes executions under law because of the inherent cruelty of the death penalty, the inherent fallibility of all criminal justice systems, and the irreversibility of executions.

PRISON CONDITIONS

The Kober Prison Population

Human Rights Watch visited Kober Prison on May 29, 1995, briefly toured the facility, spoke to prisoners at random and those chosen by us, and spoke to the prison director, Maj. Gen. Abu Bakr Mohamed Ashrriya, who had served in that position for twenty-one months, since August 1993. He said that Kober Prison had 1,066 prisoners, including sixty-four Sudan Security detainees, as of late May 1995. The prisoners included 933 convicts (of whom, they later told us, six were

---

[39]Mahmoud Mohamed Taha was executed for apostasy, the repudiation by a Muslim of his faith in Islam, on January 18, 1985 by the Nimeiri government. Taha was well known as a religious Muslim. During the Sudanese nationalist struggle at the end of World War II, Taha founded the Republican Brotherhood party, which emphasized the need for Islamic reform and liberation from domination by sectarian forces. The Republican Brotherhood was formed as an alternative to the large political parties dominated by the leaders of the traditionalist Muslim groups in Sudan. John O. Voll, "Forward," in An-Na'im, *Toward an Islamic Reformation,* pp. ix-xii.

[40]Human Rights Watch/Africa interview, Maj. Gen. Ashrriya, May 29, 1995.

political prisoners) and sixty-nine awaiting trial for culpable homicide. Those charged with lesser crimes are held in pre-trial detention in Omdurman Prison.[41]

Kober Prison, built between 1907 and 1912, is the largest prison in Sudan and has a capacity of up to 1,000.[42] According to the prison director, other prisons are located in what were capitals of states, before the recent creation of new states.[43] The total prison population of Sudan in 1995 was officially 40,500; the total prison capacity is said to be 50,000. There is a military prison at Omdurman for violations of the military code. Prisoners reportedly stay there for short periods.[44]

According to prison authorities, the inmates of Kober Prison are all twenty-one years or over, with all but four less than seventy years of age. The medical records of these four, whose age was assessed at the request of the prison director, were forwarded to the central prison authorities so that they could recommend to the president that they be released on the grounds of age.[45]

Prisoners are divided into living quarters according to their status. Generally prisoners are not permitted to move around the prison to visit prisoners of different status, the authorities told us.[46] The largest category of the 1,066 prisoners appeared to be 933 convicts, subdivided into political prisoners (six at the time of our visit), those convicted of financial crimes, those sentenced to execution or life imprisonment, and other common criminals. The common criminals occupy

---

[41]Human Rights Watch/Africa interview, Maj. Gen. Ashrriya, May 29, 1995. He told us that no prisoner had died in Kober Prison during his tenure.

[42]Technically, the name of this prison is now Home of Repentance *(Dar al Touba)*; the government changed the name from Kober, which was the name of a British inspector. The government also changed the name of the neighborhood from Hai Kober to Omar al Mukhtar, after a famous Libyan nationalist.

[43]These cities are Juba, Malakal, Wau, Obeid (700 capacity), Fasher, Kassala, Wad Medani (700 capacity), Damazien, and Port Sudan (700 capacity). There are federal prisons in Kober, Port Sudan, Suakin and Debek.

[44]Human Rights Watch/Africa interview, Maj. Gen. Ashrriya, May 29, 1995.

[45]Ibid.

[46]There is a church and a mosque inside Kober Prison. On Sundays and Wednesdays Christian ministers come to visit the prisoners and conduct services. One of the inmates in May 1995 was an Episcopal priest, convicted of financial offenses. At his request, he is permitted to remain in the common criminal section, where the church is located, rather than the financial section.

the largest facility, a two-story brick building with large rooms lined with bunk beds.[47]

The other categories are those pending trial for culpable homicide (sixty-nine), and those detained without charges by Sudan Security (sixty-four), under security jurisdiction but inside the walls of Kober Prison. The authorities allowed Human Rights Watch to walk around the prison, but not to see inside the area where the security detainees were held, nor to interview any of them without permission from Sudan Security. Our prior and subsequent written and oral requests for interviews with security officers and to visit security detainees were not responded to by the government.

Political Prisoners

It is unclear how the authorities define "political prisoners." This category does not include security detainees. It appears to include some but not all persons convicted by military tribunals of attempted coups and other anti-government activities. For instance, among those omitted from the prison director's official list of "political prisoners" were two game wardens from Juba summarily convicted by a military tribunal in connection with the SPLA attack on Juba in June 1992, who were in Kober Prison.

Political prisoners are entitled, under Sudanese law, to "special treatment." We were told this means they have the right to beds, radios, portable televisions, to wear their own clothes instead of prison uniforms, and to receive food and cigarettes from their families. The authorities permit books, except those considered "against the government." Political prisoners have their own yard and bathing facilities, which we were permitted briefly to see, but are not permitted to move about in the sections designated for other prisoners in Kober Prison. The prison director said there were only sixteen political prisoners in all of Sudan, three civilians and the rest military.[48]

---

[47]According to the prison director, there are no serious physical fights among prisoners, except small disagreements among common criminals. No guard has ever been killed or injured in the prison. Solitary confinement cells for those who break prison regulations such as bringing in drugs or attacking other prisoners are used. At the time of our visit, there were said to be four in solitary confinement, all common criminals.

[48]He gave their names as follows: in Kober Prison, six political prisoners: Osman Mahmud Ali, Abdelhadi Mekki, Abdul Rahman Khalifa, Nur Armen, Mohamed Ahmed Al Rayah, and Mohamed Ali Jaknun. A seventh, Abdul Rachman Nugdalla, was in Ibn Sina Hospital in Khartoum. In El Obeid, five political prisoners, all transferred from Kober in May 1995: Ahmed Khalid, Gimayabi, Nasr Farah, Ali Tijani, and Dr. Abdullah Hassan, and

(continued...)

Political prisoners in Kober Prison released in 1994 and 1995 and before said that the treatment in Kober Prison by prison officers is "very good," in contrast to that of Sudan Security. According to these former prisoners, prison officers are themselves afraid of security and will not interfere with what security wants.[49]

Transfers of Political Prisoners

The Kober Prison director volunteered the information that a few days before our visit, nine political prisoners had been transferred to other prisons in Wad Medani and El Obeid.[50] He said that they and 140 prisoners from the common criminal section were transferred because of overcrowding. Political prisoners, however, are housed in a special section of Kober, with ample room for the sixteen political prisoners who were there until a few days before our visit.

These transfers may have been measures intended to limit access to these prisoners by Human Rights Watch. The nine political prisoners transferred out of Kober Prison the week before Human Rights Watch visited were notified at 2:00 p.m. that day that they would be transferred. At midnight a bus arrived from security and all nine prisoners were taken from Kober. Most were still receiving medical treatment in Khartoum[51] when they were transferred, and the treatment was not complete, according to a fellow prisoner in a position to know since they were living in the same section of the prison. The transfers also represented considerable hardship for the prisoners' families.[52] One, Gaafar Yassin, comes from Atbara, according to the prison director, but was transferred to El Obeid, ten hours by car

---

[48](...continued)
a sixth already there, Omar Mahmud Omar. The three prisoners sent from Kober to Wad Medani in May 1995 were Gaafar Yasin Ahmed, Mubarak Mohamed Abdalla Gadein, and Altreifi Altahir Altreifi (all convicted in the 1994 Explosives Case).

[49]Human Rights Watch/Africa interview, Khartoum, May 6, 1995.

[50]This information dovetailed with information we had received from sources close to the political prisoners, although our sources said that some prisoners were taken to El Obeid instead of Wad Medani as the director claimed.

[51]The director said the prison service sent some political prisoners, originally confined in other prisons, to Kober for medical treatment in Khartoum. When the treatment was complete, they returned them to the prison where they belonged, he said.

[52]International standards provide that a detainee or imprisoned person shall if possible be kept in a place of detention or imprisonment reasonably near his usual place of residence. U.N. Body of Principles for the Protection of All Persons under Any Form of Detention or Imprisonment, Principle 20.

farther away from his family, although the prison closest to Atbara is Kober, in Khartoum.[53]

Other transfers may be a consequence of prisoners' contact with former associates. A former navy officer, Mohamed Ali Jaknun, convicted in connection with a 1991 coup attempt, was sent to Shalla Prison in the western state of Darfur, from which he requested a transfer to be closer to his family in the eastern city of Port Sudan. The head of the prison system agreed and he was transferred to Port Sudan prison. After one month there, security, not the prison authorities, informed him they were transferring him to Kober Prison, apparently because his former navy colleagues came to see him in the Port Sudan prison; he had served twenty-two years in the navy at Port Sudan.[54]

Omdurman Prison for Women

Human Rights Watch was not able to visit the women's section of Omdurman Prison but we spoke with people familiar with it. They told us that in 1994 this section — called Omdurman Prison for Women — had about 300 women inmates, all convicted of common (not political) crimes, usually brewing alcohol. Perhaps 75-85 percent of the female prisoners are southern non-Muslims and most of them are in jail because they are too poor to pay the fine for brewing alcohol.[55]

Omdurman Prison was built during the al Mahdiya government (1881-98) and used then as a treasury. It has a maximum capacity of about 600 people in the men's and women's sections but is usually quite overcrowded, with often hundreds more than it has capacity for. Conditions are said to be very bad; the building reportedly has no sewage facility and raw sewage flows in open shallow trenches to collection pits beyond the prison walls. The prison department has repeatedly devised detailed plans to phase out this prison and move inmates to a facility to be

---

[53]See the account of a security detainee who, with others, was moved out of Kassala prison on the dates when a visit from the U.N. Special Rapporteur on Human Rights was expected, in Chapter III.

[54]Human Rights Watch/Africa interview, May 29, 1995. This prisoner was released in the August 1995 release.

[55]Human Rights Watch/Africa interviews, Khartoum, May 1995. Brewing alcohol is an offense that is not punished in the south. Criminal Act of 1991, Accompanying Note 6 (The Southern States) says that the hudud penalties for dealing with or drinking alcohol are not enforced in the southern states. Southern women brew alcohol in the north because they know traditional alcohol recipes and have few other opportunities or skills with which to support themselves and their families; often they are the head of the household.

constructed in the outskirts of Omdurman, but failed to secure government funding.[56]

Omdurman Prison for Women houses not only women but also male juveniles (street children), because of overcrowding in the men's prison and prison regulations requiring separation of underage inmates from adults. It also houses young children living with their incarcerated mothers.

The women's branch of *Shabab al Wattan* (Organization of the Youth of the Homeland, an NIF mass organization) helps run the Popular Defense Forces (PDF) program for women inmates[57] and provides services to female prisoners. Other local NGOs work in Omdurman prison: one provides some legal assistance to the women and another maintains a nursery for children under five imprisoned with their mothers. While these NGOs are given free access to the inmates, who appreciate their services, the administration of Omdurman Prison for Women is said to provide food of very poor quality, and to have denied access to necessary health care. At least two unattended delivery cases were reported in 1994, leading to the deaths of the newborns: prisoners alleged the wardens were slow in responding to the women's request to take the mothers to the nearby Omdurman Maternity Hospital.[58]

Although benefactors have donated mattresses for women to sleep on, and cots for newborns, the prison administration is said to keep these essentials under lock and key, claiming that women would "misuse" them. Meanwhile, women sleep directly on the ground or on straw mats. Due to overcrowding and lack of hygiene, skin diseases are rampant, and infectious diseases take their toll among the vulnerable under fives who are in prison with their mothers.[59]

In 1993, on the occasion of an announced visit to this prison by Gasper Biro, the U.N. special rapporteur on human rights in Sudan, the administration hastily tried to clean up the premises: they issued mattresses to the inmates, and rolled out baby beds. Underage detained street boys living in the women's section of the prison reportedly were taken for a truck ride until the special rapporteur left the prison. Wardens went to the extent of borrowing indoor flower pots from a neighboring plant nursery to improve the look of the place. After the visit, everything returned to normal.

---

[56]Human Rights Watch/Africa interview, New York, March 1996.

[57]See Chapter 7, National Service and Popular Defense Forces. Female prisoners may be released if they attend PDF training.

[58]Human Rights Watch/Africa interview, New York, March 1996.

[59]Ibid.

During that visit, the special rapporteur picked an inmate at random and talked to her privately at length. Less than a week later, Attorney General Shiddu appeared at the prison to interview the inmate about what she told the rapporteur.[60]

Conditions Deteriorate at Omdurman Prison; Prisoner Releases

In 1994, a group of women inmates who returned to Omdurman Prison from forty five-days in training at a Popular Defense Forces camp near Wad Medani protested because the releases promised them were not forthcoming. They were reportedly angered at the conditions of their transport back from the camp site in Wad Medani, 184 kilometers from Khartoum, to the prison. They were crammed in the back of two trucks, and were exposed to the sun during the long trip. Two infants in the company of their mothers reportedly died as a direct result of the conditions of the return trip.[61] General conditions in the prison had also reportedly worsened, with overcrowding and food rations shrinking and the quality deteriorating to a point where prison food became inedible.[62]

On the day before the chief justice's October 1994 visit to Omdurman Prison, male prisoners, on the other side of the wall adjoining the women's section, protested, banging on the doors of their cells and shouting. Wardens fired in the air to break up the riot. Women joined in the protests. Prison releases ordered October 18, 1994 by the chief justice were intended to defuse this situation.[63] This order was one of the first acts of Obeid Haj Ali upon his appointment as chief justice of the Supreme Court: 102 women were released; the only ones excluded were those convicted of homicide. In addition, he ordered some 230 male prisoners released, also excluding those convicted of homicide.[64]

Conditions worsened at Omdurman and other prisons. In early August 1995 even General Administrator of Prisons Maj. Gen. al Shaikh al Rayah announced that there had been a marked deterioration in the jails, with prisoners going hungry and some dying for lack of medical care because financial assistance

---

[60]Ibid.

[61]Ibid.

[62]Many women prisoners who were trained the PDF camp at the same time in 1994 were sent to Omdurman Prison at the completion of the course, rather than back to their original places of imprisonment. The director of Omdurman Prison for Women protested this on the grounds that the prison was already overcrowded and had insufficient resources to care for them: on her insistence, these prisoners from other states were returned. Human Rights Watch/Africa interview, Khartoum, May 7, 1995.

[63]Human Rights Watch/Africa interview, New York, March 1996.

[64]"Sudan Pardons Women Prisoners," Reuter, Khartoum, October 17, 1994, quoting SUNA, the official Sudan news agency.

to prisons was totally inadequate. He said there were 1,000 sick women in jail and 300 children with their imprisoned mothers.[65] He called for the release of all prisoners with children and those serving sentences shorter than six months.[66] In late August 1995, women prisoners with children were released by order of the president, among them 101 imprisoned mothers in Khartoum State, according to the director of General Administration of Prisons.[67] The chief justice of the Supreme Court said in September 1995 that he would release 148 sick, elderly and disabled prisoners from Kober Prison.[68]

CONFISCATION WITHOUT DUE PROCESS IN SECURITY CASES

There have been many cases of home confiscations without due process as an apparent punishment for engaging in opposition politics. According to attorneys familiar with the laws governing confiscations, including the constitutional decrees issued after the 1989 coup, the president is not authorized to confiscate homes unless compensation is given and the confiscation is for the common good, public benefit, or national interest, such as use for schools, hospitals, or roads. Under laws passed prior to the coup, confiscation was considered a punishment which could only be imposed after a judicial hearing.[69]

A case of an arbitrary and unlawful confiscation was that of Omer Nour El Deim, a leader in exile of the banned Umma Party, on March 28, 1995. According to a person knowledgeable about the case, twenty security officers arrived at the house at 9:30 p.m. and asked the wife of Mr. El Deim and his two sons and two daughters, who were residing there, to vacate immediately. The officers did not identify themselves. They had no written order. They told the wife that "the president was confiscating the house" and she should leave. The family moved to the home of relatives that night. They were allowed to return to the house

---

[65]This 1,000 figure should refer to women in jail throughout Sudan, not just those in jail in Omdurman Prison for Women, where there were up to 300 in 1994.

[66]"Sudan: Jailed Sudanese Mothers and Children Set Free," Reuter, Khartoum, August 4, 1995. Although there was a general release of many women from prison in 1994, arrests of women for brewing and other offenses continued and the prison population quickly built back up.

[67]"Sudan: Former Prime Minister Sadiq al Mahdi among Released Detainees," SUNA news agency, Khartoum, in English, 1725 gmt, August 26, 1995, quoted in BBC Monitoring Service: Middle East, August 28, 1995.

[68]"Sudan adds 148 to Prisoners to be Freed," Reuter, Khartoum, September 11, 1995.

[69]Human Rights Watch/Africa interview, Khartoum, May 6, 1995.

after signing an undertaking to evacuate it in two weeks. A car owned by the older son was confiscated as well.[70]

During the two week period, the family tried many avenues of appeal, including meetings with the attorney general and minister of justice, the chief justice, and prominent NIF leaders such as Dr. Hassan al Turabi. The Attorney General admitted that he had no copy of the confiscation order, and could do nothing about it in any case because the action was initiated by the presidency. Dr. Turabi reportedly told the family that El Deim entered into "an alliance with the devil" and deserved to be punished.

This house, located in the upper-income Riyad section of Khartoum, was co-owned by El Deim and his wife. Not even her property rights could be asserted in court since there was no written order of confiscation and no written identification of who was responsible for the confiscation. No compensation was ever offered to her or the family.

The government said that the confiscation was done because Omer Nour El Deim, as head of the Umma Party in exile, had entered into an agreement with the SPLA, the armed southern rebels.[71] El Deim also testified on Sudan before the U.S. House of Representatives in March 1995. Whatever his actions, confiscation without due process is not a permissible punishment.

Since the coup, many homes of opposition leaders, both in exile and still in the country, have been confiscated. They reportedly include the houses of Amin Mekki Medani (president of the Sudan Human Rights Organisation operating in exile), Farouk Abu Eisa (now head of the Arab Lawyers Union in Cairo and recently the spokesperson for the opposition National Democratic Alliance), Mohamed El Hassan Abdullah Yassin (former DUP member of the Head of State Council and businessman, now in Cairo), Mohamed Osman al Mirghani and Ahmed al Mirghani (leaders of the banned DUP and the Khatmiyya religious sect), and Gen. Fathi Ahmed Ali, leader of the Legitimate Command (the high command of the Sudanese armed forces ousted by the coup of 1989, who have reconstituted themselves outside the country). In addition, according to opposition advocates, all land on the White Nile belonging to the family of Sadiq al Mahdi, leader of the

---

[70]Ibid.

[71] See"Declaration of Political Agreement" signed by Omer Nur el Deim for the Umma Party and by representatives of the Sudan People's Liberation Movement/Army, among others, on December 27, 1994, in Asmara, Eritrea. "Sudan: Pincer Movement," *Africa Confidential* (London), vol. 36, no. 3, February 3, 1995, p.8.

Umma Party and head of the Ansar religious sect, has been confiscated,[72] and land of the Mirghani family in Kassala, Khartoum, and northern Sudan has been confiscated. The home of Mohamed Osman Mirghani was converted to a head office for the People's Police while that of his brother Ahmed was donated to the Youth of the Homeland Organization that turned it into a private hospital.[73]

Homes and other property belonging to Sudan Security detainees and those accused of security offenses have been seized pretrial and used by security. In the Explosives Case, the property of accused Mohamed Hassan Abad, who was tried in absentia and acquitted, was seized by security before the trial. After acquittal, at the request of his advocate, the court ordered security to vacate the home and return the rest of the property, consisting of two cars and two boats. As of June 1995, this had not been done, according to those familiar with the case.[74] In some cases, agents of Sudan Security use cars confiscated from security detainees for their routine work. Houses of security detainees have been used for security work.

Security also has confiscated other items of private property at will during office and house searches conducted without warrant. Personal computers, typewriters, copiers and faxes are particularly prized. A desktop and a laptop computer were confiscated, without warrant or receipt, from the house of Abdel Rahim Min Allah during the search that preceded his arrest in April 1995. Neither were returned to him at his release four months later.[75]

Private libraries of countless security detainees have been plundered under the pretext of confiscating loosely defined "subversive literature." As a rule, this property has been taken without court order, due process, or compensation. (See Chapter VII, Freedom of Expression.)

THE LAW AND THE NORTH-SOUTH DIVIDE

Longstanding southern fears of marginalization and second-class citizenship have been sharpened by legal developments since the introduction of

---

[72]The property of Sadiq al Mahdi that was confiscated following the Ansar's armed insurrection against Nimeiri in 1976 was returned at the time of Ansar's reconciliation with Nimeiri in 1977. Peter Woodward, *Sudan 1898-1989: The Unstable State* (Boulder, Colorado: Lynne Rienner Publishers, 1990), p. 181.

[73]Human Rights Watch/Africa interview, Khartoum, May 6, 1995.

[74]Human Rights Watch/Africa interview, Khartoum, May 20, 1995.

[75]Amnesty International, "Sudan: Urgent Action," UA 184/95, AI Index: AFR 54/27/95, July 28, 1995.

shari'a in 1983, and particularly by the way the law has been administered and enforced under the current government since 1989.[76] Sudan is a highly diverse country; no ethnic group is in the clear majority and among religious groups only 60 to 70 percent are Muslim. Southerners are mostly practitioners of traditional African religions or Christianity.

The British policy was to separate southern Sudan and its African peoples from northern Arabized Sudan and Islamization. Under the British, northern Sudanese were prohibited from residing in the south except by official permission and free movement of southerners to the north was restricted. Abel Alier, a respected former judge and southern politician, wrote of British rule in the south (1898-1956):

> The spread of Arabic and Islam was curbed; even Northern Sudanese traditional dress was frowned upon and discouraged; English and the indigenous languages of the South were correspondingly encouraged and promoted. A conference organised under the auspices of the Church Missionary Society was held in Equatoria in 1928. It selected English and seven main languages for educational instruction in the Southern Sudan. Arabic was excluded.[77]

Alier believes that this separation was motivated in part by fear of revival of the slave trade, which flourished during the Turko-Egyptian administration and continued during the Mahdiya (1881-98).

> Even after the reconquest [by the Anglo-Egyptian forces in 1898], the slave trade was still alive and the slave routes from Bahr El Ghazal to Darfur and North-Eastern Upper Nile to Blue Nile were busy. The Anglo-Egyptian administration could not thus gamble with the possibility of the revival of the slave trade and so it took the steps it did in 1922.[78]

---

[76]This section is based on conversations with many southern jurists in Khartoum and elsewhere.

[77]Abel Alier, *Southern Sudan: Too Many Agreements Dishonoured* (Reading: Ithaca Press, 1990), p. 17.

[78]Ibid.

This separation of north and south did not continue after independence in 1956, and northern Sudanese replaced the British as government officials in the south, bringing Arabic and Islam with them. Foreign Christian missionaries were expelled in 1964, and the day of rest changed in the south from Sunday to Friday, as in the rest of Sudan. In 1983 shari'a was introduced as the source of law for all of Sudan. Efforts are now underway to make Arabic the language of instruction in schools in the south, where few are fluent in Arabic.

A chief concern of southern jurists is that, under certain provisions of shari'a, non-Muslims will have second-class citizenship as a matter of law.[79] They are also concerned about the lack of respect of diversity for their distinctive southern cultures, which touches on the rights of the southern peoples under Article 27 of the ICCPR:

> In those States in which ethnic, religious or linguistic minorities exist, persons belonging to such minorities shall not be denied the right, in community with the other members of their group, to enjoy their own culture, to profess and practice their own religion, or to use their own language.

Historian Douglas H. Johnson has written that southerners now feel under attack not only from a dominant religion but also from a twinned dominant culture, with steady erosion of their definition as separate peoples:

> There is a stronger feeling [in the 1990s] than in the 1970s that the south is facing an assault of religious and racial intolerance mounted by some segments of the north, often with the external support of wealthy Arab nations. Nimeiri's imposition of the shari'a is one example of this, but the election campaigns [1986] also emphasised the financial and political support some political parties receive from abroad, support which comes not so much for reasons of their proposals for foreign policy, but for their policy towards spreading Islam in the Sudan.[80]

Another historian notes that there is a large overlap of the definition of Arab and Muslim in Sudan, unlike the situation in other African countries whose

---

[79]Human Rights Watch/Africa, "In the Name of God," pp. 39-40.

[80]Douglas H. Johnson, "North-south issues," in Peter Woodward, ed., *Sudan After Nimeiri* (London: Routledge Press, 1991), p. 128.

Muslim populations do not define themselves as Arabs but rather as Kenyans, Nigerians, Senegalese, and so on.

> More than for most of the other Muslim peoples of Africa, for the Sudanese to be a Muslim is to be an Arab. It is this deep assimilation of Islam and identification with Arab culture and society which is expressed in the universal claim to Arab ancestry and the overwhelming currency of Arabic.[81]

The political debate in the north is, to a large extent, over which type of Islam is the proper form of Islam for the state to endorse, according to historians.[82] The traditional political parties that are based on Sufi sects propose one variant (with former prime minister Sadiq al Mahdi as head of the Umma Party and the Ansar sect on which it is based, for example, criticizing from a religious point of view the Islamic practices of the ruling National Islamic Front), and the nonsectarian NIF proposing a different and more rigid Islamic approach. In the south, however, "the very idea of the possibility of this kind of debate as being a 'national' stake is felt as a hegemonic attempt of the 'Arab' north to impose its political, economic and social identity upon the whole state of Sudan."[83]

Prior to the adoption of shari'a in 1983, criminal law and civil law (the laws regulating torts, contracts, corporations, banking, commercial instruments and other non-criminal matters), were not based on shari'a but on British common law (adapted for India) and Sudanese legislation. The application of shari'a was limited to personal law matters of Muslims.[84] Christians were subject to their own religious law in these matters. Those, mostly southerners, who were neither Muslims nor Christians were subject to customary law (of the Dinka, Nuer, etc.) in personal matters.

In 1983, President Nimeiri, using dictatorial powers, passed laws seemingly based on shari'a law, including the Criminal Act, the Evidence Act, and

---

[81]I.M. Lewis, "Regional Review of the Distribution and Spread of Islam, The Eastern Sudan," in I.M. Lewis, ed., *Islam in Tropical Africa*, 2d ed. (Bloomington: Indiana University Press, 1980), p. 5.

[82]Jean Francois Rycx, "The Islamisation of law as a political stake in Sudan," in Woodward, *Sudan After Nimeiri*, p. 142.

[83]Ibid.

[84]Personal law covers family law (marriage, divorce, custody) and inheritance.

the Judgments (Basic Rules) Act.[85] These laws were known as the September Laws.[86]

Nimeiri's September 1983 introduction of shari'a was the result of his political alliance with the Muslim Brotherhood. This alliance was a clear break with his southern political allies. That break was already obvious in his increasing disregard for the regional autonomy granted the south in 1972 under the Addis Ababa accords which ended the first civil war in the south (1955-72). Some southerners in the army had already gone into armed revolt in May 1983 against the central government because of the whittling away of this autonomy. The rebel Sudan People's Liberation Army was formed shortly thereafter.

This enforced turn to Islam did not prove as politically popular as Nimeiri had hoped. After introduction of shari'a hudud punishments, a wave of floggings, bloody amputations and executions took place that shocked Sudanese society and contributed to the downfall of the Nimeiri regime in April 1985. The parliamentary government was on the verge of revoking the shari'a laws in June 1989 as part of a negotiated peace with the SPLM/A, when the coup intervened, and shari'a was not revoked; instead, a 1988 draft "true" Islamic penal code prepared by the NIF became the Criminal Act of 1991 after the NIF took power, which southerners regarded as another setback for them.

Southern advocates point to various ways they believe this legal system and particularly the 1991 Criminal Act are prejudicial to non-Muslims and most southerners. First, the government claims that shari'a does not apply to the south, which is incorrect. All Sudanese legislation, including all penal law, applies in the south; the only exception is for certain penalties in the 1991 Criminal Act, which explicitly states that it is

> aimed at observing shari'a as the main source of legislation, so that its spirit shall infiltrate into the Act and its principles

---

[85]Under the Judgments Act, which deals with the sources of law to be applied, a court must apply shari'a law as established by the Qur'an and Sunna "not only in the absence of legislation but also notwithstanding any legislative provision in another law." It is also to be applied in cases not provided for by any law. Akolda M. Tier, "Islamization of the Sudan Laws and Constitution: Its Allure and its Impracticability," *Verfassung und Recht in Ubersee (Law and Politics in Africa, Asia and Latin America)* (Baden Baden, Germany: 25. Jahrgang-2.Quartal 1992), p. 208 (reprinted in English).

[86]Ibid.

intermingle with the provisions thereof, and its guidance manifest itself in the added or omitted provisions.[87]

Shari'a is applicable to virtually all matters of civil law other than matters of family and succession under the Civil Transactions Act of 1984.[88]

The 1991 Criminal Act provides only that "the Southern States are excluded from the enforcement of certain provisions," which are listed: 1) drinking alcohol, or dealing with it; 2) sale of dead animals; 3) capital theft; 4) defamation of unchastity; 5) hudud punishments in offenses of armed robbery and adultery; and 6) penalty of gisas or retribution.[89] All other parts of the Criminal Act apply in the south.[90]

This nonenforcement of hudud penalties in the south is not guaranteed and may not be permanent, southerners fear. There is no constitutional barrier to imposing the full force of shari'a on the south. Indeed, southern jurists point to an important provision in the Criminal Act that would permit northerners to impose shari'a on the south. The Criminal Act states that the shari'a (hudud) penalties will not be applied pending "completion of the federal legislative bodies, and decision on such provisions and punishments, having full regard to the recommendations of the national deliberation conference on peace problems."[91] Southerners fear that northerners imbued with the spirit of jihad who have moved and will move to southern garrison towns for commerce or government jobs, including PDF zealots and NIF militants, will elect themselves to the local legislatures and vote to apply all provisions of the Criminal Act of 1991 to the southern states. The voter turnout is low everywhere in the country, but it has traditionally been very low in the south, and as a result, the NIF has been able to elect its candidates in some southern states.[92]

The entire Criminal Act of 1991, including its ban on alcohol, adultery, and defamation of unchastity, is applicable to non-Muslim southerners and others

---

[87]Criminal Act of 1991, Accompanying Note 3, "Shari'a."

[88]Tier, "Islamization of the Sudan Laws," p. 208.

[89]Criminal Act of 1991, Accompanying Note 6, "The Southern States."

[90]Peter Nyot Kok, "Conflict over laws in the Sudan," in Herve Bleuchot, Christian Delmet, and Derek Hopwood, eds., *Sudan: History, identity, ideology* (Reading: Ithaca Press, 1991), pp. 235-52.

[91]Criminal Act of 1991, Accompanying Note 6, "The Southern States."

[92]Historian Peter Woodward wrote: "Thanks to the [electoral] rules permitting graduates to indicate whichever regional graduates' seats they wished to vote for, whether they had any connections there or not, the NIF organisation ensured that [in 1986] it won seats in [the southern states of] Bahr al-Ghazal and Upper Nile." Woodward, *Sudan 1898-1989*, p. 207.

who live outside the southern states. More than two million southerners have been displaced to the north by war and famine and most are not Muslims. Here the clash of cultures, African and Arab, is most acute. Perhaps 80 percent of women prisoners in the north are southern women who have been jailed for brewing alcohol, a livelihood that is not punished in the south. Sexual practices not punished in the south may be punishable by death in the north.

There are important differences between what shari'a outlaws in both north and south, and customary law. An example given by one southern legal scholar is the crime of adultery, which is a criminal offense (and a hudud offense under shari'a) and not part of the civil family code left to customary law.

> Shari'a defines adultery as sexual intercourse between a man and a woman without there being a *lawful [bond] between them.* What is a lawful [bond] is to be determined with reference to Islamic jurisprudence as provided by s. 2 of the Judgement (Basic Rules) Act, 1983. Accordingly, sex within a levirate relationship, or between couples in a 'ghost marriage', which are regarded as lawful under customary laws of many southern communities, can be regarded as adulterous.[93]

The penalty for adultery in the north may be death, even if both parties are non-Muslims; in the south, the maximum penalty may be three years' imprisonment and a fine, even if both parties are Muslims.[94]

Even in the south, southern jurists are afraid that the uniqueness and continued existence of southern peoples as communities will be destroyed by the imposition of a "alien" Islamic legal scheme that replaces African customs regarding family life, inheritance, custody, and other matters. Customary law of the Dinka, Nuer, Shilluk, Zande, Bari, and other southern peoples is supposed to govern in matters of family and succession. Dinka law was codified in 1984 but other southern customary laws are not codified.

Uncodified customary law will wither away. This has long been the trend, as described by one historian:

> Before and during the colonial period [in Sudan] the Arab personality imposed itself upon the perception of the history of

---

[93]Kok, "Conflict over laws in the Sudan," p. 246.

[94]Criminal Act of 1991, Article 146. Muslims in the south may elect to have shari'a applied to their crimes.

the area as a whole. The Arabo-Islamic culture derived this strong position from the successful marriage between its political and religious traditions. This domination has been facilitated by the specific gravity of an old written culture — the Arab culture — faced with the unwritten African ancestry. From such a point of view 'written history' tends to be settled in the loopholes of 'non-history'.[95]

This trend has been bucked to a certain extent up until recently by the British "indirect rule" of the south through tribal chiefs, and after independence by the efforts of southern judges to apply customary law, appreciating its importance to their communities and being familiar with its tenets from their own upbringing.

In his early days as Supreme Court chief justice in late 1994, Obeid Haj Ali showed an interest in further codifying customary law, and southerners give him credit for this. Before his appointment, he wrote on the subject,[96] and afterwards he even arranged a conference on "Native Administration" in Khartoum on January 9, 1995 to present the case for codification. Many northerners in the judicial and political systems, both at the conference and later, rebuffed the effort; Dr. Hassan al Turabi, who did not attend the conference, when consulted reportedly said that customary law was primitive and should not be perpetuated. The plans for further codification apparently died there.[97]

Since the NIF came to power in 1989, southern judges in the south have been steadily transferred north and replaced by young northern judges who have no familiarity with customary law, a subject not taught in Sudanese law schools. Nor has the Supreme Court instructed them to apply customary law. They are left to their own devices. Even the court of appeal for the largest southern city, Juba, was transferred to Khartoum in 1989 because of the war, removing the appellate court even further from the south.[98]

During the Human Rights Watch trip to Juba in June 1995, we interviewed the provincial judge, Judge Tafiq Hassan Mohamed El Nour, the highest-ranking judge in Juba. At his own initiative, the judge was making an effort to learn customary law, of which he knew nothing before arriving in Juba two years earlier.

---

[95]Rycx, "The Islamisation of law," p. 138.

[96]Obeid Haj Ali, "The Conversion of Customary Law to Written Law," Renteln and Dundes, eds., *Folklaw*, Vol. I (New York: Garland Publishing, 1994).

[97]Human Rights Watch/Africa interview, Khartoum, May 19, 1995.

[98]Human Rights Watch/Africa interview, Judge Tafiq Hassan Mohamed El Nour, Provincial Judge, Juba, southern Sudan, June 5, 1995.

This is commendable, but it is not a substitute for a judicial system that is required to know and apply customary law in family and inheritance matters — giving due consideration of those elements that, insofar as they violate international standards, should be excluded.

The judge said there were nine judges in Juba. He gave us their names; they were all Arabic names, indicating that they probably were not of southern origin. These judges sit on appeal of cases arising from local courts where traditional law usually is applied, since many of the persons chosen to fill the lowest level of judicial posts are community leaders and chiefs.[99] Whatever the decision of the local judge, the appeal goes to a judge not of southern origin and without legal training in customary law. All the law graduate judges sitting in Juba have training in shari'a law.[100] These judges have applied shari'a personal law to

---

[99]The rural court is the lowest level of court: it consists of a president (who is called "sultan") and two members. The president is elected by the people and then recommended by the (appointed) council. Those native to the area are usually on these rural courts, and apply the only law they know: customary law. There is a rural court in every council. There are 134 rural courts in the three states of Equatoria, with 134 chiefs elected, each by his own tribe. Some who were elected, however, were not approved, since the nomination by the provincial judge must be forwarded to the president of the Court of Appeal and then to the chief justice of the Supreme Court for approval. Appeals from decisions of rural courts go to a higher level of rural court and then to the provincial court in criminal matters. In civil matters, the appeal is to a higher level of rural court and then to a first class magistrate and then to the provincial judge. In both criminal and civil matters, the decision of the provincial court is final.

Apart from the rural court are three town benches or courts, consisting of a president and two members. They rule by majority vote. The members need not be law graduates and are usually chosen from among retired civil servants, police, and army personnel, and recommended for appointment by the provincial judge, who sends their names for approval to the president of the Court of Appeal sitting in Khartoum. The president of the Court of Appeal forwards their names to the chief justice of the Supreme Court for approval. The three members, who rotate in the presidency every ten months, are equivalent to third class magistrates. Rural and town courts are for "simple" cases, and the rural courts date back to the British.

Above these courts are third, second, and first class courts and the provincial court; each has graduated jurisdiction over criminal and civil matters according to the penalty or the amount of money in controversy. Their judges are all law graduates. The Court of Appeals in Khartoum is a five-judge panel with three judges sitting on each case, ruling by majority. Ibid.

[100]Ibid.

non-Muslims allegedly because they do not know any other law and are under no specific instructions from the Supreme Court to use customary law.

Southerners told of a case in which such problems arose: in shari'a the equivalent of a bride price must be returned to the husband on divorce. In Dinka customary law, bride wealth is the property of the wife's relatives and they keep it upon divorce. A northern judge sitting on such a case in the south ordered a woman jailed because her family refused to return the bride price to her husband on divorce, even though neither wife nor husband were Muslims. The judge applied shari'a, despite the fact that Dinka customary law has been codified.[101]

Southern jurists speaking on condition of anonymity, say that the future of non-Muslim judges under this system is bleak. They understand that the NIF believes as a matter of principle that justice in an Islamic state must be administered by Muslim judges.[102]

These southerners say a gradual elimination of non-Muslim judges throughout the country is going on. There are three Supreme Court judges (of eighty-seven) who are southerners, three Court of Appeals judges (of more than one hundred), three provincial judges (out of about 200), and at most twelve district judges (out of more than 400). When the NIF came into power in 1989, southern judges started to dwindle in number, although the few that are left are brought out for visiting foreign delegations to meet. Fewer southerners were admitted to universities and law faculties after 1989, so that there are fewer candidates for judicial positions, according to southern jurists.

Thirteen southern judges have been dismissed since the 1989 coup (and sixteen left voluntarily, some to join the SPLA). The thirteen were dismissed as a matter of court discipline. Southern advocates say that Supreme Court Chief Justice Jalal Ali Lufti broke with tradition to purge southern or secular judges. In the past the practice in disciplinary matters was for the judicial board to issue the punishment, quashed or confirmed by the chief justice. Under this government, however, the chief justice reportedly took the unprecedented step of imposing a higher penalty than that suggested by the board: dismissal.

---

[101]Human Rights Watch/Africa interview, Khartoum, May 27, 1995.

[102]Human Rights Watch/Africa interview, Khartoum, May 19, 1995. Disqualification from public office on the grounds of religion is discriminatory. Human Rights Watch/Africa, "In the Name of God," p.39.

6
POLICING SOCIETY

The government of national salvation brought about sweeping changes in the military, security and administrative structures in the country immediately after assuming power in 1989, with the apparent aims of ensuring its immediate and long term political survival and creating the conditions for an effective implementation of its program of reshaping and "disciplining" Sudanese society. The Sudan Police Force underwent its share of radical transformations, subjected to a dual approach consisting of selective purges and the extension or transfer of police powers to other groups. The officer corps of the regular police suffered successive waves of strategic dismissals while the government accorded police powers and authority to various civilian groups affiliated with the de facto ruling party, the National Islamic Front. At the same time, the police force was considerably enlarged through the formation of new branches. Recruits to these new branches were chosen from a narrow base of party members and sympathizers.

The government restructured the official Sudan Police Force to create a unified police force from the various autonomous regular forces that previously operated under the Ministry of Interior. The 1992 Police Force Law provides for the creation, under the direct command of the General Director of Police, of a "General Administration of Specialized Police." The specialized police units thus incorporated, under the designation of General Administrations, are: the Public Order Police, Customs Police, Prisons and Reformation Police, Civil Defense Police, Protection of Wildlife Police, and the Passport, Immigration, Nationality and Identity Police. Other units of the regular police force include the Central Reserve Police, Supporting [Administrative] Units Police and, as the 1992 law provides, "any other category that the Head of State issues a decision of incorporating in the police force."[1]

The legal structure of the regular police does not include the People's Police Force, a parallel force organized under the Order Establishing the People's Police Force of 1992. The government early on established a wide network of surveillance through neighborhood committees that go by the official name of Popular Committees for Surveillance and Services. Following protests from the regular police about unlawful use of police powers by these committees, the government introduced the semi-regular People's Police Force — whose recruits are nominated by the committees — to exercise police powers now removed from

---

[1]Article 4, definitions, Police Force Law (1992).

the committees. This force formed part of an intricate network that included the Public Order and Behavior Police which appears to have originally been conceived of as a "moral" brigade intended to enforce the provisions of the Public Order Law of Khartoum State promulgated in 1992. The last addition to the network was made in 1993 when the ministry of interior established a Deployment of Comprehensive Security Plan, and an official police force with the same name.

The overriding agenda of this network appeared to be both political and religious. On the political front, post-independence Sudan witnessed the successes of "people's power" during two historic turning points in October 1964 and April 1985, when a combination of political general strikes at places of work and scattered day-long demonstrations in residential areas resulted in bringing down unpopular military dictatorships. In 1988 similar tactics led to the weakening of the elected civilian government of Prime Minister Sadiq al Mahdi, later toppled in June 1989 by the third military takeover in Sudan's recent history. The present government took steps to prevent a recurrence of this pattern. Once it effectively stamped out free trade union activities, a primary security concern of the government remained the deterrence of spontaneous eruptions of anger and organized popular protests in the residential neighborhoods of the capital city. The stifling of unions and civic associations and the rampant persecution of union and student activists aimed at ruling out the first line of civil opposition to the military rule. The creation of the People's Police and the Deployment of Comprehensive Security Police and the dilution of police powers would bring about better control of the population in the residential areas and neutralize political opposition to the regime at that second level. In addition the Public Order, Comprehensive Security and People's Police force appear to have the combined task of ensuring a gradual tightening of religiously-based controls on Sudanese society.

Under the scheme, various security agencies routinely assume powers which prior laws of Sudan reserved to the police alone. The most damning denunciation of this trend was reportedly made by no other than the first minister of interior under the national salvation government who resigned in protest of this amid other serious matters. In mid-April 1991, Minister of Interior Gen. Faisal Ali Abu Salih presented a strongly worded letter of resignation from his ministerial position, and from the membership of the then ruling Revolutionary Command Council, the terms of which later leaked to the public. Top among his grievances was the conflict of mandates between the police, military intelligence and the sprawling branches of the security apparatus. He cited as an example of this conflict that although issuance of passports and exit visas is the prerogative of the ministry of interior, it is routine practice for other security organs to confiscate passports and annul duly obtained exit visas without referring the matter to that ministry. To this day, this abuse is a frequent occurrence in Sudanese ports of departure.[2]

Gen. Abu Salih also reportedly complained about the impunity of members of the popular committees and Popular Defense Forces, which he said was eroding the rule of law and the credibility of the regular police. This particular conflict was resolved by confirming the police powers of popular committees through the medium of the People's Police. The minister also reportedly expressed his resentment about the humiliation of police agents and officers at the hands of army soldiers who were until then in charge of the expeditious execution of rulings of the Public Order Courts.[3] One reason behind the creation of the Public Order and Behavior Police, with a mandate of carrying out such measures as evictions and floggings ordered by Public Order Courts, appears to have been the reconciliation of this conflict.

The final straw which reportedly hastened Gen. Abu Salim's resignation was a confrontation that occurred in October 1990 between police and security agents. The police raided a farm in the Khartoum suburb of Halfayia where individuals from six Arab and Islamic countries were covertly undergoing military training under the watchful eye of Sudanese security agencies, but without the knowledge of the police, according to a opposition leader.[4]

These developments have given rise to a wide range of abuses and violations of the rights of citizens to privacy, freedom of association and freedom of opinion and expression. The new police organs committed brutalities which victimized scores of individuals suspected of political or moral misconduct (the latter also having assumed "political" dimensions) or assumed guilty of some criminal offense or another. An atmosphere of fear and malaise developed in work places, where progovernment unions spied on workers, and in the residential areas as any one of the police agencies, or all of them together, lent their authority to the shadowy surveillance activities of members of NIF mass organizations.

PUBLIC ORDER AND BEHAVIOR POLICE AND THE LAWS THEY ENFORCE

In June 1992, the uniformed units of a newly created police force called the "Public Order and Behavior Police" made their first appearance in the streets

---

[2]See Chapter VII on the right to freedom of movement.
[3]Report from Khartoum, May 5, 1991.
[4]See Mudawi al Turabi, *Al Hayat*, Opinion page, p. 17, February 10, 1996 (in Arabic). Mudawi al Turabi is an academic and Assistant Secretary General of the opposition DUP.

of Khartoum. This force was a unit of the regular police force which initially had a narrow mandate. Agents of Public Order and Behavior Police wore the regular police uniform, with an added special arm band that distinguished them from other units. Among their duties are to rid the city of "vice," "corruption," alcohol consumption, to organize market places and to "discipline and control public appearance." They were usually armed with long clubs and handguns.

They used this gear soon after their initial deployment in 1992 in daily *kasha* (sweep) campaigns. These were infamous campaigns to "cleanse" the streets of the capital of petty vendors, street children, the mentally impaired and "idle" people, who are seen as scars on the face of the city. The kasha campaigns usually ended up targeting members of the displaced community and other destitute migrants from marginalized areas and minority groups.

Later in 1992, agents of the Public Order and Behavior Police were assigned to enforce the provisions of the Law of Public Order for Khartoum State, promulgated by the state government in November 1992. This local law prohibits women from selling food or drinks in the streets or in public squares between the hours of 5:00 p.m. and 5:00 a.m. Other provisions require the segregation of the sexes in public transport seating and require agencies dealing with the public to be responsible for separating men and women,[5] although enforcement of this provision is not widespread. The law also forbids holding any public parties with music except with the consent of the relevant authority. Private parties with music are also forbidden except with the consent of the local popular committee (in writing) and the local authorities,[6] which consent is usually since such parties are a firmly entrenched social institution in Sudan. The provisions of this law also require closure of all commercial shops and markets during the weekly Friday prayers.

The Law of Public Order for Khartoum State does not specifically require the enforcement of a dress code for women. There was a long, concerted propaganda campaign led personally by the governor of the capital in the early 1990s to prepare for the gradual imposition of *hejab*, a strict Islamic dress code for women involving enveloping dress and head covering.[7] This differs from the traditional Sudanese women's garment, the *toub*, a gauzy colorful cotton wrap five meters long that loosely covers the head. Authorities concurrently introduced coercive measures, requiring women workers in the public sector to adopt an Islamic style of dress. They also regulated women's access to schools, offices,

---

[5] Law of Public Order for Khartoum State, Articles 3 and 4.

[6] Ibid., Article 2.

[7]"Veiling" in Sudan refers to covering the head but not the face. It is not customary for Sudanese women to cover their faces.

buses and public parks, making it conditional upon compliance with that dress code. When Sudanese women rejected some of these dress regulations, a defacto but unstable compromise prevailed whereby the toub was deemed acceptable as long as the hair was covered by a separate scarf.

It would appear that the resistance of the regular police force to enforcing these and other new standards led several lobbying groups within the NIF ruling elite to create the Public Order and Behavior Police and the People's Police Force with missions and priorities similar to enforcing the hejab. Indeed, the energies of the Public Order and Behavior Police were largely used during its early existence to enforce the hejab. The regular police force apparently managed over time to assimilate the Public Order Police and Behavior in part, assigning to it some aspects of routine police duties such as criminal investigation and drug enforcement. The "moral cleansing" of streets, markets and neighborhood remains, however, high on the agenda of the Public Order and Behavior Police.

Outside the capital, the public order laws are stricter. In Wad Medani (Central State), the Law of Public Discipline and Conduct, Law Number 2 for 1992, regulates women's dress, and a Muslim woman on the street or in the workplace or in any public place without Islamic dress may be punished by a flogging of not more than twenty-five lashes, a fine, or both.[8] The occasions on which men and women might be in contact or alone together are also regulated in Wad Medani: men are not permitted to work in or profit from women's beauty parlors (Article 8), and the physical plant of beauty salons is regulated: "the site must have one entrance which must be the same as the exit." (Article 9). Dancing in any form between men and women at private parties is regulated by punishing — with thirty lashes or a fine or both — the person holding the party which leads to this dancing. (Article 13(1)). Any (unrelated) woman found inside the home of an unmarried man "will be punished by a flogging of no more than twenty-five lashes," a fine or both. Any man found in the home "with such a woman, or permitting her presence," will face the same punishment. (Article 14).

Women's economic activities are penalized by a prohibition on practicing her trade between 5:00 p.m. and 5:30 a.m. without a permit from the "relevant local authorities," on penalty of flogging, a fine or both, and the court is permitted to seize her work-related equipment and materials.(Article 5 (2)). This provision,

---

[8]Law of Public Discipline and Conduct for Central State (1992), Article 5 (1). The dress code for Central State requires "non-transparent or non-flimsy clothing covering all of a woman's body except the face and palms of the hands." "Repulsive or odious dress" in Wad Medani refers to "dress that is devoid of morals or that disturbs public sentiment."Ibid., Article 3.

which appears in the section dealing with women's modesty, falls hardest on women who prepare food for public consumption and sell it on the streets.

Abuses by Public Order and Behavior Police

In June 1994, the Public Order and Behavior Police made a public commitment to realize the slogan of an alcohol-free capital within one year. By November 1994, a spokesperson for the force observed that the "Year Without Alcohol" campaign had been a major success, stating that the force had destroyed 10 million Sudanese pounds worth of alcohol in two weeks.[9] On December 8, 1994, the Public Order and Behavior Police shot and killed two citizens at Mandela Camp for displaced southerners, situated south of the Green Belt of Khartoum. The two were Malual Tong Lual, a Dinka and former employee of the military corporation, and Awad Zara John, a retired soldier. An eyewitness reported that the police raided the camp in search for local brew and found nothing suspicious. They reportedly were attempting to confiscate the cooking utensils of one woman when on-lookers tried to stop them. The Public Order Police opened fire on the two victims, killing Tong instantly while Zara died from his wounds at the hospital in the same night.[10]

The targets of the Public Order and Behavior Police are mainly displaced people from southern Sudan who took refuge in the capital area from the war. Ill-adapted to the life in the north, and coming from a different cultural and religious background, they found out the hard way that being themselves may be considered unlawful behavior. The Public Order and Behavior Police has detained on charges of adultery and held for trial by the Public Order Courts scores of southern couples duly married in accordance with their own customary law, but who failed to produce written proof of the marriage "contract."[11] Southern displaced women, who due to the ravages of the war have become heads of households, often resort to the distillation and sale of alcohol as the only means available to them for making a living and supporting their families. This puts them in direct confrontation with the law. They constitute the overwhelming majority of women jailed for this crime.

---

[9]"Sudan: Anti-Alcohol Campaign in Sudan in High Gear," Reuter, Khartoum, November 7, 1994.

[10]Human Rights Watch/Africa interview, New York, March 1996.

[11]Ibid.

Public Order Courts

Public Order Courts were created by order of the chief justice of the Supreme Court to provide a fast track for the administration of justice under public order laws and related regulations. There were a number of Public Order Courts in Khartoum in 1995, including the famous ones in Khartoum 2 and another in the city center. Each court has one judge and there is one appellate judge in Khartoum to hear appeals from the Public Order Courts there. In 1995 the appellate judge was Judge Abdel Jelil, appointed by the prior chief justice, Jalal Ali Lufti.

The offenses over which the Public Order Courts apparently have jurisdiction vary. In Khartoum, they have tried cases in violation of the alcohol and theft provisions of the Criminal Act of 1991, and for violations of the Law of Public Order for Khartoum State of 1992.

Public Order Courts are supposed to provide speedy justice, but it appears that their justice is at times so hasty that the defendant is denied due process. This is routine in the case of violations of Article 79 of the Criminal Act of 1991, "Dealing in Alcohol."[12] For instance, in a morning sitting in a Public Order Court in Khartoum waiting for a case, one attorney saw fifteen southern women convicted for brewing alcohol in trials that lasted between five and thirty minutes each; they were the only persons on trial that day for that offense. The defendants were not permitted to bring in witnesses but the police testified and displayed confiscated brewing equipment (barrels). The defendants offered defenses such as denying that the equipment was their property, or asserting that others were present in the house over whom they had no control. They had been arrested the day before the trial, or on the same day as the trial.[13]

Most were sentenced to a short term in prison and a fine which they could not pay, so the time in prison was extended accordingly. The penalty for brewing alcohol was a maximum of one year's imprisonment or a fine. The maximum fine imposed in 1995 for brewing alcohol was Ls. 50,000 or 100,000 (U.S. $94.70 or

---

[12]Article 79, Criminal Act of 1991, Dealing in Alcohol: "Whoever deals in alcohol by storing, sale, purchase, transport, or possesses it with the intention of dealing therein with others, or mixing the same with food, drink or in any substance used by the public, or advertises or promotes it in any way, shall be punished with imprisonment for a term not exceeding one year or with fine. In all cases, alcohol which is the subject of dealing shall be destroyed."

[13]Human Rights Watch/Africa interview, Khartoum, May 7, 1995.

189.40), at a time when the minimum monthly wage was not more than Ls. 6,000 (U.S. $11.36); in 1993 the fine had been Ls. 5,000.[14]

The sentences are served in Omdurman Women's Prison, to which the defendants are sent the same day. Appeals are expedited but rarely taken because of the perception that they are futile; most women are released from prison as a result of pardons or clemency, not as a result of judicial appeals.

Public Order Courts also enforce the laws against drinking alcohol. Human Rights Watch takes no position on a prohibition of alcohol consumption per se, but notes that the prohibition, drafted to apply specifically to Muslims, poses problems in the fair administration of justice in a plural society.

Pursuant to the terms of Article 78 of the 1991 Criminal Act, it is a criminal offense for Muslims to drink, possess or manufacture alcohol. The punishment for this crime is "whipping with forty lashes."[15] There are many cases of enforcement of this law. In early 1995, for example, a (Muslim) policeman was with (Muslim) friends who were drinking alcohol; he said he was not drinking. At the moment that he went into a different room, the police raided the front room and took everyone in it to the station. The policeman and the families of the detainees followed. The accused were tried and flogged the same day. They reportedly received eighty lashes on their buttocks (no clothing was removed) and they did not appear to bleed.[16]

Police usually detain all people in a room or a house where they suspect there has been drinking. In another case in January 1995, a non-drinking man was sitting with his drinking neighbors. All were taken in by the police. They remained in jail for two days, but escaped punishment because they were no longer drunk by the time they arrived in court and the police forgot to obtain a doctor's certificate proving their alcohol consumption.[17]

The law prohibiting Muslims from drinking, possessing or manufacturing alcohol is not applicable to non-Muslims. (Article 78). Non-Muslims may, however, be convicted of dealing in alcohol as defined in Article 79. Non-Muslims

---

[14]Human Rights Watch/Africa interview, Khartoum, May 6, 1995.

[15]Article 78 (1) of the Criminal Act of 1991, Drinking Alcohol and Nuisance, states, "Whoever, being a Muslim, drinks alcohol or possesses or manufactures the same shall be punished with whipping with forty lashes."

[16]Human Rights Watch/Africa interview, Khartoum, May 6, 1995. There was no explanation why the sentence was eighty lashes, but it is possible to receive a sentence for drinking alcohol (Article 78 (1)) and another for being drunk and disorderly (Article 78 (2)), both of which carry a punishment of forty lashes each.

[17]Human Rights Watch/Africa interview, Khartoum, May 6, 1995.

storing or possessing alcohol for their own consumption could not legally purchase it (and no one could legally sell it to them) but could brew small quantities for personal consumption. On many occasions non-Muslim women claiming to have manufactured alcohol solely for their own consumption have been convicted of dealing in alcohol.

In some cases those drinking alcohol may be charged with drinking and creating a nuisance[18] and this crime is not limited to Muslims, so that even non-Muslims may face imprisonment for a term not exceeding one month or with whipping not exceeding forty lashes, and possibly a fine.

Public Order Courts may also enforce the laws against stealing, with the penalty of flogging. In early May 1995, an eighteen-year-old boy was flogged in the central market for theft. He had just been sentenced to sixty lashes; two men in uniform lashed him on his back as he hugged a post; he was not required to take off his shirt. The two men each gave him thirty lashes. The boy collapsed on the ground when the lashing was over, according to an eyewitness.[19]

CREATION AND POWERS OF THE PEOPLE'S POLICE FORCE

Frictions emerged between the regular police and the neighborhood Popular Committees of Surveillance and Services when the latter assumed police powers of search and arrest in many offenses. Members of these committees, invariably NIF sympathizers, formed neighborhood patrols in various residential areas of the capital to arrest patrons of alcohol brewers and to halt other practices such as prostitution and drug use and distribution. They often reported innocent social gatherings to security as "suspect," leading to many detentions. The regular police adamantly refused to recognize and cooperate with the committees on the grounds that members of the popular committees and their patrols were private citizens who had no legal capacity to enforce the law. Local police commanders went further and arrested committee members who harassed other people or who broke the law themselves.

---

[18]Article 78 (2) of the Criminal Act of 1991: "Without prejudice to the provisions of sub-Article (1), whoever drinks alcohol and thereby provokes the feelings of others or causes annoyance or nuisance thereto or drinks the same in a public place or comes to such place in a state of drunkenness, shall be punished with imprisonment for a term not exceeding one month or with whipping not exceeding forty lashes and he may also be punished with a fine."

[19]Human Rights Watch/Africa interview, Khartoum, May 5, 1995.

Underscoring the immunity of popular committee members and the legitimacy of their assumption of police powers, the attorney general issued a decree in January 1992 prohibiting police agents from arresting any member of a popular committee under any circumstances without the express authorization of the governor of Khartoum state. If the police deemed the activity of a popular committee member unlawful, the decree required the case to be reported to the governor. The attorney general had his decree posted on bulletin boards in all police stations of the capital for policemen and the public to see.

The next step in this process which marginalized and undermined the regular police was to extend some police powers to a body staffed by the popular committees, a principal objective of the order establishing the People's Police Force.

In September 1992, President Omar Hassan al Bashir issued the Order Establishing the People's Police Force (1992), whose Article 3 states: "A semi-regular force is created and called the 'People's Police Force.' It has a special emblem, and is formed from volunteer citizens who are eligible in accordance with the conditions stipulated in the regulations of the People's Police Force."

Article 7, provides: "The People's Police Force supports the police, and practices in the performance of its duties some of the authority and mandate granted to the police in accordance with the provisions of the 1991 law of criminal procedure. These are: a) arrest; b) search of persons and places and the holding of any stolen or suspected property." Article 4 specifies the goals of the force as being: to "assist the police in performing their duties and to mobilize popular energies towards maintaining security and public order, and to improve and rectify society in accordance with religious teachings and the precepts of superior morals." Article 12 of the order, entitled "Duties of People's Police Force volunteers," emphasizes, among other duties, the moral "mission" of a People's Police Force volunteer to "b) observe and uphold in his public conduct religious teachings and the precepts of superior morals" and "c) to behave according to righteous conduct which conforms with the sanctity of the tasks placed upon his shoulders." Since the enactment of this order, tens of thousands of People's Police Force members, both men and women, have been inducted into the force all over Sudan.[20]

---

[20]In Articles 9 and 11 of the Order Establishing the People's Police Force (1992), volunteers of the People's Police Force are guaranteed an official release from school or their employers in the public or private sectors for the duration of their service, and the right to return to their places in class rooms and to their jobs once their tour of duty terminates, without being disadvantaged in raises and promotions. During their service, they receive a
(continued...)

People's Police Force Compared to the Regular Police

The People's Police Force differs from the regular force in a number of ways. First, although the 1992 order does not specify this, it is mainly the popular committees that are empowered to nominate the volunteers of the People's Police Force, while aspirants to join the regular force are still required to undergo a long process of application governed by strict requirements of eligibility, qualifications and fair representation of all major population groups.[21] Second, the official discourse refers to the People's Police Force volunteer as *al Shurti al Ressali* "the policeman with a prophetic mission," while a member of the regular force remains what he has always been: a policeman. Third, an important difference between the two forces is the level of training. Members of the regular police are required to successfully complete six months of training at the police academy. People's Police Force members have only two months of training, with classes in basic law and physical exercises, during which they also receive intensive spiritual guidance. As if to symbolize this hybrid nature of the People's Police Force, its members wear a khaki uniform which is identical to that of the regular police force, but is distinguishable from it by a white badge that covers the shoulder and upper arm.

The female agents of the People's Police Force go by the evocative name of *murabitat* or "entrenched defenders of a besieged place." The murabitat are in particular responsible for enforcing women's compliance with a dress and conduct code.

DEPLOYMENT OF COMPREHENSIVE SECURITY POLICE

Starting in 1993, the government introduced a police plan purportedly aimed at the improvement of neighborhood policing. The Deployment of Comprehensive Security is a program that deploys policemen in each of the residential quarters of Khartoum, Omdurman and Khartoum North. The program required popular committees in each neighborhood to raise funds from the residents

---

[20](...continued)
regular salary, and the period of service is deductible from their obligations under the National Service Law of 1992. Human Rights Watch/Africa interview, New York, March 1996.

[21]In a statement to the government daily *Al Inghaz al Watani*, February 11, 1993, Col. Awad Wida'Attalla, the first commander of the People's Police, explained that recruitment boards for the new force were composed of police officers and civilians from the popular committees. They were to jointly decide on the eligibility of candidates. Volunteers between ages nineteen and seventy-five would be accepted.

to construct a one-or-two room station for the force, while the ministry of interior provided agents' salaries and equipment in the form of a vehicle and a radio link to the headquarters for each station. The population did its part in the program by raising funds and actually constructing the premises for the units.

By the end of 1994, at least 120 police stations sprang up all over the capital.[22] People genuinely expected that the presence of this force would deter thieves and reduce insecurity as the government promised. However, lack of resources subjected the unit to rapid wear and tear. Its equipment fell into disrepair and its personnel became demoralized.

Abuses by Deployment of Comprehensive Security Police

Human Rights Watch has a copy of the form entitled "Population Index" that police agents of the Deployment of Comprehensive Security program use to keep the entire population of the capital under their close scrutiny. Under the heading of the ministry of interior, Deployment of Comprehensive Security Project, the form comprises five sections. Information in the first two sections covers the exact location and type of each residence, and whether it was rented or owned by the occupants. Section three requires information on commercial locations, and the home addresses of business owners. The main table in the form requires the listing of members of each family, and the employment, identity, nationality and religion of each, and his or her relationship to the head of the household. The last section is dedicated to notes on changes of ownership, any family members are living abroad, recent deaths in the family, number of cars per household, and domestic help employed.

In displaced camps and suburbs of the capital, agents of the Deployment of Comprehensive Security Police, members of other security agencies who operate out of these stations and members of the local popular committee and affiliated People's Police Force operate together to keep the local population under constant security surveillance. They routinely use beatings to intimidate citizens. They make threatening visits to the homes of individuals who initiate independent community activities, such as evening classes, to coerce them into placing such activity under the umbrella of one of the NIF mass organizations or to abandon it altogether.

The Deployment of Comprehensive Security police stations of Jebel Aulia, where one of the largest displaced camps is located, and Hilat Mayo, one of the largest suburban areas to the south of Khartoum, are becoming notorious for such abuses. For example, on August 31, 1995, the People's Police patrolling the

---

[22]Julie Flint, "Sudan: Fear and Favors Keep Sudan on the Long Road to Ruin," *The Guardian* (London), December 8, 1994.

Mayo suburb shot and killed forty-five years old Ahmad Muslim, a Nuba resident who at the time of the shooting was riding his bicycle. The family lodged a complaint about his death and was told that the deceased did not stop when the patrol ordered him to.[23]

ABUSES BY NIF MASS ORGANIZATIONS AND NEIGHBORHOOD GROUPS

Chapter VII refers to the authorities' call on armed NIF party militia to maintain order in the capital during the September 1995 student demonstrations. This deployment of armed NIF mass organizations, such as Youth of the Home Land and the Organization for the Defense of Faith and the Home Land, received the sanction of the head of state who exhorted them to physically confront government opponents in the streets after various police and neighborhood surveillance mechanisms failed to predict and contain the September 1995 street demonstrations.

The call on armed civilian groups to disperse crowds, guard road blocks, guard public buildings and isolate residential areas from one another revealed the existence of this hidden parallel militia, governed by no law other than the imperative of political survival and formally accountable to no government agency for its conduct. This gives cause for concern about the lack of accountability and the potential for violence that the use of such party militia invites.

Neighborhood patrolling by civilian groups affiliated with or appointed by the NIF-dominated government continues. Inhabitants of both shantytowns and the affluent neighborhoods in the capital are daily faced with armed civilians patrolling the streets. During 1993-94, the government-appointed popular committee of Manshiya Quarter ran a patrol which stalked clients of local brewers to arrest and humiliate them.

A killing occurred in late March 1995 in block number seven of Riyadh residential area of eastern Khartoum council by patrol members appointed by the popular committee, which had introduced armed street patrols in early 1995 under the command of a member of the committee, purportedly to deter night thefts. The patrol however imposed a virtual curfew on the neighborhood and required night workers to carry special permits that it issued. Late in the night of Friday, March 24, members of the patrol shot at a crowd of angry southern citizens who were protesting in front of the local police post about the injury of a member of the group in an earlier shooting by a police agent. Sayda Mohamed Kwual, a displaced

---

[23] Human Rights Watch/Africa interview, New York, March 1996.

southerner and mother of two children, was killed by a shot fired by an unidentified member of the patrol. Despite the presence of a dozen eyewitnesses, the official police investigation avoided questioning members of the patrol, who were all civilians, and focused on the responsibility of the Deployment of Comprehensive Security police force stationed in the neighborhood.[24]

ABUSES BY THE CENTRAL RESERVE FORCE AND OTHER UNITS OF THE REGULAR POLICE

Finally, the Central Reserve Force of the regular police (the riot police) has used excessive force against unarmed civilians in a number of incidents, leading to deaths and injuries among protesters. This most frequently occurred during campaigns for the forcible resettlement of squatters and displaced people in the Khartoum area and during September 1995 street demonstrations described in Chapter VII. Coercion, torture and ill-treatment, notably floggings and beatings, are often used in ordinary criminal cases, particularly to extract confessions or to identify accomplices. This abusive conduct has become so routine that policemen do not conceal it from hundreds of citizens who daily go to police stations for ordinary business.

In February 24, 1994, the independent daily *Al Soudani al Doulia* ran a story about two incidents of police brutality to which Mirghani Hassan Ali, a regular *al Soudani* columnist and member of the Transitional National Assembly, was an eyewitness. He called for an official investigation not only of the incidents he cited but of the whole issue of police brutality, as a taboo topic in Sudan. Indeed, this was one of the rare cases in which the issue was raised publicly.[25]

Such is the degree of official tolerance of police abuses that a prompt response to this call for investigation occurred on the same afternoon the article was published, but it was somewhat different from what the journalist hoped. A security unit raided the editorial offices and the press at which the newspaper was printed, thoroughly searched both places, deliberately damaged some property in the process and arrested a reporter. Two months later, authorities closed down the newspaper altogether and confiscated its property as described below. With other

---

[24]Report from Khartoum, March 27, 1995.

[25]Report from Khartoum, March 4, 1994. See Committee to Protect Journalists, *Attacks on the Press in 1994* (Committee to Protect Journalists: New York, 1995), p. 47.

journalists, Mirghani Hassan Ali spent some weeks in incommunicado detention; he was also dismissed from the parliament.[26]

---

[26]Ibid.

7
POLITICAL AND CIVIL RIGHTS

FREEDOM OF EXPRESSION AND THE PRESS

The government of Sudan told the United Nations in November 1995 that "freedom of expression has been guaranteed by the Press and Printed Materials Law . . . . Consequently, there are many daily newspapers where opinions, different from those of the Government, are freely expressed."[1] Freedom of expression and the press, however, in fact continues to be limited, in violation of international standards. A statement by President al Bashir is more revealing of the government's position: "Press freedom must be kept within certain limits, because a madman whose profession is journalism could destroy all of society with his madness, in the form of comments and opinions."[2]

Although a few independent newspapers were allowed to open under the 1993 press law, several were later closed, their presses confiscated, and their owners and journalists arrested. In other cases, newspapers have been closed for several weeks after they published articles critical of the government. Several newspapers, including those formerly associated with political parties, have remained banned since 1989. These restrictions on the press in Sudan go far beyond what is permissible under the free expression guarantees in Article 19 of the ICCPR.

The Applicable Law

The ICCPR protects freedom of speech. Its Article 19 provides:

> 1. Everyone shall have the right to hold opinions without interference.
> 2. Everyone shall have the right to freedom of expression; this right shall include freedom to seek, receive and impart information and ideas of all kinds, regardless of frontiers, either orally, in writing or in print, in the form of art, or through any other media of his choice.

---

[1]"The Response of the Government of the Sudan," November 21, 1995, p. 11, para. 47.

[2]President Omar al Bashir, cited in International Federation of Journalists, *Directory of African Media*, Brussels, 1996, p. 287.

No restrictions are permitted on the "right to hold opinions without interference," Article 19 (1). Therefore, when the military junta that took power in Chile in 1993 limited free expression pursuant to a state of emergency, a member of the U.N. Human Rights Committee stated that

> freedom of opinion could not be restricted merely because the government considered it to be a threat to its own stability. . . . Any restriction on freedom of opinion required convincing proof that a clear and present danger could not otherwise be overcome.[3]

Authorities have concluded, "Peaceful criticism of governmental policies could never amount to such a threat."[4]

The possible limitations on free expression under Article 19 (2) are described in Article 19 (3)[5] in a three-part test: 1) any restriction must be provided by law; 2) it must serve one of the legitimate purposes expressly enumerated in the ICCPR; and 3) it must be necessary.[6] "National security," a commonly cited necessity, permits limitations on freedom of expression required to safeguard limited and legitimate national security, as by preventing publication of military secrets.

The interpretation of Article 19 over the years shows a consensus that peaceful criticism of governmental policies does not amount to a threat to national security. In 1977 the U.N. Human Rights Committee found a clear violation of Article 19 when the Iranian government permitted no discussion whatsoever about the constitution, the imperial monarchy or the "Revolution of the Shah and the

---

[3]Karl Josef Partsch, "Freedom of Conscience and Expression, Political Freedoms," in *The International Bill of Rights*, pp. 222-23., citing Tomuschat, U.N. Doc. CCPR/C/SR.128, para. 20 (1979).

[4]Ibid., p. 223.

[5]Article 19 (3) of the ICCPR: "The exercise of the rights provided for in paragraph 2 of this article carries with it special duties and responsibilities. It may therefore be subject to certain restrictions, but these shall only be such as are provided by law and are necessary:
> (a) For respect of the rights or reputations of others;
> (b) For the protection of national security or of public order (*ordre public*), or of public health or morals."

[6]Article 19, *The Article 19 Freedom of Expression Handbook, International and Comparative Law, Standards and Procedures* (Avon, U.K.: The Bath Press, August 1993), p. 16.

People."[7] Thus national security is not identical to and may not be confused with the longevity of a government.

The concept of public order when set forth together with the term *ordre public* means, in addition to prevention of disorder or crime, the general welfare and even public policy.[8] This concept of "public order" does not justify a government in repressing the speech of its critics; it is intended to protect secrets such as in diplomatic affairs, to ban pornographic materials, or to regulate false or misleading expressions about drugs in the interest of public health.[9]

Under the rubric of public order, some states have guaranteed freedom of expression only to the extent that it was deemed consistent with their philosophies of government; this approach was often used by socialist states. The freedom of expression was apparently guaranteed only if used "in order to strengthen and develop the socialist system," for instance, or as long as it was not exercised contrary to "the interests of the working people."[10] These restrictions too have been found to be a violation of Article 19, according to a legal authority:

> A state is entitled to defend the political structure enshrined in its constitution against its enemies or even against internal subversive acts, but the Covenant does not permit a state to limit political expression directed toward peaceful political or social change. Expressions of opinion favoring changes in socialism, or even from socialism, may not be limited any more than expressions threatening the stability of the regime (as in the case of Chile), or other expressions not creating a clear and present danger of some evil coming within the purposes contemplated by Article 19 (3).[11]

Freedom of expression includes the right to receive as well as impart information. (Article 19 (2)). In its case law, the European Court on Human Rights has referred to the special protection to be accorded to the press in this respect. It has found that the public's right to know is an intrinsic aspect of informed political debate crucial to genuine democracy:

---

[7]Partsch, "Freedom of Conscience and Expression," p. 222, quoting Human Rights Committee Report, U.N. Doc. A/32/44 (1977), para. 310.

[8] *The Article 19 Freedom of Expression Handbook,* p. 17.

[9] Partsch, "Freedom of Conscience and Expression," p. 221.

[10]Ibid., pp. 224-25.

[11]Ibid., p. 225.

Freedom of the press affords the public one of the best means of discovering and forming an opinion of the ideas and attitudes of political leaders. More generally, freedom of political debate is at the very core of the concept of a democratic society . . . .[12]

Controls Before the 1993 Press Law

Journalists have been under tight scrutiny and control since the coup, when the junta disbanded the independent Sudan Journalists' Union and the Writers' Union along with all other trade and professional unions.[13] An estimated 600 journalists found themselves overnight without employment.[14] Other dismissals followed: the government dismissed 200 workers from the state-controlled radio and television in 1991 alone.[15]

An average of twelve to twenty journalists annually were held in incommunicado detention in ghost houses — where many were tortured or mistreated — during the 1989-94 period. Most had been affiliated with political parties banned after the coup, and/or were suspected of involvement in the clandestine press. The authorities clamped down further by conducting warrantless house and office searches of dozens of journalists and free lance writers; in some cases property was confiscated without written order. Journalists were also routinely refused exit visas for travel outside the country. Independent correspondents of regional and international news outlets were harassed in retaliation for critical coverage of the government.[16]

After the 1989 ban on all publications was in place, the government gradually began approving the licensing, reopening, and publication of select privately-owned newspapers seen as apolitical, primarily the sports and "social"

---

[12] *The Article 19 Freedom of Expression Handbook*, p. 89, citing *Lingens v. Austria*, Judgment of 8 July 1986, Series A no. 103, para. 42,

[13] Africa Watch, "Sudan, Suppression of Information: Curbs on the Press, Attacks on Journalists, Writers and Academics," *A Human Rights Watch Short Report*, vol. 2, issue 28, August 30, 1990, p. 2 and p. 18.

[14] Ibid., p. 18

[15] Committee to Protect Journalists, *Attacks on the Press 1991* (New York: Committee to Protect Journalists, March 1992), p. 31.

[16] Africa Watch, "Sudan, Suppression of Information;" "Political Detainees in Sudan: Journalists, Poets and Writers," *A Human Rights Watch Short Report*, vol. 2, issue 6, January 8, 1990; Human Rights Watch/Africa, "In the Name of God," pp. 33-35; See Committee to Protect Journalists, *Attacks on the Press 1990* (New York: Committee to Protect Journalists, March 1991), pp. 56-57, 117; Committee to Protect Journalists, *Attacks on the Press 1992* (New York: Committee to Protect Journalists, 1992), pp. 84, 118.

tabloids and cultural and business publications. Newspapers that had been affiliated with political parties have never been permitted to reopen.

The reopened publications remained at the mercy of the executive power, represented by a ministerial committee on the media. Several ministers, as well as the directors of security and military intelligence, were members of this committee, which was created in 1989 in order to "confront the internal [clandestine] and foreign media . . . to counter lies, deceptions and rumors."[17] Fifteen of the reopened sports newspapers had their licenses revoked in February 1990 and two social tabloids and two business papers were closed down in May 1990 with no reasons given.[18]

The 1993 Press and Printed Materials Law

On the first day of the 1989 coup those who took power imposed an outright ban on all nongovernmental publications in Constitutional Decree No. 2: "All licenses and permits issued to nongovernmental journalistic establishments and publications are canceled until a new license is issued by an authoritative organization."[19] This brought to an abrupt halt the forty daily newspapers and additional weekly "social" (gossip) magazines and sports publications of the popular tabloid genre that prospered during the multi-party government of 1985 to 1989. The only newspaper left open was the armed forces' paper. This ended free expression in Sudan.

President (Lt. Gen.) Omar Hassan al Bashir declared in July 1989 that the press soon would be allowed to reopen, in accordance with a new law that would weed out "mercenary journalism," but in February 1990 the government decreed that publication of newspapers would be the monopoly of two state-owned publishing and printing houses. The media, all under government control, henceforth concentrated on the task of creating an Islamic (and Arab) Sudan, in line with the vision of the ruling NIF. The Ministry of Information publicly stated that ideological commitment was a requirement for serving in the media.[20]

The Criminal Act of 1991 contained at least two articles affecting free expression: Article 66 made it a criminal offense to publish "any news item, rumor or report knowing that the same is incorrect, intending thereby to cause apprehension or panic to the public or threat to the public peace or diminution of the prestige of the State. . . ." While prohibitions on knowingly publishing false

---

[17]Committee for the Protection of Journalists, *Attacks on the Press 1990*, p. 13.
[18]Africa Watch, "Sudan, Suppression of Information," p. 13.
[19]Constitutional Decree No. 2, Article 4 (June 30, 1989).
[20]See Committee to Protect Journalists, *Attacks on the Press 1991*, p. 31.

information are not objectionable, making illegal a publication which intends to diminish "the prestige of the State" is susceptible of political misuse. The "prestige of the State" is too often confused with the prestige of the ruling party or elite.

A second article in the Criminal Act of 1991, Article 64, makes it a crime to provoke hatred "against any sect or between sects by reason of ethnic, color, or language differences."

In July 1993 a press law was enacted that the government said was meant to allow the publication of independent newspapers. The government, in its submission in November 1995 to the United Nations, stated that

> as of 28 January 1994, the government has relinquished all control of the papers and [their] publishing houses, allowing them to compete as private entities with other privately owned publications. Already three new newspapers have emerged to compete with the privatized companies.[21]

Contrary to what this suggests, however, the government maintains a high degree of control on the press owners, publishers, editors, journalists, and the content of publications.

The government's promise in July 1993 to privatize the government-owned newspapers[22] remains to be fulfilled. The government still owns three main Arabic-language dailies, *Al Inghaz al Watani* (National Salvation), *Al Sudan al Hadith* (Modern Sudan), and *Al Gwat al Mussalaha* (The Armed Forces). It also owns two English-language publications, the daily *New Horizon* and the monthly *Sudanow*, and the Sudan News Agency (SUNA), which publishes in Arabic and English daily news bulletins of national and international news as well as weekly and monthly news summaries, specialized news reports, and documents in both languages. The Ministry of Information owns all radio and television outlets.[23]

The Press and Printed Materials Law of 1993 provides in Article 20 for the establishment of a twenty-one-member National Press and Publication Council (*al Majlis al Aala li al Sahaafa wa al Matbuuaat*) to supervise newspapers and all printed materials; the council is not independent. It is "under the supervision of the head of state" (Article 20-A), who nominates both its members and its chairperson. (Articles 21-1 and 21-2). A general secretariat conducts the day-to-day

---

[21]"The Response of the Government of the Sudan," November 21, 1995, p. 24, para. 89.

[22]Committee to Protect Journalists, *Attacks on the Press 1993* (New York: Committee to Protect Journalists, 1994), p. 92.

[23]Human Rights Watch/Africa interview, New York, March 1996.

management of the administrative, financial and technical affairs of the council, and follows up the implementation of its decisions. The secretary general of this executive body is an appointee of the head of state and reports to the council. (Article 25-1).

The powers and mandate of the council under Article 24 (1) include

> a) drawing general policies in the field of press and publications, while seeing to it that social, family, party and sectarian entities do not control any press establishment. . . .
> c) granting of licenses for the publication of newspapers and printed matters and the establishment of press houses, news agencies, press services bureaus, and binderies, [which licenses must be renewed annually in accordance with Article 33] . . . .
> j) maintenance of a register of journalists, and establishment of a commission to register journalists and to provide them with the press card which is required for practicing journalism.

The 1993 Press and Printed Materials Law contains provisions formulated in broad terms that the council can invoke to censor journalism critical of human rights abuses. Chapter 6 of the Law, entitled "Cases of prohibition of publication and Observance of Professional Ethics," prohibits the publication of information critical of the armed forces that may demoralize those forces. (Article 29-1 (h)). It prohibits publication of information that can harm national security, as may be determined by the relevant security apparatus. (Article 29-1 (b)).[24] Failure to abide by these rules is punishable by a maximum of two years of imprisonment and/or a fine of Ls. 100,000 (U.S. $189.39). (Article 36-2).

Article 30-1 defines "Duties of the Journalist and Professional Ethics," requiring journalists to abide by the following provisions:

> a) seek to realize national goals and call for peace, brotherhood and national unity,
> b) not to insult heavenly religions and honorable beliefs;
> c) observance of truth and objectivity in dealing with public affairs, through the adoption an approach of honest criticism without personal interest;

---

[24]Article 29-1 (a) also prohibits publication of information pertinent to the training, movements or plans of the army and requires journalists to refer to official army spokespersons on this matter.

d) observance of objectivity in all written and published materials criticizing individuals and public figures;

e) observance of the traditions and ethics of the profession and repudiation of insults of individuals and establishments;

f) not to receive direct or indirect funding from any local or foreign quarters in accordance with guidelines set by the Council.

The lawmakers left to fiscal and corporate provisions the task of further shortening the rope with which the council reins in freedom of expression. Articles 4 and 5 of the 1993 Press and Printed Materials Law limit newspaper ownership and publication to companies or corporations that are not owned by nor own any other persons or entities (they must be stand-alone companies), imposing such restrictions for the first time in Sudan; during the 1986-89 period of multi-party government, any individual, political party or corporation could own a newspaper. Under the 1993 law, companies owning a newspaper or other media outlet must have at least ten individual shareholders and may not be owned by another corporation. No shareholder may own more than 10 percent. Under the 1993 law, each share in a newspaper or publication company should be initially offered for no more than Ls. 100 (U.S. $ 0.19) and the initial minimum capital is to be at least Ls. fifty million (U.S. $94,697), ruling out most small-scale private publications produced in Sudan during the 1986-89 period of free press. In order to be registered, newspapers must disclose sources of funding, the breakdown of ownership of shares, and the "specialization" of the paper.

Muhammad Sa'id Ma'ruf, chairman of the National Press and Publication Council, explained the advantages that the 1993 law introduced by limiting ownership of the press to institutions only:

This was deemed necessary because institutions are more capable of sustaining strong newspapers . . . that are well edited and printed. At the same time it was important to restrict the power of individuals over newspapers, and by extension the power of families, parties and sects. . . . Newspapers articulate and shape public opinion and therefore, if we want a newspaper

which is conscious of the country's aims, that newspaper has to
speak on behalf of the majority . . . .[25]

The notion that a newspaper has to speak on behalf of the majority is a clear
violation of freedom of expression, which was conceived to protect the expression
of minority and unpopular views.

Human Rights Watch discussed the restrictions in the 1993 press law with
the government. The intent of requiring not less than ten individual shareholders
in each corporation and a minimum capitalization of fifty million Sudanese pounds
was to combat sectarianism and tribalism, we were told.[26] There is, however, no
reasonable relationship between the minimum numbers of shareholders and
capitalization, and combating sectarianism and tribalism. Those who belong to the
larger families, sects, parties and tribes will find these numerical and financial
requirements no barrier to publishing highly sectarian and tribal newspapers and
articles. The requirements are prohibitive for smaller groups or individuals wishing
to publish a newspaper, however, no matter how nonsectarian or non-tribal the
newspaper.

The names and addresses of the editor in chief, reporters and printer must
be registered with the council, which may refuse without explanation to register
anyone. Registration requirements give wide discretion to the council to discipline
not only the individuals but also to quash publications whose politics do not
conform to the government's line, and its discretion has been exercised for just that
purpose.

In September 1995 the council suspended the privately-owned daily *Al
Rai al Akhar* (The Other Viewpoint) for two weeks, purportedly because it failed
to nominate an editor-in-chief after its prior editor left the country. Even the
government newspaper *Al Sudan al Hadith* (Modern Sudan) reported that *Al Rai*
was suspended because of its September 18 article urging a referendum on self-
determination for southern Sudan.

The private press is extremely vulnerable to official pressure because of
the requirement of an initial capitalization of fifty million Sudanese pounds. To
meet what would otherwise be impossibly high capital requirements, several
private newspapers have arranged with one of the two state-owned publishing
houses to appear under their name as holding companies. This arrangement, while

---

[25]"Sudan: Press Council Chairman Explains Reasons for Banning of Two Newspapers,"
Republic of Sudan Radio, Omdurman, in Arabic, 1335 gmt, June 1, 1995, excerpts from
report quoted by BBC Monitoring Service: Middle East, June 3, 1995.

[26]Human Rights Watch/Africa interview, Dr. Elmufti, New York, November 29, 1995.

tolerated, is insecure. Should the paper cross the invisible "red line," the government may invoke the letter of the law and close down the offending newspaper, as was done with the weekly *Zilal* following its third suspension in 1995, apparently because of politically sensitive stories. (See below.)

Another move to control the press through financial requirements was the decision in mid-1995 to require all tabloid papers to publish at least twelve pages instead of four, and to employ a minimum of four reporters full time. The Press and Publication Council justified this by the need to guarantee a minimum of quality reporting in the newspapers. However, the required increase of pages and journalists on the payroll could put several smaller tabloids out of business.

Government-owned newspapers enjoy the regular flow of income from the government and the public sector's large advertising budgets. Private newspapers complain that they do not receive an equitable share of government advertising revenue. With limited possibilities of becoming self-supporting through circulation and private advertising, the private press is at a competitive disadvantage to the government-owned newspapers.

Suspension and Closure of Newspapers and Detention of Their Owners and Journalists

Under the 1993 press law, an independent press was not tolerated, although there was slightly more space to open a private newspaper. The main proponent of press reform within the NIF was Mahjoub Erwa, a journalist since 1974 and a member of the Transitional National Assembly appointed in 1992.[27] He believes that the essence of Islam is freedom, justice, equality, and tolerance, and his campaign for press reform has been consistent with this philosophy. He lobbied hard within the ruling circles to draft bills and push the reform press legislation through the TNA. The government came forward with its own less liberal draft and a compromise was reached permitting privately-owned newspapers to operate under certain limitations.

Majoub Erwa was the first to apply for permission under the 1993 press law to print his newspaper, *Al Soudani al Doulia* (Sudan International), in Sudan. Before the January 1994 date on which the press law became effective, he had printed it in Beirut.

---

[27]He had experienced problems operating as a journalist under the Nimeiri dictatorship. He was arrested, fired from his job, and went into exile, returning to work in another field. He published a magazine in Beirut but the disruption of the war there forced him to close it in 1980. He returned to Sudan and established *Al Soudani* after the overthrow of Nimeiri in 1985. Human Rights Watch/Africa interview, Khartoum, May 24, 1995.

As described in a prior Human Rights Watch report,[28] Erwa published his newspaper only a few months before it was closed down permanently by the authorities, after a warning raid and temporary closure. Following critical articles on the government policy on the war in the south, the council found in March 1994 that *Al Soudani* had violated its charter by "criticizing or undermining the moral strength of government forces."[29] Mohamed Said Ma'ruf, chairman of the council, repeatedly reminded journalists of the restrictions in the 1993 law on the discussion of matters related to security, military policy, reputations, ethnic disputes and unity of the country. Other issues covered in *Al Soudani* often cited as catalysts for its closure included strong criticism of the governor of Kordofan state for alleged corruption, the privatization of Sudatel (the telephone company) at an inexplicably low price, police brutality and cases of torture of political detainees brought to court.

In April 1994, the government permanently closed down *Al Soudani al Doulia* under the provisions of the state of emergency law — not utilizing the 1993 press law. The newspaper was accused of attempting to destroy the symbols for which the Revolution of National Salvation stands and of seeking "to raise doubts about the purpose and struggle of the armed forces and People's Defense Forces."[30]

Immediately preceding the shutdown, the newspaper published an article on April 3, 1994, about corruption in government, not naming any names. A man who concluded that the article referred to him shot at the journalist who wrote the article, Mohamed Taha Mohamed Ahmed, a regular columnist in the newspaper. The journalist complained to the police and demanded that they arrest the man, the son of a powerful political and religious leader close to the government. Instead, Taha was arrested. According to Erwa, Attorney General Shiddu arrived at the scene and tried to work out a compromise whereby Taha would not be arrested if he agreed not to press charges against the gunman. Taha refused. Three other journalists from *Al Soudani* were arrested; the four journalists were released after two weeks.[31]

---

[28]Human Rights Watch/Africa, "In the Name of God," pp. 33-35.

[29]Ibid.

[30]Amnesty International, "Urgent Action," UA 141/94, AI Index: AFR 54/12/94 (London; April 8, 1994); "Urgent Action," further information on UA 141/94, AI Index: AFR 54/14/94 (London: April 19, 1994) and AI Index: AFR 54/16/94 (London: April 26, 1994).

[31]Human Rights Watch/Africa interview, Khartoum, May 24, 1995.

Majoub Erwa, who said he was unaware of these events, was returning from a business trip to Saudi Arabia at 1:00 a.m. on April 4, 1994. He was intercepted by the authorities at the airport, presented with an order of confiscation of his newspaper pursuant to the state of emergency law, and with the permission of the speaker of the TNA to waive the immunity from arrest that Mr. Erwa enjoyed as a member of the TNA. He was arrested at the airport and spent three months in the Citibank ghost house, where he was not tortured but saw others who were. He was dismissed from the Assembly but he contends the dismissal was illegal because it was not by the required two-thirds vote.[32]

In kind of "trial by television," violating fundamental fairness and due process, the government showed Majoub Erwa on television answering questions of interrogators who contrived to convince viewers that hostile foreign powers funded *El Soudani*, and accused him publicly of a variety of crimes. Erwa later said that the session, which largely went in his favor, was filmed without his knowledge and consent.

No charges were ever brought and he was released from the ghost house without having to sign any document. Protests against his arrest within and outside of Sudan were instrumental in his release. The president issued decree 287 on August 9, 1994, authorizing his release and cessation of any criminal proceedings against him, restoring his rights and ordering the return of his personal belongings as well as compensation for the business property that was confiscated. Although Erwa was to receive financial compensation for the premises, printing press, bank accounts, all computers and other business equipment seized, as of May 1995 he had only received part payment, in land and in money. He disagreed with the government's valuation of the property, which he said was much less than the cost to him. The confiscated property, he was told, was being used by the Student Support Fund, a NIF-controlled agency that regulates the flow of public funds to student associations and activities. It also took over the printing press of *Al Soudani* as a government donation for its own printing company, run on a commercial basis.[33]

Other newspapers suspended and/or closed include:

•   In February 1995, the council temporarily closed down the two weekly magazines *Darfur al Jadidah* (New Darfur) and *Zilal* (Shadows). The

---

[32]At the airport, his luggage was searched and correspondence with the Saudi government was found. He had gone to Saudi Arabia to seek permission to distribute his newspaper there. These letters formed the basis for the unproven allegation that he was a "spy." Ibid.
    [33]Ibid.

owners of *Darfur al Jadidah* are believed to be closely associated with the ruling NIF, but published an article by a retired army officer criticizing the government. *Zilal*, which existed prior to the 1989 coup, has a sophisticated cultural and artistic content and contradicts the official line in the arts and culture. *Zilal* published an interview with Brig. Faisal Medani Mukhtar, a former member of the Revolutionary Command Council who resigned his post before the RCC was dissolved in 1993. In the interview this former health minister criticized the lack of hospital supplies, government policies and the influence of the NIF.[34]

•   The official Press and Publication Council jealously guards Sudan against press comments viewed as harmful to its foreign relations. *Darfur al Jadidah* was closed for two weeks in April 1994 for allegedly criticizing a foreign head of state, King Hassan II of Morocco. The progovernment youth publication *Al Massira* (The Procession) was permanently shut down by the council in 1994 for alleging that international terrorist Carlos the Jackal was originally sent to Sudan by Jordanian secret services to embarrass Sudan. It also reported on the arrest of Mahjoub Erwa, publisher of *Al Soudani al Doulia*.[35]

•   In June 1994, security forces raided and closed down the Khartoum offices of the independent daily *Al Khartoum*, published in Cairo.[36] Mohamed Abdel Seed, the local correspondent of *Al Khartoum*, was severely beaten and held by security for more than four months. He had been detained in 1993 when he was the local correspondent of the Saudi international daily *Al Sharq al Awsat*. Authorities took various legal and administrative measures against six other journalists who worked for *Al Khartoum*, including the confiscation of their press cards, thus barring them from practicing journalism.[37]

---

[34]See *Sudan News and Views* (London), issue no. 6, March 16, 1995.

[35]"Sudan: Two Newspapers Banned," *Africa Economic Digest,* June 5, 1995.

[36]The owner of the paper is Mohamed Abdulla, a Democratic Unionist Party supporter. This paper is distributed in the Gulf to Sudanese working there. Twenty-six of thirty issues were confiscated during this raid, but the owner did not close the Khartoum office. Human Rights Watch/Africa interview, Khartoum, May 24, 1995.

[37]Committee to Protect Journalists, *Attacks on the Press in 1994*, p. 48.

•   The aspiration of some social and sports tabloids to report and comment on "serious" political and economic events, and even to participate in an ongoing doctrinal discussion on what constitutes "true Islam," has invited the wrath of the Press and Publication Council. The council has a record of citing "ethical" arguments (the protection of public morality), however, in its public statements about suspensions and closures, as the troubles of the ill-fated *Akhir Khabar* (Latest News) demonstrate. In June 1995, the independent *Akhir Khabar* published an editorial highly critical of the 1993 press law which, publisher and editor-in-chief Nazar Awad Abdul Magid said, threatened small independent papers like his with extinction. This editorial followed the publication, in May 1995, of an interview with Mahjoub Erwa about his arrest and the confiscation of his newspaper *Al Soudani*. However, when the Press and Publications Council ordered *Akhir Khabar* off the streets for two weeks in July 1995, it publicly warned the tabloid that its coverage of the story of a woman baring herself in Khartoum street corners was too sensational and violated Sudan's Islamic morals. The council stated, "Such news is read by decent Sudanese families who would consider publication of such a story an indication of decline of the Sudanese press."[38] On January 18, 1996, the council ordered its permanent closure, accusing it of publishing articles it said "incited animosity, social disintegration and a spirit of intolerance."[39] The council also had warned the newspaper about two statements containing crude sexual puns. Its publisher Nazar Awad Abdul Magid said the real reason the paper was closed was because it had announced that it intended to publish a serialized interview with former Prime Minister Sadiq al Mahdi.[40] The council at the same time decided to bar *Sabah Al Kheir* (Good Morning), a tabloid that Abdul Magid's publishing house announced it intended to publish — but had not yet seen the light of day. This was an unprecedented step.

•   Even when tabloids stick to trivia and sensational stories, the Press and Publication Council can still step in. In June 1995, the council withdrew the licenses of *Al Kura* (Football) and *Zilal*, saying that it had given them an adequate time, two months, to defend themselves against charges that

---

[38]"Sudan: Sudanese Paper Warned for Sensationalism," Reuter, Khartoum, June 28, 1995.

[39]Nhial Bol, "Sudan-Media: No News Is Good News For Regime," January 22, 1996.

[40]Ibid.

they did not meet the ownership requirements. *Zilal* had been closed a number of times, the last in April 1995 when it and *Al Kura* were temporarily closed for carrying the story of a faith healer who was subsequently imprisoned and publicly flogged for deception and causing public disorder.[41]

Both journals had been publishing with the government's permission before the enactment of the 1993 law; after it came into effect, the council agreed to a request by Sudan House for Printing and Publishing, one of two state-owned presses, to publish both journals in its own name. The council then reversed its decision on the grounds that " it was discovered that the relationship between the publishing house and the newspapers was not one of ownership — namely, that the two newspapers had now become the property of the publishing house — but rather one of production. In other words, the two newspapers were being published in the name of the same licensed owners as before, that is before the law came into force. . . . This is a dangerous violation of the law and a punishable offence."[42]

The government-owned publishing house stopped publishing the newspapers when it learned that their licenses were withdrawn. *Zilal* and *Al Kura* finally were allowed to reopen in September 1995 under new arrangements.

Other closures for reasons that the statements of the council define only in broad moral and "national interest" terms include banning the social tabloid *Azizati* (My Dear) in June 1995, alleging infringement of unspecified regulations, and temporarily suspending three other tabloids, *Akhbar al Mujtama* (Society News), *Al Nujum* (The Stars), and *Al Kawakib* (Constellations).[43]

The progovernment Khartoum University Student Union (KUSU) publicly threatened the newspaper *Al Rai al Ahar* (The Other Viewpoint) in July 1995 for publishing a story on a demonstration by some 4,000 university students against the government, according to that newspaper, which published in full the written warning. KUSU warned the news department and the news editor "of the consequences of this," and accused the paper of working against the political stability of Sudan. This was the first such threat against a newspaper since the

---

[41]Committee to Protect Journalists, *Attacks on the Press in 1995* (New York: Committee to Protect Journalists, 1996) p. 56.

[42]"Press Council Chairman Explains Banning of Two Newspapers."

[43]"Sudan: Sudan Bans One Newspaper, Suspends Three," Reuter, Khartoum, June 29, 1995.

current government came to power in 1989, according to the paper, which said it was taking the threat seriously.[44]

Notwithstanding the above, during the March 1996 elections these limits appeared to be slightly relaxed, and the Sudanese press — with the exception of those newspapers already suspended or permanently closed — jumped into the electoral fray with articles harshly criticizing the ruling party. A nominally pro-government paper, *Al Sudan al Hadith*, even reported the opinions of some who thought the electoral exercise was a waste of time and all candidates were unfit for office.[45] This freedom is not considered a right, however, and it remains to be seen if the banned newspapers will be reopened and if this latitude continues after the elections.

Restrictions on Journalists and Writers

Starting in 1995, the Press and Publications Council decreed that all journalists operating in Sudan must be registered with the council and obtain permission to work. Sudanese nationals working as local correspondents of foreign news outlets and foreign journalists on assignment in Sudan are required to register with the council before beginning their coverage and often were denied accreditation and entry to Sudan, or suffered detention, and sometimes beatings, when the government deemed their coverage critical. Those working without registration face imprisonment for up to a month, and a fine of Ls. 500,000 (U.S. $ 947) — in a country where the average salary of a journalist is about Ls. 15,000 (U.S. $28.41) a month. In August 1995, a spokesman for the Journalists Committee, which is linked to the council, said that members of his committee plan to make unannounced visits to newspaper offices to identify journalists working without certification from the council.[46]

Up to that date the council had accredited 596 journalists, some of whom had to sit for an exam in basic linguistic and reporting skills. The licensing applications of thirty-seven journalists were rejected on the grounds that they were

---

[44]Nhial Bol, "Sudan-Media: Weeding out the Undesirables," InterPress Service, Khartoum, August 3, 1995. The demonstration occurred when President al Bashir addressed the University of Khartoum students in July 1995. "Sudan: Egyptian Radio Reports Anti-government Demonstration, Arrests in Khartoum,"Arab Republic of Egypt Radio, Cairo, in Arabic, 1400 gmt, July 29, 1995, text in BBC Monitoring Service: Middle East, July 31, 1995.

[45]Jonathan Wright, "Sudan: Sudanese Press Belies Totalitarian Image," Reuter, Khartoum, March 17, 1996.

[46]"Sudan: Unlicensed Journalists in Sudan Risk Jail," Reuter, Khartoum, August 2, 1995.

inexperienced; some of them alleged the rejection was politically motivated since they had worked as journalists for more than a decade and used to report for newspapers linked to political parties, all of which were banned in 1989. Some of the rejects said they were graduates of journalism schools or had other advanced degrees. They were given a second chance in an examination in mid-July 1995, but only nineteen of the thirty-seven passed the exam, which they said tested their knowledge of the achievements of the al Bashir government.[47]

The highly publicized detention and ill-treatment, in December 1994, of lawyer Mustafa Abdel Gadir was thought to be related to a series of historical articles he had published since October 1994 in the independent daily *Akhbar al Youm* (Today's News). The articles explained the dynamics that led to the 1985 popular uprising that toppled a military government, which, like the junta that seized power in 1989, was a close ally of the NIF.

Ali Mahmoud Hassanien, another advocate arrested at the same time as Abdel Gadir, expressed pro-democracy views in an interview in *Zilal* a few weeks prior to his December 1994 arrest. Both lawyers had infuriated the authorities in 1994 by the role they took in leading a twenty-five-strong team of advocates who defended the accused in the 1994 Explosives Trial. (See Chapter V).

The Arrest of Sadiq al Mahdi and Free Speech in Mosques

Although the government has denied it, it appears that the arrest of Sadiq al Mahdi was the result of a homily he gave on the Al Eid religious holiday (Bayram) on May 10, 1995, in his mosque in Omdurman. His arrest was an illustration of the limits on freedom of speech in Sudan in 1995, even if delivered from the pulpit.

The homily was quite critical of the government and particularly the recently-held third conference of the Popular Arab and Islamic Congress, a forum sponsored and paid for by the government. He concluded that this conference did not serve the Islamic cause in the Sudan or in the world, but was a mere waste of public funds, although some leading figures in the Sudanese regime might consider it an effective public relations platform.

Sadiq al Mahdi said it was meaningless to speak of "elections" in the context of the state of emergency, "a sword about the heads of the people of Sudan," and in the absence of basic human rights and an impartial election committee. He then lambasted the National Islamic Front as "a total failure" that

---

[47]Nhial Bol, "Sudan-Media: Weeding Out the Undesirables."

had brought economic development to a halt, was responsible for "unparalleled corruption," and had failed utterly in achieving peace in the country.[48]

Other criticisms of the government included "misquoting the Qur'an in an apparent disrespect of the Holy Text and interpreting it to serve their earthly political agenda." He concluded, "Transition to democracy in the Sudan is inevitable, all the grounds are already paved for such transition, the only argument amongst national observers is How and When?"[49]

He was detained by security a week later, on May 16, 1995, and was held in incommunicado detention without charges until his release in late August 1995. He had definitely crossed the "red line."

Attacks on Clandestine Presses, Universities and Other Unauthorized Fora

In addition to the mosque, two other limited venues for the expression of opinion opposed to the government were left after the coup: underground newspapers and university campuses. Some banned political parties continued the clandestine publication of their newspapers on a more or less regular basis. The clandestine opposition press has included *Al Maidan* (The Field, published by the SCP), *Al Shabiba* (Youth, by the banned Sudan Youth Union, an affiliate of the SCP), *Al Hadaf* (The Goal, by the Arab Ba'athist Party), *Sawt al Umma* (Voice of the Nation, by the Umma Party), and *Al Tajam'u* (The Alliance), irregularly published by the clandestine National Democratic Alliance.

In November 1994 four Umma Party leaders were arrested and questioned about the editing and location of the party's *Sawt al Umma*.[50] In April 1995 security agents raided the Khartoum home of Abdula Rahim Min Allah, believing he was in charge of typing and coordinating the distribution of *Al Maidan,* but failed to link him to it. Min Allah was only released during the general releases of August 1995. Authorities confiscated two personal computers during the house raid and tried to read the contents on the hard drive. They did not return the equipment to him at his release, in yet another glaring example of unauthorized confiscation of valuables belonging to security detainees.[51]

In parallel with their clamp-down on the underground opposition papers and leaflets, security agencies persistently attempt to silence the independent fora where free speech is still practiced, namely in some university campuses. The

---

[48]Excerpts from the speech delivered by Sadiq al Mahdi on the Eid Occasion (Bayram), May 10, 1995, Omdurman, Sudan (English translation provided by the Umma Party).

[49]Ibid.

[50]Committee to Protect Journalists, *Attacks on the Press in 1994*, p. 48.

[51]Human Rights Watch/Africa interview, New York, October 1995.

student movement jealously guards its tradition of free expression of a wide range of opinions within the imperfect sanctuary of university campuses. Student "weeks of cultural activities," posters, "discussion corners," public rallies and mural newspapers offer free outlets to a variety of student political groups. The polarization of student politics continued between the NIF supporters within the student movement and other student groups opposed to the NIF-controlled government.

The violent student clashes that occurred in Ahliya University of Omdurman in November 1995 followed a public rally organized by anti-government students on Saturday, November 25.[52] Abel Alier, a former judge and prominent southern politician, and Osman Omar Al Sharif, an attorney general during the period of multiparty government (1986-89) spoke about the war problem in southern Sudan, with the former advocating self-determination for southerners. Progovernment students did not approve of this approach to the southern problem, because in their view and that of the government the southern conflict is a true jihad, a holy war. Their displeasure irrupted on the morning of the next day and by November 28 many anti-government students were injured, and at least one hundred were arrested.[53]

Gezeira University was a fortress of free expression, militant student associations and a faculty jealous of its academic and political freedoms in the late 1980s. Authorities systematically cracked down on both faculty and students there to break these traditions and bring this institution in line after the coup, as they did at many universities. During the tenure of Professor Tigani Hassan as vice chancellor of Gezira University, particularly during 1991, the university undertook a campaign of politically-motivated dismissals of faculty members.   In 1995, Professor Tigani explained the philosophy that guided his actions at the time. He admitted that he had conducted staff purges and said that he "cleansed the Gezira University . . . because in the political context of the time, the political framework and general climate required surgical operations to eliminate corruption and opposition. I was faced as new vice chancellor with clear opposition to me and the current political order. It was an ugly and open opposition, and I represented a new order that aims to achieve change and stability. In a 'tit for tat,' it was necessary to apply the law of the jungle that the communists use in dealing with the new regime so it was necessary to uproot them."[54]

---

[52]See below, Chapter VII, Students.
[53]Ibid.
[54]*Akhbar al Youm*, October 18, 1995, p. 5 (in Arabic).

He also admitted that he applied "many steps" to eliminate those who "oppose the revolution." Sixteen staff members were dismissed from Gezeira University by the last quarter of 1992.[55]

Others, not associated with underground publications and universities, have tried to express their opinions in leaflets, with little luck. One group of thirty-seven people was arrested in Damazien in December 1994 and held for one month apparently for giving out leaflets (*munshur*, without their names on them) urging voters to boycott the 1995 elections. None was charged with a crime. This group was openly questioning the legitimacy of the elections to municipal council, the economic policies of the government, and official corruption. They spent one month in an unofficial house of detention where some were tortured.[56]

Access to Foreign News and Fax Machines

The right to receive information and ideas is an important aspect of freedom of expression under Article 19 (2). That right is stymied by security's censorship office with the innocuous name of the Import and Export Bureau, which is in charge of inspecting incoming regional and international newspapers, magazines, and books. Reporting deemed critical of the government may lead to excision of an article from a magazine before it is authorized for distribution, but in many cases, publications and books have been banned from distribution altogether. The same censorship office is in charge of inspecting incoming and outgoing mail. Customs department officials at airports and entry points to the country also are instructed to inspect all printed materials and video and audio cassettes for subversive content, political or moral.

To catch those publications that may have eluded the censor's grasp, security agents raided many private homes and offices in the capital in July 1995 in search of press clippings and opposition literature believed to be sent from abroad to activists who would then disseminate the information. Authorities were highly suspicious of fax machines. They confiscated several fax machines, and at least one person, Sid Ahmad Abdalla Akode, was detained for the ownership of a fax machine.[57]

The government has said, "As for the Licensing of fax machines . . . using a fax machine would need the availability of a telephone line and to get such

---

[55]See also Africa Watch, *Sudan, Violations of Academic Freedoms*, vol. IV, issue no. 12, November 7, 1992.

[56]Human Rights Watch/Africa interview, Khartoum, May 27, 1995.

[57]See Amnesty International, "Sudan: Crackdown on Basic Freedoms," UA 184/95, AI Index: AFR 54/27/95 (London: July 28, 1995).

service, one would need to consult the Government agency concerned which is the Ministry of Telecommunications."[58] This statement, however, creates the misleading impression that the government's role is a passive one, of "consultation" only over available phone lines. It omits to disclose that the government must consent to the licensing of a fax; the owner of a fax does not have a right to use it without government approval.

Ownership of faxes requires approval from the ministry of commerce, a license from the department of telecommunications and clearance from the security forces. This goes far beyond mere "consultation" and is a sharp limitation on the "freedom to seek, receive and impart information and ideas of all kinds, regardless of frontiers" set forth in Article 19 (2).

Lack of Remedy for Unauthorized Confiscation of Printed Materials

Even when the government admits a wrongful confiscation of books, no remedy is available. Osman Iddris Fadul Allah, owner of the now-closed publishing and book distribution house *Dar El Wae'i* (Home of Enlightenment), complained on July 10, 1994, to the Complaints Chamber that security agents confiscated imported books valued at $128,000 in a 1989 raid.[59] He complained in a letter to security that agents repeatedly beat him and threatened him with "disappearance" whenever he attempted to retrieve his books.[60]

He said he suffered serious injuries and disabilities due to these beatings. The books were confiscated, he was told, because they were considered unsuitable for distribution to the public after the advent of the national salvation government because of alleged communist content. Following this July 1994 complaint, the internal security division of the security apparatus formed an investigation committee which met with Osman Iddris Fadul Allah several times. He was informed verbally of the findings of the commission: no official authority had decided to confiscate the property of his publishing house, and what occurred was unlawful, excessive and offensive behavior. He was also verbally informed that the state was responsible for any damages resulting from the loss of the property. As

---

[58]"The Response of the Government of the Sudan," November 21, 1995, p. 25, para. 91.

[59]The Complaints Chamber is the special appeals chamber set up by the presidency to receive and review cases submitted to the head of state for special review.

[60]Letter, Osman Iddris Fadul Allah to the Internal Security Division, Khartoum, June 8, 1995.

of June 1995, however, Osman Iddris Fadul Allah had received no compensation of any kind.[61]

FREEDOM OF ASSOCIATION

Immediately after the June 1989 coup, the junta issued Constitutional Decree No. 2 banning free association. This decree stated that "all political parties and groups are to be disbanded, and it is illegal for them to be established or to remain active." Seven years later, the ban on political parties remains intact.

The 1989 decree also banned all trade unions and federations and confiscated their funds and properties, and canceled all licenses issued to non-religious institutions and societies.

Some associations have been permitted to reconstitute themselves under post-1989 laws, but their independence is severely limited and their freedom restricted by the "red line."

The Applicable Law

Article 22 (1) of the ICCPR states:

Everyone shall have the right to freedom of association with others, including the right to form and join trade unions for the protection of his interests.[62]

This right includes the right to join together with others for social, cultural, economic or political purposes. It includes association with only one other person as well as with groups, permanent and temporary associations, and organized or casual associations.[63]

The limits on the right to association appear in Article 22 (2): restrictions must be prescribed by law and "necessary in a democratic society," and "in the interests of national security or public safety, public order (*ordre public*), the protection of the public health or morals or the protection of the rights and freedoms of others."

---

[61]Ibid.

[62]This right to free association also appears in the African Charter on Human and People's Rights, Article 10 (1): "Every individual shall have the right to free association provided that he abides by the law."

[63]Partsch, "Freedom of Conscience and Expression," p. 235.

The right to freedom of association protects the right to associate in political parties. A ban on political parties is scarcely "necessary in a democratic society" since historically the development of democracy has been inextricably linked to political parties contesting power through free and fair elections in an atmosphere of free speech and assembly. This is true in Sudan as well as in other countries. Historians have noted that

> in terms of political culture, the Sudanese have ranked among the most democratic in the Arab world and Africa. . . . Multiparty elections in the Sudan have always been open and fair in comparison with other Arab or Africa states. Such is the belief in free association that elections in 1986 were contested by an astonishing 42 parties and groupings, and there were at least as many nongovernment newspapers and journals.[64]

The right to free association imposes on governments the obligation to permit and guarantee organization of all political parties, according to the Inter-American Commission on Human Rights, interpreting the free association provision in the American Convention on Human Rights.[65] The commission stated that governments have

> the obligation to permit and guarantee: the organization of all political parties and other associations, unless they are constituted to violate human rights; open debate of the principal theses of socioeconomic development; the celebration of general and free elections with all the necessary guarantees so that the results represent the popular will.[66]

---

[64]Peter K. Bechtold, "More Turbulence in Sudan: A New Politics This Time?" in John O. Voll, ed., *Sudan: State and Society in Crisis* (Bloomington: Indiana University Press, 1991), pp. 6-7 (footnotes omitted) .

[65]American Convention on Human Rights, Article 16: "1. Everyone has the right to associate freely for ideological, religious, political, economic, labor, social, cultural, sports, or other purposes. 2. The exercise of this right shall be subject only to such restrictions established by law as may be necessary in a democratic society, in the interest of national security, public safety or public order, or to protect public health or morals or the rights and freedoms of others."

[66]"Doctrine of the Inter-American Commission on Human Rights," *American University Journal of International Law and Policy*, vol. 10, no. 1 (Fall 1994), p. 335.

The right to organize political parties is also derived from the right to participate in government and to free elections, recognized in Article 25 of the ICCPR.[67]

The right to form and join trade unions is specifically protected in Article 22 (1). The U.N. Human Rights Committee noted specifically that the fact that a trade union did not share the political views of the government was not a legitimate ground for its dissolution.[68] The right to form trade unions is also protected in Article 8 of the Covenant on Economic, Social, and Cultural Rights[69] and several conventions of the International Labor Organization to which Sudan is a party.

Derogation from (or suspension of) the right to freedom of association and some other rights is permissible under circumstances set forth in Article 4 of the ICCPR:

> 1. In time of public emergency which threatens the life of the nation and the existence of which is officially proclaimed, the States Parties to the present Covenant may take measures derogating from their obligations under the present Covenant to the extent strictly required by the exigencies of the situation, provided that such measures are not inconsistent with their other obligations under international law and do not involve discrimination solely on the ground of race, color, sex, language, religion or social origin. . . .
>
> 3. Any State Party to the present Covenant availing itself of the right of derogation shall immediately inform the other States Parties to the present Covenant, through the intermediary of the Secretary-General of the United Nations, of the provisions from

---

[67]Article 25 of the ICCPR provides in part that everyone shall have the right: "(a) To take part in the conduct of public affairs, directly or through freely chosen representatives; (b) To vote and to be elected at genuine periodic elections which shall be by universal and equal suffrage and shall be held by secret ballot, guaranteeing the free expression of the will of the electors . . . ."

[68]See reports of the U.N. Human Rights Committee, 34 GAOR Supp. 40, UN Doc. A/34/40 (1979), para. 88 (strong criticism of the compulsory loyalty oath required of elected union officials), cited in Partsch, "Freedom of Conscience and Political Freedoms," p. 237, n. 131.

[69]In Article 8, the states parties to the covenant undertake to ensure the right of everyone to form and join trade unions, the right of trade unions to establish national federations and join international trade union organizations, the right of trade unions to function freely, and the right to strike, when exercised in conformity with the law.

which it has derogated and of the reasons by which it was actuated. A further communication shall be made, through the same intermediary, on the date on which it terminates such derogation.

War is not the only public emergency contemplated by Article 4 (1) of the ICCPR. But the view is that the public emergency should be of such a magnitude as to threaten the life of the nation as a whole, whose seriousness is beyond doubt and which constitutes a major threat to the nation.[70] The measures which are adopted derogating from obligations under the ICCPR are permissible only to the extent that they are strictly required by the emergency.[71]

The state party exercising its right of derogation must "immediately inform" the other state parties of the provisions of the ICCPR from which it has derogated, and of the reasons by which it was actuated. This provision "plainly calls for notice to be dispatched almost simultaneously with the proclamation of the emergency or the taking of derogating measures."[72]

The Government's Derogation from the Right to Freedom of Association

The government has not observed the required procedures for derogation from the Article 22 right to freedom of association. It notified the United Nations Treaty Office on February 14, 1992, pursuant to Article 4 of the ICCPR, that it was derogating from Article 22 (1).[73] An initial filing made on December 1991, dated August 21, 1991, failed to specify from which articles the government was derogating.[74] The government of Sudan failed to meet the requirement that the notice of derogation be timely given; its declaration of a state of emergency was June 30, 1989, almost eighteen months before the notice of derogation reached the proper authority.

The government's derogation statement does not disclose what, if any, relation political parties, trade unions, professional and other associations have to

---

[70]Thomas Buergenthal, "State Obligations and Permissible Derogations," *The International Bill of Rights*, p. 79.

[71]See A.H. Robertson and J.G. Merrills, *Human Rights in Europe* (New York: Manchester University Press, 1993), 3d ed., p. 187, citing Denmark, Norway, Sweden and Netherlands v. Greece, *Yearbook* XII, 1969, Part II, pp. 71-76.

[72]Buergenthal, "State Obligations and Permissible Derogations," p. 84.

[73]Fax from U.N. Treaty Section, Sylvie Jacque, Deputy Chief, to Human Rights Watch, August 4, 1995.

[74]Ibid.

do with the declared emergency. In its original August 21, 1991 filing of notice of derogation with the U.N. Treaty Office, the government stated in part:

> The reasons for declaring the State of Emergency were very obvious, the [National Salvation] Revolution has in June 1989, inherited a very chaotic Socio-economic and political situation with a civil war raging in the South (the Civil War started in 1983 and since then the State of Emergency was declared), and Lawlessness engulfing the North, and armed-robbery being practiced, in a serious manner, in the west (as a result of the present crisis in Tchad), and also in the east, in addition to possible threats of foreign interventions.[75]

This does not explain the necessity for the sweeping prohibition on all forms of political parties and the pervasive control of other associations later permitted to open in subsequent years. Nothing in any of the government's filings with the U.N. Treaty Office sheds any light whatsoever on the nexus between the emergency and freedom of association.

Although noting that the prior (elected) government had declared a state of emergency due to civil war, the military junta failed to disclose that under that prior state of emergency, freedom of association was not derogated from in most of the country, and political parties, trade unions, and other associations proliferated. The 1989 state of emergency declared by the junta was aimed at suppressing institutions of civil society that functioned quite apart from the war. The immediate effect and the apparent intention of suspending free association was to freeze all political opposition to the coup d'etat. The June 30, 1989, Constitutional Decree Number 2 declared:

> (1) All political parties and groups are to be disbanded, and it is illegal for them to be established or to remain active. . . .
> (3) (a) All unions and federations which have been legislated by any law are discontinued until a directive is issued for their reconstitution. . . .

---

[75]Notification in Accordance with Article (4) of International Covenant on Civil and Political Rights to U.N. Secretary General, from Ministry of Foreign Affairs, Khartoum, August 21, 1991.

(5) All licenses to non-religious institutions and societies issued by any law are canceled after one month of the date of enactment of this law, unless their license is renewed . . . .

Political Parties
Immediately after the coup of 1989, those who took power not only banned all political parties; they also detained all political party leaders. As the military leader of the coup and later President (Lt. Gen.) Omar al Bashir candidly said in 1995, those in control tried to get the approval of the detained leaders for a ban on political parties:

> We initiated the dialogue with the parties' leaderships in the first days when they were detained and told them all: Come, let us agree on how to fulfil the Sudanese people's aspirations for Islamic justice and liberate their land from the squalor of rebellion . . . . Our country has had enough division and infighting, sown by parties and factions which cannot see eye to eye and which have no time for each other. But they refused . . . .[76]

In a November 1995 human rights statement to the United Nations, the government gave its rationale for the continued ban on political associations, claiming that the continued ban on political parties had unanimous consent:

> As for the political parties . . . we once again explain that the political associations [are] regulated by law and that we believe that as long as the regulations allow free expression and full participation of all citizens without discrimination, certain types of associations and organizations, like political parties in the Sudan which are based on religious and family affiliations and which have caused universally acknowledged harm could be prohibited. It is only common sense to try to progress beyond situations that have led to repeated stalemates in the political life and harmed the progress of the country, as well as feeding strife and disharmony. For the same reason not even the opposition is

[76]"Uganda: President Bashir Accuses Uganda of Interference in Sudan," *Al Hayat* (London), in Arabic, December 4, 1995, quoted in BBC Monitoring Service: Africa, December 6, 1995.

calling for a return to the discredited party system.The opposition's programme calls for a five-year interim period in which no parties would be allowed to take part in the political life. The present government is only implementing policies which have unanimous backing in principle, and its programme differs from that espoused by the opposition in that it has more popular support. . . . In the end, the people will decide on how they want to run their country by electing the representatives they trust, and such elections have been scheduled for 1996 as we have already explained. . . . [77]

The government offered no support for the proposition that its ban on political parties has "unanimous backing in principle." Certainly the two largest parties and vote-getters in Sudan — the Umma Party and the Democratic Unionist Party — are not in agreement in principle or otherwise that they should remain banned. Nor does an opposition — referring to the National Democratic Alliance (NDA)[78] — demand for reestablishment of political parties after a five-year transition period qualify as support for the unlimited ban on political parties now imposed by the government, with no end date in sight. In fact, the government has misrepresented the opposition demand. The NDA Charter encourages political parties to be active in political life: it stipulates that during the interim period before elections the parties should deepen their commitment to democracy by reorganizing and restructuring their institutions, hold party conventions (most parties never did this in the 1986-89 period) and conduct elections for local and national party officials.[79] The opposition demand therefore does not support the government's rationale for banning political parties.

The government's statement refers to elections in 1996. But for elections to be meaningful, the full range of political and civil rights must be respected and protected by the government. Elections conducted with a blanket ban on political

---

[77]"Response of the Government of the Sudan," November 21, 1995, p. 25, para. 90.

[78]The National Democratic Alliance, based in Asmara, Eritrea, includes many banned political parties: Democratic Unionist Party (DUP), the Umma Party, the Sudan Communist Party (SCP), and the Union of Sudan African Parties. It also includes the Sudan Alliance Forces, the Beja Congress, the Legitimate Command of the Sudan Armed Forces, the Sudan Federal Alliance, the Sudanese Trade Union Alliance, and the Sudan People's Liberation Movement/Army (SPLM/A).

[79]Human Rights Watch/Africa telephone interview, New York, April 1996.

parties and with other restrictions on freedoms of association, assembly and speech cannot produce a result that is reflective of informed popular choice.

It appears from the actions and statements of the government that the ban on political parties, unlike the ban on trade unions and other associations, is intended to be permanent, not solely for the duration of the state of emergency. For that additional reason it is a violation of the derogation provisions of the ICCPR.

There is, however, a kernel of truth in the statement that political parties in Sudan have not played the beneficial and essential role expected of them in a democracy. One political analyst bemoaned political parties based on religious sects:

> No political regime, whatever its formal structures, can be dignified by the appellation 'democratic' when the life-support system of politics is based on religious sectarianism. The leaders of those sects are, by definition, immune from accountability, holding, as they are, both spiritual and temporal powers. This historic dominance, which Nimeiri's regime, in its early years, has done more than anybody else to dilute, has now resurfaced with vigor.[80]

The major Islamic sects in northern Sudan — the Ansar, Khatmiyya, Tijaniyyah, and Qadiriyyah — have deep roots in society. The Ansar and the Khatmiyya set up their own political organizations during the nationalist period before independence (1956). The Ansar established the Umma Party, with followers mostly in the central and western regions, and the Khatmiyya founded the National Unionist Party (NUP, with urban electoral support). The NUP merged with the People's Democratic Party (originally an NUP splinter group) against what they considered the overwhelming strength of the "House of Mahdi" to form the Democratic Unionist Party (DUP).[81]

> In all parliamentary elections the best performance by any party gained 42 percent of the total vote. Together, these three essentially centrist parties never obtained less than three-fourths of the votes and electoral seats. The remainder has consisted of

---

[80]Mansour Khalid, *The Government They Deserve: The Role of the Elite in Sudan's Political Evolution* (New York: Kegan Paul International, 1990), p. 431.

[81]Human Rights Watch/Africa interview, New York, March 1996; see Bechtold, "More Turbulence in Sudan," pp. 7-8 (footnote omitted).

several regional blocs in the south, east, and far west and, since the 1960s, the more radical elements of the political spectrum such as the communists and assorted socialists on the left and the Muslim Brotherhood — as the Islamic Charter Front and now as the National Islamic Front (NIF) — on the right. It is noteworthy that southern parties have never managed to organize effectively throughout the south.[82]

There were problems with some of the political parties that went beyond their sectarian or regional bases. The historian cited above comments that the problem with parliamentary democracy in Sudan was that every coalition government had a senior and a junior partner and the junior partner soon was approached by the opposition with proposals for a better portfolio, which lead to a vote of confidence and the government falling. Coalition politics deteriorated "into a game of musical chairs and, indeed, during the first six years of democratic rule every possible combination of centrist parties has been in power and each single party has been in opposition."[83] Various junior partners entered coalition governments apparently with the interest of undermining their senior partner while in office.

Precisely because smaller groupings have limited appeal, their calculations have been to discredit all rivals so that in due time the body politic would eventually look to their group as the last best hope. Perhaps even more disastrous for public policy, it appears that an overwhelming proportion of political energy expended in the capital has gone toward undermining or shoring up a coalition and deterrence of such activities, with the result that little attention has been given to, and little energy left for, the major national problems of economics, regional rebellion, and societal transformation.[84]

Political parties were discredited in Sudan, although perhaps not among the followers of the largest parties, who after all make up the majority of the electorate. The alternative to political parties, however, has been behind-the-scenes single party rule, with no real mechanism for a transfer of power. This cure for the

[82]Bechtold, ibid.
[83]Ibid., pp. 8-9.
[84]Ibid.

disease of political party ineffectiveness is not unique but — since the fall of the Berlin Wall — is definitely dated.

Narrowly tailored laws designed to protect public order or the rights and freedoms of others — for examples, anti-corruption measures — would not necessarily violate Article 22. Complete prohibition of political parties is a violation of the right to freedom of association.

Trade Unions and Professional Associations

The derogation of freedom of association was specifically aimed at political parties, but also included other associations. From its first day in power, the NIF's national salvation government cracked down on trade unions and their leaders and activists, intending to cripple the union movement and to curtail its historic role as an agent of political mobilization and change. Following the banning of unions and confiscation of their assets,[85] the new government dismissed hundreds of union leaders from the public sector and ordered the detention without charge or trial of hundreds of activists who in September 1989 began to strike in opposition to the military coup. These union activists were systematically tortured in detention in the ghost houses, introduced in the last quarter of 1989 in large part to rein in unions.

The government coupled the legal measures that it took against trade unions by exceptionally symbolic decisions, as if to signal to all concerned the real change underway. The Bar Association and the Sudan Human Rights Organization were housed in a building the transitional government (1985-86) donated to them as a gesture of recognition and support. The national salvation government decided to use the property, which it confiscated, as a ghost house in 1989-90.[86] Among those brought there for interrogation and torture were the very activists who worked with these two organizations and established their record of advocacy for the rule of law and defense of human rights in the Sudan.[87] Both organizations

---

[85]Constitutional Decree No. 2 that banned the trade unions also provided that "Funds and properties retained by unions and federations are confiscated and transferred to General Registrar Labor Organizations," and "The disposition of the funds and properties stated in item b) are to be in accordance with the directive issued by the Head of State or his representative." (Article 3 (b) and (c)).

[86]After 1990 the building was used as the operational headquarters of the Popular Defense Forces, a government militia.

[87]See Africa Watch, "Sudan: Sudanese Human Rights Organizations," *A Human Rights Watch Short Report*, November 4, 1991.

remain banned. They were replaced by the pro-government Sudan Lawyers Union and Sudan Human Rights Organization.

Since the beginning of the union movement during the colonial era, following the struggle for the establishment of the first workers' association in 1947 in Atbara, the union movement became politically active on issues of national interest. It was a major force in the nationalist drive for independence. In the post-independence era, it was in the forefront of the struggle for the restoration of democracy whenever abusive military dictatorships suppressed it. During the October 1964 popular uprising, unions orchestrated a civil disobedience campaign and a general political strike that managed to topple the military dictatorship of Gen. Ibrahim Aboud (1958-1964). Gen. Nimeiri, who led a military coup against the elected government in 1969, was only ousted when the unions combined their efforts again in April 1985, staging a successful and peaceful civil disobedience campaign and leading the population into a general strike that paralyzed the country and rendered it ungovernable until democracy was restored.[88]

A period of transition followed each of these eruptions of "people's power," during which union representatives and national figures led one-year transitional governments that prepared for elections and the reinstatement of democratically-elected governments. The medium of trade union intervention in national politics was in both cases broad alliances, called in 1964 the Front of Associations (*Jabhat al Haya'at*) and in 1984-85 the Alliance of Trade Unions (*Al Tagam'u al Naghabi*). Thus, in recognition of the union's role in bringing about the 1985 political change, the transitional government was headed by Dr. Gezouli Da'Falla, the chairperson of the Doctors' Union and of the underground Alliance of Trade Unions that spearheaded the strike against Nimeiri's military rule. This ensured a particularly harsh clamp down on the Doctor's Union following the June 1989 military coup.

The unions' role during the transitional period and under the democratically-elected government of Sadiq al Mahdi went beyond the defense of the interests of their members to also include direct participation in national affairs on a number of issues. They served as active mediators between the government of Sudan and the rebel SPLM/A in negotiations for an equitable settlement of the civil war. Union representatives and political leaders negotiated the Koka Dam agreement of February 1986, with the SPLM/A.[89] Following that initiative, union

---

[88]Human Rights Watch/Africa interview, New York, March 1996.

[89]The Koka Dam Declaration called for a "new Sudan that would be free from racism, tribalism, sectarianism and all causes of discrimination and disparity." It contained a list of

(continued...)

mediators negotiated the November 1988 agreement between the SPLM/A and the Democratic Unionist Party, the then junior partner in the coalition government, of which the Umma Party was senior party.[90] It is largely accepted by political analysts that the June 30, 1989 coup was timed to stop that government from formally adopting this second agreement, and thus achieving a negotiated end to the war. The agreement almost adopted would have required the freezing of the application of Islamic laws, a measure the National Islamic Front, the political party behind the coup, vehemently opposed.[91]

This record of activism apparently did not endear trade unions to the NIF-controlled government. The NIF tended to see the unions as dominated by communists, leftists, and secularists. While the NIF has managed to build a constituency in the student population, managing in the process to exert a quasi-control over student unions at the high school and college levels, it has performed less well among workers and professional groups.

In the last week of July 1989, hardly one month after the coup, the banned trade unions took the bold initiative of addressing a memorandum of protest to the government. A delegation of trade unionists, including representatives from the unions of intermediate school teachers, the attorney general's legal advisors, lawyers, bank employees, Khartoum University staff and the federation of civil servants and professionals, requested and immediately obtained an audience with Brig. Hamadien, a political advisor to the ruling Revolutionary Command Council, who was under the impression that the memorandum was one of allegiance to the new military order. The memorandum, instead, reminded the government of its obligations under international conventions to which Sudan remained party with regard to the freedom of association, and the prohibition of persecution of union activists; declared the banning of unions and the confiscation of their assets illegal; demanded the restoration of the banned unions as the legitimate representatives of the workers who elected them; and sought the restoration of their assets.

Upon reading the protest memorandum in the presence of the union representatives, Brig. Hamadien promised them, "We will contact you." Instead, security agents moved the same night to arrest all those who signed the

---

[89](...continued)
immediate steps to be taken, including repeal of the shari'a laws enacted in 1983 and holding a constitutional conference. It was signed by the SPLA and several political parties. Woodward, *Sudan: 1898-1989*, pp. 204-05.

[90]Human Rights Watch/Africa interview, New York, March 1996.

[91]See Gabriel R. Warburg, "The *Shari'a* in Sudan, Implementation and Repercussions," in Voll, ed., *Sudan: State and Society in Crisis*, p. 104.

memorandum on behalf of their unions, and sent them directly to Kober Prison in early August.[92]

The Sudan Doctor's Union organized a strike in November 1989 in protest against the suppression of unions and the detention of its leading members, some of whom were arrested following the submission of the July memorandum.[93] Public health services came to a stand still, except for emergencies. The government moved swiftly and ruthlessly. It dismissed leading activists from their posts and ordered the detention of many others. This wave of detainees, unlike the first, was sent to ghost houses. Many doctors were subjected to systematic beatings, torture and humiliating treatment. Security agents pulled out the fingernails of a pediatric surgeon with pliers and flogged other detainees until they bled.

Dr. Ali Fadul, a thirty-seven-year-old physician who was dismissed after the strike, a member of the executive committee of the Doctors' Union and also secretary of the League of Socialist Doctors in Sudan, went underground in fear for his safety. To force him to give himself up, security arrested and tortured his brother, Dr. Mukhtar Fadul, a veterinarian. Dr. Ali Fadul then turned himself in to security on March 13, 1990. He was severely tortured in a ghost house, and he died of internal hemorrhaging and a fractured skull on April 21, while still in the custody of security.[94] Dr. Mamoun Mohamed al Hussein, the president of the Doctors' Union, was detained following the November strike and beaten with such violence that he spent three days in a coma. He was later brought before a special security court that sentenced him to death for his role in the strike. For months, he waited in the death row, shackled, wearing the mandatory red uniform and confined to the quarters reserved in Kober for those awaiting the execution. Only a strong local and international campaign for his release managed to save him.[95]

Government Trade Union Legislation

Two years after the state of emergency was declared in 1989, the government began to issue decrees that would permit the trade unions to reopen, if they reorganized. This involved considerable manipulation of laws, people and elections. The process culminated in 1991 with the introduction of the Law for Labor Organizations. This legislation radically changed the structure and functions

---

[92]Human Rights Watch/Africa interview, October, 1995. The union leaders spent more than one year in detention without charges or trial.

[93]Ibid.

[94]Africa Watch, "Sudan, Officers Executed and Doctor Tortured to Death," *A Human Rights Watch Short Report*, April 26, 1990.

[95]Human Rights Watch/Africa interview, New York, March 1996.

of labor organizations in the country. Prior to it, unions were organized according to trade, economic sector or profession. This allowed the presence of more than one trade union in the same establishment.

The new law allowed only one union per establishment, which union must group together workers who had their own separate unions before that. This requirement diluted the influence of professional organizations, which had a record of pro-democracy activism and whose influence far exceeded their numerical strength. The law allowed the establishment of separate professional unions only as regulatory bodies for the particular profession, to serve as custodian of its norms and ethics.

Article 5 of the 1991 Law for Labor Organizations declares that

> Union organizations, being national, democratic, independent and permanent labor organizations shall have the following goals:
> a) Defend and protect rights of their members and care for their interests within the limits of the law and the requirement of national action.
> b) Improve the intellectual and artistic capacities of the membership and raise their cultural, economic and social levels.
> c) Work toward social and economic stability.
> d) Cooperate with other organs of the state to consolidate national unity, to salvage the economy and to improve services.
> e) Protect the independence of the nation and its security, and strengthen the civilizing orientation and contribute to the realization of justice among members of the society.
> f) Consolidate productivity, improve management and deploy sufficient efforts to achieve production surplus within the socio-economic development plans of the state.

An accompanying covering note from the Registrar of Trade Unions explains the underlying philosophy behind these goals. It consists of a flat "rejection of the narrow interpretation . . . which [under past legislation] considered trade unions as primarily bargaining tools, aiming at the achievement of maximum claims and sectoral gains to its membership." Instead, the memorandum explains, the legislators introduced a new understanding of unions "which is more in line with the new situation in our country; requiring union organizations to be instruments working towards economic and social stability in society."[96] One could hardly be more explicit on the limits of advocacy imposed on unions under this new law. The only unions permitted under this law would be held to the government's definition of national interest and its agenda of "civilizing orientation" — commonly used in official discourse to denote the government's strategy of Islamization of Sudanese society — and would not be permitted to pursue their members' economic or political interests.[97]

Elections for trade union offices have been marred with intimidation tactics and suppression of dissenting voices. The following testimony of a prominent union leader, whom we shall call Ahmed, illustrates the methods used to control unions and union elections and defeat the workers' right to freedom of association.[98]

Ahmed was detained for seven months in the crackdown on unions that started in September 1989. No charges were ever filed against him, and he was not questioned or tortured. He believes he and many other trade unionists were detained to prevent them from continuing pro-democracy political activism and playing their 1985 role in bringing down a military dictatorship.

Ahmed was detained again in 1991, accused of planning to assassinate government figures, taken to the Citibank ghost house and brutally tortured. He was released three months later without charges ever having been brought.

The third time he was detained, in August 1992, was directly related to his refusal to be a party to government attempts to control the trade unions. The government had issued new decrees for the reorganization of trade unions. A former independent trade unionist, who had agreed to support the government's position, was sent to feel Ahmed out about his participation in trade union elections under the new law. He wanted guarantees that Ahmed's block would vote for the NIF candidate and that the NIF man would be elected.

Ahmed assured the representative that he and his people would participate, but that he and his group would work against the NIF candidate (he proposed another candidate, a moderate Islamist, instead).

Shortly after, Ahmed and another former trade union leader were detained. He was kept in a solitary cell and accused of being a "ringleader" against the government. He was questioned very little, and although he was beaten, the treatment was not as severe as it was the year before.

---

[96]Explanatory Memorandum Attached to the Draft Labor Organizations Law, 1991.
[97]Human Rights Watch/Africa interview, New York, March 1996.
[98]Human Rights Watch/Africa interview, Khartoum, May 27, 1995.

The union elections took place in his absence and the NIF candidate was elected. When the elections were over, two and a half months after his detention, he was released without any charges. Upon release in 1992, he was required to sign a statement promising that he would not leave Khartoum without security approval.

A government labor official visited him at home, apologized to him, and explained that they had to have their man elected, and Ahmed as a politician should understand this. He worked for another union election, in which he agreed not to stand as a candidate, and his side was elected. He was fired from his job shortly after that. Security continues to visit him every two weeks, and he has been detained several times.[99]

The government maintains that professional associations are subject to their own administrative regulations.[100] But unfair tactics were used to manipulate elections to permit government supporters to take over the Bar Association in 1993.[101]

Other Nongovernmental Associations

The government of Sudan's severe restrictions on freedom of association go beyond trade unions and political parties. Registration of nongovernmental organizations (NGOs) is required by law. A special branch of Sudan Security called Security of Organizations holds veto power on the registration of any nongovernmental organization on the grounds of the supposed political affiliations of its founding members. The founders' home and work addresses must be listed in the application and Security of Organizations must provide clearance prior to approval of NGO registration. The same branch vets the names of applicants for employment with international development agencies operating in Sudan, in many cases barring those suspected of anti-government views or affiliations from these jobs. The branch closely monitors nongovernmental organizations allowed to re-register following the 1989 ban·on all associations, and frequently steps in to close down organizations it suspects of harboring opposition members. Using a formidable array of reporting requirements and surveillance of both personnel and

---

[99]Ibid.

[100]"All professions such as law, medicine, engineering . . . etc. have their own administrative regulations intended for the improvement of the profession. Furthermore, such practices are not unique to the Sudan, but are recognized almost everywhere else." "The Response of the Government of the Sudan," November 21, 1995, New York, p. 25, para. 90.

[101]Human Rights Watch, "Sudan," *World Report 1994* (New York: Human Rights Watch, December 1993), pp. 54-55.

project activities, the government puts pressure on international development organizations that support potentially opposition local organizations.[102]

Local NGOs already in existence at the time of the coup were rigorously screened, and some were not permitted to re-register. This eliminated independent and membership-elected associations such as the Sudan Human Rights Organization. In a few cases where the government suspected that a re-registered NGO had a leadership that did not agree with the ruling ideology, close security scrutiny was maintained. Official tolerance of such NGOs, viewed as "liberal," "secular," or "leftist," ran its course in several cases, and the NGOs' projects were closed, they were de-registered as organizations, and their assets confiscated.

It also proved extremely difficult for nongovernmental organizations formed after 1989 to obtain the required approvals for registration. Following the coup, new NGOs whose founding members were close to the ruling NIF won immediate approvals, while others without these political connections had to submit to the individual vetting of their founders by a special branch of security.[103]

Violations of Freedom of Association

Until 1989, the formation and registration of NGOs in Sudan was governed by a 1957 law which provided a broad framework for regulating the structure and functions of voluntary societies, and outlined their accountability to their membership and to a regulatory governmental agency, then the Registrar of Local NGOs at the Ministry of Social Welfare. The law allowed any group of seven persons to form a "charitable society" or organization for "any purpose," provided that the objective was not of an educational, religious or trade union nature, since involvement in these activities was governed by other laws. The legal requirements for the formation of NGOs were made easy by post-independence legislators to deliberately encourage popular participation in welfare and development services that the newly independent Sudan desperately needed.

The Miscellaneous Amendment (Organization of Voluntary Work) Act of 1994 increased the minimum number of people required to found a new NGO from seven to thirty. It also subjected the approval of registration to the prior clearance of Security of Organizations, which has the task of checking the political credentials and background of any persons willing to form a welfare or humanitarian association. This involves routine security checks in the places of work and residence of all founding members. A new NGO could not be registered without this clearance. This discourages the thousands of people who were purged

---

[102]Human Rights Watch/Africa interview, New York, March 1996.
[103]Ibid.

from public service, or formerly detained on the grounds of official suspicions about their affiliations, from involving themselves in any form of association. It constitutes a grave limitation on their freedom of association.

In other cases, Security of Organizations may disapprove of the objectives of a proposed NGO and deny it clearance from the outset. This happened in 1991 and 1992 when a dozen local environmental groups founded the Sudan Environmental Network (SENET) to coordinate their outreach and program work. Authorities harassed leaders of this initiative, detaining some briefly to pressure them to abandon SENET. It appeared SENET was seen as a threat to the government-controlled NGO network, the Sudan Council of Voluntary Agencies (SCOVA). This harassment continues. Leading environmentalist Professor Assim Magrhabi and his wife Dr. Alawiya Gamal were both briefly detained in September 1995, and then told to report to the head office of Sudan Security for long hours on a daily basis after that.[104] They were accused of but not charged with "espionage" activities for filming Dinder National Park, a threatened game reserve.

Church activities and all church-based organizations are the object of the specialized scrutiny of a branch of security with the telling name of Church Activities *(Al Inshita al Kanassiya)*. Saint Vincent de Paul, a charity of the Roman Catholic Church of Sudan, runs a breakfast program for more than eighty schools servicing displaced children from southern Sudan in the greater Khartoum area. It also has a street children's program which helps unaccompanied children from the south through an integrated shelter, feeding, foster parenthood and schooling approach. In April 1994 the director of both programs was detained for ten days, together with three Egyptian seminarists who were volunteers in the breakfast program (authorities initially said they were "suspected of espionage"). None was charged with a crime, but the volunteers were expelled. A vehicle they were in at the time of arrest was never returned to the program; nor was a large sum of cash, reportedly the salaries of the breakfast program workers. When the director tried in November to reclaim the assets through official channels, he was arrested again and beaten in reprisal. The Sudan Commissioner of Voluntary Agencies, the official agency overseeing NGOs, stepped in and suspended the registration of Saint Vincent de Paul on the grounds that it had violated regulations in its child residency program. Only intervention at a high level in the Ministry of Social Planning, the body to which SCOVA reports, allowed Saint Vincent de Paul to

---

[104]Ibid.

continue functioning, on the grounds that the agency was doing useful work by keeping children off the streets.[105]

In February 1995, authorities arrested Gordon Micha Kur, a retired policeman and social worker who had a close working relationship with the Sudanese Amputees Association (SSA) during its short existence from 1987 to 1989. He was detained for the first time from September 1989 to June 1991, also without charge or trial. The SSA was a welfare association set up to assist victims of hand and foot amputations following court sentences during the strict application of shari'a laws in Sudan from 1983 to 1985, a punishment the NIF actively backed. The SSA was banned at the time of the coup and not allowed to re-register, and its very mention is considered blasphemous by supporters of the NIF. It is believed that Kur's repeated detentions and the harassment he suffered are related to his involvement with this association.[106]

RIGHT OF PEACEFUL ASSEMBLY AND THE CONDUCT OF LAW ENFORCEMENT OFFICERS IN CONTROLLING DEMONSTRATIONS

The government of Sudan has stated that freedom of assembly "is fully guaranteed by law and the legal provisions governing it are identical to those applied in western countries."[107] When the U.N. special rapporteur on human rights on Sudan observed that the Criminal Act of 1991 declares as unlawful a gathering of more than five persons without prior approval, the government explained that the provision regarding unlawful assembly was originally introduced by the British during colonial rule in the Sudan (although the government has taken pride in distancing itself from the colonial past).[108] This government, moreover, radically changed the legal system, including the criminal code. The limiting of freedom of assembly by the new Criminal Act of 1991 is not, therefore, merely a holdover of the colonial past but an assertion of the new government's disregard for international standards in this regard.

At issue in Sudan is both the letter of the law and the way in which it is administered. Unofficial groups not aligned with the government rarely even apply

---

[105]Human Rights Watch/Africa, *Children of Sudan: Slaves, Street Children and Child Soldiers* (New York: Human Rights Watch, 1995), p. 19.

[106]See Amnesty International, "Prisoner of Conscience," UA 106/95, AI Index: AFR 54/13/95 (London: May 3, 1995); *Sudan Update* (London), vol. 6, no. 8, May 22, 1995, p. 4.

[107] "Response of the Government of the Sudan", November 21, 1995, p. 11, para. 48.

[108]Ibid., pp. 25-26, para. 92.

for permits for meetings indoors or outdoors, because the government will not grant permits to those considered its opponents and violently represses their meetings and demonstrations. As a consequence, outdoor demonstrations are not preannounced in order to avoid government disruption and indoor meetings take place clandestinely to prevent security from observing and arresting the participants. Citizens know where the "red line" is.

The Applicable Law

"The right of peaceful assembly shall be recognized," according to Article 21 of the ICCPR. The only permissible restrictions are those in conformity with law and necessary in a democratic society, including those necessary for public order or *ordre public*. "The right of assembly is subject only to one condition, that it be exercised peacefully," according to one legal authority.[109]

Long before the current government of Sudan came to power, it was generally accepted that a state could not restrict peaceful assembly on the grounds of deviance from or opposition to the state ideology. Public order could not be defined as conformity with the state's ideological precepts. This was the interpretation of the law on freedom of assembly,[110] and the rule applies universally, whether the ideology is communism, capitalism, theocracy, or the ideology embraced by the current or any prior Sudan government.

Peaceful assembly "refers exclusively to the conditions under which the assembly is held, i.e., 'without uproar, disturbance, or the use of arms.'"[111] This right includes the right of the individual to participate or not, and the right of groups or organizations to convoke an assembly or take part in it.[112] Peaceful assembly includes demonstrations in public places and meetings held indoors.[113]

Standards in the form of U.N. General Assembly resolutions, such as the U.N. Code of Conduct for Law Enforcement Officials, provide a practical interpretation of the norms laid down in international treaties, such as the ICCPR,

---

[109]Partsch, "Freedom of Conscience and Expression,"p. 233.

[110]In other words, "the state cannot establish the ideology of socialism as *ordre public* to justify restricting peaceful assembly expressing disagreement or even hostility to socialism." Ibid., p. 234.

[111]Ibid., p. 231 (footnote omitted).

[112]Ibid., p. 233.

[113]Article 11, African Charter on Human and Peoples' Rights: "Every individual shall have the right to assemble freely with others. The exercise of this right shall be subject only to necessary restrictions provided for by law in particular those enacted in the interest of national security, the safety, health, ethics and rights and freedoms of others."

and should guide the conduct of law enforcement officials in controlling crowds and demonstrations. Article 3 of that Code of Conduct provides, "Law enforcement officials may use force only when strictly necessary and to the extent required for the performance of their duty."[114] The commentary on that article, which forms an integral part of the code, states:

> The use of firearms is an extreme measure. . . . In general, firearms should not be used except when a suspected offender offers armed resistance or otherwise jeopardizes the lives of others and less extreme measures are not sufficient to restrain or apprehend the suspected offender. In every instance in which a firearm is discharged, a report should be made promptly to the competent authorities.[115]

A set of basic principles later clarified these guidelines further, prohibiting use of firearms except in three specific cases: 1) self-defense or defense of others against the imminent threat of death or serious injury; 2) to prevent the perpetration of a particularly serious crime involving grave threat to life; and 3) to arrest a person presenting such a danger and resisting their authority, or to prevent his or her escape.[116] Even in such circumstances, these principles permit the use of firearms "only when less extreme means are insufficient to achieve these objectives. In any event, intentional lethal use of firearms may only be made when strictly unavoidable in order to protect life." (Principle 9).

These basic principles impose additional requirements for the use of firearms: prior identification of the law enforcement officer as such, a clear warning of intent to use firearms, and sufficient time for the warning to be observed (unless it would unduly place the officer at risk or risk death or serious harm to others or "would be clearly inappropriate or pointless in the circumstances of the incident"). (Principle 10).

---

[114]U.N. Code of Conduct for Law Enforcement Officials.

[115]Ibid., Commentary (c) on Article 3.

[116]United Nations Basic Principles on the Use of Force and Firearms by Law Enforcement Officials, Eighth United Nations Congress on the Prevention of Crime and the Treatment of Offenders, Havana, 27 August to 7 September 1990, U.N. Doc. A/CONF.144/28/Rev.1 (1990), Principle 9. See Principle 4: "Law enforcement officials, in carrying out their duty, shall, as far as possible, apply non-violent means before resorting to the use of force and firearms. They may use force and firearms only if other means remain ineffective or without any promise of achieving the intended result."

There are also limits on the force that can be used even when law enforcement officials are confronted with an illegal assembly:

> 13. In the dispersal of assemblies that are unlawful but non-violent, law enforcement officials shall avoid the use of force or, where that is not practicable, shall restrict such force to the minimum extent necessary.
> 14. In the dispersal of violent assemblies, law enforcement officials may use firearms only when less dangerous means are not practicable and only to the minimum extent necessary. Law enforcement officials shall not use firearms in such cases, except under the conditions stipulated in principle 9.[117]

Even when use of force and firearms by law enforcement officials may be deemed unavoidable, law enforcement officers must consider some other factors:

> Whenever the lawful use of force and firearms is unavoidable, law enforcement officials shall:
> a) Exercise restraint in such use and act in proportion to the seriousness of the offense and the legitimate objective to be achieved;
> (b) Minimize damage and injury, and respect and preserve human life;
> (c) Ensure that assistance and medical aid are rendered to any injured or affected persons at the earliest possible moment;
> (d) Ensure that relatives or close friends of the injured or affected person are notified at the earliest possible moment.[118]

Nor may "[e]xceptional circumstances such as internal political instability or any other public emergency . . . be invoked to justify any departure from these basic principles."[119]

Relatives of Twenty-Eight Officers Demonstrate

As described above, the government summarily executed twenty-eight army officers on April 24, 1990 because of their alleged participation in a coup

---

[117]Ibid, Principles 13 and 14.
[118]Ibid.
[119]Ibid., Principle 8.

attempt that same day. The government announced on television that they had been executed, but never turned the bodies over to the relatives. The relatives formed groups inside and outside Sudan to demand that the details of the trials be made public, and that the government disclose the burial place and permit the families to rebury their loved ones if they wished.

Although civil liberties were suspended at the time of the 1989 coup and in fact have never been fully restored, the relatives of these twenty-eight army officers nevertheless attempt to publicly petition the government inside Sudan. They are among the few who have dared to try to exercise even a few of the liberties all enjoyed — for a few short years — before June 30, 1989. They attempt to exercise their rights to free expression and assembly, to commemorate and protest on or about the anniversary of the deaths. The executions took place on the twenty-eighth day of Ramadan, 1990. Therefore, the day of commemoration falls yearly on a different day of the Christian calendar.

The government has set its face against the relatives' demands. At one time it even tried to prevent them from having private meetings in their own homes to commemorate the executions. These government attempts to prevent private meetings violated the right to peacefully assemble; in addition, the authorities used excessive force in detaining and interrogating those involved.

The families organized the first commemorations in 1991 in the house of Akram al Fatih Youssif, a pilot. Family and friends of the executed officers were present and read poems and speeches eulogizing them. The next day, security called in and threatened the pilot's brother, a lawyer by the name of Eiman al Fatih. The following week, Khartoum University students organized a public rally to protest the executions. Naffissa al Mileik, a well-known professor of education and women's leader, took the podium to denounce the unfair trial of her son, officer Eiman al Mileik. Security took her in for interrogation and threats. Security agents charged into the house of Mohamed Abdel Aziz in Omdurman, where another commemorative event was underway, and arrested all young participants. Security agents severely beat the detainees while in custody, even breaking the jaw of Mohamed Ridda, who had read a poem at the event. At another event organized in al Kadru to eulogize the executed Gen. al Kadro, security agents arrested all participants and detained some for up to a week. In 1992, security agents dispersed a similar gathering convened in al Amarat residential quarter of Khartoum.[120]

It was the 1993 demonstration that the families staged in front of U.N. headquarters in Khartoum that gave their grief and protest an international resonance. Gaspar Biro, the U.N. Commission on Human Rights' special

---

[120]Human Rights Watch/Africa interview, New York, March 1996.

rapporteur on human rights in Sudan, heard the demonstration and came out of the U.N. office to receive a memorandum the families prepared for him. In front of his eyes, security agents beat up the peaceful demonstrators and arrested several women, throwing them into minitrucks.[121]

These women were within their rights to gather and present a petition to a public official. Their assembly was not violent. Preventing that meeting by detaining the demonstrators was an abuse of their human rights. The beating of demonstrators exceeded the minimum amount of force necessary to disperse an unlawful demonstration — and was further unjustified since the demonstration was lawful under international law.

In 1995, the anniversary of the execution fell on February 28, but the relatives decided to memorialize it on February 26 to avoid security harassment.[122] The force used by the authorities against the demonstrators was excessive, since by all accounts the women abandoned the demonstration when security appeared on the scene. What followed were beatings of women apparently inflicted as punishment for having held the demonstration. These beatings were not necessary to stop the demonstration, since the demonstrators had already scattered. Nor was there any justification for security's beating of women demonstrators in custody during interrogation.

On the day in question, a group of women and children gathered on University Street near the Palace of Government in Khartoum and pulled out placards with pictures of the executed men. Chanting the names of the twenty-eight victims, the women stopped cars on the street and handed out pamphlets with photographs of the executed men. They succeeded in closing the street briefly; they said the people in cars were kind but afraid to get out and join the demonstration. Symbolic coffins draped with the Sudanese flag were part of the demonstration.[123]

After a half hour at the most, security arrived to break up the demonstration. The women, who had agreed to flee when security came, did not all succeed in escaping. Six were caught. Many security cars arrived from all directions at once. Security, grabbing the pamphlets and placards, captured Samira Karrar, whom they regarded as the leader, along with her sisters Alia and Widat and three other women.

---

[121]See Report of the Special Rapporteur on the situation of human rights in the Sudan, February 1, 1994, p. 25-26, para. 85.

[122]Human Rights Watch/Africa interview, Samira Karrar, Khartoum, May 24, 1995.

[123]Ibid. The families adopted other creative forms of civil protest, including distribution of t-shirts with the photographs of the executed officers, and the unofficial renaming of certain streets.

Although Samira Karrar, sister of a slain officer, has been detained often by security for her participation in these commemorations, the 1995 detention marked the first time she and the others were severely physically abused by security. Security agents pulled her by her hair and knocked her head against a wall. They threw her and the other women inside a white Toyota vehicle of the kind used by security, and took them all to what appeared to be a private house in Khartoum North.[124]

According to her account, when agents roughly pulled them from the vehicle, she fell on the ground and the agents pulled her up by her skirt. Inside the house they slapped and kicked her; twelve agents were gathered around, some threatening her with death. One roughly grabbed her by the neck, where she was bruised for days afterward. Some took off their belts and struck her. She remained defiant. When they threatened to put her in jail with prostitutes and alcohol brewers, she said she would teach them how to work against the government — which caused another slap.[125]

One other woman, a diabetic, suffered a bloody nose from the beating. The women were in this unacknowledged place of detention from 10:00 a.m. until 6:00 p.m. the same day, and then were released, after security tried to force them to sign a document agreeing not to demonstrate or take any actions against the government.

The harassment continued; security agents entered a house where Samira Karrar and her sister were visiting and told the owner to throw the two women out. When the women left to avoid problems for their friend, two trucks followed them, one in front and the other behind them, alternatively speeding and braking. a few days later a security agent posing as a "friend" of the women came to another member of the group and sought to entrap her. He said he wanted to work with the families' group against the government and participate with them in assassinations and bombings, offering to supply them with guns and grenades. They firmly told him that they do not engage in such tactics.[126]

At the 1996 annual commemoration, the government did not repeat the 1995 brutality. The victims' families staged their demonstration in al Jumhuriyya Street, in the commercial center of Khartoum, and temporarily closed the busy street. They carried two large placards and a wreath of flowers. They shouted anti-government slogans and demands for justice for their dead relatives. They also handed out leaflets calling on the government to make public the details of the

---

[124]Ibid.
[125]Ibid.
[126]Ibid.

officers' trials, to hand over the remains to the families for decent burial, and to make public the names of those who presided over the trials and conducted the executions. Security agents were present but kept their distance.

The hands-off conduct of security during the 1996 demonstration was an improvement over the violence they unleashed on the women during the 1995 demonstration. This did not represent recognition of the right of peaceful assembly, however; before the demonstrations security summoned some family members who had been active in the past and pressured them to sign undertakings not to participate in anti-government activity, including demonstrations.[127]

Police Violence During Evictions and Demolitions of Squatter Settlements

The police shot dead at least eleven people and injured forty on October 15, 1994, during residents' resistance to the demolition of their homes in a squatter settlement in the Ghammeyer area of Omdurman, also known as Khoder.[128] The crowd, also objecting to forced relocation to remote and unserviced areas, threw stones at bulldozers arriving to destroy the homes. In response, the police who escorted the teams fired into the crowd and killed at least six people. At a second protest later the same day five more people were shot dead in the same fashion.[129] The residents complained about lack of notice, the destruction without compensation of their homes, and inferior conditions in the relocation sites.

Here, where some demonstrators threw stones at demolition teams, the applicable guideline is Principle 14 of the U.N. Basic Principles on the Use of Force by Law Enforcement Officials, referring to the dispersal of violent assemblies. Police may use firearms only when less dangerous means are not practicable and only to the minimum extent necessary. If they use firearms, they must do so under the conditions stipulated in Principle 9, whereby "intentional

---

[127]Ibid.

[128]The United Nations concluded that eleven were killed in the shooting, according to confidential sources.

[129]Journalist interviews with the residents conducted a week later indicated that "The squatters say hundreds of troops cordoned off the area before dawn last Saturday before the bulldozers moved in. a few dozen men, women and children gathered to protest the destruction of their houses. When they started throwing stones at the bulldozers the army opened fire, they said. a number of squatters said eight people were killed in the clash. They said a dozen people, including women, were injured and about 100 were arrested." Dominic Evans, "Sudan: Sudan Defends 'Brutal' Razing of Squatter Camps," Reuter, Khartoum, October 21, 1994. Later investigations established that there were two shooting incidents the same day.

lethal use of firearms may only be made when strictly unavoidable in order to protect life."

It is not clear that firing into the crowd was strictly unavoidable in order to protect life. The lives of government officials threatened by rock throwing may have been at stake; if so, less extreme means to preserve lives of officials might well have been employed before the resort to arms. It appears that no lesser measures were, however, employed.

The objective of the government action was to demolish houses. Under Principle 5, whenever the lawful use of force and firearms is unavoidable, law enforcement officials must exercise restraint in such use and act in proportion to the seriousness of the offense and the legitimate objective to be achieved.

The ministry of foreign affairs disputed the number of persons killed — claiming only one died, shot by a demonstrator — and described the killings as a result of legal police response to rioters during the removal of illegal housing. "The incident is normal, legal and usually takes place world-wide and was contained by the police,"[130] the government stated: the simple removal of illegal houses in accord with a legal process. It said a number of citizens were responsible for "some acts of riot which the police managed to control."[131] An investigation was underway into the incident's circumstances, another government statement added.[132]

There has been no investigation, at least not one made public. Nor has there been any evidence from the government that reasonable warnings of the intent to use firearms were made, or that the use of firearms was absolutely necessary.

Dr. Sharaf Eldin Ibrahim Bannaga, minister of engineering of Khartoum State and the government official responsible for the execution of the demolition program, asserted to Human Rights Watch that there were police casualties at Khoder and other sites of conflict between the police and squatters or displaced, but that no one — no international press — reported on them.[133] He also asserted that

---

[130]"Sudan: Foreign Ministry Rejects US Report on Removal of Houses," Radio National Unity, Omdurman, in Arabic, 1730 gmt, October 20, 1994, BBC Monitoring Service: Middle East, October 22, 1994.

[131]Ibid.

[132]"Ministry of Foreign Affairs Replies to American Allegations," SUNA, Daily Bulletin, Issue No. 9284, Khartoum, October 20, 1994, page 3.

[133]Dr. Bannaga also said that there were government casualties in other relocations, including in Takamel in Haj Yussef, Khartoum North in 1993; in Kurmuta in 1991; and in Angola in March 1995. Dr. Sharaf Eldin Ibrahim Bannaga, Minister of Engineering, Khartoum State, Khartoum, May 14 and 23, 1995.

police were attacked with gunfire at Khoder, although officials did not make this claim at the time.

The government was replying to an unusual storm of criticism. The shootings drew the condemnation of the U.S. government and the European Union. The U.S. State Department said the police shot into a crowd of unarmed protesters, including women and children, and called the incident "unjustifiable and a clear abuse of force by the government of Sudan. . . . The incident underscores the brutality and callousness of the policy of forcible resettlement of squatters in the Khartoum area, which has been proceeding off and on for years."[134] The government of Sudan, in turn, protested the U.S. statement.[135]

The European Union also condemned the use of violence by Sudanese security forces in Omdurman on October 15, 1994, in response to a protest by settlers there against the razing of their homes. "These clashes left at least five squatters dead and at least fourteen severely injured."[136] The European Union called upon the government of the Sudan to halt its violent campaign against the inhabitants of the squatter settlements, to compensate the victims of this campaign, and to hold accountable those responsible for the recent killings. The government of the Sudan was also called upon to investigate and fully explain the background to the incident.[137]

Dr. Bannaga said that the problems in Khoder started more than six months before the events of October 1994. Opposition parties were in Khoder, such as the "SPLA and Umma Party supporters who are army deserters."[138] He blamed them for starting the struggle. He said the government went to Khoder in early 1994 and told the people of the decision that they would be relocated. The response was that the people burned down the tent used as a temporary office by the ministry of engineering, according to Dr. Bannaga. The popular committee later contacted the ministry again, saying that everything was calm and asking the ministry to return for a celebration. They were to celebrate the day on which the people were to be informed of the place and date of relocation: the date, Dr. Bannaga made

---

[134]"U.S. Condemns Sudan Police Action," Reuter, Washington, D.C., October 18, 1994.

[135]"Sudan: Foreign Ministry Summons US Ambassador over Statement on Omdurman Evictions," Republic of Sudan Radio, Omdurman, in Arabic, 1300 gmt, October 24, 1994, quoted in BBC Monitoring Service: Middle East, October 29, 1994.

[136]European Union, "Common Foreign and Security Policy Press Release, Statement by the Presidency of the European Union on the Sudan," PESC/94/93, Brussels, Belgium, November 3, 1994.

[137]Ibid.

[138]Human Rights Watch/Africa interview, Dr. Bannaga, May 23, 1995.

clear, was not an exact date but one within a period of several weeks, so that the people did not have an opportunity to organize to oppose the move.

According to Dr. Bannaga's account, a crowd of about one hundred was present in Khoder at 10:00 a.m. on the day in early February that the forced relocation was to have been formally announced. The representatives of the ministry, the popular committee, and the few soldiers guarding the spot were "surprised" when they were stoned. The chief of the popular committee was hit with a stone and hospitalized, according to Dr. Bannaga, and they treated others who were injured at an outpatient clinic. The government representatives asked the soldiers "not to retaliate, and we left."[139]

After that, a loudspeaker on a car went through the area informing people that they would be moved within six months to a place north of Marzuk. Before the stoning incident, the popular committee and other residents were taken to see the site. They drew lots for plot numbers. "My own evaluation was that they wanted 300 meter plots, not 200 meter ones," said Dr. Bannaga. After the stoning, the government knew it had opposition to the move and decided to guard the transport used to make the relocation and "to put up a show of force by placing police around the cantonment."[140]

On October 15, the unannounced day of the evictions, Dr. Bannaga said he arrived three to four hours after the riots. He was told that at about 7:00 a.m., for fifteen or twenty minutes, the crowd shot at the police, who shot in the air. Dr. Bannaga said one man was injured and the police vehicles took him to the hospital. After that things cooled down and there were no more incidents that day. Another man reportedly died that same day, but Dr. Bannaga claims that he was killed by a type of pistol which the police do not use; police were armed with rifles.[141]

The government's account of the events leading up to the killings makes clear that the government knew that there would be a difficult situation. The plan, however, was to guard the vehicles and "to put up a show of force by placing police around the cantonment."

The statement that members of the crowd used firearms for fifteen or twenty minutes before the police responded is hard to credit. No police or army casualties were reported on the day in question. No other agencies or persons

---

[139]Ibid.
[140]Ibid.
[141]Ibid.

interviewed at that time alleged that the demonstrators used firearms, and the government did not make that allegation immediately, either.[142]

The government's version of the Khoder events is contradicted by the contemporaneous statements and research of many persons not associated with the government. We conclude that the weight of the evidence lies with the nongovernmental reports.

The next incident of resistance by slum dwellers to demolition of their homes and forcible removal occurred in March 1995 in the Omdurman area called Angola, where residents burned down a number of structures in protest. The government did not kill anyone during this forced displacement, in which police and army units collaborated. We were told, however, that the soldiers clubbed and broke the leg of a man who, like everyone else, fled when the army arrived.[143] At any rate, this eviction at Angola showed that the government can carry out demolitions and relocations without shooting into a crowd and killing protestors.

Student Demonstrations and Police Conduct

The suppression of student demonstrations at the University of Khartoum and other universities in the Three Towns, through shootings, beatings and mass arrests, is described below in this Chapter VII. Students outside Khartoum have not fared noticeably better with regard to police conduct during their demonstrations. For instance, in May 1994 students at Gezeira University in Wad Medani joined a protest demonstration started by townspeople. Security forces opened fire, reportedly wounding one medical student and a young school girl. According to our sources, they detained about 1,800 students, and tortured some, including Lubna Ahmad Hisein (Faculty of Agriculture), who was said to have received electric shocks. The university administration dismissed thirty-nine students, and gave ten a "final warning."[144] Abdel Muniem Rahma, a trade unionist detained two weeks after these demonstrations, and suspected of instigating them, died in custody.[145]

---

[142]An official statement by the government on October 20, 1994, responding to the U.S. public condemnation of the killing of squatters, did not mention any use of firearms by the squatters. It said that "a number of citizens committed some acts of riot." "Ministry of Foreign Affairs Replies to American Allegations."

[143]Human Rights Watch/Africa interview, Khartoum, May 7, 1995.

[144]Confidential communication to Human Rights Watch/Africa, February 1996.

[145]See Chapter III.

FREEDOM OF RELIGION

Religion is very high on the public agenda of the National Islamic Front-dominated government. Sudan's Constitutional Decree No. 7 (Principles, Regulations and Constitutional Developments for 1993), October 16, 1993, states in Article 1:

> Islam is the guiding religion for the overwhelming majority of the Sudanese people. It is self-generating in order to avert stagnation and constitutes a uniting force that transcends confessionalism. It is a binding code that directs the laws, regulations and policies of the State. However, revealed religions such as Christianity, or traditional religious beliefs may be freely adopted by anyone with no coercion in regard to beliefs and no restriction on religious observances. These principles are observed by the State and its laws.

Only an estimated 60 to 70 percent of the Sudanese population is Muslim, however.[146] As for the other religions, the Catholic church summarized the problem:

> Aware that the State of Sudan sponsors and promotes Islam as the religion of the country, we Christians, as citizens of Sudan, demand an equal position for Christianity and expect to be treated in the same way as the Muslims. The present policy of identifying the country and the State with one religion only, Islam, shall not promote the spirit of dialogue, understanding, and peaceful co-existence among the citizens of the country.[147]

Freedom of religion for non-Muslims has been interfered with or denied in many ways, and non-Muslims have been discriminated against on account of religion. Church leaders speak of a continual struggle for survival against

---

[146]Christians account for 4 percent of the national total (15 percent of the southern population), and traditional religions the rest. "Sudan: Country Profile 1994-95," The Economist Intelligence Unit.

[147]Sudan Catholic Bishops' Conference, "The Miscellaneous Amendment Organization of Voluntary Work Act 1994: Position of the Catholic Church," Khartoum, February 2, 1995, p. 2.

omnipresent government interference and harassment. We do not know what formal status, if any, the government accords traditional African religions; although their practitioners outnumber Christians, especially in the south, they are less organized. Those who practice other religions often have been made to feel marginal or inferior by spokespersons for the National Islamic Front which controls the government.[148]

Being a Muslim does not guarantee freedom of religion, however. Some religious groups critical of the government and the National Islamic Front — as being insufficiently religious — have been subjected to harassment and their leaders detained. The two sects on which the two largest political parties were based have been subjected to government attempts at control and even confiscation of their property.

For Muslims, religious freedom is belied by the fact that apostasy, the repudiation by a Muslim of his faith in Islam, is punishable by death under section 126 of the 1991 Criminal Act. Recent converts may be excepted from this extreme penalty but the provision remains open to abuse. The death penalty may be imposed for what the court deems to amount to repudiation of belief in Islam, regardless of the actual beliefs of the accused. It is also open to political manipulation, as illustrated by the case of Mahmoud Mohamed Taha, a religious Muslim leader and founder of the Republican Brothers movement, executed in 1985 for apostasy.[149]

The deepest conflict is between the government and the Christian churches, however. The U.N. special rapporteur on Intolerance and of Discrimination based on Religion or Belief said in his December 1995 report that there had been positive measures in Sudan as a result of the meeting between Pope John Paul II and President Omar al Bashir of Sudan, in particular the "repeal of the law relating to missionary societies, allocations of land to Christians for construction of churches, and visa issue process made easier."[150]

---

[148]One North American Muslim writer quoted NIF Politburo member Ahmad 'Abdal-Rahman in *Al Nur* (Cairo), June 17, 1987, p. 4: "Most of its [the South's] inhabitants are heathens who worship stones, trees, crocodiles, the sun, etc. . . . All this presents a civilized challenge to all of us as Arabs . . . ." Simone, *In Whose Image*, p. 165.

[149]Human Rights Watch/Africa, "In the Name of God," pp. 35-36.

[150]Report submitted by Mr. Abdelfattah Amor, special rapporteur, in accordance with Commission on Human Rights resolution 1995/23, "Implementation of the Declaration on the Elimination of All Forms of Intolerance and of Discrimination Based on Religion or Belief," United Nations, E/CN.4/1996/95, December 15, 1995, p. 12, para. 55.

It is true that the government took a step forward in its relations with the churches when it repealed the Missionary Society Act of 1962 in late 1994. It then took two steps backward when the president issued a decree that would have placed churches — but not mosques — in the same category as foreign relief organizations, required each congregation to register separately and secure approval from a minister to continue worshiping, and subjected them to numerous controls on their daily affairs which violate freedom of religion under Article 18 of the ICCPR. The churches rose in protest against its unfairness, and the decree was not enforced, but its issuance revealed the adverse and discriminatory treatment that non-Muslim religions receive from the Sudanese government despite lip service paid to the notion of respect for others' religions.

Government relations with Christian churches in government garrison southern towns have been conducted through the prism of the war. The government is constantly alert to possible rebel SPLA sympathizers and infiltrators, and church leaders figure high on its list of suspects.

The war permeates relations between the government and Christian churches because the government has characterized the civil war with southern-based rebel forces (mostly non-Muslim) as a jihad or Holy War on the part of the government and its religious adherents.[151] Christians cannot be blamed for thinking that this rhetoric is aimed at them, whether they side with the SPLA or actively oppose it.[152]

---

[151]The governor of River Nile State, Staff Brig. (Ret.) Abd al Rahman Sir al Khatim told a rally that "jihad in Sudan was a message and a duty with which we defend the faith and the homeland. He said it was a message to all the sceptics who did not wish Sudan well, conveying the courage of the sons of the north. He said the mujahidin contributed by the state to the theatres of operations had their hearts full with the Qur'an . . . ." "Sudan: Military and Food Convoy from River Nile State Arrives in Khartoum," Republic of Sudan Radio, Omdurman, in Arabic, 1300 gmt, December 4, 1995, excerpts by BBC Monitoring Service: Middle East, December 6, 1995.

[152]On the fortieth anniversary of the independence of Sudan, according to government radio, President al Bashir "reaffirmed that Sudan was entering a renaissance, which is an embodiment of real independence, so that Sudan could perform its Arab, Islamic and international roles. . . . [He] referred to the spirit of jihad which has engulfed the entire people of Sudan. He said this spirit was continuing to deepen and expand day after day and that sectors of the society were currently competing with each other in the fields of jihad in defense of the faith and the homeland." "Sudan: President Bashir Says All Citizens 'Engulfed' by Spirit of Jihad."

The army provides religious training (in Islam) to conscripts and Popular Defense Forces militia in addition to military training.[153] Christians — and practitioners of traditional African religions — are naturally out of place. There is no respect for the right to maintain one's own non-Muslim religion in this environment, and the pressure to conform by adapting to Islamic religious practices is great. Sudanese men must submit to army training if they are of the age of national military service, and both men and women must undergo forty-five day PDF training if they are government civil servants or have some other relationship with the government. Such PDF training is in addition to national service obligations for men, and is required for entry into university and professional licensing for both sexes.[154]

In this climate, where government rallies are held and the head of state addresses the participants as Muslims and encourages them to continue with the Holy War,[155] there are frequent allegations of religious discrimination and of denials of freedom of religion, including freedom to manifest one's own religion.

Even absent the war, however, the NIF aspiration to create an Islamic state with "one language, Arabic, one religion, Islam," conflicts with the demands of Sudanese that their rights to practice different religions (and to preserve languages

---

[153]A visitor to Khartoum in 1996 observed a Popular Defense Forces training camp in Markhiat outside of Khartoum, where "new recruits sang enthusiastically of Jihad — holy war — and the victorious spread of shari'a rule." The trainees "sang of Allah and the battles to be fought in his name." David Orr, "Civil War Turns against Khartoum," *The Independent* (London), February 12, 1996.

[154]Time spent in PDF training and service is deductible from national service requirements.

[155]President al Bashir addressed a mass rally held to mark the National Martyrs' Day in Kosti, according to government radio,

> stressing that Sudan would not deviate from its cultural course regardless of the conspiracies being hatched against it by the enemies of Islam and the homeland.
> . . . He said the Mahdist revolution [of 1881-98 against the corrupt Turko-Egyptian rule] would persevere for as long as the Sudanese people stuck to the principles upheld by the Mahdist revolution, which had called for the victory of the religion of truth. He called on the youth to enlist in the battalions of the jihad to defend the faith and the homeland.

"Sudan: President Addresses Martyrs' Day Rally, Says Sudan Will Protect Homeland," Republic of Sudan Radio, Omdurman, in Arabic, 1300 gmt, November 28, 1995, excerpt quoted by BBC Monitoring Service: Middle East, November 28, 1995; see "Sudan: President Says Jihad Against 'Traitors and Enemies' to Continue," Republic of Sudan Radio, Omdurman, in Arabic, 0430 gmt, November 23, 1995, excerpts quoted by BBC Monitoring Service: Middle East, November 25, 1995.

and cultures) and to be treated equally by the government be respected. It appears that there are many in government who sincerely believe that conversion to Islam of everyone — including those who already have a religion — "is for their own good."[156] Forced conversion, however, whether to a Christian sect or to Islam, violates fundamental human rights principles.

The government has pointed to the fact that the Christian population is growing.[157] This is accurate. The Catholic church says that on Easter night of 1995 for instance, there were over 6,000 adults baptized in the Catholic Church in Khartoum. Freedom of religion and religious practices cannot be measured in numbers of conversions, however, since it is impossible to say what the numbers would be if the government ceased its abusive practices.[158]

National Islamist Front ideology, according to one of its main proponents, is expressed in the preamble to its constitution:

> to group together 'all the children of Sudan, men and women,
> regardless of their historical allegiances, their class situation or
> their regions' into one comprehensive organization working for
> a Muslim Sudan.[159]

One historian described the NIF's ideology regarding treatment of non-Muslims within an Islamic state: "Starting from the customary insistence that Islamic law protects religious liberty and would encourage religious practice in general, and an acceptance that non-Muslim communities can be left free to regulate their own family laws," the NIF proposes a territorial application of shari'a, considering the prevalence of certain religions or cultures in the area at variance with the religion dominant in the country at large. Thus not only

---

[156]This sentiment was expressed to the Archbishop of Canterbury. Michael Evans, "Carey begs Sudan to stop persecuting Christian minority," *The Times* (London), October 9, 1995.

[157]"The Response of the Government of Sudan," November 21, 1993, p. 23, para. 85.

[158]The conversions are of people who previously practiced traditional African religions. Conversions from the Muslim community are extremely rare because they are punishable by death. One southern intellectual notes that Christianity combined with traditional identity among southerners to consolidate and strengthen a modern southern identity of resistance against Islamization and Arabization. Deng, *War of Visions: Conflict of Identities in the Sudan* (Washington, D.C.: The Brookings Institute, 1995), pp. 205-29. Whether there would be the same number of converts to Christianity absent Islamization forces is impossible to know.

[159]Abdelwahab El-Affendi, *Turabi's Revolution: Islam and Power in Sudan* (London: Grey Seal, 1991), p. 143.

Christians and practitioners of traditional African religions in southern Sudan were to be exempt from shari'a, but Muslims living in the south were to be similarly exempt.[160]

Theoretically, under its Sudan Charter of January 1987, the NIF accepts that a non-Muslim can be eligible for any office within the state, including head of state, although "religiousness in general may be taken into consideration as a factor of the candidate's integrity."[161] However, the same historian notes,

> Flexibility of approach seems to have existed in inverse relation to actual involvement in implementing an Islamist programme. . . . The Muslim Brotherhood [precursor of the NIF], despite its apparently flexible ideas, was effectively in alliance with Nimeiri while he was pursuing policies which were harsh, vindictive and fundamentalist. Even in the subsequent parliamentary regime, and despite the liberal ideas propounded in election programmes, NIF policies made possible the retention of the laws which Nimeiri had introduced and insisted that the courts should implement them . . . .
>
> The apparent paradox of a movement whose approach is liberal and flexible in the abstract, but capable of supporting narrow and fundamentalist policies in practice, can only be understood with reference to the dynamics inherent in religious-based political movements. The religious basis ceases to be a framework within which ideas can be developed and debated, but becomes a badge of identity — a slogan around which specific sectors of the population can be mobilized, against other movements and parties. . . . Correspondingly, to opponents the religious dimension becomes symbolic of the attempt by one part of the population to oppress another. Internal and external pressures impinge to ensure that the religious framework does not remain open and adaptive.[162]

This may explain why the theory sounds better than the practice, and how elements of religious tolerance may appear in statutes but be lacking in day to day

---

[160]Tim Niblock, "Islamic movements," pp. 262-64. See Chapter V, Law and the North-South Divide.

[161]Niblock, Islamic movements," pp. 262-64.

[162]Ibid., p. 266.

affairs. For instance, the government, defending itself against charges of forced Islamization, notes that "according to Qur'anic teachings there is no compulsion in religion, so the references [in the Special Rapporteur's report] to enforced Islamization and the killing of those who refuse to convert to Islam are against the fundamental principles enshrined in the Qur'an."[163]

What is at issue in any human rights report are government practices. The reply that "according to Qur'anic teachings there is no compulsion in religion" does not dispose of the issue; it cannot be assumed that all government practices are in complete harmony with Qur'anic teachings, since a government is only a human institution and not capable of perfection.

It is useful, however, that there is an official government statement that enforced Islamization is against fundamental Islamic principles. It would be most helpful if that statement were conveyed in a prominent way to government agencies that have been accused of using government resources and power to convert people to Islam, and to agencies with which the government contracts, including Islamic relief organizations such as *Dawa Islamiyya* (Islamic Call).[164]

Human Rights Watch has already published a report pointing out, with specific testimonies, the ways in which particular government agencies have attempted to Islamize children and adults with whom they come in contact, as in homes for street children and in the training of army recruits and the Popular Defense Forces militia.[165] When these practices are terminated, then the government will no longer be accused of forced Islamization.

There is a small space for the appearance of tolerance, usually occupied by a government-appointed Christian such as State Minister for Foreign Affairs Bishop Gabriel Rorech, who holds a visible but token position and routinely is presented to visitors as proof of the lack of religious discrimination in Sudan.[166]

---

[163]"The Response of the Government of the Sudan," November 21, 1995, p. 23, para. 84.

[164]The NIF established Islamic Dawa (Call) in the early 1980s to promote the cause of Islam in Africa. The NIF also established the Islamic African Relief Agency (IARA) to do humanitarian work in Africa. Both have their headquarters in Sudan and programs in at least fifteen countries in Africa, and a growing presence in Asia and Europe. Human Rights Watch/Africa interview, New York, March 1996. These organizations were intended to compete with parallel Christian organizations, the reasoning being that missionaries had used education and humanitarian aid to subvert African Muslims and it was necessary to provide Africans with an alternative. Francis Deng, *War of Visions*, p. 175.

[165]Human Rights Watch/Africa, *Children of Sudan.*

[166]Bishop Rorech, of the Episcopal Church of Sudan (ECS), was recently elevated to the position of archbishop. Many ECS members and clergy feel it is inappropriate for clergy to

(continued...)

The space may also be occupied by prominent foreign visitors such as the Archbishop of Canterbury Dr. George Carey, who visited Khartoum and Juba in October 1995, and exercised the right to speak publicly and freely about the difficult situation of Christians in Sudan.[167] He was quite outspoken, in what one newspaper referred to as "some of the bluntest speeches by an Archbishop of Canterbury in recent memory."[168] In the southern town of Juba the archbishop referred to the "'torture, rape, destruction of property, slavery and death' being endured by Sudanese Christians as a result of the government's Islamicisation programme. 'I challenge those who are responsible for such inhuman behaviour to stop. It is no part of any creed to treat fellow human beings with such disrespect and cruelty,' he said."[169]

Sudanese clergy, however, may not be so outspoken. They suffer from a constant campaign of harassment, most notably in the case of Catholic Archbishop Paolino Lukudu Loro of Juba, who is not even allowed to receive international visitors in private; all such conversations must take place in front of a Sudan Security agent.

Agnes Lukudu, the governor (*wali*) of Bahr El Jebel state where Juba is located, said that the Catholic archbishop takes part in politics, and "if you cannot see him, it is for the good of the people." She said that the bishop was like a king and was not in touch with the people; he did not mix with them except at mass, so "the whole story doesn't filter up." She preferred that Human Rights Watch speak to a priest. When we offered to do so if we could meet a priest privately, the offer was ignored. "If we allow anti-government people to meet with outsiders, they will say the Cabinet is dominated by Muslims," she said, then listed those in the Bahr El Jebel cabinet, herself included, who were Christians. She maintained that "it does not follow that if the area is predominantly Christian, the leadership should be held by Christians."

Many have realized that "the Church led us in Africa; we're trying to say to the Church, tell the truth," she said, ending the conversation by noting, "We [the

---

[166](...continued)
hold a government position. The bishop is outranked in the Anglican hierarchy by the Archbishop of Canterbury.

[167]Michael Evans, "Carey begs Sudan to stop persecuting Christian minority."

[168]Clifford Longley, Religious Affairs Editor, "Carey Chides Muslims for Persecuting Christians," *The Daily Telegraph* (London), October 9, 1995.

[169]Ibid.

current government] are here to help the people to come out of the darkness,"[170] a phrase frequently used by proselytizing Islamists when referring to their dealings with southern practitioners of traditional African religions and Christians.

The Catholic church in Juba is under extreme pressure from the government, even more than is visited on churches in Khartoum. Because of the archbishop's statements in homilies and pastoral letters about human rights, among other things, Sudan Security in Juba has been at loggerheads with Archbishop Paolino Lukudu Loro since 1990. He does not bend. In mid-1992, the SPLA attacked Juba twice and almost managed to reach the center of the city. Following the attacks, hundreds were rounded up by security and military intelligence and subsequently disappeared; some were tried for treason and executed but most remained unaccounted for. During that time many educated people close to the archbishop disappeared.[171]

The government's record is heavily weighted on the side of religious intolerance. Take, for example, the fury with which the government greeted the recommendation of Special Rapporteur Gaspar Biro to the government to abolish legislation contradicting provisions of international law to which Sudan is a party, referring to the hudud penalties.[172] Claiming that the special rapporteur had attacked Islam, and seeking to speak for all the faithful, the government until recently barred him from the country and engaged in ad hominem attacks on his age, educational background, experience, and other personal qualities.[173] While we believe that this is a pretext and an attempt to shield itself from criticism of human rights abuses, which Islam and all major religions condemn, the government's statements about the special rapporteur nevertheless imply religious intolerance in their reference to his commitment to observing a major Christian celebration.[174] This attack on the special rapporteur's religious practices was followed by a further statement by the government including a veiled threat against him, in the name of

---

[170]Human Rights Watch/Africa interview, Agnes Lukudu, governor of Bahr El Jebel state, Juba, Sudan, June 6, 1995.

[171]Human Rights Watch/Africa interview, Khartoum, June 9, 1995.

[172]"The Situation of Human Rights in the Sudan," February 1, 1994, p. 42, para. 133 (a).

[173]See "The Response of the Government of the Sudan," November 21, 1995, p. 3, paras. 11 and 12.

[174]"The Special Rapporteur is in no position at all to report about the rights of the child in the Sudan for the obvious reason already given that he (while in Khartoum) has turned down an official invitation to attend a seminar on the rights of the child held in Khartoum during 18-20 December 1993 . . . . He turned down the invitation as he decided to leave Khartoum on 17 December 1993 one day before the opening of the seminar, in order to meet his [C]hristmas plans." Ibid., p. 26, para. 94.

religion: "we don't want to speculate about his fate if he is to continue offending the feelings of Muslims world wide by maintaining that call [for abolition of the hudud penalties], as he did in his current interim report."[175]

Ordinary non-Muslim Sudanese may be treated considerably more harshly. Two years after barring him, the government announced that the special rapporteur would be permitted to return to Sudan.[176]

The Applicable Law

Freedom of thought, conscience and religion is protected in Article 18 of the ICCPR which provides:

> (1) Everyone shall have the right to freedom of thought, conscience and religion. This right shall include freedom to have or to adopt a religion or belief of his choice, and freedom, either individually or in community with others and in public or private, to manifest his religion or belief in worship, observance, practice and teaching.

The African Charter also protects freedom of religion.[177]

Freedom of thought, conscience and religion is so fundamental that Article 18 of the ICCPR is nonderogable, which means it may not be suspended even in time of emergency. "Religion or belief" was not limited to a theistic belief but includes equally nontheistic or even atheistic beliefs.[178]

Freedom of religion also means freedom to change one's religion, under Article 18 (2) of the ICCPR. Attempts made during the drafting of the covenant to delete freedom to change religion were defeated. The right to retain one's religion, that is, to reject zealous proselytizers and missionaries, was also confirmed in this

---

[175]Statement by Dr. Ahmed M.O. Elmufti in Response to the Statement Made by Mr. Gaspar Biro, Special Rapporteur of the Commission on Human Rights, New York, November 27,1995, p. 3.

[176]Statement by H.E. Abdel Aziz Shiddu, Minister of Justice, made before the 52nd session of the Commission on Human Rights, Geneva, April 17, 1996, p. 5.

[177]African Charter, Article 8: " Freedom of conscience, the profession and free practice of religion shall be guaranteed. No one may, subject to law and order, be submitted to measures restricting the exercise of these freedoms."

[178]Partsch, "Freedom of Conscience and Expression," p. 214.

paragraph. The clause also protects against coercion to support a religion other than one's own, "for instance by payment of church taxes or contributions."[179]

Limitations on the right to manifest one's religion — not on freedom of religion, however — are described in Article 18 (3).[180] Limitations on the right to manifest one's religion are permitted in case of public safety and order (to prevent public disorder), but not for national security reasons. Limitations may be imposed only to protect "fundamental freedoms" of others.

"A state whose public policy is atheism, for example, cannot invoke Article 18 (3) to suppress manifestations of religion or beliefs," according to one legal authority.[181] Nor can a state whose public policy is one religion use Article 18 (3) to justify the suppression of other religions.

In 1981 the General Assembly proclaimed the Declaration on the Elimination of All Forms of Intolerance and of Discrimination Based on Religion or Belief. Article 2 provides:

> (1) No one shall be subject to discrimination by any State, institution, group of persons, or person on the grounds of religion or other belief.
> (2) For the purposes of the present Declaration, the expression "intolerance and discrimination based on religion or belief" means any distinction, exclusion, restriction or preference based on religion or belief and having as its purpose or as its effect nullification or impairment of the recognition, enjoyment or exercise of human rights and fundamental freedoms on an equal basis.

The declaration lists a number of religious freedoms, including the right to maintain charitable or humanitarian institutions, to acquire materials related to religious rights, to issue publications, to teach, to solicit financial contributions, to

---

[179]Ibid., p. 211.

[180]ICCPR, Article 18 (3): "Freedom to manifest one's religion or beliefs may be subject only to such limitations as are prescribed by law and are necessary to protect public safety, order, health, or morals or the fundamental rights and freedoms of others."

[181]Partsch, "Freedom of Conscience and Expression," p. 213.

train leaders, to observe holidays, and to communicate with others regarding religion, at the national and international levels.[182]

Christians

Christian churches have been subjected to government intrusion into the organization of their religious affairs. Christian priests have been arrested on specious charges, and church leaders have been denied their right to freedom of movement. Church-state relations are at a very low ebb.

Historically successive governments both during and since colonial times interfered with and regulated the activities of religions in Sudan by dividing the country into exclusive zones of influence — with the south set aside for Christian missionaries and off limits to Islamic proselytization and public worship. Christian missionaries were forbidden any activities in the rest of the country.[183]

Since independence, there have been enormous population shifts, with millions of southerners fleeing drought, war and famine from their homes in central and southern Sudan to the cities of the north, particularly in the 1980s and 1990s. Many internal migrants — southerners — banded together and formed Christian churches throughout the north; they arrived a few years later than the several hundred thousand drought victims from western Sudan — mostly Muslims — whose path they followed into urban shantytowns. In the Three Towns (Khartoum, Khartoum North and Omdurman) slums, the dispossessed southerners built their homes as well as their own small churches/community centers of cardboard, mud and other inexpensive materials.

After the 1989 coup, the NIF came to power with an Islamist agenda, openly determined to transform Sudan from a multi religious society into an Islamic state. This pressure to Islamize (and Arabize) may have contributed to southern migrants' increasing adherence to Christianity.[184]

---

[182]Article 6 of the Declaration defines the right to freedom of thought, conscience, religion or belief to include, *inter alia*, the following:

    b. To establish and maintain appropriate charitable or humanitarian institutions;

    d. To write, issue and disseminate relevant publications in these areas;

    f. To solicit and receive voluntary financial and other contributions from individuals and institutions;

    I. To establish and maintain communications with individuals and communities in matters of religion and belief at the national and international levels.

[183]Alier, *Southern Sudan*, p. 17.

[184]Christianity has been embraced or re-embraced by southern migrants to the north because of the role played by the churches in the integration of the migrants to urban life

(continued...)

In October 1994, the government sponsored a Muslim-Christian Religious Dialogue Conference which a representative of the Vatican addressed.[185] As a concession to this forum, President (Lt. Gen.) Omar Hassan al Bashir announced that the Missionary Societies Act of 1962 would be repealed. This law, introduced by a previous military regime, was used to expel all foreign Christian missionaries from the country in 1964. One consequence of the law was the accelerated indigenization of the Christian churches in Sudan.[186]

After this conference, the government began meetings with various churches on an irregular basis in order to improve communications. Those in attendance for the government at meetings with the Catholic church included a representative of Sudan Security (on behalf of the ministry of interior), a representative of the ministry of social planning's office in charge of church personnel, a representative of the ministry of interior responsible for exit visas and other travel permits, and a representative of the Council for International People's Friendship.[187]

Most church leaders feel the dialogue is not going anywhere. One pointed to symbolic actions that are cost-free but deliberately neglected. For instance, the Kordofan governor and other officials were invited but failed to appear at the consecration of the bishop of El Obeid, Mons. Antonio Menegato, held on March 3, 1996.[188]

Arrest of Church Leaders

The government has claimed to have exposed particular priests or church leaders as rebel sympathizers and thus confirmed its suspicions that the churches

---

[184](...continued)
(material assistance, education, and continuing contacts with the village of origin and ethnic group), and the war and the reactions it engenders. Northern society is seen as aggressive and segregative. Roland Marchal, "La 'vernacularisation' de christianisme," *Sudan: History, identity, ideology*, pp. 189-90.

[185]The Vatican's representative, Cardinal Francis Arinze, a Nigerian who heads the department of dialogue among religions, called on the Sudanese to promote dialogue at home; the conference was attended by 500 people, of whom 150 were from outside Sudan. Alfred Taban, "Sudan Holds Inter-religious Dialogue," Reuter, Khartoum, October 8, 1994.

[186]The Missionary Societies Act was an attempt to regulate, by means of a system of licences, the activities of missionary society. Two prominent historians described it as "a crude device to allow unlimited interference with missionaries." P.M. Holt and M.W. Daly, *A History of the Sudan*, 4th ed. (New York: Longman, 1988), p. 179.

[187]Human Rights Watch/Africa telephone interview, New York, March 1996.
[188]Ibid.

and their followers are a "fifth column" in the Islamic state. On January 16, 1996 the government in a filmed ceremony released a Catholic priest, Fr. Mark Lotede, and a Catholic school student, Simon Peter; at the ceremony the priest, detained in Juba, "admitted" that he had been involved in sabotage plans. This ceremony took place in the presence of government officials from Sudan Security and the ministry for social planning involved in church affairs, and the papal nuncio and other Catholic officials summoned there for that purpose.

Shortly after the priest and student were released, the Vatican accused Sudan Security of torturing the priest into confessing, and of torturing a student into testifying against the priest. The papal nuncio, Amb. Archbishop Erwin Josef Ender, wrote a scathing letter to the government after witnessing the event, and rejected all statements made there by the two men as the product of torture.[189] "I was revolted by the lying and violent spectacle," the nuncio wrote. He also protested the fact that he and the other Catholic officials were brought to the ministry under false pretenses, saying he would never have attended if he had known they were going to stage such a televised spectacle.

Fr. Mark Lotede, of the Toposa tribe originating around Kapoeta in Eastern Equatoria, southern Sudan, had worked actively since 1991 against the government policy of abducting Toposa children and interning them in a camp at Qariat-Hanan where they were exposed to forced Islamization.[190] According to Catholic church sources, some of the children were sent abroad to Libya and Saudi Arabia, some were sent to work on farms, and others were given military training and sent to the front. Fr. Lotede, a teacher at St. Mary's Minor Seminary in Juba, assisted the Toposa children who escaped from the camp and helped some register in the church schools in Juba; others tried to return to their Toposa villages outside Kapoeta.[191]

The government detained and interrogated Fr. Lotede several times about his work with the Toposa children. He was detained on December 27, 1995 in Juba. Simon Peter, a Toposa youth who had recently graduated from the Comboni secondary school in Khartoum where he had lived since 1989, was detained at the

---

[189]Letter, Archbishop Erwin Josef Enter, ambassador from the Vatican, to S. Mohamed Osman al Khalifa, minister of social planning, Khartoum, January 25, 1996. This letter with a cover letter of the same date was circulated to the diplomatic corps in Khartoum.

[190]This practice is discussed in Human Rights Watch/Africa, *Children of Sudan*, pp. 14-15.

[191]Confidential communication to Human Rights Watch/Africa, March 1996.

Juba airport on December 26, 1995. Both were released at the televised ceremony on January 16, 1996.[192]

Fr. Romeo Todo, a Catholic priest from the Didinga tribe of Eastern Equatoria and teacher at the Comboni College in Khartoum, was arrested on January 5, 1996 at the college in Khartoum and released January 14. He is chaplain to the Young Christian Students in the Archdiocese of Khartoum. He was reportedly questioned with regard to the activities of those just detained in Juba. The church attempted to mediate and secure the release of the two priests, daily inquiring in many fora about their whereabouts, but failed to learn anything until the ceremony.[193] The government had an agreement with the Catholic church that no clergy would be arrested without first referring the case to the archbishop, but it did not follow the agreement, and the church did not learn of the allegations against the two priests until their release.

On January 16, the nuncio and Archbishop Gabriel Zubeir Wako of Khartoum were summoned by the ministry of social planning to come to its office to witness the freeing of Fr. Mark Lotede; the nuncio was specifically assured that there would be no television cameras present. Upon arrival, they saw that a television camera was filming all the events. In addition, the detained clerics were not turned over to the nuncio immediately, but the Catholic prelates, accompanied by the secretary general of the Sudan Council of Churches, Mons. John Dingi, were required to witness the clearly rehearsed "confessions" of the student Simon Peter and Fr. Lotede, while M. Abdin, from Sudan Security in Juba, sat in the corner to monitor events. Dr. Mustafa O. Isma'il, of the government-sponsored Council for International People's Friendship, also attended.

At the ceremony, the government charged that Fr. Lotede was planning to blow up security installations in the town of Juba, where he was based, and had set up an organization, including several politicians, to send students to SPLA-controlled Narus to the southeast of Juba.[194]

In the letter to the diplomatic corps in Khartoum, the nuncio stated that the student Simon Peter and Fr. Mark Lotede had been physically and psychologically tortured and their lives threatened by security to force them to make false statements, and that they denied to him that they had ever done what they confessed to. The nuncio firmly asserted that all the confessions made there were

---

[192]Ibid.

[193]"Vatican: Sudan Holds Three Catholic Clerics, Vatican Says," Reuter, Vatican City, January 11, 1996.

[194]Jeffrey Donovan, "Vatican accuses Sudan of torturing priest," Reuter, Vatican City, February 3, 1996.

"completely false" and did not correspond to the facts, that the whole story and its details were "pure inventions."[195]

According to information available to Human Rights Watch, Fr. Mark Lotede was tortured for three hours on the day of his arrest by Sudan Security in Juba and accused of being the "obstacle to and enemy of Islamization among the Toposa people."[196] His physical torture came to an end after a senior Sudan Security officer intervened and stopped it. According to Fr. Lotede's statement to church authorities, intense interrogation and psychological torture continued for eight days: he was told that the Toposa youth in detention would continue to be tortured and would eventually be executed if he did not accept as true the allegations against him. He could hear the cries of these youth under torture almost every night from his cell. Once he gave in to this enormous pressure, to save their lives, he was taken to a judge to plead guilty, but he was not given any opportunity to plead innocent or explain himself. He was threatened with death if he did not follow the script: the security officer who had tortured him put a pistol to Fr. Lotede's head to press this point home.

According to the accounts given to the church, Simon Peter and three other Toposa youth were detained together by Sudan Security in Juba. The four were accused of being rebels and tortured, and one was subjected to electric shocks. They were told their family members would be killed (some of the family members were even identified by name) if they did not admit to the allegations against them and Fr. Lotede. They were rehearsed with a script full of accusations against Fr. Lotede for nine days, and beaten when they deviated from it. The four were taken to the judge at the same time as Fr. Lotede and their false testimonies were videotaped and tape recorded. On January 13, 1996, Simon Peter and Fr. Lotede were flown to Khartoum.

Two weeks after the releases, Sudan Security began to search for the student Simon Peter, harassing his home in Khartoum and detaining a neighborhood girl for thirteen hours for questioning about him. The family temporarily left their home to avoid constant security visits at odd hours of the night. The papal nuncio wrote twice to the government on Simon's behalf, to no effect.[197]

---

[195]Letter, Archbishop Enter to S. Osman al Khalifa, January 25, 1996.
[196]Confidential communication to Human Rights Watch/Africa, March 1996.
[197]Ibid.

The Attempt to Register Churches as "Voluntary Societies"

In October 1994, at a government-sponsored religious dialogue conference, President al Bashir announced that the Missionary Societies Act of 1962 would be repealed. While welcoming the nascent dialogue, leaders of the indigenous Church voiced their concern for the use of religion in the war in southern Sudan, complained about the lack of religious freedoms and called for equality between Muslims and Christians.

The repeal of the Missionary Societies Act did not lead to churches finally receiving the equality under law they sought with the followers of Islam. The president instead decreed and signed new legislation in late 1994 (Provisional Order of October 4, 1994)[198] to regulate church affairs, which would have treated churches not as spiritual institutions of heavenly origin but as foreign nongovernmental organizations which must be registered with a state official, who would have the power to terminate their existence.[199] There was such resistance to the Provisional Order that it has not been enforced. No other legislation has been proposed in its place.

The Episcopal and Catholic churches responded in writing to the Provisional Order, the Catholic church condemning it as "the most comprehensive, thorough and far-reaching attempt to control (and potentially to terminate) the life and activity of the Church."[200] The Episcopal church found the Provisional Order "repugnant and irrelevant to the evangelistic mission of the church."[201]

Unlike Article 22 of the ICCPR on free association and Article 21 on peaceable assembly, Article 18 on freedom of religion is a nonderogable right — meaning it cannot be suspended even in time of war or other extreme emergency — and its limitations clause is more circumscribed than are the limitations clauses of Article 22 or 21. Therefore limits on nonreligious organizations that might be permissible under Article 22 or Article 21, such as restrictions for reasons of national security, are not applicable to religious organizations under Article 18.

The Provisional Order the government wanted to apply to the churches, however, would

---

[198]Under the 1994 procedure for legislation in Sudan, decrees are issued by the president and must be confirmed or amended by the Transitional National Assembly within two months in order to become law.

[199]Sudan Catholic Bishops' Conference, "The Miscellaneous Amendment;" Province of Episcopal Church of Sudan, Khartoum, "Provisional Order: Miscellaneous Amendment (Organisation of Voluntary Societies) Act 1994," February 2, 1995.

[200]Sudan Catholic Bishops' Conference, "The Miscellaneous Amendment," p. 2.

[201]Province of Episcopal Church, "Provisional Order," p. 1.

have amended the Alien Voluntary Work in the Sudan (Organization) Act of 1988, which regulates — tightly — the affairs of foreign nonprofit organizations. The Provisional Order would add to the definition of organization covered by the Alien Voluntary Work Act "any foreign voluntary organization whose purpose is to carry out work the nature of which is . . . religious."[202] In the past few years the number of international nongovernment nonprofit relief and development organizations have been subjected to increasingly tight restrictions by the ministry of social planning and others on their charitable activities in Sudan, to the point where many found government interference made their presence untenable, and terminated operations in the country.[203]

At the same time, the Provisional Order would have amended another law, the Societies Registration Act of 1957, which applied to national nongovernment organizations, and extended its coverage to religious organizations.[204] Prior to the Provisional Order, religious work was not covered by the Alien Voluntary Work Act or the Societies Registration Act.

The Catholic church rejected the definition of the Church as a purely human society and organization, and therefore considered that the Provisional Order did not apply to the Catholic church.[205] The Provisional Order would have required all churches existing before October 1994 to apply for registration to the Commissioner of Social Planning within sixty days,[206] according to the Episcopal Church of Sudan. It would have required each new congregation of existing churches to register as new and separate churches. That commissioner would have the power to accept or reject the application, forwarding it to the minister of social planning for approval of the rejection or registration on fulfilment of conditions.

---

[202]Provisional Order: The Miscellaneous Amendment (Organization of Voluntary Work) Act 1994, Article 2.2, signed by President (Lt. Gen.) Omar Hassan Ahmed al Bashir, October 4, 1994.

[203]Only twenty-three international relief agencies were registered by the government in 1990, a decided diminution from the mid-1980s when eighty-two were registered. J. Millard Burr and Robert O. Collins, *Requiem for the Sudan: War, Drought, and Disaster Relief on the Nile* (Boulder, Colo.: Westview Press, 1995), p. 276. Western agencies attempting to work in Khartoum were shunned by government agencies and indigenous Islamic aid agencies, according to the authors. The situation has deteriorated greatly in this respect since 1990. Ibid.

[204]Provisional Order of October 4, 1994, Article 2.1.2.

[205]Sudan Catholic Bishops' Conference, "The Miscellaneous Amendment," p. 2.

[206]Neither the Catholic nor the Episcopal Churches has ever been required to register with any government agency before, although various charitable activities are regulated by the government. Province of Episcopal Church, "Provisional Order," p. 7.

If the conditions were not fulfilled by the church within ninety days, it was to cease to function, and its assets disposed of in liquidation.[207]

The requirements for churches under the Provisional Order appear to be identical to what would be required for an ordinary foreign nonprofit corporation: submit an annual statement of accounts to the minister, hold annual meetings, file a membership list, elect officers as set forth in its by-laws, and so forth. This would not be limited to the relief and development programs of churches, but extended to them as entire spiritual institutions, according to the Episcopal Church.[208] The minister would have the power to cancel a registration if a church contravened the provisions of the act. He could cancel a registration if a church's total membership was less than thirty.[209] Although this order does not appear to have been enforced, churches are unsure of its status, and of theirs.

Church Construction and Demolition

The government has defended itself against charges of forced Islamization by pointing to the proliferation of churches in Khartoum State, with "more than 500 new churches by February 1993."[210] While there may have been 500 new churches (or congregations of existing churches) in Khartoum by February 1993, a number we cannot verify, their status was ambiguous at best. There were no church buildings for worship built with any official permission because their sponsors concluded that requests to build churches would be denied; no permission to build a church has been issued for decades, according to many church and other sources. Instead, many churches rent or share a pre-existing location.

The government denies it has destroyed places of worship.[211] If churches are built or located in "unauthorised" areas where their parishioners are, then the churches will be demolished along with all other structures when the bulldozers arrive.[212] Many churches structures have been so demolished. Human Rights Watch visited the site of a recent demolition in one of the vast shantytowns of Omdurman on May 30, 1995, and saw one church (used also as a school and community center) of mud that had recently been bulldozed; its front door was all that

---

[207]Ibid., p. 2.

[208]Ibid., pp. 3-4.

[209]Ibid.

[210]"The Response of the Government of the Sudan," November 21, 1995, p. 23, para. 85.

[211]Ibid., p. 23, para. 86.

[212]Many Christians live in the vast slum and shantytown areas of Greater Khartoum, and have few or no rights according to draconian government urban planning schemes. (See below)

remained standing. In another area of Omdurman, the shantytown parishioners were dismantling a modest church structure they had built, trying to salvage what they could, before government demolition.[213]

The situation is only slightly better in officially approved transit camps for the displaced and the peace villages for the displaced, who have been moved to these locations by the government that bulldozes their shantytown homes and churches. Whereas no permissions are forthcoming in the large "unauthorised settlement" areas, government officials will sometimes issue permits for temporary structures in the official transit camps for the displaced; these camps, however, are not designed to be permanent. Families relocated to these transit camps have no right to stay there and are subject to relocation whenever the government wants. Apparently in peace villages, where there is a right of tenure, the government may issue a permit for a multi-purpose center, which will then be used as a church and for other neighborhood activities. These are not permits for churches per se and the buildings may not have religious symbols on the outside, although inside such symbols are permitted.

Churches not only conduct religious services. They also try to provide social services for the poor. These efforts are viewed with extreme suspicion by government officials, who attempt to obstruct these activities in a variety of ways. These activities are religious practices falling within the freedom set forth in Article 18 (1) of the ICCPR, the "freedom, either individually or in community with others and in public or private, to manifest his religion or belief in worship, observance, practice and teaching," and spelled out in more detail in the Declaration on the Elimination of All Forms of Intolerance and of Discrimination Based on Religion or Belief, Article 6, specifying that freedom of religion includes the right to maintain charitable or humanitarian institutions, to acquire materials related to religious rights, to teach, to train leaders, and other activities.

Churches attempt to provide services to the very poor displaced families who live in these transit camps and peace villages. Often the communities want schools for their children.

---

[213]A recent report by a Catholic group claimed government troops destroyed two villages in the Nuba Mountains of central Sudan and bombed and desecrated a church on March 24, 1996. "Church Says Sudan Army Uproots 1,000 Families," Reuter, Nairobi, Kenya, April 16, 1996. The Sudan government denied the allegations on April 24,1996 in a statement issued by its embassy in Nairobi, Kenya.

Church Schools and Teaching of Religion in Government Schools

The government's claim that "the teaching of Christianity in government schools in the north has, for the first time, been made available by the current government so as to give equal rights to the Christian minority,"[214] is not accurate. Teaching Christianity to Christians in government schools in the north has been part of the education curriculum since before independence (1956).[215]

To graduate from secondary schools, students must pass a religion examination. The Christians must take an examination about Christianity and the Muslims about Islam. Those who practice traditional African religions, however, are not examined on their religion or any other. Instead, the government has issued a simplified paper on Islam for them, and they are required to do little more than sign their names in Arabic. Christian clergy believe that these students are registered as Muslims rather than as believers in any traditional African religion.

Christian churches must provide teachers on Christianity to the government schools. These teachers must be certified by the government to teach a subject in addition to Christianity, and the language of instruction must be Arabic. For many Christians, especially those brought up in the south, Arabic is not their native language. The difficulty of mastering Arabic has meant that there has been a lack of qualified teachers for Christian instruction in the government schools. The Catholic church started a teacher training college to meet these requirements, including Arabic-language instruction, with a four year program and 130-150 students. The first class is to graduate in April 1996, but the government still has not certified this school as a teacher training school.

Christian students are at a disadvantage in the educational system because of the shortage of teachers in Christianity. In some classes, there are few Christian students and the church makes an effort to bring them to a church on Fridays and Sundays and group them together with others scattered in other schools for instruction. Religion is not an optional subject; it is mandatory so that the Christians who do not receive adequate instruction will not graduate. This system also leaves no alternative for those who have another belief.

The government maintains that "the religious tolerance of the Government has resulted in the availability of a large number of very prestigious

---

[214]Ibid., p. 23, para. 84.

[215]This section is based on conversations with clergy inside and outside Sudan, several of whom have worked in educational institutions as teachers and administrators.

church-run schools in Khartoum and other towns."[216] While churches are permitted to run church schools, most are not "prestigious" schools. The prestigious church-run schools, with high academic standards, admit many Muslim children whose parents resisted a 1994 government decree requiring all private schools to use Arabic as the language of instruction.[217]

The need for basic instruction (reading, writing and mathematics) is most keen at lower levels. According to those who worked in the Dar Es Salaam transit camp for the displaced, most of the Christian children there, who are of southern origin, do not go to the government schools because of government-sponsored Islamization through the schools, despite the formal provision for classes in Christianity. They say there is strong pressure on the children to study the Qur'an and pressure on the girls to wear Islamic women's dress. Much depends on the person in charge of the school.[218] Another barrier for displaced children at government schools, according to a recent study, is language. Many of the children do not know Arabic well enough (or at all) to participate in government schools, where the ministry of education insists on the use of Arabic as the language of instruction in basic education.[219]

Christian churches have sponsored schools in the transit camps, but not enough to fill the gap. For many reasons, only 25 percent of school-aged children are enrolled in any school in the displaced transit camps, according to the same survey. In government schools, among the displaced schoolchildren, the enrollment of girls is half that of boys, and the teacher-student ration is 1:47.[220]

One church-run school was registered with the government as a temporary structure in Dar Es Salaam transit camp. Its Christian sponsors applied to the government for permission to build a permanent and larger (sixteen-room) structure. The popular committee,[221] whose approval was necessary, placed

---

[216]Ibid., p. 23, para. 84. In 1957, a year after independence, the government nationalized all missionary schools in the south while allowing private schools in the north, including Christian missionary schools, to continue. Deng, *War of Visions*, p. 138.

[217]Human Rights Watch/Africa interview, New York, March 1996.

[218]Human Rights Watch/Africa interview, Khartoum, May 21, 1995; telephone interview, New York, April 1996.

[219]Ushari Ahmad Mahmud and Muhammad Zaayid Baraka, "Basic Education for Internally Displaced Children," International Consultative Forum on Education for All, Country Case Studies: Sudan, Khartoum, November 1995, pp.19-21.

[220]Ibid., p. 18.

[221]Dar Es Salaam has thirty-three blocks and each has its own popular committee. For a description of the role of the popular committees in house destruction and forced relocation,

(continued...)

obstacles in the way of this improvement, complaining that the Christian leaders were "against Muslims" (although the school employed five Muslim teachers and ten Christians). The permission for a permanent structure was not issued, to the knowledge of Human Rights Watch. Church sources say that Dawa Islamiya, an Islamic NGO, has established many schools in these camps, and has easily secured the necessary government permits to do so.

Sometimes local officials give way in the face of protest, however, but permission to build schools is never easy nor routine for churches. In another block of Dar Es Salaam, where permission for a church school had been granted, two Muslim families reportedly complained to the popular committee which in turn told the church it could not build the school. In this case, however, Christian families complained that they had rights, too, and the popular committee withdrew its objections to the school. The ministry of education said that the church could continue with its activities with the proviso that no foreigners be allowed to do anything with the church except for prayers. This was apparently aimed at a foreign-born priest working in the area.[222]

In several disputes about the right to run schools in other blocks, the government ordered the church sponsors to close schools in Dar Es Salaam transit camp twice in the months between February and May 1995, on the grounds that the schools were not used properly. One school in question admittedly was used also for religious and community services, meetings and adult education, because the government would not give permission to build a church there.

On Palm Sunday of 1995 some 1,000 people attended mass held at this school. One of the priests was summoned to the popular committee soon afterward. Two police, two security officials and eleven popular committee members met with him and ordered him to close the school. A religious discussion ensued about the duty to provide food and housing for all people (the church maintains it distributes these to all regardless of religion). The church declined to close the school.[223]

Government efforts to confiscate food churches' relief arms used for school children and to incorporate the teachers from the Christian-run schools into government schools were started in 1994 and abandoned in 1995 for lack of government funding. A brief period of official recognition of the Christian

---

[221](...continued)
see Chapter VII, Internally Displaced and Squatters.
    [222]Human Rights Watch/Africa interview, Khartoum, May 21, 1995.
    [223]Ibid.

shantytown schools ensued, followed by destruction of the shantytowns and refusal of permission to build schools in some transit camps.[224]

Religion in Prisons

In an effort directed at prisoner rehabilitation through conversion to Islam, the Law for the Organization of Prisoners and Treatment of Inmates of 1992, Section 5, Article 25, provides for the early release of prison inmates who memorize the Qur'an. A religious commission convened by the administrator of prisons in consultation with the ministry of religious endowment (which oversees religious affairs) tests the prisoners and recommends those who pass for early release. No comparable legislation has been passed based on religious instruction other than in Islam, providing a powerful inducement to non-Muslim prisoners to abandon their religion. In a custodial environment, such programs place the weight of the state so firmly in favor of conversion to Islam that it is coercive, in violation of Article 18 (2) of the ICCPR that no one shall be subject to coercion which would impair his or her freedom to have a religion or belief of his or her own choice. Furthermore, this release program discriminates against those who cannot read or speak Arabic, in violation of Article 26 of the ICCPR in that it does not provide alternatives to the many prisoners, particularly women, not conversant in Arabic.

At Omdurman Prison for Women, the women's branch of *Shabab Al Wattan* (Organization of the Youth of the Homeland, an NIF mass organization) runs a program of spiritual orientation and social rehabilitation of women prisoners. Rehabilitation is provided in the formal instruction in Islam, although the vast majority of inmates are of southern and non-Muslim origin. Christian clergy ministering to prisoners however, report that they are left free to hold services and teach church doctrine in prisons.[225] In Kober Prison there is a church building.

Muslims

Not only does the government interfere with or deny the religious freedoms of non-Muslims, it also clamps down on Muslim groups it considers as too critical or ideologically out of line with its policies. Relations between the National Islamic Front, which controls the government, and various Islamic religious sects and groups have not always been smooth. Some imams (prayer leaders), who accede to this position through a consensus of community members, occasionally voice criticism of the government. Their religious obligation of advising their flock on worldly affairs, as well as on spiritual matters, leads some

---

[224]Ibid.
[225]Human Rights Watch/Africa interview, telephone, New York, April 25, 1996.

to criticize the performance of the rulers — for instance, over the high cost of living and the deterioration of public services. Other imams discuss issues of doctrine on which they disagree with government policies, such as the justification for jihad in south, and the question of whether this is a true or genuine Islamic government.

The response of the government to this criticism and challenge of legitimacy has been two-pronged. Where the opposition to the government is a matter of principle and doctrine, the government has unleashed its repressive forces against rebellious groups and imams. Groups so targeted are the Ansar, the Muslim Brothers and the conservative Ansar al Sunna. These groups have critical attitudes towards the government, from outright opposition to selective independent-minded criticism, with an occasional show of support.

The Ansar religious sect led by the Mahdi family constitutes the popular base of the Umma Party, which like all other political parties has been banned since the current government seized power in 1989. A council of religious scholars and dignitaries, the Council for Ansar Affairs (*Hai'at Shi'oun al Ansar*) oversees the affairs of the sect and the community of followers, while an executive committee runs the affairs of the party. Ex-Prime Minister Sadiq al Mahdi, who heads the Umma Party, lives in Sudan and advocates an attitude of "civil opposition" by peaceful means, although his Umma Party is a member of the National Democratic Alliance, the umbrella group of (exiled) opposition political parties and armed groups.

The government took control of the holiest shrine of the Ansar order, the Omdurman religious complex of the tomb of Mohamed Ahmed al Mahdi, on May 22, 1993,[226] and has not returned it to date. It appointed an imam to lead the prayers there, and said the move was dictated by the need to preserve the national character of the shrine, which it claimed was threatened by the way the Ansar used it. The Ansar moved their communal prayers and other community activities to the smaller Wad Noubawi mosque.

Sadiq al Mahdi has been detained several times, often following homilies critical of the government, delivered as prayer leader of the Ansar at the occasion of Al Eid religious festivities. The crackdown on the Ansar in May of 1995 involved his detention and the detentions of other prominent Ansar leaders, such as Imam Abdalla Barakat and Faki Abdalla Ishag, the leader of the cluster of Qur'anic schools attached to Wad Noubawi mosque. Elderly Ansar patriarchs who

---

[226]Lawyers Committee for Human Rights, *Critique: Review of the U.S. Department of State's Country Reports on Human Rights Practices, 1993* (New York: Lawyers Committee for Human Rights, 1994), p. 347.

submitted a memorandum of protest against the May 1995 detention of Sadiq al Mahdi were themselves detained in turn.[227] Another frequent detainee is Mohamed al Mahdi, the main imam of Wad Noubawi mosque, a well-respected religious leader. One of his favorite themes is religious justice and tolerance, against which he regularly measures government practices. The security apparatus detains him — just as regularly— for up to several months at a time for critical opinions expressed in sermons.[228] Such detentions of religious leaders for their opinions, spiritual or political, constitute a serious violation of their freedoms of religion and expression.

Ansar al Sunna is a religious group that advocates the strict interpretation of Islam, stripped of all the manifestations of what it considers popular Islam, such as sufism. Its simple version of Islam is akin to that of the Wahabi, the influential and dominant religious doctrine in Saudi Arabia. The Sudanese Ansar al Sunna has maintained a longstanding friendship with the Saudis and has been the recipient of substantial Saudi funds solicited to sponsor the spread of Islam in Sudan and neighboring African countries. Ansar al Sunna channeled these resources into the construction of nearly 400 mosques in Sudan alone, and into the sustenance of other traditional charitable and educational Islamic works, such as Islamic schools and orphanages.

Ansar al Sunna traditionally did not have a significant political profile in Sudan, but vehemently opposed the NIF on doctrinal grounds, a rivalry that has been regularly reflected in reciprocal verbal and written attacks in mosques and newspapers. For instance, Ansar al Sunna challenges the official government policy that considers war in southern Sudan a jihad, a holy war. They argue that for it to qualify as such, the war should have as sole objective the total submission of all southerners to Islam. They also dispute the Islamic credentials of the government, citing such government practices as the recruitment of women in the official PDF militia as evidence of a conduct contrary to Islamic teachings.[229]

Perhaps as a result of this rivalry, the government undertook, in mid-1993, a systematic campaign of intimidation and harassment designed to lead to the replacement of imams in mosques that Ansar al Sunna controlled. Communities in the neighborhoods of Al Thawra and Al Sahafa in Khartoum defied weeks of intimidation as truck-loads of riot police parked in front of their Ansar al Sunna

---

[227]Human Rights Watch/Africa interview, New York, March 1996.
[228]Ibid.
[229]Ibid.

mosques during successive Friday prayers to intimidate them into accepting government-appointed imams.[230]

During one phase of this campaign, security agents made a night visit to the house of the imam of the main Ansar al Sunna mosque, Shams El Din, in the populous neighborhood of the Seventh Quarter of Al Thawra. They threatened him with arrest if he did not leave his position. He replied that it was up to the community of worshipers to choose their imam. Around the same period, they kidnaped and beat up his mu'azzin, who calls the faithful to prayer. The government managed to remove the imam from his position but his followers in the neighborhood boycotted prayers called by the new government-installed imam. The government ultimately abandoned its campaign.[231]

On Friday February 4, 1994, three armed men, one Yemeni and two Sudanese, machine-gunned worshipers while they were conducting the communal prayer at the main Ansar al Sunna Mosque in Al Thawra. The leader of this Ansar al Sunna congregation, Sheikh Abu Zeid, who usually leads the prayer, was by chance not there. Followers of Ansar al Sunna and ordinary people praying there that day suffered a terrible loss in what was widely believed to be a failed assassination attempt: sixteen were killed, including children, and nineteen others were seriously injured.[232]

The attackers escaped unharmed but were captured by security forces the next day, ostensibly while seeking to enter or take refuge in the residence of Ussama Ben Lauden, a Saudi dissident deprived of his Saudi citizenship, who is a backer of the Sudan government and resides in Khartoum.[233] The two Sudanese were killed and the Yemeni seriously injured.[234]

This tragedy remains unexplained. A very speedy trial was held for the surviving gunman and an accomplice who was alleged to have participated in the preparations but did not take part in the attacks. The court found the alleged ring leader guilty, and condemned him to death. He was executed on September 19, 1994.[235]

The Muslim Brotherhood, another small religious group that focuses on doctrinal issues, breaking away from the NIF in repudiation of what it considered the NIF's political and other worldly pursuits, also has been targeted. Two or three

---

[230]Lawyers Committee for Human Rights, *1993 Critique*, p. 347.
[231]Human Rights Watch/Africa interview, New York, March 1996.
[232]Report from Khartoum, March 4, 1994.
[233]See Scott Macleod, "The Paladin of Jihad," *Time Magazine* (New York), May 6, 1996.
[234]Human Rights Watch/Africa interview, New York, March 1996.
[235]See Chapter V.

outspoken leaders of the group lead the Friday prayer in their main stronghold, the al Sababi mosque in Khartoum North. Security agents monitor this event on a regular basis. They have summoned Professor Al Hibir Youssif Nour Al Dai'eim, one of the leaders of the group, several times to appear in their offices for days at length, a form of harassment amounting to detention when prolonged.[236]

The second prong of the government's response to Islamic criticism is to implement a systematic program to bring all prayer leaders under one broad umbrella, an association of imams, and coordinate their weekly Friday sermons. Attendance of Friday mid-day prayer, a religious duty for Muslims, is the occasion for prayer leaders to deliver their homilies to an attentive and well-disposed public. Members of the public at the same time may deliver their own sermons or comment on worldly affairs to their fellow worshipers. The association is intended to coordinate the themes of the weekly sermons, so that one voice would be heard in all mosques. The government-controlled radio and television then carry this concerted message to the population through well-prepared but obviously selective coverage.[237]

RIGHT TO MOVEMENT

The right to freedom of internal movement within Sudan has been severely restricted, with the southern region placed off limits to many, including southerners living in the north whose families are in the south — particularly southerners who were politically active in the period of multiparty government. Outside the south, restrictions are also in force on movement for certain categories of people: former security detainees never charged with or convicted of any crime have been required to sign written undertakings agreeing to limitations on their residence and sometimes not to travel outside a designated city. Travel abroad is also closely controlled by means of exit visas.

Those intending to attend conferences abroad are subject to particular scrutiny and sometimes stopped even after receiving an exit visa. In other cases security has interrogated those returning from conferences or trips abroad for hours and required them to return periodically to security.

Dr. Ushari Mahmud, linguist, former lecturer at the University of Khartoum, and coauthor of a 1987 report on slavery in Sudan, has been banned from travel outside Khartoum for seven years, and his requests for exit visas

---

[236]Human Rights Watch/Africa interview, New York, March, 1996.
[237]Ibid.

ignored. In February 1996, the minister of the interior reportedly lifted the travel ban but it remains to be seen whether he will be permitted to leave Sudan.

Citizens and foreigners working in relief or development agencies, including the U.N., are subjected to very strict limitations on movement to and inside southern towns, and thus on the work they can do there. Movement to areas such as the Nuba Mountains is tightly controlled on the limited occasions it is permitted, making relief or development programs there out of the question, except in government-controlled garrison towns.

The Applicable Law

Article 12 of the International Covenant on Civil and Political Rights establishes freedom of movement as a fundamental human right, essential for the effective enjoyment of other human rights:

> 1. Everyone lawfully within the territory of a State shall, within that territory, have the right to liberty of movement and freedom to choose his residence.
> 2. Everyone shall be free to leave any country, including his own.
> 3. The above-mentioned rights shall not be subject to any restrictions except those which are provided by law, are necessary to protect national security, public order (*ordre public*), public health or morals or the rights and freedoms of others, and are consistent with the other rights recognized in the present Covenant.
> 4. No one shall be arbitrarily deprived of the right to enter his own country.

Article 12 of the African Charter protects this right in similar terms, as does Article 13 of the Universal Declaration of Human Rights.

Restrictions on freedom of movement are permissible under Article 12 (3) of the ICCPR only to protect one of the enumerated state interests and must be "provided by law." This phrase "provided by law" was used, in the words of one legal authority, "to insure that the source of a restriction is a general rule, usually announced by the legislative branch. It excludes bureaucratic caprice and administrative fiat . . . unless authorized by law and necessary for the execution of the law."[238] The same source adds that requirements apply to limitations on freedom of movement within the country. The establishment of internal security zones "cannot be used to restrict access to substantial parts of a state's territory."[239]

Restrictions mentioned in Article 12 (3) of the ICCPR refer to certain legitimate state interests. The same legal authority notes that national security was included to allow a state to protect itself from "evident and vital" political or military threats to the whole nation. "The drafters were concerned primarily with control over military personnel and the security of military installations" and they did not consider it legitimate for a state to curtail departure from a country for reasons of "security," even if an individual had been involved in activities involving work with information or projects under government secrecy rules.[240]

Political opinions are not legitimate grounds on which to deny individuals the right to leave. This scholar observes that "the fact that an individual may criticize the government while he is abroad does not pose the kind of threat to the security of his country which its government is entitled to prevent."[241] Article 12 (3) prohibits restrictions on freedom of movement that are inconsistent with other rights recognized in the ICCPR, which include the right to freedom of thought (Article 18) and freedom of expression (Article 19). Similarly, restrictions on movement based on sex also are prohibited by the nondiscrimination provisions of Article 26 of the ICCPR. Thus a woman's right to travel may not be restricted on the grounds of her sex, such as by imposing upon her restrictions for spousal or paternal approval that are not imposed upon men.

Restrictions on freedom of movement of persons who have been held in administrative detention and then released, that is, persons who have never been formally charged with a crime and never convicted or acquitted, do not bear any relation to a legitimate state interest under Article 12 (3). Those persons remain citizens and are entitled to the same human rights as other citizens; they have done no wrong in the eyes of the law.

Nor may the state achieve the same objective of restriction of freedom of movement by requiring detainees to sign an "agreement" not to leave the city or country as a condition of release. Such an agreement is not voluntary and amounts to a punishment without due process.

---

[238]Stig Jagerskiold, "Freedom of Movement," in *The International Bill of Rights*, pp.172-73.

[239]Ibid., p. 174.

[240]Ibid., p. 172.

[241]Ibid., p. 178.

Travel Bans on ex-Security Detainees

Since the coup on June 30, 1989, thousands of political party, trade union and professional association, student and other leaders and activists, civil servants and military soldiers and officers have been detained by security without court order, warrant or charges, usually incommunicado. Persons in administrative (or preventive) detention of this kind are usually released after days, weeks, or months (although some remain in custody for up to two years), without charges ever being brought against them. Many have been detained more than once. Although never convicted of any crime, most were nevertheless further punished upon release by the denial of their right to movement and travel for varying periods.

Released security detainees are usually required to undertake — in a form presented for signature before release — to reside where directed, not to leave Khartoum without the prior approval of security, and not to travel outside Sudan. They are required to give full details of their residence and in some cases are even told not to change residences without approval of security. Under the 1991 Criminal Act, Article 101, "Contravention of residence order," it is a crime for someone ordered to reside in a certain district to move, punishable with six months' imprisonment, fine, or both. Release thus is conditional on willingness to surrender the right of movement and other rights in exchange for freedom from arbitrary detention.

Enforcement of restrictions on ex-detainees' travel outside Khartoum to other areas within Sudan was coordinated by the Higher Committee on Security and Operations, under the Joint Operations Board, Command of the Central Military Zone, Sudan Armed Forces. Ex-detainees have been required to apply to the Central Military Zone, near the headquarters of the army in Khartoum, where both the higher committee and the joint operations board were housed. The request for a permit to travel to another Sudanese town is made there, and a written permission is issued, to be signed and stamped by the local police upon arrival and departure. The ex-detainee must returned to the Central Military Zone upon arrival back in Khartoum. One former security detainee, who received a permit to make a short trip to a town outside Khartoum in 1991, failed to report back to the Central Military Zone when he returned to Khartoum, and was detained for several days as a result.[242]

The Travel Ban Imposed on Human Rights Activist Dr. Ushari Mahmud

Two successive governments have imposed a travel ban on Dr. Ushari Ahmad Mahmud for his human rights work on slavery in Sudan, in violation of the

---

[242]Human Rights Watch/Africa interview, New York, March 1996.

right of free expression and the right to movement, and in reprisal for his activities on behalf of others. On several occasions the government informally offered to lift the travel ban or release him from jail (where he spent twenty-two months without charges) if he would repudiate his writing on human rights violations and slavery. They refused him exit visas and he was unable to travel outside Khartoum.

When Dr. Mahmud applied in February 1996 for an exit visa to attend a conference in South Africa on the education of displaced children, to which the U.N. invited him, not only was the exit visa denied, but the ministry of the interior confiscated his passport. Mahmud appealed by letter to several public figures and the minister of the interior informed him in writing on February 26, 1996, that the travel ban had been lifted completely. Putting this to the test, however, was not immediately possible, as it apparently came too late for him to attend the conference.

According to the letter Mahmud wrote to seek removal of the travel ban, it dates from his participation in the preparation and publication of a human rights report, *Al Diein Massacre: Slavery in Sudan* (Khartoum, 1987, in Arabic), which exposed a massacre in which more than 1,000 Dinkas, including women and children, were killed, and ongoing enslavement raids by the Rizeigat Arab tribesmen against the Dinkas. The report called for an investigation of the massacre and of the practice of slavery in Southern Darfur.

He was detained after publication of the report, interrogated by security and released two days later. The democratically-elected government of Sadiq al Mahdi banned him from travel abroad and after the report became the focus of international attention again arrested him and held him for nineteen days. During that time he was extensively and almost exclusively interrogated about the human rights report. They dropped charges that he was heading a secret organization intending to undermine the democratic system and released him.

While in detention he received an envoy from the minister of the interior who told him they would lift the travel ban if he published an article stating that the information on slavery in his 1987 report was inaccurate, according to Mahmud's 1996 letter. He refused and the ban continued in effect.

A military coup in June 1989 overthrew the democratic government and Mahmud was detained a week later, along with hundreds of political activists. The new government sent an envoy, the minister of finance, to Mahmud while he was in detention in Kober Prison and told Mahmud that they would release him immediately if he would repudiate the 1987 slavery report. He refused, was transferred to a prison with harsher conditions in western Sudan, and was held for twenty-two months in detention without charges, until the government announced an amnesty for all political detainees. Upon release he continued to be banned from travel. While he was still in detention in December 1990, Human Rights Watch honored him with a Human Rights Monitor's Award for his work.

Internal Movement

Historically the British prohibited most movement between north and south claiming this was to protect southerners from northern influences and potential abuses.[243] Because of the war, movement between north and south is now officially controlled for security reasons, but there has been tremendous migration to the north by southerners from border areas where there is fighting and raiding. Northerners friendly to the government have no problem traveling to and conducting business in southern towns, despite tight controls on others' movement.

Most garrison towns are accessible only by air and the permission of Sudan Security and military intelligence must be obtained before the ticket can be purchased or other arrangements made. Most garrison towns are accessible only by chartered flights by relief agencies and others. Only Juba had daily cargo flights in 1995, and to fly on such planes the additional permission of Civil Aviation (not a security agency) is required.

Sudanese who fly to Juba — the only way to arrive for at least the past decade, since White Nile river travel is subjected to attack and looting and land travel is subjected to rebel attack and land mines — have remarked that they feel like they are in a foreign land. They are questioned at the airport by Sudan Security and required to give names, residence, ethnic affiliation, reasons for visiting Juba, who is to be visited, and other information usually required upon entry into a foreign country.[244]

Some southern political leaders now in the north, including several who are from Juba, have not been permitted by Sudan Security and/or military intelligence to visit Juba or other southern garrison towns for several years.[245]

Even Sudanese living in Juba must have clearance and a permit each time they cross the Juba bridge over the White Nile some five miles to the east of the city, even if they are originally from the area or if they go to the area regularly on business. Permission is not always granted.

In order for citizens resident in Juba to leave Juba on a plane, they must be cleared by three agencies: Sudan Security, military intelligence, and the police.

---

[243]See Chapter V, The Law and the North-South Divide.
[244]Human Rights Watch/Africa interview, Khartoum, June 9, 1995.
[245]Human Rights Watch/Africa interview, Khartoum, May 15, 1995.

They must pay an exit fee of Ls. 5,000 (U.S.$9.46),[246] the funds ostensibly to be used to keep Juba clean. At military intelligence headquarters before going to the airport, the identity card is examined and name and number registered. Upon return, the same procedure is followed.[247]

In fact all areas affected by the civil conflict, and not only the south, are kept under the tight control of military intelligence and other security agencies. Many parts of the Nuba Mountains and Southern Blue Nile State are, for example, under emergency laws which restrict the movement of civilians. In Southern Blue Nile State, a resident spoke out in a 1992 public meeting in the village of Chali al Fil, attended by the state minister of finance. The man asked for minimum basic services for the Uduk inhabitants, who he said suffered from decades of government neglect. Military intelligence immediately detained him, held him ten days, and transferred him to Damazien, the state capital. After interrogations at security in Damazien, they banned him from returning to his village. A "travel permit" for him to return to his village was issued by the director of General Security in Damazien, dated in November 1992, as follows: "The named [man] is hereby authorized to travel from Damazien to Kurmuk to Chali for a two-month period only, for the purpose of harvesting his field there, from November 22, 1992 to January 22, 1993, and to return thereafter. Please do not stop him."[248]

Access to most of the Nuba Mountains is routinely denied to travelers and relief and development agencies alike — at least to those who are not government supporters or Islamist agencies. From time to time, in response to public criticism, the government organizes show visits to Kadugli or Dilling, the two largest towns. Even on those visits there is no freedom of movement, especially outside these garrison towns. For instance, after a human rights organization issued a report on abuses in the Nuba Mountains in July 1995,[249] the government organized a whirlwind trip to a few Nuba towns by Western diplomats accredited to Khartoum, but under controlled conditions that made independent investigation impossible, according to a participant.[250]

The night curfew in Khartoum was lifted in December 1993 in favor of a checkpoint system. Those traveling after midnight are stopped for identification checks at sensitive locations such as bridges and public buildings. These

---

[246]At the time, Ls. 528 = U.S. $1. The minimum monthly wage was Ls. 6,000.

[247]Human Rights Watch/Africa interview, Khartoum, June 9, 1995.

[248]Travel permit, Damazien, November 22, 1992.

[249]African Rights, *Facing Genocide: The Nuba of Sudan* (London: African Rights, July 1995).

[250]Human Rights Watch/Africa interview, New York, September 1995.

checkpoints are guarded by army soldiers and security agents. Checkpoints are also maintained at the entry to displaced persons camps and squatter areas. Many arbitrary killings have been reported at such checkpoints, but only a few have led to prosecutions.

Human Rights Watch's and Other Foreigners' Experience in Juba and Other Garrison Towns

Although the government of Sudan agreed to permit Human Rights Watch to conduct interviews in private and without notice to the government, and although they respected this condition of our visit in Khartoum, Sudan Security refused to permit this in Juba. This was despite promises made at higher levels, and despite the three required permissions in writing obtained in Khartoum for the visit. The visit from June 4 to June 7, 1995, was managed by Sudan Security at every turn. Its personnel did not permit the Human Rights Watch researcher to speak privately to anyone, including the Roman Catholic Archbishop of Juba, Paolino Lukudu Loro, nor to stay in the location of her choice (the U.N. compound). Instead she was forced to stay at a government hotel (the Juba Hotel, now renamed the El Salaam Hotel), was constantly accompanied by security personnel, and when she protested they terminated her visit and escorted her to the airport. Civilian government officials in Juba who initially consented to her request for private interviews and her choice of lodgings reversed themselves after security intervened. The planned visit to government-controlled "peace villages" to interview victims of SPLA abuses was canceled.

Protests to higher authorities brought apologies and assurances that it was not "government policy" to prevent free movement in Juba. Nevertheless, other foreigners have experienced similar restrictions in Juba since the end of 1994.

Foreigners who wish to visit garrison towns in the south from Khartoum must obtain the permission of military intelligence, Sudan Security, and the Alien Registration department of the Ministry of the Interior. In June 1995, foreigners had to register with Sudan Security upon arrival at the Juba airport. There a security officer informed them that they may not go anywhere without an escort from security, and that security must approve all meetings with anyone in Juba, whether government officials or private individuals. Security then sends agents openly to attend those meetings; if the agents do not speak the same language as the rest of the meeting participants, then the proceedings must be simultaneously translated for them. In the case of the Human Rights Watch mission, two security agents even attended the meeting that we tried to have with a church official even though we asked the security agents politely to leave the meeting.[251] This was the experience of all nongovernmental representatives of agencies not aligned with the government visiting Juba for at least the six months before June 1995, and we have received word that the situation is even tighter since then.

Foreigners working in Juba need clearance and a permit to go even five miles outside Juba, although government representatives in Juba in June 1995 were proclaiming that the government controlled areas up to 120 miles from Juba and this area was pacified and secure.[252] The few non-Islamic foreign agencies working in Juba must be accompanied by Sudan Security or military intelligence when they go outside the city on relief business. There are no cross-line relief operations conducted out of Juba. Relief to SPLA-controlled areas around Juba was conducted from Kenya by air, and from Uganda, overland, when the security situation in Uganda permitted; from November 1995 to March 1996 the Sudan government has imposed an exclusion zone on all locations south of the lines of Kapoeta, Torit and Juba, and Juba, Yei and Kaya, not permitting any flights in at all.[253] Although Juba receives a substantial amount of food relief, none of it is delivered across the lines. It arrives by air or on the Nile from the north, in barges that pass through SPLA-held areas and whose clearance from all parties must be negotiated well in advance. (See Chapter VIII).

Foreign clergy have not been permitted to visit Juba at all since 1993. The reason given is their security. Foreign clergy are permitted to visit some other southern garrison towns, such as Wau.[254]

When we asked the Juba authorities for the reasons they so tightly restricted foreigners (they did not allow Human Rights Watch even to visit the market, for instance), Governor (*Wali*) Agnes Lukudu replied, "You are free to move about. There are security protections for your sake, however." When we asked why they should be necessary, Governor Lukudu said, "People are very frank. They will talk to you even if security is present. We want to avoid injury to

---

[251]Human Rights Watch/Africa interview, Juba, June 5, with Archbishop Paolino Lukudu Loro and two security agents. It is not the practice of Human Rights Watch to conduct interviews of private individuals in the presence of government agents, so this interview was limited to a request to the security agent to leave and a description by Human Rights Watch of the conditions and purpose of its mission.

[252]Since an SPLA offensive in October-November 1995, the government has lost control of some of that territory.

[253]OLS (Southern Sector) Update, 9 January 1996, Nairobi, Kenya, p. 1.

[254]Human Rights Watch/Africa interview, telephone, New York, April 25, 1996.

you, our guests. The people say, 'The whites are supporting the war, we don't want to see whites.'"[255]

This explanation is inherently incredible and is unfair to the people of Juba. Personal safety of foreigners does not explain why security, before letting them board the plane, has strip-searched foreigners and read the notes of foreigners on assessment missions, nor why at the time of our visit no foreign (non-Islamic) NGOs in Juba were permitted to possess radio communications equipment commonly used in such relief locations, nor why even the UNDP radio could not be used unless security read and approved the message before it was transmitted.

We were unable to learn why our visit was so tightly circumscribed and then aborted. We were told, however, of violent attacks on Juba residents by soldiers in the week before the visit, which those familiar with Juba said were rather typical. According to reports, both of the cases involved romantic disputes.[256] In both cases, the soldier accused of killing a romantic rival was arrested and released after a short time, and reportedly transferred out of Juba upon release to protect him from the relatives of the deceased.[257] Human Rights Watch was not able to verify these accounts.

Government representatives in Khartoum assured Human Rights Watch that it was not the policy of the government to restrict our visit to Juba. Despite the presentation of our multiple written travel permits, the problem was characterized as a failure of communications with Sudan Security between Juba and Khartoum.

Restrictions on Travel Abroad

The right of movement, specifically the right to leave one's country — even on a short-term basis — guaranteed in Article 12 (2) of the ICCPR, may be denied without due process by the ministry of the interior. Citizens leaving the country must secure an exit visa from the ministry of the interior, which maintains an official list of those who have been banned from travel abroad. This is administered by a division within the ministry called Lists (*Al Gou'im*). Those on the list have been banned by court order or at the discretion of the minister of interior.

---

[255]Human Rights Watch/Africa interview, Agnes Lukudu, Juba, Sudan, June 6, 1995.

[256] In one case, we were informed that a young man was stabbed in his home near the army barracks in Atlabara by soldiers on the pretext that he had "stolen the girlfriend" of a soldier. The second case was of a young man reportedly shot dead at 5:00 p.m. in front of his family while sitting outside their home in the Kator section, also by a soldier who accused him of stealing his girlfriend.

[257]Human Rights Watch/Africa interview, Khartoum, June, 1995.

Foreign residents of Sudan must obtain an exit and reentry visa from the Alien Registration section of the ministry of interior if they wish to return. Some such visas, requested in advance, have been delayed past the date of planned vacations or conferences in the past, although practice reportedly has improved in 1996.[258]

Even if one's name does not appear on the Ministry of the interior's list, the right to leave the country may be defeated by a bureaucratic maze composed of many different security and other administrative agencies which may maintain separate lists or impose travel restrictions on certain categories of persons. Even if a petitioner is able to secure an exit visa from the ministry, he or she may find that his or her name is on another list; Sudan Security has its own list, a seemingly uncoordinated list of people banned from travel. Usually there is no notice that the person's name has been entered on any list, no reason given for any travel ban, and no procedure or criteria for removing a name from any travel ban list. Agencies and ministers are not even required to respond to a request to lift a travel ban or issue a visa. They may simply ignore such requests, neither granting nor denying them.

In October 1995, for example, the exit visa application of opposition leader Sadiq al Mahdi was ignored. Former Prime Minister al Mahdi was invited by the German government to attend a conference on "Islam and the Arabs" in November 1995 but was unable to attend because he received no reply to his request for an exit visa.[259]

There are special restrictions imposed on categories of persons such as doctors and university lecturers. Doctors may not secure an exit visa from the ministry of interior unless they secure permission in writing from the under secretary of the ministry of health, permission rarely granted even for vacations and conferences abroad. University lecturers must secure permission from the ministry of higher education even for short trips abroad.

Even if one succeeds in penetrating the seemingly chaotic bureaucracies and receives an exit visa, actual departure is never certain until the plane lifts off the ground or the border has been crossed. In some cases, travelers with exit visas have boarded a plane with other passengers, only to have security enter the plane at the last moment and force the passenger to disembark and miss the flight.

Once the traveler is abroad, he or she is faced with further bureaucratic obstacles that may be used to deny the right to movement. Sudanese passports have

---

[258]Human Rights Watch/Africa interview, New York, April 25, 1996.

[259]"Sudan reportedly 'ignoring' opposition leader's exit visa application," MENA, Cairo, Egypt, in Arabic 1420 gmt, October 12, 1995, quoted in BBC Monitoring Service: Middle East, October 14, 1995.

a ten-year life but a two-year validity. Sudanese expatriates must return to their embassy to submit the passport and pay renewal fees and additional taxes every two years. If the passport holder is a government critic, the two-year renewal period may be used to withhold the passport in punishment.

Attendance at Conferences Abroad

Those who have sought to travel abroad for short visits for business or other reasons, such as medical treatment, have sometimes come under suspicion. The questions put to travelers on their return by security suggest that the government fears that they might have exercised their freedom of expression and complained about the government.

According to the Comboni Missionary Order in Rome, Archbishop Paolino Lukudu Loro of Juba was prevented from boarding a flight in Khartoum as he was leaving for a beatification ceremony and visit to Rome on February 18, 1996. He has long been considered an opponent of the government. After he reached the airport he was refused permission to board: it was explained that he could not leave unless he had a "special permit" from security. He had been granted such a permit, he said, which had been submitted to the airport authorities the day before his departure, but they said they could not find it. He was forced to change plans to leave on that flight and stay in Sudan to secure a further "special permit." He was able to leave on February 22, after his travel problems were reported abroad.[260]

Human Rights Watch was told of the case of Episcopalian Church Bishop Renk Daniel Deng, who was leading a delegation of four church representatives to a meeting of the All African Council of Churches in Nairobi, Kenya in June 1995. He was then to travel to Ethiopia and Uganda to visit church leaders living in refugee camps in those countries. Although he was granted an exit visa, passed through immigration and customs, and boarded the plane with the rest of the passengers, Sudan Security entered the plane and took him off, thus canceling his trip. Sudan Security gave no reason for its actions at the time.[261]

Sudan Security has detained and questioned others who subsequently have been permitted to attend conferences abroad. Security has permitted some to continue, and canceled trips of others who had earlier received exit visas.

Some returning from attending conferences abroad have also been subjected to detention at the airport and held there and at other security locations

---

[260]"Missionary order says bishop detained in Sudan," Reuter, Rome, Italy, February 18, 1996; Human Rights Watch/Africa telephone interview, February 28, 1996.

[261]Human Rights Watch/Africa interview, Khartoum, June 9, 1995.

for from twenty-four to forty-eight hours, while being questioned about the conference. Since most international flights arrive in Khartoum in predawn hours, this questioning comes at a time when the traveler is already suffering from sleep disruption. One traveler told us that waiting at the security office at the airport was the order of the day for the first eight hours after deplaning, which was followed by a trip, with luggage, to security headquarters where security agents posed questions such as, "Are you an agent of the U.S.? Why were you fired [in 1990] from your job? You must be against the government. Maybe you're in the Communist Party." They asked specific questions about current employment and colleagues, the purpose of the trip and who else was at the conference. They then ordered the returning traveler to report to security offices in Khartoum North the next day. What followed was the routine of reporting daily to security offices and being forced to wait there daily, a common form of harassment. [262]

Women

The ministry of interior requires women to have the permission of a male relative, a "guardian," to travel abroad. This puts women with no husband, father, brother or son in a difficult position. Death, divorce, and migration abroad have reduced numbers of male family members available to be a "guardian" for a woman's travel. We learned of one case in which a girl aged fourteen traveled to visit her father abroad — accompanied by her nine-year-old brother, which they noted in her passport. Her mother, an employed and educated woman, was not permitted to sign permission for her daughter to travel, but the nine-year-old brother was.[263]

Other women report that, even in Sudan embassies abroad, they will not receive a passport or a passport renewal unless their heads are covered in the passport photograph they present. Some women whose heads are not covered in accord with the dress code have been prevented from boarding the plane in Khartoum.

STUDENTS' FREEDOM OF ASSOCIATION AND EXPRESSION RIGHTS AND POLICE CONDUCT

Student Demonstrations in September 1995

The largest anti-government demonstrations since the army and NIF seized power six years before occurred in September 1995, in response to the arrest

---

[262]Human Rights Watch/Africa interview, Khartoum, June 1, 1995.
[263]Ibid.

of three University of Khartoum students early that month.[264] Up to thirty demonstrators were killed and at least seventeen wounded, and many hundreds were beaten and detained without charges.

Crowd control does not appear, from press reports, to have been conducted in compliance with United Nations guidelines on use of force and firearms by law enforcement officers. In particular, the principle that "intentional lethal use of firearms may only be made when strictly unavoidable in order to protect life"[265] does not seem to have been followed. There was no claim that lives were in danger from the student demonstrations and attacks on property. Reportedly demonstrators smashed cars, motorcycles, and the windows of banks. Sudanese security forces used live ammunition on the first and second days of the demonstration to disperse the demonstrators, along with tear gas.[266] Even in the dispersal of illegal violent assemblies, law enforcement officials may use firearms only "when less dangerous means are not practicable and only to the minimum extent necessary."[267]

The government also called on armed NIF security forces and NIF youth militias, neither of which are properly constituted public forces, to assist the police and security forces. On September 13, 1995, two days after the demonstrations moved to the streets, government radio summoned Youth of the Homeland (*Shabab El Wattan*) and Defense of the Faith and the Homeland Organization (*Hei'at El Diffa'a An El Aghida Wa El Wattan*) to mobilize and "undertake the necessary steps to repulse the aggression directed at Sudan," referring to the anti-government demonstrations.[268] Where the government urges such militias to make war on their opponents on the pretext of "law enforcement," it is inviting disorder.

Human Rights Watch received reports that as many as 700 heavily armed men in civilian clothes, believed to be from the security apparatus of the National Islamic Front brought in from outside Khartoum, participated in "crowd control" by dispersing groups of pedestrians, guarding road blocks, checking identities, searching cars, and detaining people. One source described them as "very young,

---

[264]The three were Muhayyad al Siddiq (Faculty of Engineering); Murtada Abdal Raazig (Faculty of Architecture), and Majdulin Haj al Taahir (Faculty of Agriculture).

[265]U.N. Basic Principles on the Use of Force, Article 9.

[266]"Sudan: Egyptian Agency Reports Continuing Demonstrations in Khartoum," MENA news agency, Cairo, in Arabic, 1355 gmt, 1540 gmt, and 1618 gmt, September 11, 1995, quoted in BBC World Monitoring Service: Middle East, September 13, 1995.

[267]U.N. Basic Principles on the Use of Force, Article 14.

[268]*Al Asharq al Awsat,* September 14, 1995 (in Arabic).

very violent and very well-trained crack troops."[269] They were seen on the streets of Khartoum for the first time on Tuesday, September 12, a few days after the start of the demonstrations, wearing civilian clothes and carrying automatic handguns and sticks, transported into town in new Toyota minitrucks and Land cruisers. They guarded roadblocks to isolate residential areas and towns from each other, and were seen firing at crowds to disperse them. But they were not enough. On September 13, government-controlled radio called on two NIF mass organizations to mobilize and protect the government. Violent clashes between groups of students and others followed in two universities.

NIF party structures parallel to the police and army are most evident in the context of anti-government demonstrations: their use to suppress such protests reflects an awareness of the role of demonstrations in bringing down Sudanese dictatorships in 1964 and 1985. The regular police who generally conduct themselves within the law, are not entirely trusted to repress such movements by the government; nor is the army. Unlike the police and army, however, there is no hint of public accountability for members of the NIF's parallel structures, which is especially dangerous given the fervor with which NIF militants defend their cause.

The police, NIF militias and security forces gained the upper hand over the unarmed crowds. At a rally held a week after the threat to the NIF government passed, President Omar Hassan al Bashir told tens of thousands of followers, "Whoever wants to replace this government should take up arms to confront us." Culture and Information Minister Abdel Basit Sabadrat told the crowd, "The leaders of this [National Salvation] revolution will never go to prisons. Rather they will go to their graves."[270]

When the demonstrations were over, according to the government, at least three demonstrators had been killed,[271] or thirty, according to government

---

[269]Confidential communication to Human Rights Watch/Africa.

[270]Alfred Taban, "Sudan's Leader Tells Opponents to Stand Up and Fight," Reuter, Khartoum, Sudan, September 21, 1995.

[271]According to government sources quoted in the Arabic-language daily newspaper *Al Sharq al Awsat* (Cairo) of September 14 and 15, 1995, the dead were Faiz Mohamed Ali (martial arts instructor), Immad Mohamed El Amin (student, faculty of Science, University of Khartoum), and Mohamed El Tayeb Ahmed (student, University of Qur'an). Two died of bullet wounds and the third of a wound caused by a sharp instrument, according to *Asharq al Awsat* of September 14, 1995 (in Arabic). The government named Faiz Mohamed Ali as a tae kwon do (martial arts) instructor and said he had nothing to do with the university. It gave no explanation for his presence. Alfred Taban, "Sudan: Fresh Clashes
(continued...)

opponents.[272] Some of the dead were said to be street boys (*shammasa*, or "sun" boys), targeted by security and distinguishable because they are young, poorly dressed, mostly southerners. No security members or other government personnel were reported dead.[273]

At least seventeen were wounded, some with bullets[274] and at least two had their arms deliberately broken by security forces.[275] Once in detention, some reported rape, others reported beatings with black plastic pipes, thick electric cords, or whips, and burning with lit cigarette butts. The nongovernment sources estimate that groups of several hundred students and others were detained without charges; most were released after several days in incommunicado detention.[276]

The public protests began with a silent demonstration by twenty students at Khartoum University on September 9, 1995, a Saturday, the first day of the work week in Sudan, lining up along a street running through the campus and displaying banners calling for the release of three students detained a week before.[277] The

---

[271](...continued)
Around Khartoum Campus," Reuter, Khartoum, September 14, 1995.

[272]The Sudan Human Rights Organisation reported five dead: Abd al Rahman al Amin Abu al Hasan (student, High Institute of Radiology, University of Khartoum), Musa Siddiq Musa (student, Faculty of Arts, Omdurman Islamic University), Suhair Mukhtar (female student reportedly died under torture; the security forces turned her body over to her family and claimed she had a heart attack), Muhammad Fadl al Mawla (resident of eastern Dyuum, Khartoum), and Faiz Muhammad Ali (the tae kwon do instructor), the latter being the only one also mentioned by the government in *Al Sharq al Awsat*. Sudan Human Rights Organisation, "The Human Rights Situation in the Sudan, July-December 1995" (London: 1996), p. 10.

[273]In one statement, however, the interior ministry said that one of the dead, whose name was not given, was an Islamist student. Alfred Taban, "Sudan: Two Killed in Second Day of Riots in Sudan," Reuter, Khartoum, September 12, 1995.

[274]Students wounded with bullets included Musa Ahmed El Bushra, Nagm El Din El Nour, Abbas Mustafa, Mohamed Abdalla, and female students Muna Abdel Rahman and Fatima Abdel Wahab, according to *Al Sharq al Awsat*, September 14, 1995 (in Arabic).

[275]Mut'az Abdel Muneim Khalifa and Mahdi Mohamed Ahmed (law student) were reportedly victims of this practice, as was another unnamed student.

[276]Human Rights Watch/Africa interview, New York, March 1996.

[277]Alfred Taban, "Sudan: Khartoum University Students Clash with Police," Reuter, Khartoum, September 11, 1995. Amnesty International later counted twenty-two arrested at a house in Omdurman on September 2, 1995. 1995. Amnesty International, "Sudan: Possible Prisoners of Conscience/Fear of Torture," UA 222/95, AI Index: AFR 54/33/95 (London: September, 18, 1995).

government claimed the detained — whose names and numbers it did not disclose — were Communist Party members.[278]

This protest followed a week of campus marches and sit-ins that students organized to pressure the university administration to intervene for the release of their colleagues. The vice chancellor reportedly told participants in a student demonstration that he was not responsible for students who violated state security laws and were arrested outside the university.[279]

As the different schools and faculties of the University of Khartoum joined in the campaign of protest, rumors apparently spread that a captured woman student, Majdulin Haj al Taahir, was badly tortured. Students from other universities, such as Sudan University for Science and Technology and Nilein University, staged demonstrations in the streets, trying to link up with the Khartoum University students. There were also demonstrations in Omdurman on Monday afternoon, September 11.

That day, about 3,000 students at Khartoum University clashed with the police and pro-government NIF students. The student on both sides reportedly used bricks, iron bars and other instruments in the fight.[280] According to news reports, police fired teargas and bullets to disperse thousands of students, who shouted slogans against President al Bashir and Dr. Hassan al Turabi. The demonstrators spread out from various universities in Khartoum into a nearby market. They attacked cars and motorcycles, targeted because Sudan Security is popularly believed to own most motorcycles in Khartoum. As the demonstrations grew and spread, demonstrators also shattered the windows of symbols of economic wealth — such as Islamic banks associated with NIF's leader Dr. Hassan al Turabi — in protest of the deteriorating living conditions and a recent rise in the price of bread. The demonstrators shouted, "October's coming back," referring to the overthrow of past military dictatorships by popular demonstrations.[281] Eyewitnesses also reported that students shouted slogans calling for unity "against the military and terrorism" and inviting Khartoum to "revolt against dictatorial rule."[282] Following the attacks on cars and the spread of tear gas clouds, the streets of central Khartoum

---

[278]Alfred Taban, "Sudan: Sudan Police Battle Second Day of Student Protests," Reuter, Khartoum, September 12, 1995.

[279]Human Rights Watch/Africa interview, New York, March 1996.

[280]Taban, "Khartoum University Students Clash with Police."

[281]Jonathan Wright, "Sudanese Military Rulers Get Dose of Protest," Reuter, Cairo, Egypt, September 13, 1995.

[282]Confidential communication to Human Rights Watch/Africa.

emptied and cars disappeared. Most residents had to walk home for lack of transport on September 11.[283]

State-run Radio Omdurman blamed the banned Communist Party for the violence, saying communist students incited bystanders to join in, according to Reuter. It said the party was planning "destructive acts" agreed at a meeting of Sudanese opposition figures and southern rebels in the Eritrean capital Asmara in June, and that the communist plans were a response to Bashir's decision to release all political detainees in Sudan.[284]

By the morning of Tuesday September 12 plainclothes security forces had cordoned off Khartoum University, preventing anyone from entering.[285] They erected checkpoints at crossroads and security forces backed by tanks stopped students from Omdurman from trying to cross the bridge over the White Nile, to enter Khartoum and join their colleagues there. Thousands of students continued their protests, shouting, "'No' to traders of religion" and "The people are hungry."[286] For the second day the security forces used teargas, and occasionally other more lethal crowd dispersal techniques, including driving a minitruck into the crowd at full speed.

The government admitted that two people, a student and another demonstrator, were killed on September 12 in the neighborhood of Abu Hamama in Khartoum.[287] In addition Abd al Rahman al Amin Abu al Hasan, twenty-four, was killed on September 12, according to his death certificate, shot at close range in the chest.[288] He was a known opponent of the NIF. When news of his death spread, students went to the hospital morgue for his body, but security refused to hand it over and used force to disperse the students, detaining some of them.[289]

On Wednesday, September 13, the third straight day of demonstrations, security forces and police broke up clashes between rival groups of students at the Sudan University for Science and Technology in Khartoum. "Witnesses said anti-government students tried to prevent others from attending classes but pro-

---

[283]Taban, "Khartoum University Students Clash with Police."
[284]Taban, "Sudan Police Battle Second Day of Student Protests."
[285]Taban, "Khartoum University Students Clash with Police."
[286]Taban, "Sudan Police Battle Second Day of Student Protests."
[287]Al Sharq al Awsat (Cairo), September 14, 1995 (in Arabic).
[288]SHRO, "The Situation of Human Rights in the Sudan, July-December 1995," p. 22.
[289]Ibid., pp. 10-11.

government Islamic students objected and resisted," according to a news agency.[290] By Wednesday night, the Council of Ministers had announced a decision that student movements "should be free" and that meetings with students should continue.[291]

Also on Wednesday, September 13, the government-run Radio Omdurman openly called on members of two different National Islamic Front mass organizations to mobilize against the demonstrators. Leaders of one, Youth of the Homeland, said they would "come forward to confront with strength and firmness all attempts to sabotage infrastructure and foreign conspiracies aimed at destabilizing Sudan."[292]

Security forces, riot police and members of the Popular Defense Forces stormed Ahliya University in Omdurman on September 13 following the participation of Ahliya students in demonstrations. Ahliya has a reputation as an independent liberal university and militant Islamists have been in the minority in student politics at Ahliya for years. The security forces beat up at least two staff members and scores of students. Student Samira Abbas Abd al Majid was reportedly tortured, resulting in a brain hemorrhage and a coma for two days; student Edward Yasin reportedly suffered serious fractures and was still in hospital at the end of October 1995.[293] Many were detained, including Yasin Abdel Wahaab Ibrahim (Laboratory Studies), Nur al Diin Ishaaq al Daawi (Environmental Studies), Hasim Awad al Hissein (Computer Studies), Hafiz Mukhtar (Environmental Studies) and Abdel Raziq Rahama (Business Administration). At least the latter two were reportedly severely tortured.[294]

The security agents also went on a rampage. They stormed a computer laboratory and reportedly destroyed twenty-seven computers, then ransacked the office and property of the Student Union. Photographs taken immediately after show the extent of the damage. The raiding party mounted waiting vehicles and toured the main streets of Omdurman in a motorized show of force, shouting religious slogans.[295]

On the morning of Thursday, September 14, security forces and others moved into the Khartoum campus of Sudan University for Science and Technology

---

[290]Alfred Taban, "Student Unrest Flares for Third Day in Sudanese Capital," Reuter, Khartoum, Sudan, September 14, 1995.

[291]Ibid.

[292]Ibid.

[293]SHRO, "The Situation of Human Rights in Sudan, July-December 1995," p. 10.

[294]Human Rights Watch/Africa interview, New York, March 1996.

[295]Ibid.

and arrested male and female students in lecture halls and dormitories which led to more violent clashes between the government forces and students. Reportedly, some 450 Science and Technology students were arrested. Following the mass detentions the situation quieted down.

On September 16, 1995, an Ahliya student was alleged to have torn a page out of the Qur'an and stepped on it, in front of other students. According to the government, the student was attacked by fellow students said to have witnessed the act, and was hospitalized.[296] In a September 16 leaflet, the Student Islamic Movement of Omdurman Ahliya University identified that student as Shihab Ali Youssif — although it has never been independently verified that the incident even happened. It accused other unnamed students of having smoked and chewed tobacco in the mosque. The authors of the leaflet declared their intention of fighting to the death to defend the faith and the motherland, using threatening language.[297]

Detentions Following Demonstrations, and Due Process

Under Sudan's system of "preventive detention," anyone can be held without charges, in incommunicado detention, for six months without any judicial supervision whatsoever. This is a violation of Article 9 (4) of the ICCPR. Torturing and beating detainees violates Article 7's prohibition on torture and cruel and inhuman treatment.

Human Rights Watch received reports from nongovernment sources that several hundred, and perhaps up to 2,000, were detained. They were all held without charges. Several hundred were held in the headquarters of Sudan Security in Khartoum, and reportedly hundreds more were held incommunicado in tents inside Kober Prison, where many were reportedly whipped. Some security agents reportedly promised individual students they would stop beating them if they would write down the names of ten other students who played a role in organizing the demonstrations.[298] After local and international protests, most detainees were

---

[296]Alfred Taban, "Sudan: Sudanese Television Shows Arrested Demonstrators," Reuter, Khartoum, September 19, 1995, quoting the newspaper *Akbar al Youm* that said police rushed the student to Omdurman hospital for treatment after he was attacked by his colleagues.

[297]"Criminal complaint lodged against university student who tore the Holy Qur'an," *Akhbar al Youm* (Khartoum), September 19, 1995, p. 1 (in Arabic).

[298]Human Rights Watch/Africa interview, New York, March 1996.

released after a few days, but the government reiterated its determination to try several.[299]

Several prominent advocates, including Mustafa Abdel Gadir, [300] Mohamed Ali al Sayid (also a member of the banned Democratic Unionist Party), and Bushra Abdel Karim,[301] were detained, reportedly in connection with the student protests, and were released without explanation a few days later.

Minister of Justice and Attorney General Abdel Aziz Shiddu, quoted by the government newspaper *Al Ingaz al Watani* on September 18, said that violent demonstrators would be tried within days, and compensation would be paid for property damage. Fifteen were charged with illegal assembly, use of force, resisting authorities, criminal opposition, attacks, and disturbing public peace, carrying sentences of up to five years in prison and twenty lashes, according to one press account.[302] The swiftness of expected trials and the possible punishment of lashing suggested that some of the accused would be tried in Public Order courts. Attorney General Shiddu also said security forces had seized knives, petrol bombs and leaflets from a Communist Party hideout.[303]

State television on September 18 showed some of the seventeen people who it said would be prosecuted for "plotting acts of sabotage and participating in these acts."[304] Some were shown being interrogated by uniformed police, and others simply stood facing the camera. At least one had a swollen face, apparently from beating. Several Ethiopians and Eritreans, said to have confessed to participating in the demonstrations, also were shown on television.[305] Charges were not, however, brought against most of these detainees.

Some eighteen persons detained in connection with the demonstrations were still being held in the security section of Kober Prison, and another at an unknown security location, two months after the incidents, still without having been charged with any crime. Most were eventually released. By early February 1996, three demonstration-related detainees remained in security detention (in the

---

[299]"Sudanese Rioters Face Trial within Days: Minister," Reuter, Khartoum, September 18, 1995.

[300]See Chapter V.

[301]Amnesty International, "Sudan: Prisoners of Conscience/Fear of Torture," UA 218/95, AI Index AFR 54/31/95 (London: September 15, 1995).

[302]"Sudanese Rioters Face Trial within Days," Reuter.

[303]Ibid.

[304]Taban, "Sudanese Television Shows Arrested Demonstrators."

[305]Ibid. Sudan's relations with its neighbors Eritrea and Ethiopia were already at a very low ebb, with charges and countercharges of interference in the internal affairs of each.

security section of Kober Prison): Awad Bashir, Adlaan Abdel Aziz,[306] and Al Sir Ossman Babu. They are all university graduates apparently considered by security to have been leaders of the student demonstrations.[307] Adlaan Abdel Aziz was released on April 25, 1996, and Al Sir Ossman Babu was still being detained.[308]

Influential religious and political leaders, as well as government supporters at rallies, called for the punishment for apostasy of Shihab Ali Yusif, the third-year student at Omdurman Ahliya University College in the Faculty of Environmental Studies, accused of having torn a page from the Qur'an. Apostasy, the repudiation by a Muslim of his faith in Islam, is punishable by death. The crime of apostasy, as defined in Article 126 of the Criminal Act of 1991, however, is subject to political manipulation. It also violates freedom of religion in Article 18 of the ICCPR.[309] It appears, however, that no charge of apostasy was brought against the student. Government-owned Sudan TV reported on September 18 that Shihab Ali Yusif and another student, Nader Bashir Youssif, were to face criminal charges of possession of a pistol and other (unspecified) fire arms. According to the independent daily *Akhbar al Youm* of September 19, a highly placed security source said that the authorities lodged a "criminal charge" against a student in Omdurman who tore a page from the Qur'an, and intended to try the student as soon as he recovered from injuries.

The vice chancellor of Ahliya University established a committee to investigate the allegations against Shihab Ali Yusif. The young man's family was not allowed to see him in detention and wrote a letter to the United Nations representative in Khartoum asking for his intervention. The family was unable to locate Shihab in a thorough search of the hospitals in the Three Towns although the local media reported that he was taken to a hospital after being beaten by witnesses.[310]

Apparently Shihab Ali Yusif was beaten so badly at the time of his detention and in security custody that he was in and out of different hospitals during the first few days of his detention. Reportedly he was detained with two colleagues on September 16, 1995, as they were leaving the university. They were

---

[306]Awad Bashir and Adlaan Abdel Aziz were among the twenty-two arrested in a security raid on a house in al Thawra, an Omdurman suburb, on September 2, 1995, which arrests sparked the student demonstrations. Amnesty International, "Sudan: Possible Prisoners of Conscience," September 18, 1995.

[307]Confidential communication to Human Rights Watch/Africa, February 1996.

[308]SOS-Torture, "Follow-up of Cases SDN 301095.1," May 3, 1996.

[309]Human Rights Watch/Africa, "In the Name of God," pp. 35-36.

[310]See SHRO, "The Situation of Human Rights in Sudan, July-December 1995," p. 11.

thrown into a vehicle by security agents, who started beating them while they were driven to security offices in Omdurman. At those offices, Shihab was blindfolded then tortured by security agents, who suspended him from a tree and beat him, causing him to black out more than once. He was reportedly beaten with sticks and thick plastic water pipes. He was taken to a security hospital in Khartoum North. Upon return from the hospital, he was reportedly beaten again and passed out again; he was taken to a different hospital. After three days of this rotation from hospital to ghost house to security offices, he was taken to another ghost house.[311]

The purpose of his torture was reportedly to pressure him to admit that he tore pages from the Qur'an, as other evidence of these acts was apparently lacking. He was interviewed by the prosecutor on the third day of detention. He reportedly told the prosecutor he wanted to make a statement about the torture he suffered, and bring charges against the torturers (three security officers whom he named), but he was rebuffed. Almost a month after his arrest, he was moved to the security section of Kober Prison in poor conditions, having only the floor to sleep on despite his injuries.[312]

Four months after his detention, Shihab Ali Yusif was called into the security office in Khartoum North and released on condition that he make certain undertakings: 1) to discontinue his studies at Ahliya University; 2) not to appear in public places (under the implied threat of liquidation by an extremist group which security named[313]); and 3) to agree not to participate in any form of opposition to the government, inside or outside Sudan. He was threatened that his father and brother could be arrested in his place (or worse) if he went underground or did not live up to these undertakings.[314]

Further Targeting of Ahliya University

The allegations against the Ahliya student accused of apostasy were just the tip of the iceberg of bad relations between the government and Ahliya University. Security forces again raided Ahliya on Saturday September 23 and

---

[311]SHRO (London), press release, "Torture of Shihab Ali Yusif," London, February 26, 1996.

[312]Ibid.

[313]This group was *al Takfir Wa al Higra* (Repudiation and Exodus). Ibid. According to Reuter, this group clashed with police in January 1996, leaving nine dead, including one policeman. "Sudanese Islamists Clash with Police, Nine Killed," Reuter, Cairo, January 2, 1996. The ministry of the interior said the group was trying to convert residents of a town one hundred kilometers south of Khartoum to Islam, and that it attacked the policemen.

[314]SHRO, press release, February 26, 1996.

brutalized a student named Abdel Hafiz Saad, according to the leftist Democratic Front *(Al Gabha al Demogratiya)*, an Ahliya University student political group. An Omdurman Hospital medical report of September 23 shows he was treated on that date for injuries, including a left leg broken in two places, a left arm broken at the elbow, and a broken left shoulder bone.[315]

Ahliya University, a private university, is on the government's hit list for a number of reasons. First, it failed to enforce the policy of Arabization of instruction which the ministry of higher education decreed mandatory throughout Sudan. Repeated direct pressures on the Ahliya vice chancellor and faculty failed to shake their commitment to their decision on this and other academic policy matters. Second, Ahliya University College employed lecturers purged from public sector universities. It received repeated warnings, which it disregarded, to stop this practice, to dismiss purged lecturers already in its service, and to dismiss others whom the authorities considered undesirable. A third point of tension was the liberal attitude of the university administration toward the issue of women's dress.[316]

The greatest issue of contention between the university and the government was the tolerance of a student movement that the authorities considered too rebellious. For instance, the university recognized the Democratic Front, a leftist student political group. The Student Union of Ahliya is controlled by an alliance of student political groups who identify with the opposition.

In a provisional order of August 15, 1995, signed by President al Bashir, the institution was renamed Ahliya University instead of Ahliya University College. Under this order, the minister of higher education has the power to appoint all sixty members of the board of trustees of Ahliya, and this body appoints the vice chancellor.[317]

On November 21 the minister of higher education in an official letter informed the board of trustees that he was appointing Abdel Wahab al Khalifa, ex-minister of interior, as chair of the board of trustees, and Yassin Omar al Imam, a founding member of the Islamist movement in Sudan, as his deputy. He also

---

[315]Human Rights Watch/Africa interview, New York, March 1996.

[316]Ibid. Women's dress is frequently a point of contention at universities. Minister of Higher Education Ibrahim Ahmed Omar announced in April 1996 that women who want to attend public or private universities in Sudan would be required by his ministry to wear Islamic head coverings. "Sudan May Mandate Student Garb," Associated Press, Khartoum, April 14, 1996.

[317]Provisional Order of August 15, 1995, section three, Article 8-1 and 8-2 and Article 18.

appointed Mohamed al Hassan Abu Shanab, a known NIF cadre, as deputy vice chancellor. A retired general was appointed director general of finance and administration, by-passing the existing director.[318]

Ahliya faculty members and administrators considered this to be direct intervention in the affairs of a private university and a step toward the liquidation of the university. They refused to cooperate and sent a memorandum of protest to the government-appointed officers.

Progovernment students began to disrupt classes at the end of November. For instance, a female faculty member had an altercation with some of her progovernment students who entered her class and ordered her to cover her head and to stop teaching. A few days later, a security officer reportedly made threatening remarks to her: "We will burn down Ahliya University and close it down."[319] The disruption of classes later seemed part of a NIF campaign to take over the student movement and to prepare for the complete takeover of the university by the government.

The clashes of September were renewed in late November with more violence. The trigger this time was the Third Cultural Week of the Ahliya University Student Union. It featured a public lecture by Abel Alier, a prominent southern leader, and Osman O. al Sharif, an ex-attorney general, on the prospects for a peaceful solution for the war in southern Sudan.[320]

This discussion was not to the liking of pro-NIF students. On the following day, November 26, they attacked the wall newspaper posted by the leftist Democratic Front, leading to violent confrontations between the two groups.

According to the vice chancellor, on Tuesday, November 28, 1995, "an unidentified group . . . broke into the university and attacked, without apparent reason, students, employees and some faculty members," causing some to be hospitalized. A group of university students joined the attacking group and started setting university property ablaze.[321]

On this day, non-NIF students were at the Student Union Activities Center, which had become a prime location for free expression, debate and criticism of the NIF interpretation of jihad, martyrdom and the war in the south.

---

[318]Human Rights Watch/Africa interview, New York, March 1996.

[319]Ibid.

[320]Abel Alier's remarks are reprinted in "Abel Alier Explains Self-Determination at a Student Rally in Khartoum," *Sudan Democratic Gazette* (London), February 1996, pp. 7-10.

[321]"The vice chancellor of Ahliya to Al Rai al Akhar: Freezing of Studies Occurred Due to Recent Disturbances: An unidentified group breaks into the University and Attacks Students," *Al Rai al Akhar* (Khartoum), December 3, 1995. p. 1 (in Arabic).

There was an exhibit of Sudanese arts and artifacts at the Activities Center, including rare manuscripts borrowed from the Sudan National Museum.[322]

According to eyewitnesses, three different groups of twenty-five NIF men each started parading in military fashion — a familiar sight — in front of the mosque one hundred meters from the Activities Center. Most were armed with four-foot iron bars and plastic and metal bicycle locks. They were believed to be NIF security and students from Ahliya, Khartoum, Sudan and other universities. Students watching thought it was just a show of force.

At about 12:30 p.m., the three NIF groups moved toward the Activities Center and encircled it. The anti-government speeches inside continued. A fourth NIF contingent surrounded the mosque, as guards.

Pandemonium broke out as a fire started in the Activities Center, the NIF men started to go after particular students, seemingly targeting them, and students began shouting and running to the university gates to escape. They were chased by NIF security and NIF students. Eyewitnesses reported violent scenes of street battles as riot police and security forces joined in the hunting of opposition students. Some students were beaten and roughed up by the NIF, especially women not wearing Islamic dress, whose uncovered hair was pulled. These women also were slapped and, if their skirts were considered short, the skirts were pulled down.

This reached a point where students confronted each other in quasi-military formations and brigades of various names, armed with sticks, bricks, iron bars, plastic pipes and, in the case of at least some of the pro-NIF students, as reported by eyewitnesses, firearms.

Dozens of students were seriously injured, and security forces arrested many others. One Christian student was hit in the face with a bicycle lock and hurt badly. Many students had blood on their faces and clothes.

Several cars pulled up outside the gates to pick up the wounded and take them to hospital. NIF men were at the gates of the university, inspecting cars that started to leave to escape the fighting. They searched the cars and the students leaving on foot.

The NIF contingent occupied the Activities Center and broadcast over the loudspeakers a statement that declared: 1) their occupation of the cafeteria for three days; 2) banning of all political activities of "Communist students;" 3) denial of entry to the university premises to all members of the Democratic Front; and 4) a proclamation of jihad.

The culmination was the destruction of many cultural artifacts on display at the Activities Center in the fire that the NIF groups apparently set as they entered

---

[322]Ibid.

the center. Fire trucks rushed to the scene were denied access to the campus. By the end of the day the art exhibit was in ruins. Following these confrontations, the university was ordered closed down until January 6, 1996.[323]

Background: The University of Khartoum

The student movement in Sudan, and other political movements as well, traditionally has been focused on the University of Khartoum. In what became known as the October Revolution, student rallies that voiced opposition to the government's war policy in southern Sudan triggered mass demonstrations and a civil disobedience campaign that brought down the military government of General Aboud in October 1964. The faculty lounge of Khartoum University became the prime meeting location for government opponents during the demonstrations that succeeded in toppling unelected President Nimeiri in 1985.

The University of Khartoum has played an important role in the political life of Sudan. Many of the country's political and intellectual leaders graduated from the University of Khartoum, at one time considered to be one of the best universities in Africa and the Middle East.[324] Graduates were in effect members of the small Sudanese elite. Although the student body was about 15,000, students who were politically active came to know each other, and to know those who were in the opposing camp. Years later, purges of secularists were based on their activities as students, and secularists identified many men in power after the 1989 coup as Islamists, based also on their student records.

The fate of independent student organizations after the coup in 1989 is a study in tactics used to undermine and destroy civil society and freedom of association of all independent organizations — that is, those organizations independent of the de facto ruling party, the National Islamic Front. Similar tactics have been used to destroy other independent nongovernmental organizations, such

---

[323]"Vice Chancellor of Ahliya to Al Rai al Akhbar," December 3, 1995.

[324]Since instruction was in English, and the native language of the majority of students was Arabic, most graduates were bilingual in two difficult tongues in addition to being taught by faculty selected according to high standards: at a minimum the staff had to have two higher degrees. A person with a masters degree would be only a teaching assistant. For the position of lecturer, a Ph.D. was required, as well as high grades (honors), according to one graduate. Human Rights Watch/Africa interview, Khartoum, June 7, 1995.

as the trade unions and the professional associations, with force employed where banning the organizations, detentions, manipulation and dirty tricks have failed. [325]

The National Islamic Front formed its own student organizations, recruiting many youth disillusioned with secular society and with political corruption and confusion under Nimeiri and during the multiparty interlude from 1986-89. They and rival student groups clashed both rhetorically and physically; one man now in power was said to have been nicknamed "the steel bar" (al tayeb seikha) after the implement he used against his secular opponents in student demonstrations.[326]

Militant Islamic students were recruited as early as 1990 to join militias and fight in the south. Large pictures of twenty who were killed in battle there were displayed on the outside walls of Khartoum University's main campus in 1995.

On December 9, 1989, a few months after the NIF-dominated coup ousted the democratically-elected government, a third-year student in the Faculty of Arts and member of the organization Islamic Orientation (Al Itigah al Islami), Faisal Hassan Omer, killed Bashir al Tayyib, a fifth year arts student, with a knife inside the Faculty of Economics building. Although he was convicted of murder, as described above (Chapter IV), the appellate court overturned this on the grounds that he was found to be "on jihad." The Supreme Court reinstated the guilty verdict, but on a second Supreme Court appeal, the guilty verdict was quashed by a different panel and Faisal Hassan Omer was freed in 1992. He reportedly was later killed in battle in the south.

The killing was controversial at the time and was followed by two to three days of student protests and demonstrations seeking to force the government to punish the guilty. In the course of putting down these demonstrations on December 11, 1989, security used firearms and killed two more students, Salim Muhammad Abu Bakr (third year, Faculty of Arts) and Al Taaya Ahmad Abu Bakr (second year, Faculty of Education). Twelve other students were injured by the gunfire.

In January 1991 Student Union (Council of Forty) representatives were elected; the anti-NIF coalition received 73 percent of the votes, in what may have been the last student union democratically elected at Khartoum University. A pro-democracy demonstration was held the same month by the Neutralist students (al

---

[325]This account of student struggles at the University of Khartoum from 1989 to 1995 is based on interviews with several participants in Khartoum, May 24 and 30, 1995.

[326]Human Rights Watch/Africa interview, Khartoum, May 6, 1995.

Muha'ideen),[327] followed by security arrests of the head of the Council of Forty Hashim Ahmad Taha (fourth year, Faculty of Arts), Hasim Ibrahim al Faadil, also a student union officer (third year Law Faculty), and fifteen other students. All were reportedly beaten by security.

On July 17, 1991, security occupied the Faculty of Medicine at the University of Khartoum, arresting twenty students following student demonstrations protesting the administration decision to end free room and board for Khartoum University students. Security, armed with firearms, entered the campus to put down the demonstration, shooting at the demonstrators: Tariq Muhammad Ibrahim (student, Faculty of Science) was shot dead. Tariq was hiding behind an empty water tank when he was spotted by a security agent and shot from a short distance.

He apparently did not die immediately. One student, who told Human Rights Watch that he among others accompanied Tarik to the hospital, said that Tariq died three minutes before they reached Khartoum Hospital. After one hour two army officers arrived at the hospital, took away Tarik's body as well as detaining some of the students who had gone with Tarik to the hospital. Other students ran back to the university to tell the others what had happened: Tarik died and the army took his body. Within two hours of the killing, large numbers of students (some say up to 2,000) were detained by security, no doubt to put a damper on further protests.

The body was taken to the army hospital and then in an ambulance for the four-hour drive to Kosti, where Tarik's family lived. Two buses full of students tried to go to Kosti for the funeral. They were stopped forty kilometers south of Khartoum, at the military base at Jebel Aulia, by security men with guns who ordered them out of the buses, hands on necks. The students were insulted and ordered to turn around and go back to Khartoum, to security headquarters, the Red Building (*al Amar al Hamra*) inside the army headquarters, where other students detained on the day of the killing were held.

Some students were taken from security headquarters to the Citibank ghost house. Security members reportedly beat the students on the body with hands, sticks and wires as the students were getting out of the bus, according to one who was there. According to later accounts by some of them, the students were forced to write a guarantee not to participate in any political activities against the government. They were warned that if they were arrested for a second time, "we'll

---

[327]Another grouping of students who also are not aligned with either the Islamists or the leftist Democratic Front are the Independent students (al Mustaghileen). For convenience, we refer to these nonaligned groups as Neutralists/Independents.

kill you." Some were held for seven days, others for three weeks. Among the detainees were ten members of the executive committee of the Student Union (Council of Forty) elected in January 1991.

In September 1991, students, acting through the elected Student Union again, protested against the decision of the administration to suspend free room and board for university students. This was the first action taken by the Student Union representatives elected in January 1991. The NIF students, who before the coup had joined in such protests, now tried to prevent the other student from protesting. The NIF student organization Islamic Orientation readied itself to attack the Student Union building. Using the radio, the group claimed it had stopped SPLA leader Garang in the south and now had to stop the students in the north; the organization described its mission at the university as a jihad. The NIF students, armed with sticks and steel bars, occupied the Student Union offices, but only for a brief time. The Neutralist/Independent Students, as those opposing the NIF called themselves, joined forces and drove the Islamic Orientation students out of the Student Union building. The vice chancellor, Professor Muddathir al Tingari, was asked by the Neutralist/Independents to call the police but he refused to do so.

The Neutralist/Independent students, who outnumbered the NIF students, then attacked with sticks, stones and chairs and drove their foes out of the Student Union building. Many were injured, but there were no deaths.

The Islamic Orientation group retreated to the Khartoum University mosque, where they allegedly kept their weapons; their opponents claimed they illegally had access to firearms. They stayed there three days, where they were visited by NIF leaders Dr. Hassan al Turabi, Ali Osman Taha (now minister of foreign relations), and others.

Three days after the Neutralist/Independent Students entered and occupied the Student Union building the university administration closed the university, suspended the (non-NIF) Student Union, and dismissed fourteen students who were on the executive committee of the Student Union. The university was closed for five months, until February 8, 1992.

On the day the university was reopened, the university administration reportedly dismissed seven students for their participation in a political forum on the problems at the university shortly before its reopening. The Student Union, in turn, organized a sit-in, a boycott of classes and a referendum to ask students whether they wanted to boycott examinations until all dismissed students were reinstated and the university permitted student activities to resume. The vote registered a high percentage in favor of a boycott of examinations, participants said.

The boycott started on February 13, when the Faculty of Arts students were the first students slated to take examinations. In an operation called Beginning of the Morning *(Falaj al Sabah)*, about 200 security agents occupied the university, starting with the student dormitories located under the Blue Nile Bridge at 3:00 a.m. The students were forced out of the buildings and those who resisted were beaten. About 300 students were detained. Security also entered the women's dormitory and forcibly removed the female students, in what was reportedly security's first raid of this kind.

One student in the dormitory at the time said that he awoke to a noise at about 3:30 a.m. and ten minutes later looking out of his window saw security men with guns and students with their hands up. By 5:00 a.m. security had been to every room in the dorm. He said three agents entered his room, accompanied by a student who was wearing a mask, one of the informers. One of the security men had a walkie-talkie, the masked student had a gun, and a drunken security agent had a pistol. They asked for the students' identification cards and searched their rooms. They were apparently focusing on the Arts students since their examinations took place first.

Students who were picked out by the informers were taken to the Student Union building, beaten, questioned, and forced to write a guarantee *(ta'ahud)* that they would not cause any problems and would take the examinations, on threat of serious measures against them.

At 6:00 a.m., a police general arrived with two men wearing jellabiya; the student later said he recognized the two men as Fateh Erwa and Ibrahim Shams al Din.[328] The authorities brought a bus and three pickup trucks in which to take the students to their examinations, which were being conducted in an unusual location: the police academy. Some of the students were still in their nightshirts. The authorities told the students, "This truck is going to the examination. The other truck is going to the Red House [the name of Sudan Security headquarters]; you choose which one you want to get in."

The examinations at the police academy were monitored by security men. Not all the students went to the examinations, however. Many went to the Red House.

That evening on television, the vice chancellor said that those who did not take the examinations would be "dismissed forever" from the university. So many

---

[328]Fateh Erwa was presidential security advisor and Ibrahim Shams al Din was an army officer and the youngest member of the junta's Revolutionary Command Council reportedly in charge of the enforcement of security measures. The jellabia is a long white garment traditionally worn by men in northern Sudan.

refused to sit for the examinations, however, that the problem continued for another month. Hundreds who refused to sit for examinations were arrested and nine were definitively dismissed from school. Student union activities were suspended again until 1993.

In September 1993, the Student Union executive committee called on students to commemorate Tariq Muhammad Ibrahim's death. The university administration dismissed nine members of the executive committee and suspended various student activities, including cultural, political and social events and sports. The student newspaper was suspended. Gatherings of more than ten students were harassed. Many students were taken to Citibank ghost house during this time. Yet the administration announced it would allow the Student Union to reopen, and elections to be held in November 1993. The administration and a committee of students reportedly picked by it proposed several amendments to the constitution of the Student Union. Some amendments, including one to enlarge the elected Student Union (Council of Forty) from forty to sixty members, were voted on by all the students. The Neutralist/Independents campaigned for forty members and the NIF for sixty members. According to Neutralist/Independent students, the vote was 71 percent for their position, and only 12 percent for the NIF alternative.

Although NIF students appeared to be in a minority, in subsequent November 1993 elections where police intervened NIF candidates prevailed. The elections for Student Union held after the vote on the amendment were marred by irregularities, according to the Neutralist/Independent students, including the extension of the customary one-day election to two days. At the end of the first day, the twenty ballot boxes were taken to the Student Union, which was surrounded by police. Those losing the election allege that the ballots were tampered with and changed that night.

The announced results were that the NIF won by a margin of 1,000 votes, or 64 percent of the 15,000 students. Surprisingly, the Muslim Brothers, who opposed Dr. Hassan al Turabi and the NIF after a jurisprudential difference in 1979, were not credited with any votes at all in the Arts Faculty, although they told the Neutralist/Independent students that they had voted for themselves. A group of students sat in the vice chancellor's office, demanding abolition of the results and a new election. The vice chancellor refused and called in security; tear gas was used, the students nicknaming it "Iranian gas for God." Some 2,000 students reportedly were detained. Many were beaten and all but thirty-five released after a few days. Thirty-five students were dismissed, however, and held for a month without charges by security.

The vice chancellor established a committee to investigate the fraud allegations, but the opposition students alleged the committee consisted solely of NIF loyalists.

A new election for the Student Union was held in April 1995, with a one-day format. These elections were held without the gross fraud that marred the 1993 elections. But the Student Union, then controlled by the NIF, announced the elections on extremely short notice, so that the other students had only forty-eight hours to organize their slates. The main opposition to the NIF, the Neutralist/Independent student block, was composed of many different parties and tendencies, which could not be organized into one slate in such a short time. Therefore instead of one united slate, several slates were run, by the Umma Party, the DUP, the Neutralists, and the Communist Party (all officially disbanded parties, as was the NIF). The opposition was at another disadvantage: since meetings and rallies were banned, they could not notify their followers how to fill out registration lists. All meetings had to be held secretly outside the university.

Neutralist student leader Ismael Wadi was detained when the elections were announced, and held for three days. According to his fellow students, he had no sleep for forty-eight hours and was beaten and questioned about the source of financial support of the Neutralists, which security assumed to be political parties inside and outside the country. He was held in the security office building in Khartoum North. At this time, arrested students were generally subjected to the same treatment: first beatings, then interrogation sometimes while being filmed with a video camera, then beaten again, then forced to write their biographies, then to sign guarantees of future cooperation with security. They were deprived of sleep throughout their periods in detention.

Today, NIF supporters control the Student Union at the University of Khartoum, but the September 1995 student demonstrations showed that the student body remains politically divided. Opposition students do not enjoy freedom of speech, assembly, or association.

SQUATTERS AND INTERNALLY DISPLACED PERSONS IN KHARTOUM

The internally displaced and squatters comprise approximately 1,900,000, or 40 percent of the total population of Greater Khartoum (or the Three Towns, as Khartoum, Omdurman and Khartoum North were called), according to 1995 estimates.[329] Among the 1.9 million people an estimated 800,000 were displaced as a direct result of the conflict in the south, and more than 350,000 were displaced from the west because of drought in the mid to late 1980s. The traditional economically-motivated squatters comprise the balance of 750,000 persons.[330]

The government's urban renewal plan — drawn up by a European firm in 1985 under a prior government, the current government is fond of pointing out[331] — designated the places where squatters and displaced lived as "unauthorised and squatter settlements."[332] This master plan has not even been modified much, according to one official, despite the fact that since it was drawn up in 1985 about one million people have migrated to Khartoum.[333]

The population of the Three Towns has grown rapidly: in 1983, it was 1.8 million.[334] By 1990 those displaced and squatters living in "unauthorised and squatter settlements" alone numbered 1.8 million and the entire urban population was over 3.3 million.[335] A 1987 sampling of 800 displaced persons' households revealed that southerners made up at least two-thirds of the population living in displaced persons camps (later demolished by the government).[336] By 1990, relief workers considered that southerners composed 90 percent of the displaced population in the Three Towns. Most of the displaced from western Sudan (i.e., the non-southern parts of Darfur and Kordofan) were said to have returned home when

---

[329]United Nations, Office of the U.N. Coordinator for Emergency and Relief Operations in the Sudan, "Briefing Notes about the Khartoum Displaced Population," Khartoum, January 1995, p. 1. This would make the population of Greater Khartoum about 4.75 million.

[330]Ibid., and other agency documents.

[331]Human Rights Watch/Africa interview, Dr. Bannaga, May 18, 1995.

[332]Dr. Sharaf Eldin Ibrahim Bannaga,"Unauthorised and Squatter Settlements in Khartoum: History, Magnitude and Treatment," 2d ed. (Khartoum: Ministry of Engineering Affairs, 1994), p. 17. In this publication, the number of squatters and displaced is given as 1.8 million.

[333]Human Rights Watch/Africa interview, Dr. Ibrahim Abouf, State Minister of Social Planning, Khartoum, May 7, 1995.

[334]The Economist Intelligence Unit, "Country Profile: Sudan 1994-95," p. 8.

[335]Dr. Bannaga, "Unauthorised and Squatter Settlements in Khartoum," pp. 17-18.

[336]Some 29 percent came from Upper Nile, 25 percent from Bahr El Ghazal, and 8 percent from Equatoria; the total from the three southern states was 62 percent. Some 26 percent of the displaced surveyed were from Kordofan, but their numbers were not broken down by ethnicity and many were southerners from the Abyei plain and non-Arabs from the Nuba Mountains. U.S. Committee for Refugees, "Khartoum's Displaced Persons: A Decade of Despair" (Washington, D.C., August 1990), p. 9.

the drought subsided after 1986 or to have been integrated through kinship ties into the non-displaced population.[337] Even at the height of the drought in western Sudan, however, the numbers of its victims reaching the Three Towns was not as great as the numbers of southerners who arrived yearly beginning in 1986, fleeing war and war-caused famine.[338]

Those who arrived up until 1984 were referred to by the government as squatters, who were primarily economic migrants and integrated themselves into the city.[339] Those fleeing the 1984 famine and an escalation of the war in the south in 1986 were displaced persons, that is, "temporary residents in the city."[340] Those arriving in 1986 and later, also displaced, were in the vast majority southerners and Nubas, and thus there was a clear racial/cultural/religious difference between the two government-created categories.

According to the London-based Minority Rights Group, the democratically-elected government of Sadiq al Mahdi (1986-89) took draconian measures to force squatters and the displaced out of Khartoum, starting with a campaign of forced expulsion. This was in the context of a deterioration in economic conditions in the country and increased crime rate in the towns which coincided with the flow of migrants from the war, militia raids, drought and famine into northern cities, particularly Khartoum. Long-term residents put the blame on the newcomers.[341]

Due Process Rights for Squatters and Displaced

Dr. Sharaf Eldin Bannaga, minister of engineering affairs of Khartoum state and government czar of slum clearance, said in 1995 that 90 percent of the targeted "unauthorized" areas have been demolished, and some 2,080,000 people on that land "treated" by being relocated to government transit camps and "peace cities."[342] Despite international uproar over violent evictions and conditions of

---

[337]Many from these states began migrating seasonally to the agricultural areas of the Nile decades earlier, and some settled in the Three Towns.

[338]See David Keen, *The Benefits of Famine* (Princeton: Princeton University Press, 1994).

[339]Dr. Bannaga, "Unauthorized and Squatter Settlements in Khartoum," p. 10.

[340]Ibid. Technically, squatters are those who occupy land without permission. Internally displaced persons are those who have had to leave their places of origin because of, among other things, conflict or natural disasters such as droughts.

[341]Verney,"Sudan: Conflict and minorities," pp. 24-25.

[342]Human Rights Watch/Africa interview, Dr. Bannaga, May 18, 1995. He said that the 2.08 million were "disposed of" as of late May 1995 as follows:
"Peace cities"(Dar Es Salaam) (for those arriving 1983-1990)

(continued...)

relocation that were significantly harsher than the demolished shantytowns, the government has literally bulldozed its way to its goal, which appears to be cleansing Khartoum of "undesirable" poverty-stricken, uneducated migrants who arrived because of drought, famine, and war from their rural places of origin, mostly from the south and the Nuba Mountains.

The current government has removed pre-existing due process rights and undertaken to provide its own version of due process to those mostly southern and Nuba displaced persons in the shantytowns who are to be relocated and whose homes are going to be destroyed. The government's own due process rules are rarely followed, however, and most of the relocations and subsequent destruction of the homes of the poor have been conducted in violation of elementary international standards of due process.

The revocation of judicial redress was accomplished in two decrees of 1990, as described in our 1992 report, "Sudan: Refugees in their own Country." In Decree 941 of May 20, 1990, entitled "Approval of Some Procedures to Contain Squatter Settlement," Article (d) states that the authorities are "to *immediately* demolish squatter settlements on planned residential and agricultural land and are to *immediately* give the land to its rightful owners" (emphasis added).[343] As almost all the land on which people had been squatting was either designated as

---

[342](...continued)

Omdurman	100,000 families (7 members/family)	= 700,000
Jebel Aulia	25,000 families	=175,000
Khartoum North	15,000 families	=105,000

                                                                                980,000

Official displaced "transit camps" (As Salaam)
                    (for arrivals 1990 and later)

                                                                                385,000

Mayo Farms ("awaiting treatment")   715,000
                                                                              2,080,000

NGO records suggest a smaller total number in part because they use a smaller number of family members per household.

[343]In this legislation the term squatter refers to those occupying the land without permission, not the narrower definition used by Dr. Bannaga's agency. It would thus include those arriving after 1986.

residential[344] or agricultural[345], this article was authorization to immediately evict and demolish.

The second decree was passed in response to previous legal challenges to the government's squatter relocation program.[346] An amendment to the Civil

---

[344]During the colonial period, all the land in and around Khartoum was designated as residential, industrial, agricultural, etc. Not all the land designated as residential has been developed, though individuals may own the plots. Some squatter and displaced settlements have grown up on this land.

Sudanese urban planning distinguishes four classes of residential area. Planned neighborhoods are designated class one, two or three, according to the standard of housing and services. All land in these areas is registered with the Registrar of Lands. In addition, the law tolerates building on other land.

A de facto fourth class of residential area has been created over the last two decades as demand for low-income housing has outstripped the supply in class three residential areas. In years prior to 1992, new residents of these areas have commonly paid a nominal fee for a plot of twenty meters by twenty meters, on which they are allowed to build with mud-bricks.

The poorest fourth class areas (sometimes referred to as fifth class) are settlements for the displaced where no services are provided, and no building in semi-permanent materials is permitted. Africa Watch, "Sudan: Refugees in their own Country," *A Human Rights Watch Short Report*, vol. 4, no. 8, July 1992, pp. 6, 8.

[345]Agricultural land was designated as such during a time when Khartoum received enough rainfall to make cultivation possible. In the last three decades, the climate has changed so that only irrigated farming, chiefly along the banks of the Nile itself, is possible; rain-fed cultivation has entirely ceased — but the land designation has not changed. Thus, there is no case for returning this land to its "rightful use." In past years, other "agricultural" lands that were built on, such as in parts of Shajara, Soba, Gerief, adjacent areas along the Blue Nile, and al Menshiriya, have subsequently been changed to registered residential areas. Ibid.

[346]In 1981, the Khartoum Bar Association mounted a legal challenge to the expulsions then underway, claiming that the Sudanese constitution guaranteed freedom of movement and residence for all citizens. The government responded that there was a caveat, "except for reasons of security and public health," both of which it argued were applicable in this case, as "the resultant decrease in urban crime, lessening of the pressure on urban food supplies, and reduction of the danger of urban unrest justified the measures taken."

None of the challenged expulsions of 1979-84 involved Sudanese citizens who had lived in the Three Towns for more than a year or so, or who had built semi-permanent houses. The relocation of squatters who had been resident for longer promised far more formidable legal obstacles. In addition, the government's 1980s defense of its expulsions made further actions dependent on programs to improve sanitation and security. Subsequent

(continued...)

Transactions Act on October 10, 1990, cut through the Gordian Knot of potential land disputes, giving absolute and arbitrary power to the government to deal with the squatters and displaced. The fact that the government needed to legislate such extreme powers suggests that, under previous land law in Sudan, its current actions would be illegal.

The first provision of the 1990 Civil Transactions Act decrees that all non-registered land (whether residential, agricultural or commercial) should be considered as if registered in the name of the state. This automatically negates any rights under customary law that squatters may have obtained by having occupied a certain piece of unregistered land, unchallenged, for a certain length of time.

The second provision is the key to the government's intentions. It decrees that no judicial recourse is possible for those subjected to expulsion from "state-owned land." This was even made retroactive.

Faced with enormous international pressure as a result of hasty evictions in 1991-92 that forced tens of thousands of people to move to unprepared settlements far from water sources or places of employment,[347] the government responded by drawing up a brochure outlining the procedures to be used in relocations. The government's brochure on its program for the squatters and displaced of the Three Towns states:

> A popular committee is formed to reflect the opinions of the settlers and to convey the Ministry policies to the people. It also participates in the negotiations and the alternatives given for those who are to be relocated. . . . In the case of relocation the popular committee helps in confirming the period of residence of the people . . . . All settlements undergo a social survey prior to any action taken.
>
> Replanning and incorporation of the settlements in the urban fabric is always carried out in consultation with the popular committee. . . .
>
> **Relocation:**
> The popular committee will be notified by the date of the start of relocation. All people have the right to appeal to the Higher Relocation Committee and finally to the Minister. . . .

---

[346](...continued)
relocation programs have had precisely the reverse effect. Ibid.
[347]Ibid.

Squatters moving to Dar-es-Salaam will be handed over their plots in the new sites before demolition and they will be given ample time to pack their belongings. . . .

Demolition is done under the supervision of the Ministry social surveyors, . . . witnessed by the assigned judge or a representative of the Attorney General. . . . [T]he judge is the only person authorised to stop demolition or delay it. He also decides when police should use force.[348]

Lack of Due Process in Relocation from Khoder, October 1994, and Other Sites

This official procedure is not honored. At least eleven people were shot dead by police and forty injured during protests against demolitions without notice of mud homes in the Ghammeyer-Khoder area of Omdurman on October 15, 1994. The demolitions were to be of homes owned by those who had property rights under the government's own scheme. Bulldozers escorted by People's Police trucks entered and began demolishing mud houses marked with "Xs."[349] The residents protested to the police that they did not have any notice and there was no time for them to remove their personal belongings. They also objected to being moved to Sita Abril (Thowra 48), a site on the periphery of Omdurman, some four kilometers from a macadam road.

Their pleas were ignored and some residents threw stones at the demolition teams and police who then turned their automatic weapons on the crowd, killing six. Later that morning, a second protest flared up, and the police again used their automatic weapons, killing five. No judge or attorney general's representative was on the scene, as far as the residents could tell.[350]

Government officials admitted that there are no hearings held prior to relocations and demolitions, no judge involved in adjudicating rights, and specifically, there was no court order of eviction in the Khoder case.[351] Indeed, judicial recourse was removed by 1990 legislation. Minister of Engineering Affairs Dr. Bannaga himself said that the government gives little or no notice of the

---

[348]Dr. Bannaga, "Unauthorised and Squatter Settlements in Khartoum," pp. 28-30.

[349]The government began using "X" to mark some houses — but not all the houses to be demolished — in 1989 as a device to scare people into moving. In some locations, as in Omdurman in 1990, this panicked whole communities.

[350]Confidential communication to Human Rights Watch/Africa, May 1995. For a discussion of police conduct here, see Chapter VII, Freedom of Assembly.

[351]Human Rights Watch/Africa interview, Dr. Ibrahim Abouf.

relocation, so that the people will not have time to organize to resist the move. "We do not specify the date, because if we do, people will make this sort of thing [resistance in Khoder]. They'll be organized and make an organized opposition. They were told [in Khoder] three weeks ahead that from now to three weeks they would be relocated."[352]

The demolitions of homes in Khoder continued from October 15 through at least October 24, 1994. The People's Police Force trucks were loaded with personal belongings such as utensils, mattresses, and wood salvaged from the structures. A total of 750 to 800 families were to be relocated as follows: 140 families, who arrived in Khartoum before 1976, and were to receive the right to buy a plot of land within the area, were to live with friends or family; those who arrived in Khartoum between 1977 and 1982,[353] about 350-400 families, were relocated to Sita Abril (Thowra 48) where each was to receive a plot about 200-300 square meters; the rest, who arrived after 1982, were sent to Dar Es Salaam, an official displaced camp in Omdurman.[354]

The residents insisted they had been given no notice; their leaders were arrested two days before the eviction by men in plain clothes. Some heard about the evictions on the radio on October 15. Others were unaware, and when they saw the People's Police move in, assumed they were searching for criminals, arms, or marijuana.[355]

Sita Abril (Thowra 48) was virtually without basic services at the time of relocation: the nearest market and health center were three kilometers away, water was provided only by vendors selling from donkey carts, and the five-room school in the area was full.[356] After the forced relocations from Khoder, an NGO extended the services of a health clinic in another location to Sita Abril. Within two months of the international attention attracted by the shootings, NGOs had built an eight-room school house, dug a borehole, and distributed non-food relief (blankets, kitchen utensils, jerrycans, soap) to 643 families, but the first two months were hard going for the new residents.[357]

---

[352]Human Rights Watch/Africa Interview, Dr. Bannaga, May 23, 1995.

[353]Sic. The year should be 1983, according to the government's own scheme. Agency records, November 1994.

[354]Agency records, October and November 1994.

[355]Human Rights Watch/Africa interview, Khartoum, May 6, 1995.

[356]Agency records, October and November 1994.

[357]U.N. Emergency Unit, Khartoum, "Khartoum Displaced, 1994: Year in Review," pp. 3-4.

Khoder was described as a pretty area, with rolling hills, on the Nile. With its narrow arcades, it had an old Middle Eastern look, and the surrounding area was a "first class" residential area.[358] Khoder, alleged one government official, had been a hotbed of Ansar activity, the religious sect on which the banned Umma Party is based. Many long-term residents had come to Khartoum from the west of Sudan, also historically an Ansar area. As in most marginal areas, poorly-paid soldiers and police lived there, and the authorities may have believed the people were armed. The government had demolished the cardboard shelters in Khoder of about 1,000 families, more recent arrivals in Khartoum from the south and the Nuba Mountains, in early 1994.[359] These people had no property rights by government definition, and no rights to compensation for their demolished houses. The housing remaining on the site in October 1994 was mud houses.

The stated purpose for evicting 750-800 families in October without notice, destroying their homes, and relocating them to a remote site without any water or health facilities and far from a paved road, was ostensibly to clear the area pursuant to an urban renewal plan. Part of the area is designated for a hospital, but one minister had no idea if there was any money in the budget to build the hospital,[360] and the other affirmed that it did not matter if there was no money in the budget for the hospital, the demolitions would go ahead anyway. "That's not my problem. I have to clear the sites," said Dr. Bannaga. "If I have squatters grabbing land next to the Nile, even if I don't have any project, I will not leave it [the land]."[361]

A second case — of many — of relocation without due process occurred in the Angola area of Omm Badda, Omdurman.[362] According to Dr. Bannaga, everyone in that Angola area was a new squatter, having arrived there after 1992. This class of people has no rights, regardless of what is suggested in the

---

[358]Dr. Abouf explained that "first class" land was that allocated for "people like me, in government, with limited incomes." Human Rights Watch/Africa interview, May 7, 1995. Much of Khoder was designated "first class" land. Those persons living in Khoder who have property rights there (because they arrived in Khartoum in 1983 or before) were subjected to house demolition if they were in a "first class" plot. They have rights to buy a "third class" or 200 or 300 square meter plot, Dr. Abouf said.

[359]Human Rights Watch/Africa interviews, Khartoum, May 15 and 17, 1995.

[360]Ibid.

[361]Human Rights Watch/Africa interview, Dr. Bannaga, May 23, 1995.

[362]Many of the squatter or slum neighborhoods have popular names reflecting residents' attitudes to the conditions. Angola and Texas, for instance, were said to be named after "bad" or "rough" places: there has been a decades-long bloody war in Angola, and Texas was known as the violent place where U.S. President Kennedy was shot.

government brochure on relocations. In such cases, no social survey is taken "because we already know they are new," according to this minister. The government does not usually count the displaced; it just takes them to transit camps. The government knew these were new residents because the government dug a trench around the area surveyed for demolition before these people moved in.[363] Dr. Bannaga claimed that the popular committee in Angola was given notice of the relocation, but it did not inform the residents. (See below)

On May 22 and 30, 1995, Human Rights Watch visited another site in Omdurman before and after eviction. The location was next to a dump and seemingly unused industrial buildings in a sector descriptively dubbed by its residents *Zagalone* ("We were thrown away").

A Dinka resident sat amid the rubble of his house, a few mattresses, and salvaged doors. He said that the government had given them seven days notice and come in two days to demolish the houses. They had little time to salvage the doors and other usable materials from their homes; if they did not dismantle them they knew from experience that the bulldozers would crush everything. So preoccupied, the residents had little time to organize a protest.

The Dinka family to whom Human Rights Watch talked had lived in Khartoum since 1977, and so were entitled to the highest class of property rights possible for the poor in these areas: they were told they had the right to buy a new plot in this area — for a price of Ls. 40,000 (U.S. $75.75). The minimum monthly wage was Ls. 6,000 (U.S. $11.36), and the head of this household, which consisted of five adults and ten children, made about Ls. 14,000 (U.S. $26.51) a month. To avoid going to a transit camp far from his work, he had to pay transport to a place where the family could stay - either with relatives or renting. He did not know when he could move back or how he was going to afford the plot of land and the construction of a new house. "They want us blacks to be poor," he concluded.[364]

Usually the first bulldozing done in an area — of houses, schools, and churches — is for the construction of roads. The bulldozing, of a swath sixty meters wide, is worthy of a boulevard. It is first cut through an area, then left unpaved and desolate. This begins the carving up of communities.

The existence of an urban renewal plan does not dispose of the issue of due process for individuals who are to be forcibly evicted and lose their homes. Even the government's own guidelines contemplate some consultation and notice,

---

[363]Human Rights Watch/Africa interview, Dr. Bannaga, May 23, 1995. One person familiar with the area pointed out that the wind and other elements quickly erase lines drawn in the sandy soil.

[364]Human Rights Watch/Africa interview, Zagalone, Omdurman, May 22, 1995.

with the right of appeal for "all people" to a committee and finally to the minister, and the process on the eviction day supervised by a judge or attorney general representative who is to control the police. None of the government's own rules have been followed, with the possible exception of the appeal to Minister Bannaga. On the days designated for appeal, hundreds of people gather outside his office, regardless of the heat.

The social cost is enormous: migrants who have been in Khartoum as long as ten years are nevertheless uprooted, often more than once, and have to start again from scratch. They are relocated to unprepared areas on the periphery of the city, far from sources of employment and far even from public transport to work. Their communities are dispersed and debilitated, as individuals become preoccupied with staying one step ahead of the bulldozer. Their churches and schools, "illegal" because no government agency will permit their construction on land "planned" for another use, are demolished and their members have to try to start up again — not as a group, but scattered to many different locations. The impact on the children who have managed to attend school is devastating; the school year may be interrupted or lost completely. Only 25 percent of school-aged children are enrolled in school in the displaced transit camps.[365]

The constant threat of removal, finally, makes community building among Nubas and southerners in Khartoum extremely difficult, and costly. As one relief worker said, "through relocation, the infrastructure we have established for (the displaced) is broken down and we have to follow them again to build new structures — it's very expensive."[366]

Persons living in what the government calls "unauthorised settlements" are subject to eviction and house demolition without due process as described above. A mix of persons were living in the demolished areas: some arrived earlier in Khartoum and were never able to afford any better housing, some arrived because of the war, and some are recent arrivals. All have had their property destroyed and are denied due process. Some are compensated and some are not, however. Some are given tenure rights and some are subjected to relocation at the will of the government, forbidden to build even semi-permanent structures on the site to which they are forcibly relocated, and denied any right of tenure. They may be evicted and their homes destroyed again without due process, if the government so chooses.

---

[365]Mahmud and Baraka, "Basic Education for Internally Displaced Children," pp. 18 and 21.

[366]Obinna Anyadike, "Sudan: No Home-Sweet-Home for Displaced Southerners," InterPress Service, Khartoum, March 6, 1996.

The government has constructed three categories of displaced and squatters, according to their year of arrival in Khartoum, and allocated or denied benefits accordingly. Those who arrived before 1983 generally receive the right to buy, at a reduced price, a plot of land in the area from which were evicted; those who arrived between 1983 and 1990 receive some rights to settle in government-established camps on the outskirts of the city; and those who arrived in 1990 and after have no property or tenure rights whatsoever and may be relocated on a moment's notice. The current government established the following criteria for access to tenured land for those living in "unauthorised settlements": Sudanese nationality, head of family; resident prior to 1990; gainfully employed, and no residence elsewhere in Khartoum.[367]

As for those who were not resident prior to 1990, the government established transit camps.[368] There, construction may not even be semi-permanent (mud) shelters but must be huts of sticks or branches covered with grass, plastic or burlap.[369] This downgrades their housing, since many built semi-permanent houses on the sites that were later demolished. The evictees also must build their own housing. When they arrive at the new site, there is nothing prepared for them. Finally, starting over in a transit camp is a tremendous financial set back to the displaced, who live well below the poverty line. Those who arrived in Khartoum in 1990 and later receive no government compensation for the destruction of their homes. One man, who lived in Angola with his family in a three-room hut made of mud bricks, said it took fifteen days years ago to build one room; he had to make the bricks because they had no money to buy bricks. To replace the house now, he

---

[367]United Nations, Office of the UN Coordinator for Emergency and Relief Operations, "Briefing Notes about the Khartoum Displaced Population," p. 1; Dr. Bannaga, "Unauthorised and Squatter Settlements in Khartoum, pp. 27 and 13 ("No land rights for 1990 squatters and afterwards.").

[368]A census taken in March 1995 of the official displaced transit camps showed the following:

Jebel Aulia As Salaam	34,220
Omdurman As Salaam	26,075 [+ 24,500]*
Mayo Farms	27,618
Wad Al Bashir	N/A
	87,813 [+24,500 = 112,313]

While numbers are always elusive, it appears that one reason this number is lower than the government's is that this census used 3.5 family members per home, not 5-8 as was used in prior counts. Agency records, July 19, 1995.

*Plus an estimated 24,500 beneficiaries yet to be registered.

[369]Ibid.

estimated, would cost Ls. 30,000 (U.S. $56.82) for one room; the biggest cost is for the walls, about Ls. 20,000 (U.S. $37.88) per wall. It costs about Ls. 1020 (U.S. $0.02-0.04) to buy one brick.[370] The minimum monthly wage in Sudan is Ls. 6,000 (U.S. $11.36).

In addition, health conditions in the transit and other camps are very poor. A 1995 survey in the Al Salaam transit camp showed "an unacceptably high malnutrition rate among children," prompting the need for an NGO wet supplementary feeding center for severely malnourished children.[371] The highest malnutrition rate of all Khartoum displaced camps was at the Wad al Bashir transit camp.[372]

The problems typically faced by these families moved to unprepared sites were illustrated by the arrival of some 600 families, many from Khoder at Dar Es Salaam official displaced persons camp (peace village), in November 1994. Of these, 400 families were allocated land within the camp. Another 200 families were sent to an area to the north of the displaced camp but not given any land there. They were told that the land inside the displaced persons camp had not yet been surveyed for them, and in the meantime they were directed to this area and told to build temporary housing there. Relief workers were able to provide blankets, food, kitchen utensils, plastic sheets and so forth for these 200 families and others in need. Then one Sunday in January 1995, about a month after these 200 families built their temporary housing, bulldozers and police arrived unannounced and destroyed all the structures in the area where they were living. The government officials told the families to go where they wanted or to go live with relatives, but to go. One hundred families left but one hundred stayed in the area since they said they had nowhere else to go, according to a relief worker who witnessed their problems.[373]

---

[370]Human Rights Watch/Africa interviews, Khartoum, May 7 and 25, 1995.

[371]U.S. Agency for International Development, Bureau for Humanitarian Response, Office of U.S. Foreign Disaster Assistance, "Sudan Situation Report #2," Washington, D.C., February 20, 1996. Wet supplementary feeding is designed for the most severe cases of malnutrition. Those in such programs are fed food prepared by health care workers in the feeding center, where the patients live or spend the day. This assures they receive the kind and amount of food required.

[372]Ibid.

[373]Human Rights Watch/Africa interview, Khartoum, May 21, 1995.

Popular Committees and Freedom of Association: Angola

Freedom of association of the displaced had been violated by the government's manipulation of some popular committees. A popular committee, appointed by the government, figured in the March 1995 resistance by slum dwellers to demolition of their homes and forcible relocation from the Angola section of Omm Badda, Omdurman.

The role of the popular committee was spelled out by the government in its brochure on squatter and displaced ("illegal") settlements in Khartoum:

> A popular committee is formed to reflect the opinions of the settlers and to convey the Ministry policies to the people. It also participates in the negotiations and the alternatives given for those who are to be relocated. . . .
>
> Replanning and incorporation of the settlements in the urban fabric is always carried out in consultation with the popular committee.[374]

The popular committees, modeled on the neighborhood organizations installed in Libya under the military rule of President Qaddafi,[375] receive their income from government allocation of sugar at subsidized prices. The committees resell the sugar to the residents at lower than market prices pursuant to a rationing system for which each household must sign up, thus giving the committees some measure of control over the neighborhood. These popular committees received many food staples at subsidized prices before Sudan's economic crisis lead to a phasing out of subsidized food — the phase out also reduced the power of the popular committees. In return for their appointment and power over the neighborhood, the popular committees are expected to be instruments of government policy, i.e., " convey the Ministry policies to the people."[376]

The authorities responsible for the forcible relocation of hundreds of thousands of poor residents of Khartoum, and the destruction of their homes, have been accused of manipulating the popular committees so often that they have inserted defensive paragraphs in the government brochure on squatters and displaced in Khartoum:

---

[374]Dr. Bannaga, "Unauthorized and Squatter Settlements in Khartoum," pp. 28-29.

[375]Human Rights Watch/Africa interview, New York, March 1996.

[376]Dr. Bannaga, "Unauthorized and Squatter Settlements in Khartoum," pp. 28-29.

Squatters are usually very pleased when they are informed by their popular committee that their site will be replanned. They will definitely be displeased in case of relocation and they tend to disassociate themselves with the committee thus paving the way for rumors and for land speculators to step in and fill the gap. The land speculators will then do all their best to unite the squatters against the Ministry decision. In addition the speculators mobilize all interested parties from other squatter settlements in an endeavor to stop relocation.

When relocation is completed and the squatters settle in their new site they come and associate themselves again with the old popular committee and then organize a big ceremony and declare that they were misinformed.[377]

Angola was considered an illegal settlement, so there was no infrastructure put in by the government and no nongovernment organizations were allowed to work there to fill the gap. It had no boreholes (wells) and no water, except that brought in for sale in donkey carts. There was never electricity but each house had its own latrine. Residents had built their own homes and had lived there from the mid-1980s. Despite these drawbacks, the residents did not want to move to a site that was worse. We visited the location on May 6, 1995, and talked to residents who had moved back after they were evicted and built temporary shelters.

The population of the Angola area had grown so that it was divided into one zone that was to be demolished and one that was not, according to one resident. They told us that the popular committee serving the entire area was assigned to the not-to-be-demolished area, where the members of that popular committee had their homes, and a new popular committee was appointed by the government to serve the Angola section targeted for demolition.[378]

We were told that the minister of engineering met with the new popular committee, and informed them that Angola would be demolished. This committee, whose members' homes were all in the targeted area, objected to the plan. They

[377]Ibid., p. 32.

[378]Dr. Bannaga acknowledged that there were two Popular Committees in Angola, the old and the new, but he said that the old committee did not want to represent "the newcomers." The new Committee applied for and was granted recognition by the Assembly of Khartoum State, a few months earlier. Human Rights Watch/Africa Interview, Dr. Bannaga, May 23, 1995.

were to receive no compensation and would have no right to buy lots on the cleared land or anywhere else. They were simply to be moved to a transit camp far from their places of employment. After their foreseeable objections to these plans for their future, the ministry of engineering conducted its Angola business with the old popular committee, ignoring the new committee.

The old committee received notice of the demolition and gave "approval" to the government to proceed, according to civilian officials who accompanied the bulldozers to Angola on March 8, 1995.[379] The attorney general's representative told the crowd the old popular committee had approved this.[380] This caused an outburst of anger and the residents went to the office of the old popular committee, the homes of four of its members, and the local office of the ministry, and set them on fire. No one was injured and no shots were fired by any side,[381] as the two police at the office left when the crowd of 200 appeared, according to Dr. Bannaga. Thereafter the police arrested some forty-one to sixty people, members of the new popular committee and members of a neighborhood security committee,[382] identified as leaders by some of the old popular committee members. The detainees included government clerks, police and army soldiers, since wages are low for government employees, and many cannot afford anything other than slum housing.

They were taken to the police station and interrogated about the reasons for the resistance to the demolitions and the burning of the office, according to one man who was detained. Some police rebuked the new popular committee members, saying, "We chose you and you betrayed us." [383]

A former Angola resident told us that he visited the jailed men; one Nuba from his tribe told him he had been beaten for the first two or three days of detention.[384] Many detainees were still awaiting trial in Omdurman Criminal Court in June 1995.

---

[379]Representatives of the Ministry of Engineering, police, a judge, and a representative of the Attorney General's office came, saw "an unhappy crowd of 700," and left. Ibid.

[380]Human Rights Watch/Africa interview, Omdurman, May 6, 1995.

[381]Alfred Taban, "Sudan: Over 60 Arrested After Sudan Land Office Razed," Reuter, Khartoum, March 9, 1995.

[382]Dr. Bannaga said fifty-five were arrested. Human Rights Watch/Africa Interview, Dr. Bannaga, May 23, 1995.

[383]Human Rights Watch/Africa interview, Omdurman, May 6, 1995.

[384]Human Rights Watch/Africa interview, Khartoum, May 7, 1995.

The demolition continued and some 2,000 mud houses were totally destroyed, affecting an estimated 3,000 families. Of those some 900 who had rights to land in the area would be allowed to return eventually.[385]

The contents of the homes were not destroyed by the bulldozers unless residents refused to pack up and move out of the house. The mosque and church were left standing, as was the Comboni-run school,[386] but nothing else. As well as the homes, all shops were destroyed.

Some of the residents were taken by the police in trucks to *Jeberone* ("they dumped us here") further out in Omdurman. Dr. Bannaga was not sure where they were taken or if there were any services there, although he said, "The government would not take them to a place that was not serviced."[387] The minister has been contradicted by scores of witnesses on this point, however.

Other residents refused relocation and stayed in the area; they returned to their demolished homes when the bulldozers left and built temporary structures on top of the rubble. On March 20 the government ordered the families who had built temporary shelters to pull down these shelters and prepare to be moved to As Salam transit camp in the next two days.[388] Residents still on the site in May 1995 told Human Rights Watch that the soldiers went away when the 1995 national elections started and did not return.

NATIONAL SERVICE AND POPULAR DEFENSE FORCES

National service is the duty of all men in Sudan between the ages of eighteen and thirty-three years. At times, due in part to the failure of young men to respond to calls to register for the service, the army has undertaken campaigns to capture young men in random sweeps. Some of these campaigns, conducted through checkpoints and house-to-house searches, have employed excessive force and some have resulted in the induction of below-age boys. The army maintains that service at the front in the civil war in Sudan is voluntary pursuant to Sudanese law, but many young men have been sent to the front against their will. Doctors are required to complete their national service obligations after finishing their residencies, and before they can be certified by the Ministry of Health to practice medicine.

---

[385]U.N. Office of the UN Coordinator for Emergency and Relief Operations in the Sudan, "Memo to All NGOs," Khartoum, March 20, 1995.

[386]The Combonis are an Italian order of the Catholic church with a long history in Sudan.

[387]Human Rights Watch/Africa interview, Dr. Bannaga, May 23, 1995.

[388]U.N. "Memo to All NGOs," March 20, 1995.

Parallel to national service is service in the Popular Defense Forces, a militia since 1989 under army jurisdiction, that is intended to support the military effort in the civil war. PDF training is in addition to military national service obligations. PDF service is credited against the national service. The PDF, although is said to be voluntary, but in fact PDF training is required for certain segments of Sudanese society regardless of their obligations to serve in the army: university students, civil servants, and others. Recent medical school graduates, male and female (who have not received PDF training), reportedly are required to undergo PDF training as a condition of being licensed to practice medicine. In some regions considered strategic, whole villages have been required to undergo PDF training and participate in defense measures.

Women are trained separately from men. Even middle-aged women in academia are required to participate, on penalty of losing their jobs or sanctions such as docking pay (having the fine taken out of the salary).

One principal objective of the PDF is to indoctrinate its "volunteers" with the spirit of jihad (holy war) so that they become mujahedeen (holy warriors), volunteer to fight in the south, and are ready to become martyrs for Islam. Thus PDF training is imbued with Islamic religious themes, religious songs, and chants and non-Muslims are subjected to coercion to change their religions, in violation of Article 18 of the ICCPR.

President (Lt. Gen.) Omar al Bashir admitted the religious objectives of PDF training. Government radio reported that he said the PDF military camps were "used to provide spiritual and religious lessons to recruits to help create a prudent Muslim society."[389]

National Service

The compulsory national military service was introduced under Nimeiri's government in 1972 and revised in a 1989 law, but was never strictly enforced. A new law adopted in February 1992, the National Service Law, states a religious and ideological agenda in its Article 4:

> The National Service aims at the following: a) to implant the spirit of jihad and its traditions, and to disseminate the models of martyrs and the qualities of boldness, firmness and readiness to offer oneself in martyrdom, and to reject the spirit of relaxation

---

[389]"Bashir Says Amnesty Allegations about Sudan Include Lies and Contradictions," Republic of Sudan Radio, Omdurman, in English, 1800 gmt, February 24, 1995, text quoted in BBC Monitoring Service: Middle East, February 27, 1995.

and fear of danger; b) to promote the spirit of discipline and commitment within a cohesive group and the qualities of obedience and cooperation and leadership and to deny the inclination towards selfishness through individual demarcation from the rank and file; c) to consolidate the spirit of giving and loyalty and belonging to the group and the homeland and the religion; and the bypassing of narrow allegiances to the family, the professional group or the region; d) preparation of regular forces for military and defense work, or for involvement in development work and social work or any other task aiming at the general good; and e) train the youth so that they may be raised in proper health and conduct and be proficient in any trade or job or to improve any of their skills or readiness.

Notwithstanding its religious references, national service is compulsory for Sudanese men of all religions from the ages of eighteen to thirty-three years. The length of conscripts' service is a function of their educational status: the more educated serve less time. Thus, university or college graduates serve twelve months, high school graduates eighteen months, and those with less than a high school diploma must serve twenty-four months.[390]

Enforcement mechanisms include a prohibition in Article 20 on men of eligible ages leaving the country for any reason, unless they obtain certificates of exception, postponement or fulfilment of military obligation issued by the Ministry of Defense under Article 27. They may not receive diplomas of graduation from universities, colleges or schools unless they produce one of these certificates, under Article 22.

Doctors will not be licensed to practice medicine unless they meet national service requirements. In other professions, one may be licensed to practice without having complied with national service obligations. Essential work experience such as residencies (housemanships) is conditioned on compliance with national service requirements. Female doctors may apply for jobs with the army's medical corps and serve as army doctors, but on a voluntary basis.[391]

The Association of Islamist Doctors has a program, run not by the military but by NIF doctors, to recruit doctors for volunteer work for the Ministry of Health, often in war zones.

---

[390]Articles 7 and 9 of the National Service Law.

[391]Recent female medical school graduates, like all others receiving university education, must complete PDF requirements, however. See below.

The Association of Islamist Doctors benefits from government support for its initiatives to widen its membership base and to recruit doctors to volunteer for service in the war.

In 1994-95 pressure from the war led the government to fully enforce the 1992 National Service Law. The first large-scale campaign was launched in early March 1995. Army and PDF soldiers set up checkpoints throughout Khartoum, mainly around low income residential areas. At checkpoints, they searched for youth in buses and other vehicles, and went on patrol in business and recreation areas such as markets, cinemas and sports stadiums to find draft dodgers. The recruiters checked identities in mobile tents, and apprehended youth suspected of dodging the service. They trucked these young men immediately to training camps in military bases around the capital and elsewhere. Among them were boys under eighteen years, the minimum age for national service in Sudan.[392] According to testimonies Human Rights Watch received, soldiers guarding the checkpoints were rough and in many instances violent in picking out members of the target group and checking identities.

The minister of defense replied to complaints from the government-appointed Transitional National Assembly on May 31, 1995, explaining that only eighty-nine youth responded to the army's most recent call to the draft, addressed to 10,000 people. Since the enforcement of the national service law, he told the TNA, only 26,079 out of the estimated 2.5 million Sudanese of draft age had turned up for training, and less than half of them had actually completed the course.[393]

In this address, the defense minister admitted that "individual and isolated" errors were committed during the roundup of youth. He sought to calm public anxiety about alleged high losses in the ranks of conscripts sent to the war zone, telling the parliamentarians that under Sudanese law conscripts could only be sent to the front if they volunteered to go.[394] The minister of defense denied that the government was sending conscripts to the south. He said, however, that 1,850 recruits were sent to the "operations zones," all at their own request, and that fifty-four of them had been killed in action.[395]

In an address to a freshly-recruited group of conscripts at Fatasha military training camp in the outskirts of the capital in late 1994, the commander of the

---

[392] Human Rights Watch/Africa, *Children of Sudan*, pp. 54-65.

[393] "Sudanese Rounding Up Draft-Dodgers in Khartoum," Reuter, Khartoum, June 5, 1995.

[394] "Sudan: Defense Minister Reportedly Admits Some 'Errors' During Roundups for Military Service," KNA news agency, Nairobi, Kenya, June 5, 1995.

[395] Ibid.

national service also asserted that only volunteers would be sent to the war zones. Immediately after their graduation two months later, however, some 750 of them (those who had only a high school education) were airlifted to Juba for combat duties in spite of their protests citing the commander's opening address. Instructors and political coordinators, who oversee the military instructors, threatened them with arrest if they failed to get into the truck going to the airport.[396]

In response to an SPLA October 1995 offensive in the south, the government began stepped-up conscription efforts. According to reports, thousands of young PDF and conscripts were sent in eighty-two groups to the front in just a few weeks of the airlift.[397]

Human Rights Watch received reports that in the early hours of November 20 and 21, 1995, the People's Police raided the houses of residents of the Helfayat al Muluk and Droshab residential areas of Khartoum North, searching for young men of conscription age. On November 26 young boys rounded up from street checkpoints were taken directly to Khartoum airport. They were told that they would be sent immediately to the south for training and fighting. The boys panicked and ran out in all directions, with Sudan Security and military agents running after them and dragging some from the airport offices where they tried to hide. Other boys scaled the airport wall and escaped.[398]

The airlifts of soldiers, volunteer mujahedeen and national service conscripts to the front increased. We received one report, however, that in the southern garrison town of Wau in 1995, men who were Christian were turned away although they wanted to volunteer "for economic reasons — for the army. Where the economy is bad, there is no forced recruitment."[399]

Human Rights Watch recognizes the clear right of governments of states to raise armies and provide for national defense, but is also mindful that conscription, albeit lawful, is always a deprivation of personal liberty, and during armed conflict subjects conscripts to direct attack by virtue of their status as combatants. Consequently, where governments utilize conscription, Human Rights Watch opposes practices that do not comply with international and domestic law; that are not explicitly authorized by domestic law; and/or that are grossly inequitable in distributing the burden of military service.

---

[396]Report from Khartoum, March 27, 1995.

[397]Nhial Bol, "Sudan-Politics: Islamist Warriors Battle 'Infidels,'" InterPress Service, Khartoum, November 28, 1995.

[398]Confidential communication to Human Rights Watch/Africa, November 1995.

[399]Human Rights Watch/Africa interview, Khartoum, May 26, 1995.

We believe that the domestic laws that regulate conscription should meet reasonable standards of fairness in apportioning the burden of military service; conscription should be carried out in a manner that gives the conscript notice of the period during which military service will be required and an opportunity to communicate promptly with family or friends that the conscript is being required to serve, and an opportunity to secure a fair and prompt review of any claim that the conscript or potential conscript is not required to serve or to serve at that time; domestic law should provide for alternative service based on religious or conscientious opposition to military service, and the conscript should be permitted by law to secure a fair review of a claim of right to engage in such alternative service; and conscription should not be left to the unfettered discretion of local authorities or press gangs, but should be carried out according to nationally prescribed and enforced standards.

The Popular Defense Forces Militia

In 1989 a law was passed setting up a militia under army control. Article 4 of the 1989 Popular Defense Forces Law states, "A paramilitary force is hereby established to be called 'Popular Defense Forces' under the command of the General Commander [of the regular army]." The purpose of the PDF is set forth in Article 5 as the "training of its members in civil and military defense and raising of their security awareness as well as spreading the spirit and traditions of military discipline among them so that they become able to assist the People's Armed Forces and other regular forces when required."

PDF training is in addition to national service. Any period of time spent in the service of the PDF will be credited toward the national service obligations.[400]

The PDF member must be "a) of Sudanese nationality by birth, b) of 16 years of age minimum, c) medically fit and d) of good conduct and reputation." (Article 5) Women may join; and certain categories of women and men (university students, civil servants and others) are required to join.

The general commander of the army appoints the commander of the PDF, and is empowered to appoint any number of army officers to serve under that appointee. Orders of the PDF commander are subject to the approval of the general commander of the army.[401] The general commander of the army is empowered to call PDF members to duty in any of the following situations: "a) for training

---

[400]Popular Defense Forces Law (1989), Article 16-3.

[401]Popular Defense Forces Law, Articles 7 and 8. The chief of staff of the army chairs the PDF Advisory Council established under Article 9.

purposes, b) during crisis and disasters, c) when war breaks out or is expected to, and d) any other situations he considers appropriate." (Article 12)

Tribal PDFs

From the very beginning of the civil war in 1983, under the military rule of Gen. Nimeiri (1969-85), the army adopted a counterinsurgency strategy of using tribal militias in the south and north to stem the rebel tide. Political parties during the short-lived period of elected government (1986-89) sought to gain support of peoples in north-central Sudan by playing up fears triggered by the penetration of southern rebels into the northern border town of Kurmuk.[402]

The National Islamic Front was the junior partner in various ruling coalitions in 1986-89, and occasionally crossed over to the opposition when the ruling Umma and Democratic Unionist parties frustrated its Islamist agenda. To widen its power base, the NIF initiated the call to "popular defense" in the heartland of the Baggara (meaning cattle herders in Arabic) Arabs of Southern Darfur who were traditionally an ally of the Umma Party of Prime Minster Sadiq al Mahdi. The NIF organized a conference in Southern Kordofan in 1986 and invited representatives from some forty Baggara Arab tribes. The NIF advocated and won the support of the tribal representatives for the concept of a "human belt" running across Sudan from Geissan on the eastern border to Um Dafaug on the western border. The implication was that this cordon sanitaire would defend the cultural and religious purity of the north.[403]

The NIF formed a committee of nationally well-known persons to raise funds for the purchase of arms and ammunition for the Baggara tribes. Members of the committee, including well-respected retired army officers and state officials, toured Gulf countries to raise funds from Sudanese expatriates to arm the tribes.

This alarmed the ruling Umma Party, which suspected the NIF of trying to win over its traditional allies. Starting in 1987, the Prime Minister Sadiq al Mahdi's Umma Party minister of defense, Gen. (Ret.) Fadlalla Burma Nasir (a Misseiriya Baggara himself), gave unequivocal political approval to the army to use tribes from these border areas in its counterinsurgency campaign, particularly the militia of the Baggara tribes: the Misseiriya in southern Kordofan, the Hwazma in the Nuba Mountains, and the Rezeigat in southern Darfur. The armed horsemen

---

[402]Simone, *In Whose Image?*, p. 57.

[403]The Fund For Peace, "Living on the Margin: The Struggle of Women and Minorities for Human Rights in Sudan" (New York: The Fund For Peace, July 1995), pp. 18-19.

of the Baggara tribes were known as the *murahiliin*.[404] These tribes have a long history of co-existence and interaction with their neighbors the Dinka to the south and the Nuba to the east, with whom they share grazing and water resources. Conflicts over these resources were resolved in the past through inter-tribal peace conferences in which the local government authorities played the role of the arbitrator and enforcer, but in the mid-eighties the resolution mechanism broke down as drought drastically decreased the Baggara cattle herds and the SPLA gained control of their summer grazing lands in Bahr El Ghazal.

In November 1989, a few months after the NIF came to power through a military coup, the new government promulgated the Popular Defense Forces Act, which legitimized pre-existing tribal militias such as the murahiliin.[405] The first PDF commander announced a target of enlisting 100,000 PDF elements by the end of the first year. This was achieved by absorbing pre-existing militia in the PDF. In late 1989 and early 1990, the PDF commander toured the areas where tribal militia were active. They were issued arms and considered to be PDF units without further ado. The first militia absorbed in this manner were the murahiliin militia of the Misseiriya tribe, in El Muglad, Kordofan (December, 1989); the Peace Army militia of the Fertit tribe, in Wau, Bahr El Ghazal (December 1989); and the *fursan* (cavalry) militia of the Rezeigat tribe in Al Dien, Southern Darfur (March 1990).[406]

The underlying assumption in placing the PDF under the control of the regular army was that the professional army would help to discipline the tribal militia, direct their energies for defense purposes, and check their destructive inclination towards looting, burning of villages, killings and abductions of southern civilians as hostages and war captives destined for domestic enslavement, all practices for which the tribal militia became renowned prior to the promulgation of the 1989 PDF law.[407] The continuation of these atrocities under the current law defeated this purpose. This expected moderating role of the army proved illusory.

Relations between the army and tribal militias were rife with conflicts and tensions all along. Leaders of tribal militias who agreed to submit to the control of the army did so only after the government conceded a high degree of autonomy to them, including remaining in command of their own men. They obtained government recognition of tribal militia leaders as PDF officers with a hierarchy

---

[404]Ibid.

[405]Ibid., p. 21.

[406]Ibid., pp. 21-22.

[407]Africa Watch, *Denying "The Honor of Living,"* pp. 65-102. Ushari Ahmad Mahmud and Suleyman Ali Baldo, *Al Dien Massacre: Slavery in Sudan* (Khartoum: 1989), p. 19-22 (English summary).

identical but parallel to that of the army. Tribal militias also pressed for and obtained permission to confine their operations to their traditional areas of raiding, to the exclusion of unfamiliar terrain. They also demanded and obtained equal treatment with regard to the benefits that the army law guarantees to professional soldiers and their dependents in cases of war-related injury, disability, captivity or death.[408]

Although the army conceded all these conditions, problems recurred, as tribes wanted to campaign according to their own seasonal agendas and not in relation to the army's military priorities. Some PDF tribesmen struck peace agreements with local SPLA rebel commanders, usually in exchange for access for their people to grazing lands for their animals. Such localized agreements led to the appearance of "peace markets" where traders and militiamen bartered goods with villagers in rebel-held areas, their safety being guaranteed by the local rebel units.[409]

There were other tensions between the army and PDF generally. The regular army provided the logistics and supplies of the PDF during its first year of existence (1989-90). As the PDF forces grew in size, and their functions became more diversified, they developed their own purchase and supplies department in Khartoum, leading some in the army to complain that badly needed resources were diverted to paramilitary groups at the expense of the regular forces.[410]

In February 1990, the state government of Kordofan convened a regional conference in El Obeid to set its war policy toward Southern Kordofan, where the SPLA had maintained a presence since 1986. A confidential document written by the subcommittee on Popular Defense for this conference reported on the merits of murahiliin involvement in the civil war: they managed to revive in people the value of defending the land and honor, they used tactics identical to those of guerrilla warfare against the rebellion and thus managed to repel the rebels in the western area of Kordofan, and the militia aided the armed forces in military operations in a way that makes them a defense line that can be called upon when need arises.[411]

According to the same report, however,

---

[408]Human Rights Watch/Africa interview, New York, March 1996.

[409]Ibid.

[410]Ibid.

[411]Report of the Sub-Committee on Popular Defense, The Regional Conference on National Dialogue for Peace, Development and Rehabilitation, Kordofan State, El Obeid, February, 1990, cited in The Fund For Peace, "Living on the Margin," p. 19.

since these militia are irregular and undisciplined, they have indulged in some operations that may be counted as a negative record. These were:

a) being inclined to loot, without achieving the security aim, which is defense;

b) non-adherence to the discipline that binds unified regular forces in the area, even when they are in joint operations;

c) in certain cases, they deliberately give wrong information to achieve specific purposes, and the truth is veiled through certain behavior and patterns of conduct;

d) they often get diverted from the main objective contrary to specific orders;

e) [they lead to] the spread of animosity and loss of trust between people;

f) fueling of tribal and racial hatred. As an example of this what happened in Lagawa area and also in the eastern area.[412]

In Lagawa, in the Nuba Mountains of central Sudan, according to the report, the Misseiriya tribal militia burned down and looted twenty villages inhabited by Nuba and Daju people, both considered non-Arab, in October - November 1989, because of suspicions that rebels were hiding in these villages. An inter-tribal peace conference held in Lagawa in January 1990 listed the fatalities as eighty-two Nuba, ten Daju and thirty-eight Misseiriya.[413]

Although this report put the Sudanese government authorities on notice of the grave human rights problems caused by arming these tribes against others, it nevertheless continued its policy under the Popular Defense Forces Act of legalizing and arming tribal militia.

Where existing tribal militia were not sufficient for military purposes, the government created new tribal militia. Gen. Al Huseini, the governor of Kordofan state, officially declared a state of jihad in 1992 and asked the Arab tribes of northern Kordofan to raise an army of 40,000 fighters to chase the rebels from the southern provinces of the region.[414] He was able to meet this target in a matter of a few weeks through winning over the tribal chiefs of northern Kordofan by restoring to them the judicial powers that earlier governments had revoked, giving each chief a symbolic government salary (and the highest chiefs a prestigious four-

---

[412]Ibid.
[413]Ibid., p. 20.
[414]Ibid., p. 25.

wheel drive vehicle) and appointing the chiefs and their agents as collectors of the religious tax (Zakat), permitting them to keep a percentage for themselves.[415]

Kordofan state organized a huge public rally in El Obeid in May 1992 for the induction of these freshly-trained tribal militia into the ranks of the PDF. President (Lt.-Gen.) Omar Hassan al Bashir attended, and on national television handed assault rifles over to tribal chiefs who had met their quotas of volunteer youth. He told the crowd, "the banner of jihad which was declared by Kordofan will never stop until the war comes to an end."[416]

The jihad campaign that followed was one of the most abusive on record in Sudan. One person who exposed the atrocities that government troops and allied militia committed in the Nuba Mountains was a senior Sudan Security official who defected and sought asylum in Switzerland, Khalid Saleh, the younger brother of the governor. Saleh told the press that in the war against the civilian population of the Nuba Mountains

> there are no rules, no human rights. . . .The government wants to
> finish the name of the Nuba, without distinguishing who belongs
> to the SPLA and who is just an ordinary citizen of the area.[417]

While tribal militias enjoyed impunity in their assaults on southern and Nuba civilians, the government promptly intervened to contain clashes when the same militias turned their weapons against each other. In July 1993 a minor family feud rapidly degenerated into a major confrontation between two sub-clans of the Misseiriya tribe, the Zeyoud and Awlad Omran. In a deadly rampage that spread over a wide area in two days, July 16 and 17, 1993, the two clans suffered 108 dead and fifty wounded. Cattle was looted, villages were burned to the ground. The government promptly dispatched army and police troops from neighboring garrisons to separate the warring factions. Vice President (Gen.) Zubeir Mohamed Salih and Brig. Abdel Rahim Mohammed Hussein (then minister of interior and secretary of the Revolutionary Command Council) hurriedly flew to the area to

---

[415]Ibid., p. 26. This incentive proved effective. There was no way for the nomadic rural populations of the region to hide their real wealth in livestock herds from these well-informed tax agents, as they could have done with urban civil servants. The scheme allowed the government to recycle part of the returns into the war effort to sustain the "holy warriors" of the PDF.

[416]Report from Khartoum, September 1992.

[417]Quoted in Julie Flint, "Hidden Holy War in the Hills," *The Guardian* (London), July 22, 1995.

oversee the containment campaign and to lobby tribal leaders to settle the dispute. An ad hoc tribal conference was convened in their presence and that of Kordofan state authorities. The conference reached an agreement allowing local tribal chiefs and PDF commanders to disarm the two sub-clans. A special court was formed to try those responsible for the incident, identified to the court by their chiefs and village elders.[418]

The minister of interior publicly expressed his regrets that a tribe upon which the Islamic state so depended had to waste its energy in fratricidal quarrels. He recalled the PDF campaigns where the Misseiriya played a leading role: they participated in the opening of the militarily-essential railroad from El Muglad to Wau, they were the first to introduce cavalry raids in the south in a return to the fighting traditions of early Islam, and they "raised the banner of Islam and Arabism against the rebellion."[419] The minister said the tribes formed a "human belt" against the spread of the rebellion, and stood firmly in the first defense line of the Islamic faith. He said the arms collected from the Misseiriya tribesmen "will be kept in a safe place with tribal chiefs and local PDF commanders and will be handed back to them at times of campaign and jihad."[420]

He could not have been more explicit: arms are for use against southerners but may not be used in tribal conflicts in the north. No attention at any level was ever paid to well-known attacks committed by the same militiamen against southern civilians, including the killing and atrocities that accompanied the opening of the railroad from El Muglad to Wau.[421] Army units and PDF troops accompanying the train along the vital Babanusa to Wau route have a record of scorched earth tactics along the tract. Their priority is to defend the route and the flow of supplies to the garrison towns of Gogrial and Wau. In the process, soldiers and militiamen protecting the train have plundered Dinka land and abducted women and children.[422] To date, the government has not punished or even investigated these atrocities.

---

[418]Confidential communication to Human Rights Watch/Africa.

[419]Confidential communication to Human Rights Watch/Africa, regarding notes of statement made by the minister of interior at a televised press conference on Sudan TV, July 29, 1993.

[420]Ibid.

[421]See Amnesty International, *The Tears of Orphans, No Future Without Human Rights in Sudan* (London: Amnesty International Publications, 1995), pp. 71-78.

[422]See Chapter VII.

Controlling Minority Populations

The PDF system has also been employed some in non-Muslim areas to regiment and control the populations. In areas of southern and central Sudan, the government is increasingly relying on the rigors of military discipline to control the population and to convert non-Muslims to Islam. In the Nuba Mountains of southern Kordofan, an area inhabited by African peoples of whom half are Muslim and the others Christians and practitioners of traditional African religions, the state government forcibly relocated an estimated 40,000 Nubas from their homes to six towns in northern Kordofan in 1992.[423] State agencies organized a relief and rehabilitation program in 1992-93, called "the Rehabilitation of the Returnees Program." It required displaced Nubas to take regular adult classes in Arabic and Islam.[424] When the same villagers were relocated for the second time to the peace villages, they were organized as units of the PDF, allegedly to defend themselves against rebel attacks.[425] In reality, this allowed closer control of them.

In the Ingessana Mountains of Southern Blue Nile province, another area inhabited by African peoples with a late exposure to Arabic-Islamic culture, whole villages were considered closed PDF training camps for periods averaging two months in 1993. This program, called *El Da'awa El Shamla* (Comprehensive Islamic Call), was addressed to some 60,000 people who previously lived in rebel-controlled areas. The government employed national service conscripts to give all age groups, men and women, classes in Arabic language and Islam. While adult villagers were allowed to leave for their work during the day, children were taught elementary Arabic and made to memorize the Qur'an. The instructors led both adults and young people in intensive afternoon military training exercises and evening cultural classes.[426] Movement of civilians between the various villages, turned into PDF camps for the purposes of these programs, was permitted only with the approval of local PDF commanders.

When the SPLA advanced on Kurmuk in Blue Nile province of eastern Sudan in late 1995, the governor ordered a general mobilization of citizens into

---

[423]Fund For Peace, "Living on the Margin," pp. 32-35.

[424]Ibid.

[425]Minister of housing and coordinator of the program in Kordofan state, interviewed in the government-owned daily *Al Sudan al Hadith* (Khartoum), September 30, 1992 , p. 5 (in Arabic).

[426]Commissioner of Damazien and coordinator of the program, interviewed in *Al Sudan al Hadith* (Khartoum), October 4, 1993, p.1 (in Arabic).

forty-two PDF camps in that province. Civilians were to receive military training at these camps and assist the army in defense.[427]

PDF Training

Article 14 of the 1989 PDF law provides that PDF training shall include the following programs: military training, training on civil defense activities, patriotic education, and cultural education. Article 13, entitled "release of volunteers," requires that all public and private sector employers "shall release any person accepted or called upon to join the Popular Defense Forces." Women as well as men are eligible, and PDF training for women as well as men is mandatory if they belong to sectors of society targeted for recruitment such as university students or civil servants.

PDF trainees are trained in their own groups, not with the army, and they receive training which is different from army training — although PDF officers may be assigned from the army — in that they learn much more about jihad and are given Qur'anic lessons. Their training is to become holy warriors.[428]

Under the cultural and patriotic aspects of its training program, the PDF serves as an instrument of religious indoctrination and militarization of Sudanese society. In the opening day of the training, male recruits are made to shave each other's heads with hand-held blades.[429] During the line-up that follows, instructors and political cadres let them know that if they had any pride or self esteem they should bury them and start a new page of humility, discipline and obedience of their superiors. To bring the message home, the instructors resort to a symbolic ritual: they instruct new volunteers, including students and professional people, each to dig a hole in the ground and to simulate burying in it their diplomas, pride and other achievements.[430]

Forty-five days to two months of harsh, degrading treatment and insults follow this opening ritual. Recruits and volunteers must do strenuous physical exercises during the day, with little time off, except for meals and prayers. NIF cadres and political leaders lecture or show political and religious videos to the

---

[427]"Sudan: Government Forces in 'Fierce Fighting' Near Ethiopian Border," Arab Republic of Egypt Radio, Cairo, Egypt, in Arabic, 1500 gmt, October 5, 1995, quoted in BBC Monitoring Service: Middle East, October 7, 1995.

[428]Human Rights Watch/Africa interview, Khartoum, May 26, 1995.

[429]Human Rights Watch/Africa interview, New York, March 1996. Graduates were concerned both at the humiliation of the process and the health risk: no special measures were taken to ensure the blades were clean.

[430]Ibid.

trainees in the evening. The trainees are required to memorize parts of the holy Qur'an and to pray late into the night. While non-Muslim participants sometimes may be permitted — but not always — to stay in their tents during Muslim prayers, the religious nature of the training program and lectures create an atmosphere where non-Muslims are subjected to coercion impairing their freedom to hold their own beliefs, in violation of Article 18 of the ICCPR.

The whole program is imbued with religious militancy. The overall premise is that the trainees are aspirant mujahedeen (holy warriors) who must make the sacrifices required by that status. Lectures teach that Sudan is a pioneer Islamic state, threatened by a hostile world. This is repeated by the head of state.[431] PDF troops are intended to throw fear and disorientation in the hearts of the infidels and enemies of Islam, recruits are told. The rebels of southern Sudan are depicted as outlaws and agents of the enemies of the Islamic state and faith, who have to be fought in a holy, total war, according to lecturers. Marching and jogging songs are all intensely religious and glorify martyrs of Islam.[432]

Dr. Hassan al Turabi, the spiritual leader of the NIF and now speaker of the national assembly, had this to say about the philosophy underlying the induction of civilian groups into the PDF:

> The trouble of comparing and contrasting what is military with what is civilian has been largely bypassed by the time of arrival of the revolution. Of course the best thing that occurred since then was the idea of popular defense that was also proposed by the Islamic movement. In this it was seeking to follow the Islamic example where all Muslims are conscripted soldiers, ready for jihad, and not exercising it as a profession; but if the call arose for jihad, they all mobilized, and no one remained behind. These were their aspirations when they were not in control of power, but when they were able to establish a state nearer to the Islamic spirit, this state opened the door to the popular defense so that each citizen or each cultured person who

---

[431]President (Lt.-Gen.) Omar al Bashir, at a mass rally held to mark the National Martyrs' Day in 1995, stressed that "Sudan would not deviate from its cultural course regardless of the conspiracies being hatched against it by the enemies of Islam and the homeland. . . .He called on the youth to enlist in the battalions of the jihad to defend the faith and the homeland. "Sudan: President Addresses Martyrs' Day Rally."

[432]Human Rights Watch/Africa interview, Khartoum, May 7; 1995.

belongs to the elite in particular would have a military qualification. Presently, at all the entry points to elite positions, in public service and universities, a person passes through the military life that exposes him to a shock so that he emerges from it as a soldier not seeing any difference between himself and the other soldier who remained there [in the front line]; since he will be called at times to join him and to fight with him there also. This is one of the largest projects to unify Sudanese society, so that it may not be divided into military and civilian, leading to the dissipation of its power and to its weakness. And the other great project is to unify the Sudanese society so that it may not be divided into elites and commoners.[433]

As the PDF expanded, it had to accommodate the growing numbers of people for whom the government required training. Training for some began to be held on a part-time basis. For instance, in Wau the PDF has four training camps with part-time training, lasting three to five months, to permit the trainee to continue to go to his job part time.[434]

In the Khartoum area, open training camps made their appearance in 1994, while the original closed training camps at places such as El Quoteina, fifty kilometers south of Khartoum on the White Nile, and the military base at Fatasha on the outskirts of the capital, remained operational. Trainees parade, chanting religious songs and conducting physical and military exercises in full view of residents all afternoons for the duration of the training period. Refresher training cycles for senior civil servants take place in the afternoons on the football grounds of the University of Khartoum. Women had their PDF training as a day-time activity in such places as an unused hangar at Khartoum airport or a high school during recess. Even in villages PDF volunteers conduct their afternoon PDF training in the village football field.[435]

The open camp considerably cuts the maintenance costs since no food, accommodation or transportation expenses are required. The show of parading youth and elders naturally attracts the curiosity of neighborhood people. For the PDF commanders and cadres, this accomplishes the objective of "show of force," a central theme in the official discourse about the PDF.

---

[433]Dr. Hassan al Turabi, interviewed in *Qira'at Siyasiya* (Political Readings), Washington, D.C., vol. 2, no. 3 (Summer 1992), p. 18 (in Arabic).

[434]Human Rights Watch/Africa interview, Khartoum, May 26, 1995.

[435]Human Rights Watch/Africa interview, Khartoum, May 7, 1995.

Students in the PDF

In the first few months after the establishment of the PDF, the task of recruiting the first group of volunteers for the PDF in the capital area was left to the NIF student organizations, especially at Khartoum University. The student group erected a tent in the middle of the university central campus. Similar tents were erected in other areas of the capital. A banner explained to passers-by why it was necessary to volunteer: "to crush traitors and dissidents." This first group consisted of 5,000 civilians, in the majority students.

Human Rights Watch talked to some students who were among the first group who had PDF training as a condition of university attendance. The training was announced to them on November 26, 1990, for all students starting college then. They were required to report for PDF training on December 1, 1990, and had two months of training in closed El Quoteina camp south of Khartoum.[436]

The location was not an army base but was especially created as a PDF camp for the University of Khartoum. Other students, not from the University of Khartoum, were sent to Jebel Aulia military base for training. The students in this first class had to wear a long white shirt and pants of a coarse cotton cloth (*damouriya*) as a uniform.

There were daily lectures by Islamists, by government officials, and by NIF leaders. They talked about "the Islamist attitude." These speakers told the students that they wanted to defeat the West and Russia. They referred to the new civilization of Sudan, an Islamic civilization, and said the "whole world is against us because of our Islamic attitude."[437] The lecturers included al Taib Mohamed Kher, minister of interior, who came to the camp every Wednesday; Amin Hassan Omar; Dr. Hassam Muki, International African Islamic University president; Mohamed Amin Khalifa, president of the Transitional National Assembly; Salah Karrar, minister of mining and power; Ali Osman Mohamed Taha, the NIF leader who is now foreign affairs minister. The students we interviewed considered this to be "brainwashing to prepare mujahedeen to go on holy war in the south."[438]

At other times, the army officers threatened the student trainees, warning that if they demonstrated on return to Khartoum University, they would be beaten. The students were told that when they finished training they would have an army number and an army record, and could be ordered by the army to do anything. Those orders must be obeyed; any mistake and the trainee or PDF graduate would be tried under military laws, not under civilian laws.

---

[436]Human Rights Watch/Africa interview, Khartoum, May 30, 1995.
[437]Ibid.
[438]Ibid.

According to former trainees, the daily schedule of training was to rise at 4:00 a.m. to pray. Then into the field to march with weapons. Breakfast was at 9:00 a.m. and after that, back to the field and training. Lunch was at 1:00 p.m. The trainees were then required to stand at attention under the sun until 3:00 p.m. There was a rest period from 3:00 to 4:00 p.m.

At 4:00 p.m. they were again sent to the field to train and march. Sunset prayers were at 6:00 p.m. and dinner was at 7:00 p.m. From 8:00 to 9:00 p.m., or sometimes until 2:00 or 3:00 a.m., they were forced to stand at attention, depriving them of sleep.

Prayers were by order, except for the Christians, who were permitted to stay in their tents during prayer time. One student said he was a practicing Muslim, but he tried to stop praying during this training period because of the way it was forced on him.

This rigorous training schedule went on for one month then became less intense. The army officers said that they wanted to change the students from civilians into military, so that when they heard an order, they would comply without any negotiations. "Brainwashing was easy after this. You would accept anything," one student remarked. They joked that the lectures were the best time to sleep.

By 1992, PDF training had become mandatory for higher education students, male and female. All candidates accepted to attend colleges were required to undergo a two-month training course in the PDF before they entered college. Students who matriculated before that date were required to complete PDF training before graduation. The training usually took place during summer break. Those who were trained were not obliged to participate in military activities with the PDF after the training period, although there was pressure on them to volunteer for the war in the south, the jihad. (Students who did not volunteer were not sent with the PDF to fight in the war.)

For the academic year 1994-95, Professor Ibrahim Ahmad Omar, the minister of higher education and scientific research, again stated that PDF training attendance was a precondition for entering institutes of higher education throughout Sudan. Application forms for universities and higher educational establishments, both public and private, could only be obtained inside the PDF training camps once the training was completed.

Professor Omar explained to a press conference called for this purpose that the ministry prepared twenty-two PDF camps to receive 26,987 students (who had been admitted to higher education in the academic year 1995-96) all over the country, for a training period of forty-five days.[439] He asked holders of foreign school certificates to enlist in the Khartoum camps.[440] Brig. Mohamed al Hassan al Fadil, commander of the PDF, explained that all students admitted to higher education who failed to attend the training within a week of the opening day of the training camp on October 28 would lose the opportunity to proceed with their university education for that year.[441]

In November 1995 Uthman Bashir Abu Agla, a fourth year student at the University of Khartoum, died in Abdullahi Ibn Abi Rwaha PDF Training Camp. Authorities reportedly informed his family two days after the death, by which time an official autopsy had already established the cause of death as natural. They then delivered his remains to the family. According to the Sudan Human Rights Organization (U.S. Chapter), other students informed the family after their discharge from the training camp that Abu Agla actually died under torture by an agent of Sudan Security named in SHRO's press release. The agent reportedly was punishing the victim for anti-government campus activism.[442]

At least at two occasions, in 1993 and 1994, students broke out from the PDF camps and marched in protest demonstrations in the main streets of Khartoum to denounce the poor conditions of the camps and the degrading treatment that was their daily lot. The minister of higher education and scientific research warned students and their parents that the training remained mandatory, and gave ultimatums for the students to return to the camps or risk loosing their chance to complete university education. According to a student leader, students constituted 70 percent of seven PDF brigades fighting in the south in 1996, and a total of 670 students had been killed in battle in southern Sudan.[443]

---

[439]"Minister of Higher Education: More than 26 thousand students join PDF camps; PDF Cmdr.: Denial of access to Universities beyond one week of delay," *Akhbar al Youm* (Khartoum), October 18, 1995, p.1 (in Arabic).

[440]The Sudanese national high school certificate, Sudan School Certificate (SSC), is awarded by examination taken when high school course work is complete. Sudanese students who attend high schools in Saudi Arabia and other Gulf countries, by agreement among Sudan and the Gulf countries, will receive a certificate equating their high school degree with the SSC. They may therefore compete for admittance to Sudanese universities and upon admittance are obliged to attend PDF training.

[441]"More than 26 thousand students join PDF camps," October 18, 1995.

[442]Sudan Human Rights Organization-U.S. Chapter, press release, November 29, 1995.

[443]*Al Hayat* (London), April 15, 1996, p. 5 (in Arabic), quoting student leader Zuheir Hamid.

Civil Servants, Doctors, Women and Tribal Leaders

In 1995 Wahid Taj El Sir, a senior official in the Ministry of Work and Administrative Reform, said that the government wanted all its employees to receive military training by the end of 1996 so they would become imbued with the spirit of jihad, and that the PDF would undertake this training. The official warned that any person who dodged the training would not be promoted.[444]

While PDF service in the south is said to be voluntary, officials stated in November 1995 that a PDF battalion consisting of civil servants had been "sent to the southern states to take part in reconstruction efforts and the efforts aimed at bringing about peace from within." This statement was made at graduation ceremonies for PDF civil servant recruits from the Farouq-7 detachment, the Nusaybah-4 and the medium-level civil service cadres number 9.[445]

Civil servants, judges, diplomats, university faculty, physicians, and other professionals must attend a mandatory PDF training program. The training program for civil servants targeted senior government officials at first, so that they would set an example, and an example could be made of them if they failed to accept PDF training. Promotion in public service was conditional on such attendance. Refusal to attend has led to some employees' dismissal from public service. For example, eight lecturers from Gezira University, including the deputy vice chancellor, were dismissed in 1991 for refusing to attend PDF training.[446] In Wau in 1994, reportedly an older man who was director of fisheries in the Ministry of Agriculture was retired the day after he said he was too ill to attend PDF training.[447]

We interviewed one man who had spent forty-five days in one of the first PDF training programs for senior civil servants in 1993. They were grouped according to rank. Many were older men unaccustomed to hard exercise, raised in the capital and used to drinking cold water from the refrigerator. The conditions in which they trained, arising at 3:00 a.m. and training until 1:00 p.m., and then later in the day until late at night, were very difficult for them. Some used every excuse they could to find to be away from the training.

During this PDF training, there were political and patriotic lectures. One of the constant themes that was reiterated was the undesirable possibility of "Dinka domination" unless the SPLA was defeated. Some of the Dinka civil service

---

[444]*Al Hayat* (London), September 9, 1995, p. 5 (in Arabic), quoting Wahid Taj El Sir.

[445]"Sudan: President Attends Passing Out Popular Defense Recruits to go to Operation Zone," Republic of Sudan Radio, Omdurman in Arabic, 1700 gmt, November 9, 1995, quoted in BBC Monitoring Service: Middle East, November 11, 1995.

[446]See Africa Watch, "Sudan: Violations of Academic Freedom."

[447]Human Rights Watch/Africa interview, Khartoum, May 26, 1995.

trainees protested because of the repetition of "Dinka domination, Dinka domination.[448]

The emphasis of the training of civil servants, as with other groups, is ideological and religious. The trainees are strongly encouraged to join fighting units in the civil war. Those who do join receive career advantages, such as quicker advancement.[449] The training also helps authorities identify people who resist regime propaganda and religious indoctrination.

Even justices of the Supreme Court, many of them advanced in age, have been asked to join the PDF. At present, Supreme Court and regional judges may volunteer for PDF training. New members of the judiciary may not sit as judges until they complete the forty-five days of PDF training.

In June 1995 the chief justice, at a regular meeting of the justices, urged them to enlist for PDF training. Pressures on the judges to "volunteer" took various forms, including arguments by militant Islamist justices that all should participate in jihad and that only those trained in Europe would not want to follow suit. A true Muslim judge would not object to PDF training, they said, arguing that the judges were "enjoying life while the Muslims in Bosnia are fighting." Several judges objected that the training was improper and military exercises are inconsistent with the dignity of their offices. They noted that PDF trainees have to have their heads shaved and are subjected to harsh training by young military men.[450]

In recent years, doctors who had completed their residency were required by the Ministry of Health, prior to being certified to practice medicine, to register for and attend PDF training. This has included women doctors. In 1995, apparently this system was revised slightly with regard to women in the medical profession. In 1995 those women and men who had graduated from medical schools in 1992, 1993 and 1994 were reportedly required by the Ministry of Health to register for the PDF; this included graduates from 1994 who had not yet completed their residency. In June 1995 the Ministry of Health posted the names of those in these classes who were required to sign up with the PDF section in the Minister of Defense headquarters. Those subjected to this requirement believed that medical graduates who supported the government were not required to join the PDF but were given instead hardship posts in western Sudan that did not expose them to any

---

[448]Human Rights Watch/Africa interview, Khartoum, May 11, 1995.
[449]Fund for Peace, "Living on the Margin," p. 22.
[450]Human Rights Watch/Africa interview, Khartoum, June 1995.

military risk. Those who were believed to be anti-government reportedly were threatened with posting to the front line in the war in the south.[451]

A group of about 300 women, mostly civil servants and many in the health profession, was given notice to start training on July 1, 1995, at the Jebel Aulia camp near a military base to the south of Khartoum. According to one woman, the program was to be PDF training for six months, with a graduation from the PDF in December at a ceremony to be attended by the president, then national service for six months.[452] Since the women did not have to perform military duties in the army, for the second six months they would be required to report daily to officers at the military headquarters.[453]

In the PDF camp which she attended, ten women slept in each tent and every seventy women had a female instructor assigned to them. The instructors slept in the buildings at the training camp. The routine was to arise at 4:00 a.m. daily for prayers in the mosque, and to receive military/Islamic training from 6:00 a.m. until 9:00 a.m. This training included military training such as use of firearms, and Islamic songs and chants of a military nature.

At 9:00 a.m. daily the women trainees would be addressed by an imam — usually the only male instructor they had — on religion and politics and the formation of a new Sudanese society under an Islamic state. Reportedly the Christian women were required to participate in the Islamic activities, including prayers five times a day and Islamic songs. When they refused, they were punished by being forced to stand in the sun and then assigned the most distasteful duties to perform, such as cleaning latrines and washing dishes. One Christian woman reportedly was punished by being locked in her room for twelve hours, for reading a Bible and not listening to the instructor during a lecture. The Christian women reportedly thereafter were separated from the other women at mealtime and harassed verbally by an instructor, including statements such as "We are going to the south to kill your people — our men will kill them."[454]

In March 1995, the government invited tribal leaders from all over Sudan to a three-week conference it said was designed to bring harmony and better understanding among them. In addition to listening to public lectures and participating in discussions, the leaders were also required to undergo a PDF training course of fifteen days — not previously announced as part of the

---

[451]Human Rights Watch/Africa telephone interviews, New York, September 19, 1995 and February 12, 1996.

[452]Human Rights Watch/Africa telephone interview, New York, February 12, 1996.

[453]Ibid.

[454]Ibid.

conference. Discipline was adapted to their status and condition since many were elderly. The announced aim of this exercise was to bring about national unity through the acceleration of understanding among the main tribes in the country.[455]

Prisoners

Women prisoners may win their release if they attend PDF training for forty-five days through the Zahra program initiated in 1993 for the rehabilitation of women prisoners.[456] This program, called *Mu'askar al Zahra llilta'ibat* (Zahra Camp for Repenting Women), is under the joint supervision of the ministry of interior and the governor of Khartoum State and is a collaborative effort between the General Administration of Prisons under the ministry of interior, and the Coordination Department of the Popular Defense Forces. While there is no specific provision in the law for release of prisoners who have completed PDF training, this is probably covered under the provisions for release on the grounds of good conduct.[457]

The first forty-five day Zahra Camp PDF training program began in February 1993 at Soba Youth City, a facility for youth activities in the outskirts of Khartoum. Two hundred and fifty participants from Omdurman Prison for Women took part in it, and graduated on April 8, 1993.

The statements of the camp's director, prisons warden Captain Hamid Kabar, revealed that Christians were in fact converted to Islam during the PDF training:

> Participants are of different ages, ethnic groups and religions. The crimes for which they have been convicted were mainly alcohol brewing, gambling, forgery and adultery. The camp offers participants a spiritual rehabilitation and vocational training such as in sewing and needle work to prepare inmates for their reintegration in the community after their release. All participating agencies, plus Zakat Chamber, Islamic Call Organization and the Fund to Sponsor the Application of Shari'a, plan to extend support to the participants after their release to ease their reinsertion. The camp includes both Muslim

---

[455]Human Rights Watch/Africa interview, New York, March 1996.

[456]The Zahra program is in addition to the provision for release of prisoners who memorize the Qur'an while in prison.

[457]Law for the Organization of Prisons and Treatment of Inmates (1992), section 5, Article 26.

and Christian women, and some of the latter converted to Islam at the end of the period. [458]

He repeated this observation at the end of the interview: "I draw your attention to the presence of some Christian inmates who converted to Islam inside the camp and memorized the Qur'an, and conduct their daily prayers timely."[459]

According to the government press, inmates of the camp said that Muslim prayers are part of the daily routine of the camp. "W.A." explained that she and many other participants learned how to reject the Devil. They were taught how to pray, memorize the Qur'an and fast, and were introduced to discipline and other beneficial things. Seven other inmates had only positive things to say about the camp, expecting that after forty-five days there they would be freed.[460]

The representative of the Popular Defense Forces operational department explained that the camp's day starts at 3:00 a.m. for morning prayer. A session of collective reading of the Qur'an follows. Inmates clean the place in time for their morning parade that takes place at 6:00 a.m. In the evening they follow religious and cultural orientation programs delivered by instructors from the Africa University, previously the African Islamic Center, a training institute for proselytizers from Sudan and various other African countries.

The Zahra program was repeated in 1994 and in 1995; in early May 1995 another group of women prisoners were taken for PDF training. Hundreds of convicts have benefited from this offer of early release in exchange for PDF training, and groups of graduated ex-convicts are occasionally shown on national television.

Mass Mobilizations

At a mass rally in Port Sudan on January 1, 1995, President (Lt.-Gen.) Omar al Bashir called upon citizens to join the PDF at its training camps, which in 1995, he promised, would train "more than one million recruits to defend the country against the machinations of the enemies lying in wait to detract from its unity and sovereignty."[461] To meet this target, he directed all state governors to recruit and train at least 30,000 mujahedeen in each state. Since he issued this

---

[458] *Al Inghaz al Watani* (Khartoum), April 8, 1993, p. 5 (in Arabic).

[459] Ibid.

[460] Ibid.

[461] "Bashir says one million popular defense recruits to be trained this year," Republic of Sudan Radio, Omdurman, in Arabic, 1300 gmt, January 1, 1995, quoted in BBC Monitoring Service: Middle East, January 3, 1995.

directive, the president has been touring the country to swear graduating trainees into the PDF. Campaigns for the recruitment of national service soldiers were concurrently launched and intensified.[462]

The president inducted some 60,000 volunteers into the PDF in Kassala state, eastern Sudan, on February 15, 1995. A week earlier, some 55,000 recruits were inducted in Gedaref state, also in the east.[463]

At the end of October 1995, the SPLA overran several strategic government garrisons in Eastern Equatoria, in southern Sudan. President al Bashir, in response, called for mass mobilization against the SPLA rebels and "the foreign armies" allegedly supporting them.[464] He called on all sectors of the population and youth to head immediately to the popular defense camps and enlist in the jihad battalions to protect the faith, the country and its territory, according to national radio.[465]

---

[462]"Sudan: Sudan to Boost Militia Force to One Million," Reuter, Khartoum, February 16, 1995.

[463]Ibid.; "Sudan: Flash Points-Death Toll Reaches 1.3 Million," Reuter, Khartoum, February 16, 1995; "Sudan: Bashir Rejects Human Rights Report, Says Islamic Nation Reborn," Republic of Sudan Radio, Omdurman, in Arabic, 1300 gmt, February 15, 1995, BBC Monitoring Service: Middle East, February 17, 1995.

[464]Alfred Taban, "Sudanese President Calls for Mobilization," Reuter, Khartoum, November 8, 1995.

[465]Ibid.

8
ABUSES BY ALL PARTIES IN THE WAR

Cease-fires for two months in 1994 and four months in 1995 brought a much-needed breather to the thirteen-year civil war in the south but no lasting solutions. In 1995 former U.S. President Jimmy Carter convinced the government and the rebels to halt hostilities so health workers could conduct a campaign against guinea worm[1] and river blindness [2]in conjunction with the international health component of the Carter Center. A two-month cease-fire was agreed to on March 27, 1995, and was renewed once, expiring on July 28, 1995.

A rapprochement in 1995 between the two main rebel factions, the Sudan People's Liberation Movement/Army (SPLM/A) and the South Sudan Independence Movement/Army (SSIM/A), permitting displaced civilians to return to their homes without attack by either faction, was seriously undercut by the splintering of the SSIM/A into many different factions. In early 1996, SSIM/A founder Riek Machar Terry Dhurgon and Bahr El Ghazal commander Kerubino Kuanyin Bol, signed a peace agreement with the government.

Cmdr. Kerubino, whose forces functioned as a government militia since about 1994, attacking Bahr El Ghazal Dinka villages and SPLA targets, caused substantial civilian casualties, food shortages and other hardships by his loot-and-burn tactics in 1995-96. Fighting in Jonglei and Upper Nile between Riek's SSIM/A and a breakaway commander, William Nyuon Bany, caused enough

---

[1]Guinea worm or *Dracunculus medinensis* disease is caused by a parasite whose larvae enter the human body usually in drinking water and manifest themselves as blisters and ulcers. The number of infected persons is estimated to be nearly 50 million in Central Africa and elsewhere. The provision of a safe drinking water supply is essential in the control and eradication of the disease. Water protected at the source from contamination by individuals shedding the parasite, or water boiled or filtered before it is consumed, is considered safe. See Michael Katz, Dickson D. Despommer, and Robert W. Gwadz, 2d ed., *Parasitic Diseases* (New York: Springer-Verlag, 1989), pp. 41-46.

[2]River blindness or *onchocerca volvulus* disease results from a severe inflammatory reaction elicited by the foreign protein of a worm which is carried by the black fly whose breeding habitat is rivers and streams, hence the term river blindness. Man is the only host of this worm. It is a major cause of blindness in Africa and elsewhere, often affecting more than 50 percent of the inhabitants of towns and villages in endemic areas. Approximately 17 million people throughout the world are infected, with over 330,000 cases of blindness. The Carter Center effort focuses on preventing the progression of the disease to the stage where blindness becomes a reality; by administering one dose of Mectizan per year, the disease is arrested. See ibid., pp. 50-53.

civilian casualties and damage to return that Upper Nile area designated in 1993 as the "Hunger Triangle" to its unenviable status of the past.[3]

In addition to its sponsorship of Cmdr. Kerubino, the government has continued a policy, established under the prior government, of counterinsurgency operations against the Dinka of Bahr El Ghazal in which the army and the Popular Defense Forces (PDF), including former Arab tribal militias of communities that are neighbors and traditional competitors of the Dinka, raid civilian Dinka villages and take women and children as slaves — as well as loot cattle and other possessions, burn the villages, and kill anyone who gets in their way. The women and children are taken far from their homes and are forced to work (with beatings) for no pay. Some are sold. This practice has spread beyond the area of Bahr El Ghazal, and some soldiers, officers and PDF from garrison towns in different parts of the south take their captives home with them — on government transport, almost always air — when they return north.

Indiscriminate bombing by the government continued to claim civilian casualties in the south. The secretary-general of the United Nations took the unusual step of issuing a press release expressing his concern over two incidents in February 1996 in which government planes bombed airfields used by relief agencies, endangering the lives of civilians in need as well as the lives of international relief workers and flight crews. These bombings occurred in Akuer and Paluer, on Feburary 17, and in Paluer on February 22, both near Bor in Jonglei. The bombs fell within 300 meters of a clearly marked relief aircraft in Paluer on February 17, and within 300 meters of a relief building in Akuer.[4]

The rebel attacks in which humanitarian standards were most severely breached occurred in October 1994, with 106 mostly civilian dead in Akot, and in July 1995, with 210 mostly civilian dead in Ganyliel. It appeared that the SSIA was implicated in the first and the SPLA in the second, which had all the hallmarks of retaliation for the first. Neither movement has investigated or issued a satisfactory report on these devastating attacks.

A persistent problem for relief providers — and thus for some of the civilian population in southern Sudan — is the frequent looting of relief supplies and hostage-taking of relief personnel. Almost forty relief workers were taken hostage in 1995. There were many incidents of looting occurring after military attacks, and several involved looting not by the attacker but by the rebels based in

---

[3]See Human Rights Watch/Africa, *Civilian Devastation,* pp. 146-74.

[4]Press Release, "Secretary-General Gravely Concerned Over Bombing in Southern Sudan," SG/SM15904, New York, March 1, 1996; OLS (Southern Sector) Update 96/09, 5 March 1996, p. 1.

the area. In July and August 1995, the SPLM/A and SSIM/A signed separate humanitarian ground rules with Operation Lifeline Sudan (OLS),[5] promising not to attack civilians, among other things.[6]

Fighting in southern Sudan caused significant civilian hardship in 1995, more than in 1994 — and perhaps less than in 1993.[7] The U.N. noted that intensified fighting in three areas of the south, northern Bahr El Ghazal, Jonglei and Upper Nile, threatened the precarious health and nutritional status of vulnerable people there. OLS (Southern Sector) director Philip O'Brien said that "these areas have been arenas of war for various militia leaders. People are facing insecurity in all forms. In parts of Bahr el Ghazal, militia raids destroyed up to three-quarters of people's grain stores; and in the Sobat [Upper Nile] region, we know that fighting forced people away from their traditional grazing and fishing grounds."[8]

Almost one million more people in southern Sudan will require relief food in 1996 than in 1995, according to the United Nations. Priority activities would include emergency food aid for an estimated 2.1 million war-affected people throughout Sudan.[9] There are an estimated 556,000 Sudanese refugees in

---

[5]OLS is the U.N. umbrella agency responsible for emergency relief in Sudan. Its southern sector is based in Nairobi, Kenya, and its northern sector in Khartoum. As for the southern sector, its humanitarian programs are coordinated by UNICEF. The World Food Program manages air operations on behalf of the U.N. and NGOs. More than thirty-five international and Sudanese NGOs operate under the OLS umbrella, for which UNICEF also provides full-time security services. On average, some 200 U.N. and NGO relief workers are stationed inside southern Sudan. OLS (Southern Sector) news release, "Increased Fighting in Southern Sudan Threatens Humanitarian Conditions," Nairobi, Kenya, February 7, 1996.

Other NGOs such as Lutheran World Federation and Norwegian People's Aid operate in southern Sudan but outside of the OLS umbrella.

[6]OLS (Southern Sector) July 1995, p. 2 (SPLM/A); OLS (Southern Sector) Update, 29 August 1995, p. 1 (SSIM/A).

[7]See Human Rights Watch/Africa, *Civilian Devastation*.

[8]Moyiga Nduru, "Sudan-Politics: Ethnic Conflict Devastates the South,." InterPress Service, Nairobi, Kenya, March 19, 1996.

[9]OLS (Southern Sector),"Increased Fighting Threatens Humanitarian Conditions." In 1995, the United Nations agencies identified 719,460 displaced and war-affected persons in southern Sudan in need of food assistance. Report of the Secretary-General, Emergency assistance to the Sudan, Fiftieth session, Agenda item 20 (b), U.N. General Assembly, A/50/464, 22 September 1995, p. 3, para. 5.

neighboring countries, on account of the war, and at least 2.5 million Sudanese in Egypt, which does not recognize Sudanese as refugees.[10]

Southern Sudan is about three times the size of the United Kingdom and has only forty kilometers of paved road. Air transport remains the primary means of delivering humanitarian assistance and personnel, and it is also the most costly component of OLS.[11] Complicating this relief task, the government has imposed increasing restrictions on OLS flight operations, in stark contrast to the approval in November 1994 of flight access for all 104 locations requested. In the first half of 1995 the government refused clearances for flights to twelve established OLS relief bases in areas controlled by SPLM/A, putting in jeopardy those needy populations,[12] and indicated a continued willingness to disregard human need in favor of military considerations.

In October 1995, the SPLA attacked Sudan government positions in Eastern Equatoria, beginning an offensive that took back territory from the government for the first time since the rebel split in 1991.[13] The SPLA ultimately claimed its forces took control of thirteen villages or towns and destroyed three brigades in Eastern Equatoria province in the course of the campaign, leaving the government with control of only Kapoeta, Torit and some villages between Torit and Juba.[14] The government thereafter clamped down on all relief air access to southern Sudan in late 1995, imposing an exclusion zone (not permitting any flights to land at all) on all locations south of the lines of Kapoeta, Torit and Juba,

---

[10]The refugees include 27,000 in the Central African Republic; 320,000 in Uganda; 60,000 in Ethiopia; 112,000 in Zaire; and 37,000 in Kenya. US AID, Office of U.S. Foreign Disaster Assistance, "Sudan Situation Report #2."

[11]Report of the Secretary-General, "Emergency assistance to the Sudan 1995," p. 16, para. 67.

[12]Ibid., p. 7, paras. 22 and 23.

[13]Louise Tunbridge, "Ugandans 'helping rebels' in Sudan," *The Daily Telegraph* (London), October 31, 1995.

[14]Youssif Khazim, "Sudan People's Liberation Movement leader details areas under its control," *Al Hayat* (London), in Arabic, January 23, 1996, quoted in BBC Monitoring Service: Middle East, January 26, 1996; "Rebel movement says government forces in the south have been 'wiped out,'" Egyptian news agency MENA, Cairo, Egypt, in Arabic 2010 gmt, November 17, 1995, quoted in BBC Monitoring Service: Middle East, November 20, 1995. The SPLA advance on Juba in mid-November was reportedly only stopped by the retreating government forces' destruction of the Kit bridge. Khazim, "Sudan People's Liberation Movement leader details areas."

and Juba, Yei and Kaya.[15] The exclusion zone remained in place until March 1996, when it was lifted in favor of specific restrictions within that area.[16]

The government continued to restrict access to the Nuba Mountains, an area long forbidden to international relief efforts, regardless of documented need. The United Nations managed to conduct assessments in April 1995 in government-held areas of southern Kordofan and estimated there were 100,000 Nuba displaced persons in peace villages established by the government. Many locations were assessed for the first time in several years. Despite the identification of extensive needs, follow-up assessments and overall humanitarian assistance were severely curtailed by the lack of flight approval by the government to the requested locations.[17]

The war, showing no signs of abating,[18] spread from the south and the Nuba Mountains[19] to the east of Sudan in early 1996. The SPLA captured a small town, Khor Yabus, in Blue Nile province in eastern Sudan, and recaptured Pochalla on the Ethiopian border of Upper Nile province, in mid-March 1996.[20] In mid-April, 1996, a northern rebel group, the Sudan Alliance Forces, announced its first major operation in Sudan, claiming it attacked a military camp near Kassala in eastern Sudan and killed fifteen government forces. This marked the first real military operation by any northern opposition force to date.[21]

---

[15]It also restricted flight clearance to the U.N., NGOs, and the ICRC on a daily basis only from November 22, 1995 until early December. OLS (Southern Sector) Update, 9 January 1996, p. 1.

[16]OLS (Southern Sector) Update 96/09, 5 March 1996, p. 1.

[17]Report of the Secretary-General, "Emergency assistance to the Sudan 1995," p. 6, para. 18.

[18]The Bonn International Centre for Conversion, a disarmament group, reported that "conflict-ridden Sudan, one of the world's poorest states," showed the biggest relative arms build-up in the world in 1995, at 44 percent. Kevin Liffey, "Decade of Disarmament Brings Slow Peace Dividend," Reuter, Bonn, Germany, April 16, 1996.

[19]The Sudan Catholic Information Office reported fighting affecting civilians in the Nuba Mountains in March 1996. "Church Says Sudan Army Uproots 1,000 Families."

[20]"Kenya: Sudanese Rebels Says 1,500 Troops 'Annihilated,'" Reuter, Nairobi, Kenya, March 28, 1996. According to Reuter, the government acknowledged the SPLA capture of these towns. Pochalla had been in SPLA hands since 1986 and was recaptured by government forces in March 1992. Human Rights Watch/Africa, *Civilian Devastation*, pp. 37-38.

[21]"Sudanese Rebels Say They Kill 15 Government Troops," Reuter, Cairo, Egypt, April 22, 1996. The Sudan Alliance Forces is one of four military factions grouped under the National Democratic Alliance, an opposition umbrella movement, according to Reuter.

THE APPLICABLE LAW

The conduct of government armies fighting an internal conflict against insurgent forces is governed by the rules of war, also called international humanitarian law, which comprise the four 1949 Geneva Conventions, the two 1977 Protocols to those Conventions, and the customary laws of war. The rules of war, whose basic provisions are not derogable (may not be suspended) are primarily intended to protect the victims of armed conflicts.[22] They complement those standards of international human rights law that are nonderogable and remain binding upon governments.

The armed conflict between the government of Sudan and dissident forces, principally the SPLA, is an internal (non-international) armed conflict,[23] although over the years the government and apparently the rebels have requested and received military assistance, advisers and training from various countries. As an internal armed conflict, government and insurgent forces' conduct is governed by common Article 3 of the Geneva Conventions and customary international law. The 1977 Protocol II to the Geneva Conventions contains rules providing authoritative guidance on the conduct of hostilities by the warring parties.

Article 3 applies when a situation of internal armed conflict objectively exists in the territory of a state party; it expressly binds all parties to the internal conflict, including insurgents although they do not have the legal capacity to sign the Geneva Conventions.[24]

The obligation to apply Article 3 is absolute for all parties to the conflict and independent of the obligation of the other parties. Application of Article 3 by the government cannot be legally construed as recognition of the insurgent party's belligerence, from which recognition of additional legal obligations beyond common Article 3 would flow..

---

[22]See Human Rights Watch/Africa, *Civilian Devastation*, pp. 257-79.

[23]This applies to the fighting between factions of insurgents and to fighting between rebels and government-supported militia.

[24]As private individuals within the national territory of a state party, certain obligations are imposed on them. International Committee of the Red Cross, *Commentary on the Additional Protocols of 1977* (Geneva: International Committee of the Red Cross, 1987), p. 1345.

The law governing internal armed conflicts does not recognize the combatant's privilege[25] and therefore does not provide any special status for combatants, even when captured. Thus, the Sudan government is not obliged to grant captured members of the rebel forces prisoner of war status. Similarly, government army or militia combatants who are captured by the rebel forces need not be accorded this status. Either can agree to treat its captives as prisoners of war, however, and the SPLA has recently permitted the ICRC to visit its prisoners. The Sudanese government has refused access to the ICRC, however. Since the rebels are not privileged combatants, they may be tried and punished by the Sudan government for treason, sedition, and the commission of other crimes under Sudanese law. They may not be tortured, held in secret detention, disappeared, or summarily executed; to do so is forbidden by common Article 3 and international human rights law.

Article 3 common to the four Geneva Conventions,[26] virtually a convention within a convention, states:

> In the case of armed conflict not of an international character occurring in the territory of one of the High Contracting Parties, each Party to the conflict shall be bound to apply, as a minimum, the following provisions:
> (1) Persons taking no active part in the hostilities, including members of armed forces who had laid down their arms and those placed *hors de combat* by sickness, wounds, detention, or any other cause, shall in all circumstances be treated humanely, without any adverse distinction founded on race, colour, religion or faith, sex, birth or wealth, or any other similar criteria.
>   To this end the following acts are and shall remain prohibited at any time and in any place whatsoever with respect to the above-mentioned persons:

---

[25]The combatant's privilege is a license to kill or capture enemy troops, destroy military objectives and cause unavoidable civilian casualties. This privilege immunizes members of armed forces or rebels from criminal prosecution by their captors for their violent acts that do not violate the laws of war but would otherwise be crimes under domestic law. Prisoner of war status depends on and flows from this privilege. See Solf, "The Status of Combatants in Non-International Armed Conflicts Under Domestic Law and Transnational Practice," *American University Law Review*, vol. 33, p. 59.

[26]The Sudan acceded to the four Geneva Conventions on September 23, 1957.

(a) violence to life and person, in particular murder of all kinds, mutilation, cruel treatment and torture;
(b) taking of hostages;
(c) outrages upon personal dignity, in particular humiliating and degrading treatment;
(d)the passing of sentences and the carrying out of executions without previous judgment pronounced by a regularly constituted court, affording all the judicial guarantees which are recognized as indispensable by civilized peoples.

U.N. General Assembly Resolution 2444,[27] adopted by unanimous vote on December 19, 1969, expressly recognized the customary law principle of civilian immunity and its complementary principle requiring the warring parties in all armed conflicts to distinguish civilians from combatants at all times. It affirms

the following principles for observance by all government and other authorities responsible for action in armed conflicts:

(a) That the right of the parties to a conflict to adopt means of injuring the enemy is not unlimited;
(b) That it is prohibited to launch attacks against the civilian populations as such;
(c) That distinction must be made at all times between persons taking part in the hostilities and members of the civilian population to the effect that the latter be spared as much as possible.

---

[27]"Respect for Human Rights in Armed Conflicts," United Nations General Assembly Resolution 2444, G.A. Res. 2444, 23 U.N. GAOR Supp. (No. 18), p. 164, U.N. Doc. A/7433 (1968).

In situations of internal armed conflict, generally speaking, a civilian is anyone who is not a member of the armed forces or of an organized armed group of a party to the conflict. Accordingly, "the civilian population comprises all persons who do not actively participate in the hostilities."[28] Civilians may not be subject to deliberate individualized attack since they pose no immediate threat to the adversary.[29] Civilians lose their immunity from attack for as long as they directly participate in hostilities.[30] "[D]irect participation [in hostilities] means acts of war which by their nature and purpose are likely to cause actual harm to the personnel and equipment of enemy armed forces," and includes acts of defense.[31]

Persons protected by Article 3 include members of both government and SPLA forces who surrender, are wounded, sick or unarmed, or are captured. They are *hors de combat,* literally, out of combat, until such time as they take a hostile action such as attempting to escape.

Children are especially protected under the rules of war and under the Convention on the Rights of the Child. Article 4 (3) (e) of Protocol II to the 1949 Geneva Conventions states that children shall be provided with the care and aid they require, in particular measures with the consent of their parents "to remove them temporarily from the area in which hostilities are taking place to a safer area within the country and ensure that they are accompanied by persons responsible for their safety and well-being." States parties to the Convention on the Rights of the Child — of which Sudan was an early ratifier — shall take "all feasible measures to ensure protection and care of children who are affected by an armed conflict."[32]

Sudan is obligated under this Convention to take all appropriate measures "to prevent the abduction, the sale of or traffic in children for any purpose or in any form." (Article 35). Equally, it is required to "protect the child against all other forms of exploitation prejudicial to any aspects of the child's welfare." (Article 36). Sudan has recognized the right of the child "to be protected from economic exploitation and from performing any work that is likely to be hazardous or to interfere with the child's education . . . ." (Article 32). It also is obligated to take all appropriate legislative, administrative and other measures to "protect the child

---

[28]Robert K. Goldman, "International Humanitarian Law and the Armed Conflicts in El Salvador and Nicaragua," *American University Journal of International Law & Policy,* vol. 2, p. 553.

[29]Bothe et al., *New Rules,* p. 303.

[30]Ibid.

[31]*ICRC Commentary on the Additional Protocols,* pp. 618-19; Bothe et al., *New Rules,* p. 303.

[32]Convention on the Rights of the Child, Article 38 (4).

from all forms of physical or mental violence, injury or abuse, neglect or negligent treatment, maltreatment or exploitation including sexual abuses, while in the care of . . . any other person who has the care of the child." (Article 19 (1)). Children separated from their parents shall be assisted by the state in protecting their identity, including nationality, name and family relations. (Article 8).

Under the laws of war, military objectives are defined expressly only as they relate to objects or targets, although it is clear that members of the armed forces are also permissible targets. To constitute a legitimate military objective, the object or target, selected by its nature, location, purpose, or use, must contribute effectively to the enemy's military capability or activity, and its total or partial destruction or neutralization must offer a definite military advantage in the circumstances.[33]

While not an all-encompassing list, customary and conventional (treaty-based) international law prohibits the following kinds of practices, orders, or actions:

- Orders that there shall be no survivors, such threats to combatants, or orders to conduct hostilities on this basis.

- Attacks against combatants who are captured, surrender, or are placed hors de combat.

- Torture, any form of corporal punishment, or other cruel treatment of persons under any circumstances.

- The infliction of humiliating or degrading treatment on civilians or combatants who are captured, have surrendered, or are hors de combat.

- Hostage taking.[34]

- Shielding, or using the presence of the civilian population to immunize areas from military operations, or to favor or impede

---

[33]See Protocol I of 1977 to the Four Geneval Conventions of 1949, Article 52 (2).

[34]The *ICRC Commentary on the Additional Protocols*, p. 874, defines hostages as "persons who find themselves, willingly or unwillingly, in the power of the enemy and who answer with their freedom or their life for compliance with the orders of the latter and for upholding the security of its armed forces."

military operations. In addition, the parties may not direct the movement of civilians in order to attempt to shield legitimate military objectives from attack, or to favor military operations.[35]

- Pillage.[36] This includes looting or taking booty or spoils of war. This prohibition is designed to spare people the suffering resulting from the destruction of their real and personal property: houses, furniture, clothing, provisions, tools, and so forth.[37] Pillage includes organized acts as well as individual acts without the consent of the military authorities. The ordering or authorization of pillage is forbidden, and the parties are obliged to prevent or, if it has commenced, to stop pillage. All types of property, whether private, communal, state or other are protected, although the military authorities retain the right to requisition goods under certain conditions.[38]

- Destruction of property not absolutely necessary on account of military operations.[39]

- Slavery and the slave trade in all their forms.[40] The prohibition on slavery is one of the "hard-core" fundamental guarantees, universally accepted.

There are only two exceptions to the prohibition on the deliberate displacement, for war-related reasons, of civilians: their security or imperative military reasons.[41] Displacement or capture of civilians solely to deny a social base

---

[35]See Protocol I, Article 51 (7).

[36]IV Geneva, Article 33. This is a reflection of customary law.

[37]ICRC, *Commentary on the IV Geneva Convention* (Geneva: ICRC, 1958), p. 226.

[38]Ibid., pp. 226-27.

[39]Both pillage and unnecessary destruction are forbidden by customary international humanitarian law governing internal armed conflicts. Theodor Meron, *Human Rights and Humanitarian Norms as Customary Law* (Oxford: Clarendon Press, 1989), pp. 46-47; see IV Geneva, Article 53.

[40]See Protocol II of 1977 to the Four Geneval Conventions of 1949, Article 4 (2) (f).

[41]Article 17 (1) of Protocol II states: "The displacement of the civilian population shall not be ordered for reasons related to the conflict unless the security of the civilians involved or imperative military reasons so demand. Should such displacements have to be carried out,

(continued...)

to the enemy clearly has nothing to do with the security of the civilians. Nor is it justified by "imperative military reasons," which require "the most meticulous assessment of the circumstances"[42] because such reasons are so capable of abuse. One authority stated: "Clearly, imperative military reasons cannot be justified by political motives. For example, it would be prohibited to move a population in order to exercise more effective control over a dissident ethnic group."[43]

The civilian population and individual civilians are to be protected against attack. The laws of war implicitly characterize all objects as civilian unless they satisfy the two-fold test required of military objectives (see above). Objects normally dedicated to civilian use, such as churches, houses and schools, are presumed not to be military objectives. If they in fact do assist the enemy's military action, as through the placement of guns in a bell tower, they can lose their immunity from direct attack.

Even attacks on legitimate military targets, however, are limited by the principle of proportionality. This principle places a duty on combatants to choose means of attack that avoid or minimize damage to civilians. In particular, the attacker should refrain from launching an attack if the expected civilian casualties would outweigh the importance of the military target to the attacker. The attacker also must do everything "feasible" to verify that the objectives to be attacked are not civilian. "Feasible" means "that which is practical or practically possible taking into account all the circumstances at the time, including those relevant to the success of military operations."[44]

Prohibited indiscriminate attacks are defined in Protocol I, Article 51 (4), as

> a) those which are not directed at a specific military objective;
> b) those which employ a method or means of combat which cannot be directed at a specific military objective; or
> c) those which employ a method or means of combat the effects of which cannot be limited as required by this Protocol; and consequently, in each such case, are of a nature to strike military objectives and civilians or civilian objects without distinction.

---

[41](...continued)
all possible measures shall be taken in order that the civilian population may be received under satisfactory conditions of shelter, hygiene, health, safety and nutrition."
[42]*ICRC Commentary on the Additional Protocols*, p. 1472.
[43]Ibid.
[44]Bothe et al., *New Rules*, p. 362 (footnote omitted).

Starvation of civilians as a method of combat has become illegal as a matter of customary law.[45] The ICRC defines starvation as the term is used in Article 14 as "the action of subjecting people to famine, i.e., extreme and general scarcity of food."[46] Starvation is prohibited "when it is used as a weapon to destroy the civilian population."[47] This prohibition on starving civilians "is a rule from which no derogation may be made."[48] No exception was made for imperative military necessity, for instance.

Article 14 lists the most usual ways in which starvation is brought about. Specific protection is extended to "objects indispensable to the survival of the civilian population," and a non-exhaustive list of such objects follows, including foodstuffs, agricultural areas for the production of foodstuffs, crops, and livestock. The article prohibits taking any destructive actions aimed at these essential supplies.

Sieges are considered a form of starvation by omission: "Starvation can also result from an omission. To deliberately decide not to take measures to supply the population with objects indispensable for its survival in a way would become a method of combat by default, and would be prohibited under this rule."[49] It is therefore incumbent upon the attackers, in sieges and blockades as well as in other methods of combat, to take actions to ameliorate the effects upon civilians. The Protocols suggest various alternatives, among them permitting relief supplies to or evacuation of the civilian population.[50]

Depriving the civilian population of objects indispensable to its survival often results in the population moving elsewhere to find food. Since the provision of relief is often inadequate or uncertain in amount and timing and may even be blocked by an army or rebel group, there may be no other alternative for civilians than to move. "Such [population] movements are provoked by the use of starvation,

---

[45]Protocol II, Article 14 (" Protection of objects indispensable to the survival of the civilian population") states: "Starvation of civilians as a method of combat is prohibited. It is prohibited to attack, destroy, remove or render useless, for that purpose, objects indispensable to the survival of the civilian population, such as foodstuffs, agricultural areas for the production of foodstuffs, crops, livestock, drinking water installations and supplies and irrigation works."

[46]*ICRC Commentary on the Additional Protocols,* p. 1456 (footnote omitted).

[47]Ibid., p. 1458.

[48]Ibid., p. 1456.

[49]Ibid., p. 1458.

[50]See Protocol I, Articles 70 and following.

which is in such cases equivalent to the use of force."[51] Forcing civilians to move by attempting to starve them out is therefore prohibited.

VIOLATIONS BY GOVERNMENT ARMY AND MILITIA

Bombing

The government began its 1994 dry season offensive into Western Equatoria[52] with bombing by military aircraft of Mundri in Western Equatoria, hit several times between October 1 and 10, 1994.[53]

On February 21, 1995, government planes bombed Chukudum. According to an eyewitness, there were many explosions, much smoke, and many delayed detonations. Frightened civilians fled to the security of the mountain. This was the second bombing in a week, and these bombs fell very close to the dispensary run by Catholic sisters.[54] Although the SPLA headquarters is in Chukudum, this is a preexisting village, the largest in the area inhabited by the Didinga people, and still has a civilian population. It is the duty of the government to exercise care in attacking military targets within Chukudum, and to refrain from such attacks if it cannot avoid or at least minimize civilian casualties or damage to civilian property.

Twenty-three civilians reportedly were killed in a government aerial bombing of Ombaci in Yei County on September 14, 1995 and thirty-four wounded. The next day, four of the injured died.[55]

The government stepped up its bombing in Eastern and Western Equatoria in September through November 1995, hitting the Lui/Amadi junction and the Mundri/Gulu junction and Kotobi camp, Chukudum and Yambio in November. There were casualties in Yambio, where two died and five were wounded when the bomb landed between the airstrip and the village center.[56]

The day after the visit of Archbishop of Canterbury Carey to Juba, on October 9, 1995, two displaced persons camps near Nimule, south of Juba, were bombed by a Sudan government Antonov plane, leaving two civilian dead and others injured. According to one witness, one civilian lost his leg, one woman lost an eye, a small child had a piece of shrapnel through his upper arm, among others.

---

[51]*ICRC Commentary on the Additional Protocols,* p. 1459.

[52]The dry season starts in November and lasts until about May.

[53]OLS (Southern Sector) Update, 11 October 1994, p. 1.

[54]Confidential communication to Human Rights Watch/Africa, June 1995.

[55]Statement, Msgr. Peter Dada, Vicar General, Diocese of Yei, "More than 27 Civilians Killed by the Sudan Government in Ombaci, Yei County," Nairobi, Kenya, October 2, 1995.

[56]OLS (Southern Sector) Update, 7 November 1995, p. 1.

The government seemed to be using a smaller bomb that threw more shrapnel and caused much more injury.[57]

Labone, inside the exclusion zone imposed on November 22, 1995 by the government (barring relief flights), was bombed by government planes three times, on November 21, 25 and 30, 1995. Around 50,000 displaced civilians were estimated to live in Labone.[58] Two persons, a woman and a child, died during the November 25 bombing by an Antonov.[59]

Taking Children and Women Slaves as War Booty

The practice of government soldiers, officers and militia (Popular Defense Forces) who take women and children captive, to be used or sold as household slaves, has persisted almost since the beginning of the war, in violation of the most fundamental and universally-accepted human rights concepts, the prohibition of slavery and slave-trading. In the face of mounting evidence, including NGO and journalist interviews with escaped slaves in many different places,[60] the government asks the world to believe that these practices are nothing more than hostage-taking, done by both sides. Nothing could be farther from the truth.

Troops have regularly accompanied supply trains from Babanusa to Wau, on what the government of Sudan insists on referring to as "a noble mission of protecting the relief routes and fighting banditry and outlaws who regularly interfere with the relief operations . . . ."[61] Indiscriminate attacks by government forces conducted on villages near the railway in the Babanusa-Wau route, however, are routine. Those troops and PDF militia capture civilians as war booty, providing

---

[57]Confidential communication to Human Rights Watch/Africa, October 21, 1995.

[58]Human Rights Watch/Africa interview, Labone, southern Sudan, March 15, 1995. Human Rights Watch/Africa visited southern Sudan in March 1995.

[59]Confidential communication to Human Rights Watch/Africa, December 4, 1995.

[60]U.N. Commission on Human Rights, "Situation of human rights in the Sudan," February 1, 1994, pp. 16-18, paras. 62-65; Mahmud and Baldo, *Al Dien Massacre: Slavery in the Sudan;* Africa Watch, *Denying "The Honor of Living,"* pp. 139-51; Christian Solidarity International, "Widespread Enslavement of Black African Southern Sudanese by Arabic Northerners and Attempted Genocide of the Africans of the Nuba Mountains by the Government of Sudan" (London, August 1995); Human Rights Watch/Africa, *Children of Sudan,* pp. 31-53; Sam Kiley, "Sudanese Children Sold as Slaves, Say Christian Groups," *The Times* (London), March 16, 1996; Tim Sandler, "Africa's invisible slaves," *The Boston Phoenix,* June 30-July 6, 1995, pp. 16-20; Shyam Bhatia, "Sudan revives the slave trade," *The Observer* (London), April 9, 1995.

[61]"The Response of the Government of the Sudan," November 21, 1995, p. 22, para. 83.

a financial incentive for impoverished Baggara (Arabized tribes of western Sudan) PDF militia and soldiers. The government ensures their impunity for these acts.

One letter from Wau states that, in the second week of December 1994, a train carrying military supplies arrived at the government garrison town of Wau. "Instead of following the railway line," the letter continued,

> the government forces raided the villages far away from the railway line, even across the River Jur, and robbed cattle, goats, chickens and food items. The worst thing is the number of small children taken from their relatives who were either killed or had run away and left the children behind.
>
> Most of the children are now in Wau under the control of those mujahedeen who captured them. Some of them were left at Gette, 25 miles northwest of Wau town under the custody of the army there. Their owners will pick them up from there on the return journey.
>
> The civil authorities in Wau are afraid to question the mujahedeen and the army who have brought the children and the cattle of the innocent people in thousands. Soon the train will leave Wau for Babanusa, and the children, cattle and goats will find their ways into the northern Sudan markets.[62]

The following year, 1995, the supply train from Babanusa to Wau again was guarded by soldiers and militia who looted and captured women and children from villages along the way. The SPLA attacked the train and its armed "protectors," who fled with their captors to the closest garrison town, Aweil, not on the railway line. There, a southern police chief prevented the militia and army personnel from taking the women and children with them when they left for the garrison town of Wau. It was estimated that 500 captured women and children were left behind in Wau. The militia and soldiers, however, managed to hold on to the 3,000 head of cattle they pillaged from the villages.[63]

In late 1995, meetings reportedly were held between representatives of the Dinka and the Rizeigat (Arabized western tribes, originally nomads in Darfur), a subgroup of the Baggara. In exchange for access to the fresh pasture land and water controlled by the SPLA, the Rizeigat agreed to release Dinka "prisoners" captured during their raids. They reportedly brought with them to a meeting a list of 674

---

[62]Confidential communication, December 16, 1994.
[63]Human Rights Watch/Africa, *Children of Sudan,* pp. 41-42.

children already identified and whose release has been promised. They were given Ls. 250,000 (U.S. $473) for the immediate transport and clothing of twenty children said to have been gathered in Nyala in Southern Darfur. In Nyala, a court case was opened by the relatives of two young Dinka women of about seventeen years of age, impregnated by their masters, for the return of the two to their families. A report of these events was said to have been taken to Khartoum for presentation to Angelo Beda, Fathi Khalil and an army officer, all members of the assembly and on its committee for human rights, who were in the region in February 1996 investigating reports of slavery.[64]

In mid-March 1996, a government column consisting of PDF and army and including many Baggara on horses, fled east from an SPLA ambush on the railway to Lake Keilak and on the way, not far from Abyei in Southern Kordofan, reportedly attacked the village of Mabior, established in 1995 by the government to encourage the displaced to settle and become self-supporting. Many women and children were said to have been captured as war booty, although ten women with eight children managed to escape.[65]

In a sign that international pressure has had some effect, the local authorities in El Diein in Southern Darfur were believed to have ordered the release of dozens of Dinka children brought to El Diein and surrounding villages by raiders who had captured them from the area around Aweil in Bahr El Ghazal in early 1996. Those children were handed over to the care of the Dinka community in El Diein. In another case, a Dinka boy, captured at age six in 1986 near Abyei by a Baggara raider and taken to Nahud, was located by his uncle, who complained to the police. The police issued a warrant for the release of the boy to the uncle (the boy's parents were dead). The person who allegedly purchased the boy from the raider did not want to give him up without a payment of money, and threatened the uncle with death, but because of the police warrant eventually released the boy to the uncle without compensation. The boy reportedly does not remember anything about his family or background, knows very few words of Dinka, and has never been to school.[66]

The government is under pressure on the slavery issue, and has been under investigation by several U.N. bodies and mechanisms with regard to the allegation of condoning slavery and forced labor for several years: the ILO, the U.N.

---

[64]Confidential communication to Human Rights Watch/Africa, May 9, 1996. It is not clear if this committee had any relation to the government committee officially charged with investigating slavery on or about March 22, 1996, referred to below.

[65]Ibid.

[66]Ibid.

Committee on the Rights of the Child, the U.N. Working Group on Contemporary Forms of Slavery and the U.N. Commission on Human Rights. Finally in 1996, the government of Sudan notified the U.N. on March 22, 1996 that it was extending the mandate of an existing special committee to investigate alleged cases of slavery and related practices in the Sudan. This committee is composed of representatives of the ministry of justice and interior, internal and external security, and military intelligence.[67]

The government claims that with regard to slavery, "the element of intention is decisive." In the Sudan, it maintains, tribal fights normally result in captives and prisoners of war on both sides of the conflict, but there is no intention to take slaves. It adds that collecting slaves was the practice of the "white man decades ago."[68]

The history of slavery in Sudan, however, is more complex. The southern peoples of what is now Sudan were subjected to slave raids by the Turko-Egyptian forces (and northern Sudanese) starting in 1820 during their colonization of the vast land south of Egypt. Slave raids continued during the 1881-98 independent Sudanese (Mahdist) state; by the end of the nineteenth century the Shilluk, Dinka, Bari, Latuka and Azande peoples (the last three from areas around Juba far from Bahr El Ghazal), as well as many others, "had all been subjected to devastating raids from Mahdist garrisons established inside their countries or along their borders."[69]

Southerners, however, were not colonized; they were raided and raided again but their peoples remaining in the south remained free.[70] After the reconquest of Sudan in 1898 by the Anglo-Egyptian forces, slave-taking diminished but never entirely died out. Even in the border areas most prone to raiding, such as the Dinka/Baggara border in northern Bahr El Ghazal and southern Darfur, however, the resistance of the southerners and the raiding ability of the Baggara tribes were in rough parity, until the mid-1980s.[71]

---

[67]U.N. Economic and Social Council, Commission on Human Rights, Fifty-second session, Agenda item 10, Letter of 29 March 1996 from Sudan to the U.N., E/CN.4/1996/145, April 2, 1996, annexes 2 and 4. Originally, this committee was set up to investigate 249 cases of disappeared Nubas.

[68]"The Response of the Government of the Sudan,"November 21, 1995, p. 22, para. 82.

[69]Alier, *Southern Sudan*, p. 13.

[70]Deng, *War of Visions*, p. 6: "'southern Sudanese' are the progeny of those Africans who escaped enslavement."

[71]Keen, *The Benefits of Famine*, pp. 21-31.

The resurgence of slavery in modern times is a direct result of war and government policy in that war, as described in a 1987 report researched and written by two northern Sudanese intellectuals on the faculty of the University of Khartoum.[72] The report pointed out that since a conciliation accord in 1976, relations between the Dinka in northern Bahr El Ghazal and the Baggara people, specifically its Rizeigat subgroup (originally nomads in Darfur), to their north were good. The Rizeigat groups settled on Dinka land during the famine in the north of 1985 and their presence was not disturbed by the (largely Dinka) SPLA units in the area.

The Transitional Military Council — which came to power for a year (1985-86) after Nimeiri was deposed — devised a comprehensive strategy toward the area, based on the understanding that the Dinka civilian population there constituted the major potential support for the SPLA and that it was essential to undermine such support. "The core of the strategy to undermine SPLA support in the Dinka was to resurrect and fuel the historical Dinka-Rizeigat strife which was put to rest by the accord of 1976 in Babanusa," according to the authors.[73]

The government's method of forcing the Rizeigat and the Misseiriya to the east into the war included arming their tribal militias. The first attack by these forces took place at the end of 1985 to the north of Aweil. The governor of Bahr El Ghazal at that time was a Dinka with the rank of general in the army, however, and a small army unit chased away the attackers and returned the cattle stolen during the attack. A few weeks later large numbers of armed tribal militias attacked several Dinka villages, killing 612 Dinkas, looting a large number of cattle, and kidnaping more than 700 women and children. Similar attacks continued until May-June 1986 when the SPLA deployed heavier forces in the area.[74]

In January 1987 another Rizeigat militia attack on a number of Dinka villages occurred. Hundreds of women and children were kidnaped and taken as slaves. Another attack in the same month was blocked by SPLA forces, with heavy casualties. The SPLA and the Rizeigat militias fought in March near Sahafa, in southern Darfur, and the SPLA caused heavy casualties and returned south with large numbers of Dinka cattle taken in the January 1987 attack from the Dinka.[75]

The government tried to excuse as revenge for the Rizeigat defeat at Sahafa a massacre in 1987 at El Diein — a commercial center in Darfur with rail and lorry links in many directions, one day south of Sahafa by lorry. On March 27-

---

[72]Mahmud and Baldo, *Al Diein Massacre: Slavery in the Sudan*, pp. 17-18.
[73]Ibid.
[74]Ibid., p. 18.
[75]Ibid., pp. 18-19.

28, 1987, about 1,000 unarmed Dinka were slaughtered in El Diein by Rizeigat and some local officials while the police fled or participated.[76] The Rizeigat took Dinka children and young girls into slavery during this massacre. The authors of the report were told by survivors that their children were being sold and others were held in servitude in Rizeigat homes; the survivors had the names of the captors. They said that the government officials and police did not respond to their complaints and requests to rescue their children.[77]

> The kidnaping of Dinka children, young girls, and women, their subsequent enslavement, their use in the Rizeigat economy and other spheres of life, and their exchange for money — all these are facts. And the government has full knowledge of them. Indeed, the perpetrators of kidnaping and slavery are its allies in the armed militias.[78]

This report, published in Arabic in Khartoum, was controversial among the political class in Khartoum. The *Sudan Times,* an English-language newspaper published in Khartoum by Bona Malwal, a southern politician and former minister of information, took up the cause, and began publishing stories of escaped slaves on a frequent basis.[79] Abel Alier, a former judge and vice president of Sudan and still the most respected southern politician in Sudan, investigated some cases of slavery and concluded:

> The Baggara [the tribal grouping to which both the Misseiriya and Rizeigat belonged] regard the captured children as part of the war booty. . . . The Baggara support the government in Khartoum. The Southerners are generally assumed to support the SPLA. The captured people are labeled 'prisoners of war' and as such belong to the 'soldiers' who captured them. But this is reminiscent of the Turco-Egyptian and Mahdiya administrations and hardly acceptable practice in modern times even in civil war.[80]

---

[76]Ibid., p. 16.
[77]Ibid., p. 20-21.
[78]Ibid., p. 20.
[79]See Alier, *Southern Sudan,* p. 284.
[80]Ibid., p. 286.

Those who spoke out against the resurgence of slavery were punished, however. As one historian wrote,

> The study of slavery in what is now the Republic of the Sudan ... is a politically charged topic; especially so now when slave-raiding has been revived both as a strategy of war and a tactic in large-scale labour mobilization for the agricultural schemes which dominate the economic planning of one half of the nation. To investigate slavery and the trade in slaves is to court unpopularity in the Sudan. Those who have written on past slavery have frequently been resented as discourteous; those who try to document present slavery are now denounced as 'enemies', 'traitors', and 'spies.'[81]

In a footnote the historian states:

> Before the June 1989 coup, Ushari Mahmud [an author of the 1987 study in Arabic on slavery] was regularly arrested and harassed by the police for his part in investigating the al-Diein massacre and subsequent slaving; the *Sudan Times* was threatened with liquidation by the Prime Minister [Sadiq al Mahdi] and its editor, Bona Malwal, denounced in parliament as an enemy of the Sudan for documenting cases of slavery. Even I was identified by some sections of the Sudanese press as a public enemy and a spy for reporting the evidence provided by the above. At the date of writing (early 1991), Ushari Mahmud is in prison and Bona Malwal is in exile.[82]

After twenty-two months in warrantless detention, and a visit from a government emissary who said he would be released if he recanted the slavery study (which he refused to do), Dr. Mahmud was released in a general prisoner release in May 1991. He was, however, subjected to a travel ban forbidding him from leaving Sudan or even Khartoum without government permission, which was never

---

[81]Douglas H. Johnson, "Recruitment and Entrapment in Private Slave Armies: The Structure of the *Zara'ib* in the Southern Sudan," *Slavery & Abolition*, vol. 13 (London: April 1992), p. 162 (footnote omitted).

[82]Ibid., p. 172, fn. 1.

forthcoming. The government offered him the same proposition, a trade of his civil liberties for renouncing the slavery study, which he again refused.

After the coup d'etat in June 1989, the government incorporated the Baggara tribal militias into its Popular Defense Forces, under the authority and supervision of the army. The raiding and capture of women and children to use as slaves continued, however. The evidence of this comes from international nongovernment human rights or other organizations and journalists traveling to sites where slaves had recently been taken,[83] interviewing escaped slaves elsewhere, and even filming the exchange of money for slaves.[84]

Having largely prevented Sudanese from speaking, the government has taken the inexcusable attitude that slavery must be "proven" to it, instead of living up to its obligations under international human rights law to seriously investigate grave and often well-documented reports,[85] and protect its citizens from this abuse. Its attitude toward the allegations is so negative that the victims of slavery practices who have managed to escape from their owners are most unlikely to come forward to offer "proof" to a hostile government. These victims are very poor, uneducated people (denied education by their owners) whose only protection against possible harassment, detention or torture is anonymity. In general, because of government intimidation and denial of freedom of speech, assembly and association, only a handful of persons — not former slaves — have come forward in public under the current government to provide testimony of any government abuses, and they have suffered for it.[86]

The government's most recent defense is to claim that the allegations of slavery were invented by those who want to prevent African Americans from supporting the government of Sudan. As described above, modern slavery was brought to international attention in 1987 — before the current government took power — by a study by two northern Sudanese intellectuals, but this government is well aware of this since it detained one of its authors, Dr. Ushari Mahmud. Attempts to bring the slavery issue to Sudanese public attention through letters to newspapers in 1996 have not been successful, and discussion of slavery remains beyond the "red line."

---

[83]Christian Solidarity International, "Widespread Enslavement of Black African Southern Sudanese," pp. 31-53.

[84]"The Slave Trade in Sudan," shown on Channel 4, London, in November, 1995, produced by Damien Lewis.

[85]E.g., Africa Watch, *Denying "The Honor of Living,"* pp. 139-51; .

[86]See the case of Brig (Ret.) al Rayah, who complained he was tortured in detention, Chapter V.

The Government's Garrison Towns

Juba, the largest town in the south, continued to be held by the Sudan government and run by military intelligence and Sudan Security. In the first week of December 1994, fourteen Juba residents were detained by military intelligence and Sudan Security, three were subjected to torture by Sudan Security, and all were finally released without charges after two months. (See Chapter V).

On September 7, 1995, government troops moving from Yei to Dodo along the Yei/Kaya road entered the village of Alero, where a service of the Episcopal Church of Sudan (ECS) was in session. According to the vicar general of Yei, the troops attacked the congregation, killing two on the spot and taking eighty captives to the garrison town of Yei. The Reverend Yoane Akule of the ECS and another man escaped from the army barracks in Yei, reporting that the captives were treated most inhumanly, and were constantly called *abit*, or slaves.[87]

Conditions in southern garrison towns held by the government but ringed by rebels, where the only access in and out was by air, are harsh, and strict control is the order of the day. In Wau, Bahr El Ghazal, security even went so far as to put a Sudanese relief worker under house arrest for three days in May 1995 to prevent her from meeting with Chip Carter (son of former U.S. president Jimmy Carter), who was in Wau for the campaign against guinea worm. A foreigner notified Chip Carter of this arrest, but the worker was held until Mr. Carter departed.[88]

In late April 1995, several persons associated with the university in Wau were detained by security without warrant and without charges for as long as sixteen days. Apparently one instructor and a few students were believed to have left Wau to join the SPLA, and consequently others at the college were picked up. One, a teaching assistant named Isak Makur Boc, had arrived in Wau only in February 1995 when the first two years of the four year course of the Faculty of Education, to which he was attached, were transferred there as a result of the decentralization of the universities.[89]

When Nasir in Upper Nile fell to the government at the end of March 1995, the Islamists organized a celebration at the university. Makur asked a southern student at that celebration why he, as a southerner, was reciting a poem to celebrate the fall of Nasir. This apparently made security suspicious of Makur.

---

[87]Msgr. Peter Dada,"More than 27 Civilians Killed by the Sudan Government in Ombaci, Yei County."

[88]Human Rights Watch/Africa interview, Khartoum, May 1995.

[89]The faculty was renamed the University of Bahr El Ghazal. There were about 200 students and thirty-three staff (including administrators) at the university. Students included northerners and southerners mostly from Equatoria, and both Islamists and non-Islamists.

According to one account, Makur was kept alone in an unventilated three by four meters windowless cell, locked up continually except for a few minutes at night, without water for two days and without washing or changing clothes for fifteen days. He was threatened with beating but not beaten. Arrested at the same time were six students who were beaten, one severely, and questioned about Makur's "connection" to the SPLA. No charges were brought but Makur was obliged by security to leave Wau and return to Khartoum upon his release.[90]

Under the government's "Peace from Within" plan, displaced southerners in Khartoum and other northern cities would voluntarily return to or near their homes in "pacified" areas of the south. The Sudan Council of Churches, an umbrella agency of Protestant Christian churches in Khartoum, assisted in the transport of those voluntarily returning to the south, arranging up to two flights a day to various southern towns.[91] A government spokesperson noted that 6,003 families were moved in fifteen trips to different states in the south in almost four years.[92]

The return was in many cases not successful because of unfavorable conditions in the towns to which the displaced were returned. For instance, in Juba, aid agencies reported that there was little work for the returnees and they were a burden on their relatives, and as a result many of them returned to the north. Juba experienced a very difficult year in 1995. A food assessment by the World Food Program in early 1995 revealed that Juba had a population of only 148,000, not the 300,000 previously estimated. WFP therefore cut back the rations in Juba, and the staples prices in the market skyrocketed: a fifty kilo sack of sorghum was Ls. 22,000 (U.S. $41.66) in Juba, compared to only Ls. 6,000 ($11.36) in Khartoum.[93] The hardship was increased when, as in other regions, civil servants — including medical doctors and most employees below the ministerial level — were not paid for months on end in 1995. The lack of cash meant that prices dropped, however. By October, 1995, the situation worsened and people began to leave Juba in search of food. The urban plots they cultivated had been exhausted, and the price of a fifty

---

[90]Human Rights Watch/Africa interviews, Khartoum, May 26 and June 11, 1995.

[91]Others involved in the repatriation program included the government's Peace and Development Fund, headed by Mustafa Gismallah, a Muslim from Malakal in Upper Nile and the founder of Islamic NGO *Dawa Islamiyya* (Islamic Call), and the government's Relief and Rehabilitation Commission.

[92]Mustafa Ismael, "Displacement in Khartoum State and the Related Humanitarian Assistance," paper given at the 24th Ordinary Session of the Organization of African Unity, Coordinating Committee on Assistance to Refugees in Africa, September 20, 1995.

[93]The May 1995 rate was $1 U.S. = 528 Sudanese pounds (Ls.).

kilo bag of sorghum shot to between Ls. 30,000 (U.S. $ 24.65) and Ls. 36,000 (U.S. $29.58).[94]

Relocation of displaced southerners back to Wau did not proceed smoothly. As much as the Khartoum state government was eager see the displaced southern population return home, whether the war was over or not, military intelligence and security in Wau and elsewhere did not like the idea. For instance, many of the displaced did not stay under government control in Wau but returned home, to rebel-controlled areas. The local officials were very suspicious of these returnees, accusing them of having joined the SPLA, and the repatriation flights to Wau were canceled as a result.[95]

There are about ten Islamic organizations administering World Food Program aid in Wau. Reports allege that some food aid to non-Muslims was conditioned on conversion to Islam. According to an account told to Human Rights Watch, a Dinka police officer based in Wau was put under this pressure.[96] According to the account, this policeman had gone without any salary for three or four months prior to August 1994 — a not uncommon situation for government employees. He asked Dawa Islamiyya for food assistance for his children. When he was asked his religion, he replied he was a Christian. The aid was reportedly refused, with the person in charge telling the sergeant, "We do not give food to Christians, only to Muslims. If you accept conversion, we will give you everything, food, clothes, money." The sergeant agreed but was told he must be circumcised and then the next day, Friday, he would have to declare in the mosque that he had changed his religion. According to this account, related by a close friend, he was given an amount of food, clothes and money before he undertook these steps.

He reportedly went to the mosque without having been circumcised; it is not the tradition of Agar Dinka men to be circumcised; some other sections (or groups)[97] of Dinka are traditionally circumcised. When the official at Dawa still insisted on his circumcision, the policeman discussed the matter with his wife, who was strongly opposed to it. "What would our people think?" (We were told that, to insult an Agar, one accuses him of being circumcised.) The policeman said he had

---

[94]Using the free market rate of $1 US = Ls. 1217; Nhial Bol, "Sudan-Food: Hunger Stalks Southern Town," InterPress Service, Juba, Sudan, October 11, 1995.

[95]Human Rights Watch/Africa interview, Khartoum, May 16, 1995.

[96]Human Rights Watch/Africa interview, Khartoum, May 26, 1995.

[97]Sections are the largest tribal segments within the Nuer, based on place of origin. E.E. Evans-Pritchard, *The Nuer* (New York: Oxford University Press, 1969), p. 5. This term is used in a similar fashion to describe the Dinka groupings. Dinka, Nuer, Shilluk and Anuak are all Nilotic peoples.

already accepted some relief and was afraid of being jailed if he did not do what they asked. The wife told him to ask for a delay, which he did on the pretext that he was sick. The wife sold all their belongings in the market and they left town.[98]

Government Militia

The government continued to pursue a divide and conquer approach to southern rebels. Playing on ethnic divisions among southerners, and particularly fostering anti-Dinka feeling with claims of "Dinka domination," the government entered into what was originally a clandestine arms-supplying alliance with several factions of the SSIM/A to fight the SPLA. At least two of those alliances were never publicly recognized until a peace agreement, termed the Political Charter, was signed in Khartoum on April 10, 1996 by the government, Cmdr. Riek Machar of the SSIM/A, and Cmdr. Kerubino Kuanyin of the SPLM/A (Bahr El Ghazal), an SSIA splinter group.

Cmdr. Riek Machar had led a rebellion against the leadership of SPLA Cmdr.-in-Chief John Garang in 1991, and formed a separate rebel force that Cmdr. Kerubino joined in 1993. Fighting between Riek's and Garang's forces in 1991-93 took several thousand civilian lives in a series of human rights abuses,[99] but in early 1995 they ceased hostilities. On January 25, 1995, Cmdr. Riek Machar dismissed Cmdr. Kerubino, at the time deputy chairman of SSIM and deputy Cmdr.-in-chief of SSIA, and Cmdr. William Nyuon Bany[100] from the SSIM/A for their alleged signing of military and political agreements with the government of Sudan between November and December 1994, and attempting to form a faction with the support of the government between January 8-16, 1995.[101]

The abuses described below, committed by troops of Cmdr. Kerubino, are attributable to the government of Sudan in that they occurred while his forces functioned as a government militia.

Cmdrs. Kerubino and Faustino Atem Gualdit, both Dinkas from Bahr El Ghazal, were among the founders of the SPLM/A in 1983-84. Accused of plotting

---

[98]Human Rights Watch/Africa interview, Khartoum, May 26, 1995.

[99]Human Rights Watch/Africa, *Civilian Devastation*, pp. 90-173.

[100]The SSIM announced that its forces killed Cmdr. William Nyuon in the course of an attack on Nyuon's hideout at Gul in the Waat area, Eastern Upper Nile, in mid-January 1996. "Kenya: Sudan Rebel Group Says it Kills Commander Nyuon," Reuter, Nairobi, Kenya, January 16, 1996.

[101]OLS (Southern Sector) Update, 31 January 1995, p. 1, quoting a SSIM/A press release; Buchizya Mseteka, "Kenya: Sudan Rebel Group Splits Further, Sacks Officials," Reuter, Nairobi, Kenya, January 25, 1995.

a coup against SPLA Cmdr.-in-Chief John Garang, they were jailed by the SPLA from 1987-92, when they escaped from SPLA custody,[102] and in 1993 joined the forces of SPLA-United under the leadership of Cmdr. Riek Machar; since they and their followers are Dinka, their participation in SPLA-United significantly broadened this rebel movement beyond its basic Nuer base.

Kerubino and Faustino returned to their native Bahr El Ghazal in late 1993 and with their followers started participating in hostilities — not against the government but against the SPLA. It was long rumored that Kerubino and others in the SSIA and its predecessor SPLA-United were receiving weapons and ammunition from the government in order to fight Garang. Indeed, this area of northern Bahr El Ghazal is so far from any border that military resupply would pose a major problem to rebels there had they had not assistance from Gogrial, the nearby government garrison town on the Babanusa - Wau railroad, where government supplies were ferried in by plane, as well as rail.

Repeated attacks in northern Bahr El Ghazal by the forces of Cmdr. Kerubino Kuanyin Bol caused many civilian casualties. These attacks violated rules of war prohibiting targeted attacks on civilians and destruction of civilian property, as well as indiscriminate attacks causing civilian casualties.[103]

Starting in June 1994 Kerubino attacked and took Mayen Abun and other villages in the Wunrock County area, until then in the hands of the SPLM/A (Garang). Mayen Abun, a village seventy-five kilometers from government-held Gogrial, was Kerubino's home town. The village was the scene of repeated attacks by both sides and it swung back and forth from the control of one band to the other.[104]

The Diocese of Rumbek denounced the fighting led by Kerubino and Faustino in Wunrock County in 1994 because of its devastating impact on civilians. The diocese, estimating that other commanders and over 2,000 Dinka and Nuer soldiers joined in the Kerubino attacks on these villages, deemed the location "a

---

[102]Human Rights Watch/Africa, *Civilian Devastation*, pp. 228-35. Their five-year detention without hearing or trial violated the customary law prohibition on prolonged arbitrary detention. They were subjected to cruel and inhumane treatment in detention as well.

[103]See Human Rights Watch/Africa, *Civilian Devastation*, pp. 228-35.

[104]*The Guardian* (London) reported that on June 29, 1994, the SPLA ordered Alek and Akon evacuated because of an imminent attack by Cmdr. Kerubino, who claimed he seized Alek on July 14. *Sudan Update* (London), vol. 5, no. 12, July 14, 1994; see OLS (Southern Sector) Update, 5 July 1994 (UN/NGO staff relocated from Akon and Mayen Abun in the last week of June 1994).

new fratricidal area."[105] Between the end of June and July 14, peaking on July 13, 1994, the two rebel fighting forces confronted each other in Wunrock villages, Turaiel, Maper, Aweng, Major, Pannyok and Mayen Abun, causing civilian deaths in the thousands, according to the diocese. Many died in the attempt to escape across the swollen Lol River.

Mayen Abun was looted and relooted. On July 3, 1994, when the SPLA withdrew from Mayen Abun, it looted the town of household goods, cattle, and anything else portable. The troops also took several women and children.[106] Kerubino's forces quietly took over Mayen Abun on July 5, 1994, and held it until after the fighting died down on July 14, when they left the village with 5,000 rebel soldiers, many having come to Mayen Abun to join this band. Kerubino's forces looted Mayen Abun down to the bones, taking everything that had not been removed by the SPLA two weeks before.

SPLA forces moved back into Mayen Abun the next day, in the early hours of July 15, finding that the civilian population had been evacuated or fled except for a few elderly people.[107] In this changeover from one band to the other, NGO equipment and supplies were destroyed and looted.[108]

Interfactional fighting north of Mayen Abun started again on September 4, 1994[109] and lasted about a week. SPLA-United forces under Kerubino gained control of Mayen Abun again. Civilians fled the area, walking two to three days away, and stayed there for some weeks. [110]

By October the village had reverted to SPLA control. Nhomo Kot Deng was badly injured in the fighting in that month. A native of Mayen Abun and at twenty-five a mother of four, she said that Mayen Abun was attacked one morning by "Kerubino," who came from outside Mayen Abun. He fought and withdrew the same day. She was in her *tukl* (hut) when the attack started and she was hit with a bullet. Four months and a skin graft later, her left leg was still in a cast. She believes she was the only civilian wounded that day, although she saw the bodies of two small boys who were killed.[111]

---

[105]Caesar Mazzolari, Apostolic Administrator, Diocese of Rumbek, "Sudan: The Pace of War and Division Is Relentless," Nairobi, Kenya, July 17, 1994.

[106]Ibid.

[107]Ibid.

[108]OLS (Southern Sector) Update, 19 July 1994, p. 1.

[109]OLS (Southern Sector) Update, 6 September 1994, p. 1.

[110]OLS (Southern Sector) Update, 4 October 1994, p. 1.

[111]Human Rights Watch/Africa interview, Lokichokio, Kenya, March 18, 1995.

Mayen Abun was the scene of fighting between the SPLA and SPLA-United, renamed Southern Sudan Independence Army (SSIA), again in late October 1994, resulting in the flight of about 5,600 people to SPLA-held Akon.[112] Kerubino then advanced on Akon and Lietnhom, and the SPLA warned the people and the NGOs to evacuate.[113] The SPLA pushed Kerubino's band out of Mayen Abun in November, and it took refuge in government-controlled Gogrial.[114]

The government forces also committed abuses in Mayen Abun. A twenty-two-year old woman was injured in a 5:00 a.m. attack on a cattle camp near Mayen Abun in February 1995. "The *Moram* (Arabs) came to attack. I was in the cattle camp," she said. "They did not come to take the cows; they left the cattle. They came just to attack."[115] In this attack she saw four children killed, with her own eyes. A pregnant woman was killed in the same camp. The injured woman was hit by a bullet in the right knee. Her three children remained in Mayen Abun, where she was born.[116]

OLS head Philip O'Brien reported after visiting Turalei that Kerubino, with a force of 200, had devastated that village, taking all the crops and robbing the people. "Nothing was left standing," he said, calling Kerubino "pettily vindictive," apparently acting in revenge against those civilians who did not support him.[117]

On April 27, 1995, the SPLA and SSIA reduced their cease-fire to writing in the Lafon Declaration.[118] This had no benefit, however, for the people of northern Bahr El Ghazal, where Kerubino — having been expelled by the SSIA — continued to fight Garang. A U.N. assessment visit to Mayen Abun (one of several locations in Bahr El Ghazal to which there had been no access for months because

---

[112]OLS (Southern Sector) Update, 1 November 1994, p. 1.

[113]Buchizya Mseteka, "Kenya: Aid Workers Ordered to Evacuate South Sudan Towns," Reuter, Nairobi, Kenya, November 4, 1994.

[114]"Kenya: Sudanese Rebels Deny Mass Exodus," Reuter, Nairobi, Kenya, November 10, 1994.

[115]This camp was not a military base. Human Rights Watch/Africa interview, Lokichokio, Kenya, March 18, 1995.

[116]Ibid.

[117]Aidan Hartley, "Kenya: Marauders Devastate Villages in Sudan War - U.N.," Reuter, Nairobi, Kenya, March 20, 1995.

[118]The Lafon Declaration, signed in Chukudum, Eastern Equatoria, Sudan, on April 27, 1995, by Cmdr. Oyay Deng Ajak, chairman, SPLM/SPLA Committee and Cmdr. Gatdor Kiec Wuor, Chairman, SSIM/SSIA Committee, approved on the same day by Dr. John Garang de Mabior, Chairman/C-in-C, SPLM/SPLA, and Cmdr. William Nyuon Bany, Chief of Staff, SSIM/SSIA, p. 3, para. V.3.

of the fighting) in March 1995 revealed "widespread damage to Tukuls [huts]."[119] Displaced people from Mayen Abun moved in May to Mankien and other locations.[120]

Fighting continued in northern Bahr El Ghazal, in Wau County and in Gogrial area where government militias raided and torched many villages in April and Babanusa May 1995.[121] As the train carrying government military supplies and food proceeded south from to Wau, it was heavily guarded by government militias and army who spread terror in their path, causing residents to escape[122] or suffer capture or enslavement.[123] In fighting near the railway between Aweil and Wau, there were an unconfirmed thirty-seven dead and twenty seriously injured, both soldiers and civilians.[124]

Kerubino was again reported to be fighting against the SPLA in the Gogrial/Panliet area in early July 1995.[125] On July 21, he attacked Panliet, forcing two WFP and two UNICEF staff members to flee by road and on foot to Wunrok.[126] In August 1995 the government of Sudan announced that Mayen Abun and three other destinations in southern Sudan (Akon and Lietnhom, in Bahr El Ghazal, and Kongor in Jonglei) must be sent relief supplies only from northern Sudan, indicating it was or hoped to be in control of these locations.[127] This change of relief arrangements was rejected by the SPLA on the grounds that no change in the point of origin for relief flights could be negotiated without its consent.[128]

An aid worker captured by Kerubino in September 1995 was released by the Sudan Foreign Ministry in Khartoum a month later. Kerubino told the Medecins Sans Frontiers-Belgium employee, a Kenyan, that he had "negotiated" the release, but MSF said that the Kenyan aid worker had been held in the government town of Gogrial, from which he was flown to Khartoum. Eleven aid workers escaped after they were captured by Kerubino during a September 16 attack on Panthou village in northern Bahr El Ghazal, but the Kenyan had sprained

---

[119]OLS (Southern Sector), March 1995, p. 4.
[120]OLS (Southern Sector) Update, 9 May 1995, p. 2.
[121]OLS (Southern Sector) Update, 30 May 1995, p. 2.
[122]OLS (Southern Sector) Update, 6 June 1995, p. 1.
[123]See Human Rights Watch/Africa, *Children of Sudan*, pp. 31-53.
[124]OLS (Southern Sector) Monthly Report, May 1995, p. 2.
[125]OLS (Southern Sector) Update, July 4, 1995 p. 1
[126]OLS (Southern Sector) Monthly Report, July 1995, p. 5
[127]OLS (Southern Sector) Update, August 8, 1995, p. 2
[128]Report of the Secretary-General, "Emergency Assistance to the Sudan 1995," pp. 7-8, para. 23.

his ankle and was unable to flee with them.[129] The aid worker, Stephen Gatuma Kamau, told journalists he was held in a fenced enclosure and given two meals a day before being taken to Khartoum for the last week of his captivity, where he was interrogated by the government on suspicion of spying.[130]

Kerubino attacked Lietnhom on December 9, 1995, with three killed and several tukuls destroyed,[131] and attacked Akon on January 12, 1996, capturing it the same night.[132]

VIOLATIONS BY THE REBEL FORCES

Nuer/SSIA Attack Akot in October 1994, Killing 106

Akot, a town in the Agar Dinka area of the Lakes district of Bahr El Ghazal, and a nearby cattle camp Theragap, were attacked on the morning of October 22, 1994 by heavily armed men. The attack, carried out by Nuer forces with reported assistance by the SSIM/A, resulted in 106 deaths and eighty-nine wounded, according to local officials. This indiscriminate attack, with its disproportionate effect on civilians, was followed by extensive SPLA looting.[133] (See below.)

Akot was the most serious attack by a faction in eighteen months. Some 35,000 people were believed to have fled the attack and the cattle camp was looted of almost 10,000 head of cattle, of which 7,500 were recovered afterwards.[134]

According to eyewitnesses, the raid was conducted by a government-backed Nuer militia group. They were armed with weapons believed to have been supplied by the government of Sudan (sixty millimeter mortars, Kalashnikovs, broken-down antiaircraft artillery guns). There is some indication that the raid was lead or joined by some SSIM/A forces based in Ganyliel. There were also reports that the attackers were in radio contact with Cmdr. William Nyuon, then an SSIA commander, during the attack. Documents reportedly found on one of the dead

---

[129]"Kenya: Sudanese Rebels Free Kenyan Aid Worker," Reuter, Nairobi, Kenya, October 24, 1995.

[130]Sonya Laurence-Green, "Sudan Rebel Offensive," Voice of America, Nairobi, Kenya, October 27, 1995, 1406 UTC.

[131]OLS (Southern Sector) Update, 16 January 1996, p. 2

[132]Ibid., p. 1.

[133]This account draws on confidential communications to Human Rights Watch/Africa and interviews in Nairobi, Kenya in March 1995.

[134]OLS (Southern Sector) Update, 1 November 1994, p. 1.

raiders identified him as an SSIA member.[135] The U.S. government, strongly condemning the killing as a massacre of civilians, claimed that 300 SSIA soldiers participated in the attack.[136]

The SPLA garrison forty-five kilometers east of Akot had heard that an attack was coming, and warned the people two days before. The SPLA's efforts to intercept the attackers were unsuccessful, however, because the grass at that time of year was eight feet high, thus providing ample cover for raiders.

According to a witness, the attack on Akot town commenced at 5:30 a.m. on October 22 and the attackers entered the town from the north and east. The SPLA briefly fended off the attack, enabling some civilians to escape to the south. Not only the SPLA soldiers from the garrison participated in the defense of the town; the local security and armed population, including Sudan Relief and Rehabilitation Association (SRRA, relief wing of SPLA) officials, joined in.[137]

After Akot town was attacked and the defenders drawn away from the cattle camp, a second prong of the attack was aimed at the main cattle camp Theragap, fifteen to eighteen kilometers from the town. Thousands of cattle were stolen by the attackers. At this time of the year, at the end of the rainy season, there were some 40,000 cattle in the camp along the river.

The women and children in the cattle camp (as well as the cattle), however, were unprotected from the attack. A local chief, hearing that an attack was coming, had warned the young men at the camp but they nevertheless went to Tonj, a nearby town, for a party — marriage parties being common at the end of the rainy season. Other civilians were warned of a coming attack by their Nuer relatives in Akot; intermarriage is not uncommon.

The dead and wounded were disproportionately women and children and most of these losses took place at the cattle camp. Of the 106 bodies counted, fifty-eight were men (twenty of them SPLA soldiers) and the rest, forty-eight, were women and children. There were eighty-nine injured in the attack (including eighteen SPLA soldiers); many children had been shot in the foot. The injuries were mostly gunshot wounds to the head and abdomen.

To the north of Akot is the Nuer/Dinka border, where rustling and looting have gone on back and forth for a long time. The rustling is now being done with automatic weapons instead of spears. In the past, cattle camps were the targets.

---

[135]Julie Flint, "Sudan: Dawn Raid Dims Hopes for Unity," *The Guardian* (London), November 9, 1994.

[136]"USA: U.S. Condemns Massacre of Civilians in South Sudan," Reuter, Washington, D.C., November 3, 1994.

[137]Human Rights Watch/Africa interview, Nairobi, Kenya, March 9, 1995.

Akot town was never attacked before, and traditionally, women and children were not the targets. The border chiefs of the Dinka and Nuer used to negotiate and settle accounts after raids, but since the commencement of the armed conflict their power, as well as traditions protecting women and children, has eroded.

After the attack, local Agar Dinka youths armed and said they were going to avenge the attack in the Nuer areas, and to retrieve their cattle. Fifty kilometers or two days' walk north of Akot is the Lake Nubor grazing and fishing area used by both Dinka and Nuer, to which heavily armed men now escort the cattle.

Some looting in Akot appeared to have been done by the local SPLA soldiers and garrison after the attackers withdrew and before most civilians returned to the town. Some SPLA soldiers forced civilians to porter the looted goods for them back to the garrison to the east of Akot; large quantities of relief food were taken, including twelve tons of salt that would have been very hard for the original attackers to move with them as they withdrew. The relief organizations lost almost everything in the looting, including the personal possessions of aid workers that later turned up for sale in the Akot market.

The local SPLA commander denied that his troops had anything to do with the looting, adding, "These things happen in war." He told the relief organizations that this was "none of their business." NGOs and churches which had also been looted complained officially to the SRRA, the relief arm of the SPLA. SPLA's chief John Garang sent a team of civilian police to investigate the looting in February 1995, over three months later. They questioned the local residents and relief personnel. This investigation was never finalized and very few looted goods were ever returned.[138]

SPLA-aligned Raiders Attack Ganyliel in July 1995, Killing 210

The residents and soldiers of Akot and elsewhere attacked Ganyliel nine months later, on the night of July 29-30, 1995, in what was probably a retaliatory raid. Ganyliel is in Western Upper Nile, in Nuer territory, then loosely controlled by the SSIM/A. The manner in which this attack was carried out, with indiscriminate and deliberate attacks on civilians and destruction and looting of civilian property, was a violation of the rules of war. The attack, carried out by civilians aligned with the SPLA and most likely in conjunction with SPLA forces,[139] was the first serious violation of the Lafon Declaration's cease-fire signed

---

[138]Ibid.

[139]Although not part of an organized militia, these civilians from time to time before and during this conflict armed themselves to carry out raids on other villages, often in

(continued...)

on April 27, 1995, by the rebel two groups. It also violated the humanitarian ground rules that the SPLA had signed with the OLS in July 1995. The SPLM/A, responding to an SSIM/A press release accusing it of the attack, denied that its forces were involved.[140]

The attackers apparently came from Akot to the southwest, under SPLA control. There was no discernible military target in the area. There was a small SSIA garrison stationed about twelve kilometers from Ganyliel, but the attackers went straight for the villages where there were people and cattle.

The raid on Ganyliel killed 210 people, mostly civilians (thirty men, fifty-three women, and 127 children), and destroyed a total of forty-one villages.[141] The victims were shot in their huts as they slept or shot or macheted as they fled the attack, which occurred between 3:00 a.m. and 6:00 a.m. on July 30. Since the bodies of the unaccounted-for children were not all found, it is possible that some were abducted. An unknown number were injured, of whom twenty-five were injured badly enough to require evacuation to the ICRC hospital near Lokichokio, Kenya. The ICRC flew in a three-member medical team to treat the injured from August 3-5.[142]

On the night of the attack, there were reportedly twelve Dinka chiefs and traders staying in Ganyliel village (a Nuer village) as guests of Chief Daniel Malualwon. This was part of a peace process between the SPLA and SSIA and their adherents which the chiefs had been promoting for several months. After the attack, these Dinkas were said to have been escorted to the border between the Nuer and Dinka on their way back to Yirol. Other reports, however, indicate that none of these twelve men ever returned home. They are suspected of having been killed, after being taken to SSIA security for interrogation.[143]

The property losses included 2,060 dwellings, burned after looting. The looted items included household possessions such as blankets, cooking pots, clothes, and the all-important mosquito nets and fishing equipment. Heavier items such as clay cooking pots and water pots were smashed on the ground. Reportedly

---

[139](...continued)
connection with cattle raiding or retrieval.
[140]"Sudan Rebel Group Denies Attacking Rivals," Reuter, Nairobi, Kenya, July 31, 1995.
[141]OLS (Southern Sector) Update, 22 August 1995, p. 2.
[142]OLS (Southern Sector) Update, 8 August 1995, p. 2.
[143]Confidential communication to Human Rights Watch/Africa, September 1995.

over 3,500 head of cattle were looted and scores of goats taken.[144] UNICEF said that a school serving 290 pupils was burned and two other schools serving 340 pupils were looted during the July 30 attack.[145] The property of the relief staff working in Ganyliel, however, was not looted.[146]

The attack was believed to have been led by Cmdr. Daniel Aywal of the SPLA, based in Akot, where celebrations were heard the following day when the men returned with their booty. A large group of armed men, half wearing camouflage and olive green uniforms and boots, the rest wearing black garments and carrying *pangas* (spears) and machetes, descended first on the villages of Manyal and Guk north west of Ganyliel, then spread out in three directions, to the south, south east and east, hitting the villages along the way. The uniformed men were carrying radios as well as rocket-propelled grenade launchers and automatic weapons.

The OLS (Southern Sector) asked for an accounting from the SPLA of the breaking of the terms of the humanitarian ground rules. The U.S. condemned the killings and called on the SPLA to investigate and take appropriate measures against those responsible.[147] Human Rights Watch/Africa sought to know the results of the investigation. To date, there has been no report of any investigation undertaken or completed.

The Forcible Disappearance of Dr. Karlo Madut

Dr. Karlo Madut Deng, a medical doctor formerly affiliated with the relief wings of both the SPLA and SPLA-United (now SSIA), was taken from the home of his wife in the Adjumani, Uganda refugee camp on the night of August 28, 1994, by a group of armed men allegedly including Ugandan National Resistance Army and SPLA members. He has never been heard from since. The family learned, indirectly, that he was taken to the SPLA base in Nimule, southern Sudan,

---

[144]OLS (Southern Sector) Update, 22 August 1995, p. 2. Further surveys identified additional villages burned, bringing the total to forty-one, six more than the original estimate. The total number of *luaks* (large houses) destroyed and looted was 2,060. Ibid.

[145]Ibid.

[146]The six relief staff of the International Rescue Committee and their cook were evacuated from Ganyliel on July 30. OLS (Southern Sector) Update, 1 August 1995, p. 1. When they returned on August 5 they found that none of the items in their compound had been looted. OLS (Southern Sector) Update, 8 August 1995, p. 1.

[147]"United States Condemns Southern Sudan Massacre," Reuter, Khartoum, August 23, 1995.

and executed there by the SPLA. The SPLA denies any responsibility, and the Ugandan government has failed to answer our inquiries.

A relief agency sent an urgent message to the UNHCR on the detention, requesting that the UNHCR security officer investigate and that the incident be brought to the attention of the UNHCR protection officer in Kampala.[148] There was reportedly no response.

Dr. Madut, a Nuer, was practicing medicine before November 1992 at the Aswa Hospital north of Nimule, southern Sudan, according to family members.[149] The area was then controlled by the SPLA and Dr. Madut worked with the relief arm of the SPLA, Sudan Relief and Rehabilitation Association (SRRA).[150] While in that hospital, he had disagreements with SPLA Cmdr. Kuol Manyang, who as the ranking military commander in the area gave orders to Dr. Madut relating to medical affairs. Dr. Madut felt Cmdr. Manyang was interfering in his work by recommending inexperienced men for work in the hospital, commandeering cars, and directing how drugs should be distributed, according to an associate of Dr. Madut who was in Nimule at the time.[151] Cmdr. Manyang appointed a pharmacist, Dr. Manyang (no relation) in place of Dr. Madut at the hospital and ordered Dr. Madut to go to the front near Juba, which Dr. Madut did not do. Instead, he received permission to go to Nairobi and did not return.

Before Dr. Madut went to Nairobi, Dr. Timothy Tutlam, also a Nuer, escaped from Nimule because he had received threats from SPLA leaders.[152] While in Nairobi, Dr. Madut was contacted by the top two SPLA commanders, John Garang and Salva Kiir, about returning to Nimule or to the front. He declined. In March 1993 he joined the faction opposing the SPLA, then called SPLA-United and led by Cmdr. Riek Machar. Dr. Madut became director of the SPLA-United relief arm, Relief Association of Southern Sudan (RASS).

In April 1993, according to relatives, he went to the Adjumani refugee camp in Uganda to visit his first wife but while there was alerted by friends that the

---

[148]Confidential communication to Human Rights Watch/Africa, July 1995.

[149]Human Rights Watch/Africa interviews, Nairobi, Kenya, March 9 and 10, 1995.

[150]Many Nuers deserted this displaced persons camp in late August 1992 when a leading Nuer commander in the SPLA, William Nyuon, defected with his forces to SSIA's predecessor. The Nuer feared retaliation by the mostly Dinka SPLM/A leadership in the area. Human Rights Watch/Africa, *Civilian Devastation*, p. 136.

[151]Human Rights Watch/Africa interview, Nairobi, Kenya, March 9, 1995.

[152]Human Rights Watch/Africa, *Civilian Devastation,* p. 136.

SPLA was going to kidnap him. He returned hastily to Nairobi. Later that year he received a scholarship to study gynecology in Zimbabwe, and left Nairobi.[153]

When he returned to the region in August 1994, he decided to try to visit his wife in Adjumani again. He arrived from Nairobi to Adjumani refugee camp on August 26, 1994, at night. The next day, August 27, a Saturday, he spent the whole day visiting without any incident or warning. He did the same thing on Sunday.

He returned to his wife's house in Adjumani after visiting friends at 5:00 p.m. on Sunday night August 28. He was captured from this house at 8:30 p.m. Others in the camp heard gunshots and shouting.

Family members investigating the matter were told by witnesses that there were several SPLA men involved in the abduction: Cmdr. Ubote (Isaac) Mamur based in Nimule, who drove a Toyota pickup, and 2d Lt. Modi, based in Gulu, who drove a green Land rover. Their cars were recognized and Ubote's driver said that Ubote had come on a "mission." Also used in the mission was a Tata lorry, a vehicle used by the Ugandan military. Another source told the family that a Ugandan security man, identified only as "Ben," based in Adjumani, knocked at the door of the house where Dr. Madut was and said they wanted to search. Whey they refused to open the door, the abductors broke it down.

Dr. Madut's wife is reported to have followed the group who kidnaped Dr. Madut to the Ugandan army (NRA) barracks in Gulu, where she was told he had been taken to Nimule and handed over to the SPLA.[154] She apparently went to the office of the UNHCR in Adjumani and described the cars and what happened. After reporting the abduction, Dr. Madut's family left the area immediately.

The family later received information, supposedly from persons who defected from the SPLA, that Dr. Madut was killed and his body thrown into the river (White Nile) when the abductors reached Nimule. The family wrote letters and attempted to find out about the case from various SPLA officials, but no answer was forthcoming; the SPLA continued to deny any knowledge, referring all inquiries to the Ugandan authorities and saying that the SPLA was not responsible for what happened in Uganda. Cmdr. Deng Alor, secretary of foreign affairs for the SPLA, told a relative in September 1994 that Dr. Madut had been captured by Ugandan authorities and the SPLA was doing its very best to secure his release. The family wrote to the Ugandan authorities in early September 1994 asking them

---

[153]Human Rights Watch/Africa interview, Nairobi, Kenya, March 9 and 10, 1995.

[154]Confidential communication to Human Rights Watch/Africa, April 5, 1995. According to other family sources, Dr. Madut allegedly was delivered to Cmdr. Kuol Manyang who was waiting in Bibia, Uganda.

to protect Dr. Madut's life. Uganda denied any knowledge or involvement. One relative in the United States reportedly even called a contact in Uganda security, Jim Katung, who also denied that Uganda was involved.[155]

Finally SPLA's Deng Alor told a relative in February 1995, "Dr. Madut is not a living man any longer."[156] The family then held a memorial service for Dr. Madut in Nairobi.

Human Rights Watch questioned Cmdr. Kuol Manyang, the third highest officer in the SPLA, about the case. He denied any involvement.[157] The Ugandan Embassy in Washington, D.C., failed to respond to our letters and calls about this case.

At the First SPLA National Convention in Chukudum, Eastern Equatoria in March-April 1994, Dr. John Garang, the commander-in-chief of the SPLA, announced the death of Martin Majieur Gai, said to have been shot escaping from his SPLA jail near Kaya, Western Equatoria, in 1993.[158] Garang told the conference he had a report that reached this conclusion. That report was not made public and it was unclear if the report was even in writing.[159] Martin Majieur, a former judge, advocate, member of parliament for Bor South and regional minister, and a Bor Dinka, was the attorney who drafted the first SPLA criminal code before his 1985 arrest by the SPLA over political differences with John Garang.

Looting and Taking Hostages by All Parties to the Conflict

Looting of civilian property and of U.N. and NGO relief supplies by the opposing forces has continued, often on a large scale. The record to early 1996 for looting any one relief barge is the 1,800 tons of food taken from four barges in June 1994 in Jonglei state at Dhiam Dhiam, by a Dinka militia which held ten U.N. staff and a barge crew of twenty-two for ten days without any radio contact. The captives were not harmed nor were they robbed. The OLS (Southern Sector) protested to the SPLM/A.[160]

---

[155]Human Rights Watch/Africa interview, Nairobi, Kenya, March 9, 1995.

[156]Human Rights Watch/Africa interview, Nairobi, Kenya, March 10, 1995.

[157]Human Rights Watch/Africa interview, Labone, Eastern Equatoria, March 16, 1995.

[158]Steve Wondu, spokesperson for SPLM/A, Nairobi, Kenya, March 8, 1995. See Human Rights Watch/Africa, *Civilian Devastation*, p. 224. Our information was that several SPLA long-term political detainees escaped prison near Morobo close to the Uganda border in July 1993.

[159]Ibid.

[160]Human Rights Watch/Africa interview, Khartoum, May 21, 1995; OLS (Southern Sector) Update, 17 June 1994.

When the OLS evacuated relief staff from Nasir on February 10 because of insecurity, their equipment and property were extensively looted, including boats and generators,[161] almost certainly by SSIA forces. Protests were lodged with RASS and SSIA authorities, but few items were returned.[162]

Another SSIA splinter, also backed by the government, attracted attention on February 8, 1995, with the abduction of eleven aid workers from Waat, Upper Nile. Cmdr. Gordon Kong Banypiny of Waat, who defected to the government from the SSIA a few months earlier, sent word to Waat he was leaving the government stronghold of Dolieb Hill (under the command of government militia) because he had not been treated well by the government, and was returning to SSIA territory, to Waat.

When Cmdr. Kong Banypiny reached Waat he revealed his true purpose and attacked the village. All civilians had fled, but he captured eleven NGO workers, one tractor and three vehicles. By the end of the third day, he had released all the aid workers, who were not mistreated.[163] Riek's SSIA forces pursued him and he withdrew to Malakal, from which the government bombarded and repelled the attackers.[164]

In 1995 almost forty relief personnel were taken hostage in three separate incidents, according to the OLS. In addition to the above eleven hostages, twenty-two were captured on a barge in May 1995 and three in June in Pariang, both described below.

Looting of Relief Barge and Holding Crew and Relief Personnel Hostage in May 1995

After lengthy and tortuous negotiations, all sides to the conflict approved the movement of a WFP food barge up the White Nile from Kosti to Juba in early May 1995. Most barges, however, had been plagued by a series of attacks for the purpose of looting as they passed in and out of territory controlled by the Sudan government, its militias, and various rebel factions. This barge suffered the same

---

[161]OLS (Southern Sector) Monthly Report, February 1995, p. 7.

[162]OLS (Southern Sector) Update, 7 March 1995, p. 1.

[163]OLS (Southern Sector) Monthly Report, February 1995, p. 2.

[164]Human Rights Watch/Africa interview, Kakuma, Kenya, March 17, 1995. Another version of the story is that the government of Sudan launched surprise attacks on SSIA bases south of Malakal, in Abhong and Baliet, and dislodged the SSIA after fighting. The SSIA then joined with SPLA Cmdr. George Atar of Baliet (a Dinka enclave) to protect his home village and to push out the Sudan government. This counterattack was successful. Human Rights Watch/Africa interview, Lokichokio, Kenya, March 16, 1995.

plague; it was attacked by two different groups, and its twenty-two crew and passengers taken hostage while the barge's relief food was looted. Article three common to the four Geneva Conventions of 1949 strictly forbids the taking of hostages, and looting is a violation of customary rules of war.

This barge to Juba began to run into trouble on May 7, 1995, a Sunday, at Barboi on the White Nile, one hundred kilometers (sixty-two miles) west of Malakal. A Nuer militia, probably aligned with the government, fired into the path of and over the barge with automatic weapons and rocket-propelled grenades. The militia demanded that the barge change course to a location convenient for this militia to off-load the food, to Pakan.[165]

A WFP food monitor, Mark Rizzuto, of Italian nationality, went off the barge to discuss the situation with the militia. They did not permit him to reboard. They took a small amount of food, saying it was for civilians in Barboi, and removed the barge's radio to prevent communication. Rizzuto and one Sudanese WFP employee were taken hostage to insure that the barge would be taken where the militia directed. The two hostages were walked to Pakan and held there two days.

The Nuer militia wanted the barge to divert its course up a side river, Bahr el Zeraf. Before it reached its militia-dictated destination, however, the barge was stopped by a rebel faction, SPLA-United (Western Upper Nile), headed by Dr. Lam Akol in Tonga. Lam Akol, a Shilluk, had been an SPLA political advisor to Garang before he joined Riek Machar's breakaway faction known after October 1994 as SSIM/A. Cmdr. Riek Machar expelled Dr. Lam Akol in early 1994 and Akol retreated to the Shilluk area of Upper Nile, where he established his own movement.

Dr. Lam Akol's soldiers did not fire at the barge but displayed their arms, indicating that the barge was to stop; a man in a canoe with a flag also signaled them to stop. The Akol soldiers boarded the barge and made the crew (thirteen men) and staff (seven: one Filipino and one Sudanese WFP staff and five Sudanese UNICEF staff) spend the night on land while the soldiers looted the barge. They took 250 tons of foodstuffs, mostly sorghum, lentils and vegetable oil. They also took their global positioning device, a computer, a printer, a boat with an outboard motor and all the personal items belonging to the crew and staff .

---

[165]Human Rights Watch/Africa interview, Khartoum, May 21, 1995.

The following day, May 8, the barge with its crew and all staff but one person, Filipino citizen Rimi Delos Santos, were permitted to leave.[166] Some speculated that Santos was taken hostage in order to pressure the U.N. to recognize SPLA-United (Western Upper Nile) as a party to the conflict, and to bring relief to the civilians living in its jurisdiction. Dr. Lam Akol had already taken a hostage a few months earlier, a doctor on a consulting mission for UNICEF in Tonga.[167] Santos was held for seven days by the faction, during which time the U.N. was not permitted to see him. He was not mistreated.

The remaining WFP staff members convinced the barge crew to go on to Pakan, where Rizzuto and one other WFP staff member still were held hostage. When they reached Pakan, Rizzuto and the other staff member were allowed to get back on the barge and were able to persuade the militia to permit them to use the barge's radio to contact WFP in Khartoum, which they did on May 8 and 9.

The barge was looted again while the staff was on it, on May 8 and 9, by the Nuer militia that had originally captured the barge. It took about one hundred tons of foodstuffs.

In New York, Peter Hansen, U.N. Undersecretary General for Humanitarian Affairs, condemned the abduction "in the strongest possible terms" and called for immediate and unconditional release of the staff and immediate restitution of looted food and other relief goods.[168]

On the afternoon of May 9 another armed group arrived in Pakan, apparently government soldiers, and shooting broke out. The Nuer militia that was holding the U.N. workers fled, as did the civilians who were looting the barge. The U.N. staff and barge crew, and the barge, were set free.[169] Rizzuto was taken again overland to the White Nile. The rest were cast adrift on the barge on Tuesday night, coming ashore near Malakal on Wednesday morning May 10,[170] where Rizzuto met up with the barge. Only about 235 tons of foodstuffs had been saved from looting,

---

[166]See Alfred Taban, "Sudan: Kidnaped Aid Workers in Sudan in Good Health," Reuter, Khartoum, May 9, 1995.

[167]Dr. Peter Adwok Nyaba, a Shilluk who went to Tonga as a consultant for the OLS, was captured upon arrival in late 1994 and put on trial before a military court, which found him guilty of subversion and sentenced him to life in captivity. Dr. Peter Adwok, who was handicapped by a foot injury, was pardoned and freed in May 1995. *Sudan Update* (London), vol. 6, no. 13, August 24, 1995, p. 2.

[168]"Sudanese Rebels Release 21 Aid Workers," Reuter, Rome, Italy, May 10, 1995.

[169]Alfred Taban, "Kidnaped Aid Workers in Sudan in Good Health."

[170]"Sudanese Rebels Release 21 Aid Workers."

and taken back to Malakal. By May 10, all but one relief worker, Santos, had been freed,[171] and he was released after seven days' captivity.[172]

Looting of relief barges continues; on March 15, 1996, a World Food Program barge with some 350 tons of food was attacked and looted by "an unknown group of armed militia" four to five kilometers southeast of Doleib Hill near Malakal in Upper Nile, long the base of a Nuer government militia. The barge was stripped clean of computers, solar panels, batteries, satellite communication equipment, and the personal possessions of the seventeen staff and barge crew, who were released unhurt the next day. Fifty tons of relief food were taken.[173]

Doctors Captured in Upper Nile by Government and Released in Exchange for SPLA Hostages, May-June 1995

On May 25, 1995, a plane took off from Lokichokio, the OLS (Southern Sector) base camp and airstrip in Kenya, near the Sudan border. The plane was being chartered by the Italian medical relief organization, Comitato Collaborazione Medica (CCM), an OLS member, and was heading for Pariang in Western Upper Nile, a destination the government had declared off limits since November 1994 to OLS organizations. In the plane were two medical doctors. Pariang was in the hands of the SPLA when they landed, but a few days later the government attacked, in violation of the cease-fire, and captured the two doctors. In order to free them, the SPLA violated the rules of war by taking hostage three U.N. employees and two government employees of Sudan Security.

Because the plane had been sitting on the runway in Lokichokio for months (it was chartered by the U.S. relief organization World Vision until November 1994) and was familiar to the flight controllers, and because it did not use fuel from OLS storage, little attention was paid when it took off among many other relief flights leaving that morning for approved destinations deep within southern Sudan's rebel-controlled areas. CCM, however, had filed a false flight plan with the Kenyan air traffic controllers at Lokichokio, and had not disclosed its plans to the OLS.

CCM's destination, Pariang, had been specifically rejected as a relief destination by the government of Sudan. Pariang, in Western Upper Nile, is about 100 kilometers south of Talodi, in Southern Kordofan in the Nuba Mountains, where the government of Sudan has long prohibited any international relief

---

[171]Ibid.
[172]"Sudanese Rebels Release Filipino Aid Workers," Reuter, Rome, Italy, May 15, 1995.
[173]OLS (Southern Sector) Update 96/11, 19 March 1996, p. 1

whatsoever. Pariang was ravaged by an epidemic of the kala azar disease.[174] The epidemic, which started in the early 1990s, had not been effectively treated because Pariang had been off limits — by the government — for relief flights for some time.[175] Under the OLS rules, both the government and the rebel groups must approve OLS destinations, and flight plans are announced in advance to all sides.

CCM personnel, however, had been making surreptitious trips to Pariang to try to treat victims of kala azar. The May trip, to last less than a week, was for two doctors, Dr. Giuseppe Meo, age fifty-seven, from Turin, Italy, and Dr. Hashim Mohamed Zeyada, a Sudanese citizen from the Nuba Mountains, also in his fifties. They would be dropped off by the CCM-chartered plane which would return at a specified time to pick them up again.

This trip went wrong. Although a cease-fire was in effect to facilitate treatment of the guinea worm disease at the request of former U.S. President Jimmy Carter, Sudanese government soldiers nevertheless entered Pariang and captured the two doctors. The doctors landed in Pariang on May 25 and were captured by the government on May 28.[176]

When the CCM-chartered plane landed to pick up the doctors at the Pariang airstrip at the appointed time on May 29, 1995, the pilot was told by SPLA forces that the area was extremely insecure and there was fighting nearby. He was advised that it was too dangerous for him to stay on the ground any longer. There was no sign of the doctors. The pilot took off.[177]

---

[174]Kala azar means "black fever." It is a protozoa. Symptoms of the disease, after incubation of three to eighteen months, include fever, diarrhea, coughing. In advanced stages, the patient suffers enlarged spleen, liver, lymph nodes, and anemia. Left untreated, 75 to 85 percent of children will die, and 90 to 95 percent of adults will die, within a course of three to twenty months. The disease is more common in children. See Katz et al., *Parasitic Diseases.*

[175]We noted in our report *Civilian Devastation* that the kala azar epidemic around Pariang was worsened by militia and government raids. Ibid., pp. 149-51.

[176]OLS (Southern Sector) Monthly Report, June 1995, p. 2; see Amnesty International, "Urgent Action: Sudan," UA 127/95, AI Index: AFR 54/20/95, London, June 8, 1995. Amnesty gives the date of detention as May 29, 1995.

[177]"Italian, Sudanese Doctors Abducted in South Sudan," Reuter, Nairobi, Kenya, May 30, 1995.

CCM advised OLS of what had happened.[178] The Italian Embassy asked the Sudan government for information about Dr. Meo. The government denied knowledge of the affair until June 1, when it admitted that it had detained two doctors in Pariang, which was under Sudan government control, and asked the U.N. to bring the two to Khartoum for interrogation. The OLS suspended CCM for violation of OLS ground rules.[179]

The Sudan government seized upon the capture of the two doctors as an opportunity to renegotiate the entire OLS program. The government had long chafed under the presence of nongovernmental organizations working in rebel-controlled areas of southern Sudan, most of them working under the OLS umbrella. Sudan's previous refusal to countenance more than a trickle of flights to the disease- and famine-struck south turned around after the U.N. Security Council approved U.S. and other foreign troops' entry into Somalia to protect relief deliveries to the civilian population in December 1992. Immediately after that Security Council resolution, Sudan approved numerous destinations in rebel territory, and each year since then, granted more and more access. The government also gained ground militarily in the south following the SPLA faction fighting in 1991, so that it was interested in securing relief flight access to its increasing number of garrison towns as well.

The government became convinced, however, that the relief operation to rebel areas was permitting the SPLA and others to continue the war by delivering food to civilians under rebel control, food which allegedly was being diverted to rebel use. The capture of the doctors led to a reiteration of two government demands: to fire OLS (Southern Sector)'s effective director, Philip O'Brien, and to relocate the base for relief operations from Kenya to Sudan government-controlled soil, to Malakal or El Obeid.[180] The U.N. through its Department of Humanitarian Affairs examined the government's allegations "and the Government was informed that the allegations had proved to be unfounded."[181] The U.N. resisted giving any government a veto over its personnel, and also resisted

---

[178]OLS (Southern Sector) Update, 30 May 1995, Nairobi, Kenya. The OLS reported that according to CCM, two doctors working with them were taken into custody by unknown forces in Pariang, a highly insecure area which "has not been approved for aircraft landings since November 1994. According to recent reports, there has been fighting in the area between SSIA and GOS [government of Sudan] forces." Ibid.

[179]OLS (Southern Sector) Update, 6 June 1995, Nairobi, Kenya.

[180]Human Rights Watch/Africa interview, Khartoum, June 2, 1995.

[181]Report of the Secretary-General, "Emergency assistance to the Sudan," p. 4, para. 10.

relocation of the relief operations.[182] One reason was the cost but, most important to western nongovernmental organizations that had worked or tried to work inside government-controlled Sudan, a second reason was the long track record of this government's extreme obstruction of all relief work except for that conducted by Islamic nongovernmental organizations.

The U.N., the Sudan government, and the SPLA agreed that the U.N. would send a plane to pick up the two doctors in Pariang and transport them to Khartoum. The WFP plane left Khartoum on June 7 and went to Juba where it picked up two government officials who were to accompany the doctors on board from Pariang to Khartoum, and three U.N. relief workers (one FAO staff and two WFP staff) who were catching a ride from Juba back to Khartoum. The plane refueled in Malakal then took off for Pariang.

The three U.N. relief workers happened to be in the wrong place at the wrong time. When the plane landed in Pariang, SPLA Cmdr. John Mayak met the plane and ordered everyone out.[183] The pilot and the five passengers, who spent the night sleeping on the ground, were forced to walk the next day about fifteen kilometers southeast, while the commander radioed back and forth to SPLA headquarters. Water was in short supply and the sun was hot, so some of the captives were reduced to drinking from pools on the ground. The two CCM doctors were no where in sight.

That afternoon, back at the airstrip, the pilot and five passengers were ordered by the SPLA to fly to Chukudum, the SPLA's headquarters hundreds of kilometers to the south. They were joined by three armed SPLA guards whose mission was to make sure that they went to Chukudum, and to guard the five captives. The plane landed at dusk in Chukudum.

The five passengers were taken captive and the pilot, at machine gun point, was forced to take off without them the next day. He flew to Lokichokio

---

[182]Ibid. The U.N. informed the government that its request for a restructuring of OLS would take place in consultation with all concerned parties.

[183]Some have suggested that part of the confusion was caused by Cmdr. Mayak, who controlled the Pariang area, switching sides during this affair, from the SPLA to the government and back to the SPLA. This remains unclear but there was gunfire and fighting on May 29 when the CCM-chartered pilot landed at Pariang, and when the WFP plane arrived on June 7 Cmdr. Mayak was in charge and in close radio contact with SPLA headquarters.

nearby on Friday, June 9, 1995.[184] The WFP was allowed to bring food to the five captives left behind.[185]

The SPLA, whose bargaining position vis-a-vis the CCM doctors held by the government was improved by the capture of the five hostages, two of whom were government employees, called for negotiations on release of hostages; it claimed the two government officials in its custody at Chukudum were the heads of Sudan Security in Juba and Malakal.[186] Human Rights Watch was later told that one official was indeed the head of Sudan Security in Juba.[187]

After negotiations, the Sudan government freed the doctors in Khartoum on July 18, 1995, saying the Italian had entered the country illegally and both broke the law but would be freed anyway.[188] The doctors had only been brought to Khartoum ten days before they were freed.[189] The following day the SPLA announced that it had freed the three U.N. relief workers and would shortly release the two Sudanese government employees, which it did.[190]

Combatants Captured by the SPLA and SSIA

Several hundred northern army and PDF combatants captured by the SPLA or SSIA are in SPLA custody; some are periodically shown to journalists and other visitors. In a positive step, the SPLM/A, for the first time since 1994, permitted the ICRC to visit 229 captured combatants in January 1996. Another visit, this time to 102 prisoners, was permitted in April 1996.[191]

The reason the ICRC was not able to visit the SPLA's captured combatants between 1994 and January 1996 was that the SPLA authorities would

---

[184]Human Rights Watch/Africa interview, Khartoum, June 12, 1995.

[185]"U.N. Workers, Sudanese Officials Held by Rebels," Reuter, Nairobi, Kenya, June 12, 1995.

[186]"Sudan Rebels Call for Talks on Hostages," Reuter, Nairobi, Kenya, July 14, 1995.

[187]Confidential communication to Human Rights Watch/Africa, December 1995.

[188]Alfred Taban, "Sudan Sets Free Italian Doctor and Colleague," Reuter, Khartoum, Sudan, July 18, 1995.

[189]David Orr, "Doctors Free After Ordeal in Sudan Civil War Zone," *The Independent* (London), June 19, 1995.

[190]"Sudan Rebels say They Released Three Aid Workers," Reuter, Nairobi, Kenya, July 19, 1995.

[191]"Red Cross Visits 102 Prisoners in Southern Sudan," Reuter, Nairobi, Kenya, April 12, 1996.

not permit ICRC delegates to interview captives in private.[192] The ICRC, however, does not visit places of detention unless the following criteria are met: its delegates must be allowed to see all the detainees and talk freely to them without witnesses, to have access to all premises used for detention and to repeat their visits, and must be provided with a list of the persons to be visited (or be permitted to draw up such a list during the visit). The ICRC delegates hold discussions at various levels of the government or detaining rebel forces before and after these visits.[193] The SPLM/A now permits private interviews by ICRC delegates, and the ICRC has been able to continue the visits.

Although the ICRC secured the agreement of the SSIA to visit the sixty or so government soldiers it captured in Lafon in late March 1995,[194] the government capture of Lafon intervened and the prisoners ended up in the hands of the SPLM/A.

A correspondent who visited SPLA territory in early 1996 reported that the SPLA said they had captured 246 prisoners of war since October 1995, of whom the reporter for an Arabic-language newspaper in London interviewed

---

[192]Letter, Steven Wondu, representative of SPLM/A, to Human Rights Watch/Africa, February 26, 1996.

[193]International Committee of the Red Cross, *Annual Report 1994*, p. 8.

[194]The prisoners were captured in an unusual manner, according to one source: There had been tension between Cmdr. William Nyuon's mostly Nuer soldiers and Pari soldiers, all in the SSIA. The Pari, an Equatorian people, live in Lafon; the Pari Ruling Committee (age class) appointed a Pari officer as commissioner and area commander there, replacing a Nuer SSIM officer. Cmdr. William Nyuon found tensions between the Pari and his Nuer soldiers so high when he visited Lafon in March 1995 that he decided to pull his Nuer forces back to Magire. On March 31, 1995, 200 SSIM soldiers under Cmdr. Thomas Gador were sent as an advance force to Lafon with three lorries and two tanks plus a small number of government soldiers, according to this source, who believed the SSIM leadership intended to re-install the SSIM as the authority in the Lafon area, relying on the power of the Sudan government. Lafon is in a strategic location, since government convoys originating in Juba pass through Lafon to reinforce Kapoeta. On the way, however, SSIM commanders changed their minds and decided to arrest the outnumbered government soldiers among them and they did so, without any fighting, also taking over the lorries and tanks. Cmdr. William Nyuon and a brigade of government soldiers were stationed about six kilometers from Lafon, at Chol River. He was dispatched to Lafon on April 1 to negotiate the release of government soldiers and equipment, but the young SSIM officers forced him to join them instead. The government plans to reinforce Kapoeta were stymied and government troops attacked and took Lafon on April 10, 1995, in violation of the two-month cease-fire that had just been agreed to by the government. Confidential communication to Human Rights Watch/Africa, April 14, 1995.

fourteen.[195] SPLA Cmdr. Oyoung Deng Ajak said there were an additional 300 prisoners of war and another fifty captured during the battle for Aswa, making a total of almost 600. Most are reportedly held near Labone. This commander said that the government has refused to exchange prisoners of war with the SPLA, which released ten prisoners of war, among them a brigadier and other officers.[196]

Lafon Declaration Purportedly Grants Amnesty to Both Sides in Faction Fighting

On April 27, 1995, the SPLM/A and SSIM/A leadership signed the Lafon declaration, agreeing to a cease-fire between their forces and free movement of people, goods and services all over southern Sudan, Southern Kordofan and Southern Blue Nile.[197] Unfortunately, the declaration also provided "a general and unconditional amnesty, covering the period from 28/8/1991 to 27/4/95, to all sides of the split, so that nobody may be prosecuted or punished for actions committed during this period."[198]

This attempt to amnesty persons — mostly armed rebels — responsible for serious crimes against the civilian population and against other combatants is in total contradiction to the statements by leaders of both movements promising respect for human rights and the rules of war. These international laws must be enforced by the rebel armies if they want their promises of compliance with human rights to be taken seriously by the international community.

SSIM/A Court Martials Struck down by Convention

At the October 1994 South Sudan Independence Movement/Army convention at Akobo, amnesty for all persons in SSIM/A custody was declared.[199] This included amnesty for SSIA rebel military commanders who were being held or had been convicted in connection with the fighting among Nuer sections in

---

[195]Thirteen of fourteen said they had been forcibly conscripted. They complained they had not received correspondence from their families because the families did not know they were held as prisoners of war. Khazim, "Confrontation in a Box."

[196]Ibid. "Sudan: Southern Rebel Group Says Government Has Refused to Accept Released POWs," Voice of Sudan, Voice of the National Democratic Alliance, in Arabic, 1715 gmt, January 9, 1995, quoted by BBC Monitoring Service: Middle East, January 11, 1996.

[197]The Lafon Declaration, April 27, 1995.

[198]Ibid., p. 3, para. V.1.

[199]At the time the SSIM/A apparently held no government prisoners.

February 1994.[200] This amnesty was a setback for efforts at the rule of law and accountability for SSIA troops. Reportedly, Cmdr.-in-Chief Riek Machar opposed the amnesty, but it carried anyway.

The fighting among Nuer sections, which was not believed to have any SPLA or government overtones, resulted in the burning and destruction of many villages along the Sobat River in Upper Nile. This intersectional fighting, which went on from February to May 1994, resulted in almost 1,400 civilians dead. The destruction began in a quarrel over fishing in the Sobat River between the Lou Nuer from Waat, who customarily migrated to the Sobat River in the dry season with their cattle, and the Jikany Nuer in Nasir on that river. SSIA commanders in the area became involved in the fighting to protect their own people.[201]

Apparently this quarrel over fishing rights escalated to the point where the Jikany Nuers shot three Lou Nuers, who in turn burned Ulang village on the Sobat River to the ground. SSIA Cmdr.-in-Chief Riek Machar ordered Cmdr. Gordon Kong Chol, a Jikany Nuer and the SSIA commander of Waat and Nasir, to defend Nasir. Instead that commander left Nasir and launched a retaliating attack on Lou civilians after Ulang was burned, using heavy weapons.

The Lou Nuer reportedly called upon a Lou Nuer commander in the SSIA, Gordon Kong Banypiny, and he then took charge of the Lou men who went to Nasir and burned it down in retaliation. Three SSIA commanders from Nasir (said to be Biel Joak, Buny Muol, and Opal Lual) then reportedly defected to the Khartoum government in order to get arms to fight the Lou Nuer.[202]

Cmdr. Riek Machar detained about eleven commanders who had taken part in the intersectional fighting, and at least three, including Gordon Kong Chol and Gordon Kong Banypiny, were tried by a special military tribunal of the SSIA. The judges were Cmdr. Africa (from Equatoria), Cmdr. Elijah Hon (of Ayod), Chol Dhuor (from Bentiu) and others. Some participants were sentenced to imprisonment and others to death.[203]

---

[200]Sections are the largest tribal segments within the Nuer, based on place of origin. Evans-Pritchard, *The Nuer*, p. 5.

[201]Human Rights Watch/Africa interviews, Lokichokio, Kenya, March 12 and 16, 1995.

[202]This is according to advocate John Luk of Waat, also of the Lou section, who later was detained by Riek for other reasons. Human Rights Watch/Africa interview, Nairobi, Kenya, March 7, 1995. Since then, Luk became a leader of the SSIM/A splinter group headed by Cmdr. Nyuon before his death. *Sudan Update* (London), vol. 6, no. 16, October 20, 1995, p. 3.

[203]Human Rights Watch/Africa interviews, March 7 and 12, 1995.

This punishment of military commanders for abusing their positions and attacking civilians and destroying civilian property was commendable.[204] However, the SSIM convention destroyed this important precedent and deterrent when it amnestied all these prisoners. Cmdr. Riek Machar opposed the decision to amnesty them, but was overridden by the convention.[205]

One of those amnestied was Cmdr. Gordon Kong Banypiny. After he was amnestied, he and other Lou from Waat defected to the government at Malakal.[206] His supporters say that Riek transferred Gordon Kong Banypiny to Maiwut, far from his people in Waat, but that he refused to go. While the convention was still in session, Riek dispatched several elders to talk to him outside of Akobo.[207] Although they reported back to Riek that Cmdr. Gordon Kong was still resisting, Riek did not order his arrest.[208] After being in the vicinity of Waat for a few weeks and failing to rally support there, Cmdr. Gordon Kong and three or four others fled to government-held Dolieb Hill near Malakal, commanded by Mabur Dhol, a former Anyanya (rebel) soldier heading a government militia. From there the defectors went to nearby Malakal, where they were armed by the government.[209]

Afterwards, Cmdr. Gordon Kong conducted several attacks on Waat, including taking eleven relief workers hostage in Waat in February 1995. His release pursuant to the amnesty made these later abuses possible.

SPLA and Looting in Labone: the Duty to Investigate

In February 1995, the NGO compounds in Labone were thoroughly looted by SPLA troops following a government army attack on the area; government troops never reached the compound. The looters took medical supplies and equipment, camping equipment, personal belongings, and even stripped the plastic from under the thatched roofs.

---

[204]Human Rights Watch opposes the death penalty in all cases and does not commend the death sentence here.

[205]Human Rights Watch/Africa interview, Nairobi, Kenya, March 7, 1995.

[206] Human Rights Watch/Africa interview, Lokichokio, Kenya, March 16, 1995.

[207]Cmdr. Gordon Kong Banypiny had been commander of Yuai south of Waat for two years but wanted to be commander of Waat, which was then commanded by Johanes Yual Bath, according to one of the elders who talked to him.

[208]Human Rights Watch/Africa interview, Kakuma, Kenya, March 17, 1995.

[209]Ibid. SSIA Cmdr. Peter Manyol attacked Gordon Kong Banypiny at Dolieb Hill on February 8 or 9, 1995. Human Rights Watch/Africa interview, John Luk, Nairobi, Kenya, March 7, 1995.

The NGOs protested and the SPLA sent to Labone an investigative team of five police usually based in Nimule. They managed to recover some of the stolen property.

We spoke to this team, headed by Cmdr. Maluk Aketch Deng, the chair of the investigating board and SPLM/A director of public security in Nimule, when we visited Labone.[210] Public security is a directorate or branch of the SPLA's directorate general of the police. This is an agency that is separate from the army and is under civilian supervision of the SPLA secretary of the interior. It was created by the SPLM/A convention of July 1994, which also created the directorate general of prisons, also under the secretary of the interior. The director general of prisons was Cmdr. Agasi Akol, and the director general of police was Cmdr. Magni Poch.

Cmdr. Aketch said he had been acting as a policeman for some time but that position was only formally created after the SPLM/A convention in July 1994. Cmdr. Aketch is himself a graduate of the police college in Khartoum, which he attended from 1978 to 1980. He was then stationed in Gezira, Wau and Bor, until he joined the SPLM/A in December 1984.

He said that the movement was serious about stopping looting, and they had detained fourteen persons, both soldiers and civilians, involved in the looting. He said they would be tried, and that some of the stolen goods had been recovered and returned to the owners.

With regard to the charges against the detainees, Cmdr. Aketch stated that charges of looting of civilian goods would be tried in a civilian court. If it were a military crime, it would be investigated by a military delegation which would report to the commander who ordered the formation of the board of inquiry.

We requested a visit to the place where the fourteen men were being held in detention. Although this request was unexpected we were courteously shown the detention area, which was a large tukl of branches with a fence around the perimeter. The fourteen men were passing time outside the tukl. Security was minimal. In fact, we were not sure the tukl was a detention facility at all when we saw a rifle propped up against the inside wall where the detainees slept. The fourteen men there indicated they were detainees.

We were told in March 1995 that this investigating commission would write a report that would be published in the next issue of SPLM/A Update, which was not available. We await that report. We also await the report of the incident at Ganyliel, and the looting of Akot, as well as other cases mentioned in this report.

---

[210]Human Rights Watch/Africa interviews, Labone, Eastern Equatoria, March 15 and 16, 1995.